AFRICAN ETHNOGRAPHIC STUDIES OF THE 20TH CENTURY

Volume 27

THE DYNAMICS OF CLANSHIP AMONG THE TALLENSI

THE DYNAMICS OF CLANSHIP AMONG THE TALLENSI

Being the First Part of an Analysis of the Social Structure of a Trans-Volta Tribe

MEYER FORTES

LONDON AND NEW YORK

First published in 1945 by Oxford University Press for the International African Institute.

This edition first published in 2018
by Routledge
2 Park Square, Milton Park, Abingdon, Oxon OX14 4RN

and by Routledge
711 Third Avenue, New York, NY 10017

Routledge is an imprint of the Taylor & Francis Group, an informa business

© 1945 International African Institute

All rights reserved. No part of this book may be reprinted or reproduced or utilised in any form or by any electronic, mechanical, or other means, now known or hereafter invented, including photocopying and recording, or in any information storage or retrieval system, without permission in writing from the publishers.

Trademark notice: Product or corporate names may be trademarks or registered trademarks, and are used only for identification and explanation without intent to infringe.

British Library Cataloguing in Publication Data
A catalogue record for this book is available from the British Library

ISBN: 978-0-8153-8713-8 (Set)
ISBN: 978-0-429-48813-9 (Set) (ebk)
ISBN: 978-1-138-59188-2 (Volume 27) (hbk)
ISBN: 978-0-429-49023-1 (Volume 27) (ebk)

Publisher's Note
The publisher has gone to great lengths to ensure the quality of this reprint but points out that some imperfections in the original copies may be apparent.

Disclaimer
The publisher has made every effort to trace copyright holders and would welcome correspondence from those they have been unable to trace.

Due to modern production methods, it has not been possible to reproduce the fold-out maps within the book. Please visit www.routledge.com to view them.

Na Naam Bioŋ, Chief of Tongo (d. 1941), wearing his red fez (*muŋ*) the chief emblem of his office, and clad in his finest ceremonial robes.

THE DYNAMICS OF CLANSHIP AMONG THE TALLENSI

*Being the First Part of
an Analysis of the Social Structure of
a Trans-Volta Tribe*

BY

MEYER FORTES

M.A. (CAPETOWN), PH.D. (LONDON)

*Sociologist to the Institute of
West African Industries, Arts, and Social Science
Accra, Gold Coast*

Published for the
INTERNATIONAL AFRICAN INSTITUTE
by the
OXFORD UNIVERSITY PRESS
LONDON NEW YORK TORONTO
1945

PRINTED IN GREAT BRITAIN

2044.S.B.459

TO

BRENDA Z. SELIGMAN

Hui Tzu said to Chuang Tzu, 'Your teachings are of no practical use'. Chuang Tzu said, 'Only those who already know the value of the useless can be talked to about the useful. This earth we walk upon is of vast extent, yet in order to walk a man uses no more of it than the soles of his two feet will cover. But suppose one cut away the ground round his feet till one reached the Yellow Springs, could his patches of ground still be of any use to him for walking?' Hui Tzu said, 'They would be of no use'. Chuang Tzu said, 'So then the usefulness of the useless is evident'.

ARTHUR WALEY: *Three Ways of Ancient Thought in China*

FOREWORD

I

THE writing of this book has been a harder task than I anticipated when I began it in 1938. It has taught me that the hardest part of an anthropologist's work begins after he leaves the field. In the field he is engrossed in concrete human activities. It is true that he can never feel himself completely at one with the people he is studying, however gifted he may be, linguistically or psychologically. He may make some real friends among his hosts; but he can never adopt their cultural values. If he did, he would lose that detachment without which anything he wrote would be of no scientific value. All the same, he is carried by the living stream of social life. He hardly has to stop and think. Thus the crucial scientific task begins when he starts to write up his field material. It is not merely a question of putting his observations on record. Writing an anthropological monograph is itself an instrument of research, and perhaps the most significant instrument of research in the anthropologist's armoury. It involves breaking up the vivid, kaleidoscopic reality of human action, thought, and emotion which lives in the anthropologist's note-books and memory, and creating out of the pieces a coherent representation of a society, in terms of the general principles of organization and motivation that regulate behaviour in it. It is a task that cannot be done without the help of theory.

The task would be easier if social anthropology had a well-founded body of principles to which every new observation in the field could be related. This is not so; and though we all build on the shoulders of our predecessors, working out our problems with their hypotheses and findings implicitly or explicitly in mind, yet every new piece of field-work is unique in some respects, and every new monograph raises unique problems of analysis and exposition. There is inevitably, therefore, a large personal element in an anthropological monograph.

One of my difficulties lay in the complexity of the material I have tried to present. It is commonly accepted that primitive societies are much simpler than ours, both in their cultural make-up and in their social and economic structure. But even a very simple cultural heritage or social organization may be composed of a large number of strands and elements whose interrelations make up a very elaborate pattern. Simplicity in this context is much more a value concept than a scientific category. In social science it is partly a question of how closely and with what discipline one examines the data. I should have found it much easier to write this book at the end of my first tour among the Tallensi, but it would have been inaccurate in some points and defective in many. I did not know enough about the External *Bɔyar* cult of the Hill Talis, for example, at the end of my first tour, to understand its significance in the social structure. Indeed, this and many other matters only became clear to me in the course of writing this book.

viii FOREWORD

There were extraneous difficulties too. In 1938, to quote Lord Hailey,[1] there was 'no systematic demand for research workers' in anthropology in Great Britain. Then came the war, bringing with it issues of far greater moment than the study of the social structure of a remote and unimportant African people.

The requirements of war-time publication have made it necessary to publish separately the two parts of which this study of Tale social structure consists. Though each part is self-contained, I had hoped that they could appear together in one volume. A considerable amount of compression has been necessary in order to fit the book to the Procrustean bed of austerity printing. As my concern in this book is with Tale social structure, I have preferred to leave the descriptive data pertaining to my central theme fairly full, and to compress material that can be more fully dealt with in later studies. This applies particularly to what I have written about Tale religion. It is sometimes said that anthropological monographs tend to be too long. Unfortunately, in descriptive work of this kind brevity is not always reconcilable with accuracy, however attractive it may be from the literary angle. As it is, anthropologists have to exercise rigorous selection in presenting the small fraction of their field material that it is physically possible to publish. One of the objects of any descriptive monograph must be to record material that can be used for comparative and theoretical studies. Excessive brevity (which easily lapses into facile generalization) has often proved a more serious defect, from this point of view, than an inelegant multiplicity of detail. Failing statistical devices, there is no alternative for the anthropologist who wishes to support his general statements with the evidence of observed fact, but adequate descriptive detail. I fear that I have not obeyed this rule as strictly as I should have liked to, owing to lack of space.

My object, however, has been a limited one. I have not attempted to give an 'outline' of 'the whole culture'. I consider that a work of that kind is best done in the traditional ethnographic manner of such classics as Junod's *Life of a South African Tribe* or Smith and Dale's *Ila Speaking Peoples*. It is a different thing to study those attributes of a social system that pertain to it *as a whole*, by contrast with those attributes that pertain to a limited sector of the society or a single institutional complex. Malinowski's *Argonauts of the Western Pacific* and Evans-Pritchard's *Witchcraft, Oracles and Magic of the Azande* are examples of the latter type of study. But all studies in social structure or political organization or economic structure, being concerned with the factors of social integration, are necessarily concerned with attributes of the whole society. It is chiefly because these categories of social relations are the constant elements in all social activities and constitute the common medium through which social activities are articulated with one another that we can speak of a society as a unit, or of its different aspects as being functionally interrelated or mutually consistent. What I have tried to do in this book is to give a descriptive analysis of Tale social structure at the level of corporate

[1] Lord Hailey, 'The Role of Anthropology in Colonial Development', *Man*, xliv, 1944, No. 5; cf. also A. I. Richards, 'Practical Anthropology in the Lifetime of the International African Institute', *Africa*, xiv. 6, 1944.

FOREWORD ix

group organization. This is the framework of the political system of the Tallensi, which I have described briefly elsewhere[1] and hope to write about more fully later; and it is in its turn built up on the system of inter-personal social relations which I have called kinship in the narrow sense and describe in the second part of this study.[2]

As I am analysing Tale social structure in this book I treat Tale culture primarily as the content of social relations and not in its own right. I discuss customs, beliefs, conventional usages, religious values, and so forth, principally as indices of social relations. That is why I have not been able to make use of the concepts and methods of the students of culture history and of the psychology of culture. The recent work of Benedict, Mead, Bateson, Linton, and others in the United States promises to revolutionize the study of the psychology of culture; but as Bateson argues,[3] with admirable cogency, both the approach and the aims of that study differ from those of the study of social structure.

Except for one or two topics where they seemed apposite, I have made no use of comparative data, because my aim is entirely different from that of a comparative study. Actually, there is extremely little in the literature on the Voltaic region, apart from Rattray's and Labouret's works,[4] that is relevant, and the mere citation of information from other parts of West Africa would have no value in an analytical study. Africanists will see, however, that many features of Tale social organization are typical of patrilineal societies in West Africa and some Tale institutions have parallels in South, East, and Central Africa.

I have also kept general theoretical discussions out of this book as far as possible. It was Poincaré, I believe, who remarked that whereas physical scientists have a subject-matter, sociologists, for lack of a subject-matter, spend most of their time discussing methodology. I have tried to stick to my subject-matter, using whatever theoretical guidance I could find to make it clear and to interpret it to the best of my knowledge of the Tallensi.

Observation in the field showed that every significant social activity among the Tallensi is tied up with the lineage system. I set out, therefore, to investigate the function of the lineage in Tale social organization, and the result is this book. I consider that it should be the first task of every field-worker to give an account of the social structure of the people he has studied. On this foundation he can subsequently build his studies of separate functional systems, such as law or economics or religion, of particular institutional complexes or social mechanisms, or of the culture as a whole. As regards the Tallensi, I have no hesitation in saying that it is impossible fully to understand their economic, jural, or ritual institutions without a grasp of their lineage system.

While avoiding theoretical discussions I have drawn attention to characteristics of Tale society that have a wider theoretical interest. I was impressed, in the field, with the apparent stability of Tale society over

---

[1] In *African Political Systems*, edited by M. Fortes and E. E. Evans-Pritchard.
[2] Forthcoming under the title of *The Web of Kinship Among the Tallensi*.
[3] Gregory Bateson, *Naven*.
[4] Cit. *infra*.

a 3

FOREWORD

the historical time span consciously recognized by the natives, that is, five or six generations, and probably for a much longer period. I have tried to show how this is associated with the lineage system.

At the same time it was clear that stability did not mean stagnation in Tale social life. Nothing could be farther from the way of life of the Tallensi than a rigid regimentation of social behaviour. Observation of the lineage system in action suggested that its distinguishing characteristic, as a regulating factor in the social structure, was its tendency towards equilibrium. This operated in such a way as to leave room for continual internal adjustments in the social organization without endangering its long-term stability.

The tendency towards equilibrium is marked in every sector of Tale society and in the society as a whole; and it is clearly a result of the dominance of the lineage principle in the social structure. Looking at Tale society in this way has helped me to see how the social structure is built up and how its parts are integrated with one another. The factors that determine this equilibrium require further study. But for this a full analysis, firstly, of the economic organization, and secondly, of the religious system of the Tallensi is necessary.

It seems to me that the equilibrium in the social structure is made possible by the conditions of Tale economic life. The almost complete absence of economic differentiation, by occupation or by ownership of resources, and, in particular, the absence of both material and institutional possibilities for capital accumulation or for technical advance, mean that economic interests do not play the part of dynamic factors in the social structure. We do not find permanent social groupings or classes organized solely on the basis of common economic interests, nor do economic differences decisively influence the incidence of political power or of leadership in public affairs. This is one of the major distinctions between Tale society and more highly differentiated West African societies such as the Nupe[1] or European peasant societies. There are no rich peasants and poor peasants, no landlords and tenants, no craft specialists, public officials or money-lenders, among the Tallensi. Economic factors are neutral, so to speak, in relation to the social structure, the primary constitutive factors of which are genealogical, local, and ritual relations.

But if the equilibrium of Tale society is made possible by the economic structure, and if the lineage system is the chief mechanism of social organization by which it is maintained, the system of religious values is undoubtedly the supreme sanction of its existence. I have been able to give only an indication of this as there has not been space in this book for an extensive treatment of Tale religion. Ritual activities are so conspicuous and so frequent in Tale social life that I was bound to give a great deal of attention to them in the field. One cannot understand the springs of conduct among the Tallensi without a good knowledge of their religious values.

The structural equilibrium of Tale society is associated with its segmentary form, which I regard as a particularly important characteristic of the social structure as a whole. Elsewhere[2] Evans-Pritchard and I have

[1] Cf. S. F. Nadel, *A Black Byzantium.*   [2] *African Political Systems,* Introduction.

FOREWORD xi

tentatively described two main types of political organization found in Africa, a segmentary type and a pyramidal or centralized type. Among the Tallensi, who belong to the first type, it can be seen that the segmentary principle operates right through the social system as a dynamic factor of social organization. From one point of view it can be regarded as simply the obverse of the principle of equilibrium. It is connected, also, with the idea of polarity which plays a very big part in all Tale institutions.

These characteristics of Tale society are perhaps merely aspects of a common principle of social organization. I do not think there is anything novel or abstruse about them. Every anthropologist knows that kinship systems are built up on the complementary relationships of the two sexes in marriage and parenthood. The concept of segmentation derives from Durkheim.[1] So also does the concept of social equilibrium, via Rad-cliffe-Brown's and Malinowski's theories of structure and function. These or analogous concepts are common currency in contemporary social anthropology, and their virtue lies not in their explanatory but in their exploratory value. It is in this sense that I have used them.

There are other subjects of general theoretical interest for the study of which Tale society affords useful data. There is the problem of the range of social relations, in space and in time, consciously recognized in a primitive society without a centralized form of government and without permanent records of the past. I have touched on one side of this problem in discussing what I have called the field of social relations. The function of time in a segmentary social structure has recently been investigated by Evans-Pritchard,[2] and I have referred to it in this book. People like the Tallensi do not have the idea of historical time as a specific dimension of their social life. They do not think of the lapse of time as being associated with cumulative changes in their culture or social structure but rather as a periodical or cyclical rhythm of eternal repetition. They do not think of their history as something separate from, and leading up to, their con-temporary way of life. They seem to live wholly in the present and im-mediately recollected past. But social life is a pattern of processes, and the time dimension is a significant factor in social structure everywhere. Among the Tallensi the time factor is, as it were, embedded in the social structure and, as with the Nuer, there is a direct correlation between the time perspective recognized by the society and the social structure. This suggests that the absence of a consciousness of history in primitive societies like the Tallensi is not due solely to lack of permanent records. There are primitive societies, especially those that have royal dynasties, in which a sense of history exists and is kept alive through folk-tales, ritual chants and heirlooms, royal ceremonies and praise songs, and so forth.[3] The political and social structure, including the principal political values of a people, directly shapes the notions of time and of history that prevail among them. Traditions of migration and of origins fall into place

[1] Durkheim, E., *La Division du travail sociale.*
[2] Evans-Pritchard, E. E., *The Nuer*, ch. 3. Cf. also my paper on 'The Significance of Descent in Tale Social Structure', cit. *infra*.
[3] The large West African kingdoms—Ashanti, Yoruba, Dahomey, Mossi, and others—are good examples of such societies.

xii FOREWORD

as myths that sanction or reflect contemporary social relationships and usages.[1]

In short, my chief aim has been to give a descriptive analysis of Tale social structure; but I hope that the material will also be useful for comparative and theoretical studies.

II

My wife and I spent nearly two and a half years in the Northern Territories of the Gold Coast, between January 1934 and April 1937. For most of that time we were amongst the Tallensi.[2] Our head-quarters were at Tongo, which proved to be an ideal base for our work. There we were at the hub of Taleland and within a few hours' march or ride of any part of the country we might wish to visit. We trekked over most of Taleland and also visited the chief centres of the neighbouring tribes, in particular the Mamprusi. As there is no linguistic literature for the Tallensi, we had to learn their dialect from scratch, with the assistance of a semi-literate interpreter and the scanty literature on Mole and Dagbane. It took us about six months to learn enough Talni for workaday communication with the people. By the end of our first tour we became proficient enough to dispense with an interpreter. Nevertheless, I know only too well that we reached but a moderate standard in our vocabulary and in our appreciation of the finer shades of thought and feeling that can be expressed in Talni.

We were the only white people who had ever lived among the Tallensi for any length of time and the first to speak their dialect. After their initial suspicions had been allayed, we were quickly accepted and soon had many friends. Our first informants soon got to understand our aims and entered into the spirit of our work with sincerity and zeal. They were mostly men and women who assisted us out of friendship and trust in our good faith. I wish to thank them for their confidence in us and for the devotion with which they instructed us in the way of life of their people. We remember with gratitude the patience, tolerance, tact, and friendliness of many dozens of Tale men, women, and children. They welcomed us to their homes, their domestic occasions, and their esoteric and public religious gatherings. We learnt more from them about humanity than I have the skill to write of. Tɔŋ-Yikpɛmdaan, my first friend and mentor and one of nature's gentlemen, was a fount of wisdom. The late Chief of Tongo, Na Naam Bioŋ, was a proud, intelligent, and forthright man whose support stood us in good stead and whose great store of knowledge was freely opened to us. Many others, too numerous to mention, were our faithful friends and zealous helpers.

My field-work among the Tallensi was made possible by the grant of a fellowship from the International Institute of African Languages and Cultures. I appreciate the privilege of having held this fellowship and record with gratitude the unfailing interest which the Directors (Dr. J. H.

[1] As Radcliffe-Brown showed in *The Andaman Islands*, and Malinowski in *Argonauts of the Western Pacific*.

[2] In 1943, in the course of other duties, I had occasion to spend some time in the Northern Territories. I found that no social changes of significance had taken place among the Tallensi since 1937.

FOREWORD xiii

Oldham and later Professor Sir Reginald Coupland) and the Secretary-General (Sir Hanns Vischer) took in the work of the Institute's fellows. I appreciate, in particular, the freedom they allowed us in carrying out the research entrusted to us and the encouragement they gave us to aim at high scientific standards. I am greatly indebted to Professor D. Westermann, who was one of the Institute's research directors. His great scholarship in West African languages and cultures made his counsel of exceptional value. The success my wife and I were able to achieve in learning Talni owed much to a short course we were fortunate enough to have with him. This, like my preliminary training at the London School of Economics, was made possible by a grant from the Rockefeller Foundation.

I chose the Northern Territories of the Gold Coast for my field-work on the advice of the late Captain R. S. Rattray. His name is written in indelible letters in the annals of West African ethnology and I was proud to follow in his footsteps. His pioneer ethnographical survey of the Northern Territories saved me months of labour.

I made Tongo our head-quarters on the advice of Administrative and other Government officers working in the Northern Territories. My wife and I owe a special debt of gratitude to the then Chief Commissioner Mr. W. J. A. (now Sir Andrew) Jones for the keen interest he took in our work and for many helpful arrangements he made to facilitate it. We have also to thank Sir Andrew and Lady Jones for many personal kindnesses. I owe my understanding of the spirit and methods of colonial administration chiefly to Sir Andrew and his officers.

My wife and I also remember gratefully the unfailing kindness and hospitality of Colonel G. H. Gibbs, M.C., Sir Andrew's successor as Chief Commissioner of the Northern Territories, who was District Commissioner, Mamprusi, in 1934–7, and of Mrs. Gibbs. A visit to them was a heaven-sent rest from the strenuous routine of field-work. Many discussions with Colonel Gibbs helped to broaden my understanding of the problems of government and social development in the Northern Territories.

Captain J. L. Mothersill, Mr. E. W. Ellison, and Mr. A. F. Kerr, who were in charge of the Zuarungu district at various times during our stay there, put us greatly in their debt by their readiness to help us.

Our nearest European neighbour was Mr. C. W. Lynn, M.B.E., Superintendent of Agriculture at Zuarungu. Mr. Lynn's friendship was a great stand-by to us at all times. He was at that time engaged on his now well-known survey of native agriculture in the Zuarungu district and we had many long talks on this subject. Farming is a subject of supreme interest to the natives; and though it does not come into this book very much, I should have made little progress in the field without some knowledge of Tale agriculture. I received great help from Mr. Lynn on this side of my field-work.

I have, in this study, stuck to my last and dealt with an anthropological problem from an anthropological point of view. But I hope that what I have written will also be of service to Government officers in the Northern territories.

xiv FOREWORD

My first teachers in anthropology were the late Professor C. G. Seligman, F.R.S., and the late Professor B. Malinowski. Both were unorthodox teachers, in different ways, and the power of their influence lay as much in the points of view as in the subject-matter they taught. An anthropologist has to be in sympathy with the people he is working amongst; but he has to view their ideas and values objectively. He can succeed in this only if he has the conviction that his work is not only immediately useful, but represents a contribution to the general body of science by which his work is nourished. Both Seligman and Malinowski had the gift of making one feel this. Seligman's catholic conception of anthropology, backed as it was by great learning, enabled him to show his pupils what a vast and exciting field of study lay open to them. I owe more to him than I can speak of here, and without his encouragement would probably never have finished this book.

My debt to Malinowski is writ large in this book. My field-work was done under the inspiration of his teaching, and I have drawn heavily on his writings and on ideas debated in his classes.

My debt to Professor A. R. Radcliffe-Brown is as great. The final draft of this book was written while I was working with him at Oxford and every significant problem in it was discussed with him. The results are obvious in every chapter. My approach to the study of social structure in primitive society is basically derived from him.

I have to thank Professor Raymond Firth for opening up many new and fruitful lines of thought to me, both in discussion and through his writings.

Dr. E. E. Evans-Pritchard has a special place in my regard. I look upon him as my older brother in anthropological studies. I have, in this book, followed where he has led. His preliminary reports on the Nuer[1] gave me the clue to the lineage system among the Tallensi. He was working on his Nuer book at the same time as I was struggling with my Tale material, and there is very little in this book that does not owe much to discussion with him.

Mrs. B. Z. Seligman, Dr. Lucy Mair, and my wife read the manuscript of this book with critical attention. I wish to thank them for this most valuable service, by which they helped me to rescue many passages from needless obscurity. My wife has not only contributed some of the field data for the book but has also materially assisted in its authorship by comment and criticism. I am very happy to be able to dedicate this book to Mrs. Seligman both as a mark of esteem from a fellow anthropologist, and as a token of friendship.

I have also to thank Miss Phyllis Puckle for secretarial assistance; Captain V. G. L. Sheddick for help with maps; Mrs. B. Wyatt for her careful editing of the book; and Dr. Alice Meinhard for compiling the index.

Lastly, there remains a friend who has to be anonymous and to whom the quotation from Arthur Waley's book is addressed. Like many people concerned with practical questions of colonial government he has doubts about the practical usefulness of anthropology and, in particular, of a

[1] Published in *Sudan Notes & Records*, xvi–xviii, 1933–5.

FOREWORD xv

work of this kind. I consider it futile to debate this question and can think of no more apposite answer to him than the Chinese philosopher's retort to a similar doubt.

NOTE ON ORTHOGRAPHY

I have kept vernacular terms and phrases down to a minimum using English equivalents, however approximate, for preference. But I have had to retain a few native words as special terms for lack of satisfactory equivalents. I have used the orthography recommended by the International African Institute, with one exception. I have used the symbol *h* medially and finally to represent a very open velar fricative. This consonant is interchangeable with *s* in Talni. Initially, this consonant is pronounced as in English, and is not interchangeable with *s*. Talni has neither semantic nor grammatical tone.

The Tallensi often drop a final vowel if it is not semantically significant and I have automatically followed this habit. Thus Tallensi, say *Gɔris* or *Gɔrisi*, *tɛndaan* or *tɛndaana*, *Yinduur* or *Yinduuri*, *yir* or *yiri*, *biis* or *biisi*, *na'ab* or *na'aba*, *Tɔŋ* or *Tɔŋo* according to the context.

OXFORD
December 1944

CONTENTS

FOREWORD vii

CHAPTER I. INTRODUCTORY I
The Natural Environment of the Tallensi
Cultural Affinities of the Tallensi
General Characteristics of the Tallensi
British Rule and Contact with Western Civilization

CHAPTER II. THE MEANING OF 'TALLENSI' . 14
Tribal Divisions
Cultural Segmentation of the Tallensi
The 'Real Talis'
Nomenclature and the Structural Scheme
Myths of Origin
The Major Cleavage in Tale Society

CHAPTER III. PARADIGM OF THE LINEAGE SYSTEM 30

CHAPTER IV. CLANSHIP: THE NAMOOS . . . 39
The Dispersion of Mosuor biis
The Chain of Sub-clans
The Critical Norms of Clanship
Mosuor biis a Maximal Lineage
The Lineage Principle in the Structure of the Clan
The Internal Differentiation of the Clan: (A) Sie
The Internal Differentiation of the Clan: (B) Tongo and the
Status of Accessory Lineages
The Nexus of Clanship Ties
The Field of Clanship

CHAPTER V. THE DISTRIBUTION OF THE NAMOOS 66
The Distinctive Ritual Observances of the Namoos
Significance of the Totemic Taboos of the Namoos
Other Namoo Clans
The Meaning of 'Namoo'

CHAPTER VI. THE STRUCTURAL RELATIONS OF THE
TALIS 78
A General Point
The Clan Structure of Zubiuŋ
Ritual Differentiation and Integration of Zubiuŋ
Linked Maximal Lineages and the Field of Clanship

xviii CONTENTS

The Gradation of Clanship Ties
The Pattern of Clanship among the Talis
The Mesh of Clanship among the Talis
Quasi-clanship: Joking Partnership
Privileged Moral Coercion
The Rationalization of Clanship Ties

CHAPTER VII. CLANSHIP AND RITUAL COLLABORA-
TION 98
The Significance of Sacrificing Together
Ritual Relations in Namoo Clans
Ritual Collaboration among the Talis: The External *Bɔyar* and
the Earth
The Underlying Principles of Ritual Collaboration
The Scheme of Ritual Collaboration among the Hill Talis
The Network of Ritual Ties between Talis Clans
Native Thought and the Realities of Social Structure
The Network of Structural Ties among the Gɔrisi and in the
Sie District

CHAPTER VIII. TOTEMISM AMONG THE TALIS AND
OTHER NON-NAMOOS 121
The Unity of all the Talis
Funeral Customs as Criteria of Social Alinement among Talis
Clans
Totemic Avoidances and Clanship Ties
Totemic Myths
The Totemic Avoidances of the Talis as a Reflex of the Social
Structure
Totemic Taboos and the Patrilineal Principle
Totems, Clanship, and External *Bɔyar*
The Significance of Animals as Totems
Taboos of the Earth
Functional Differentiation and its Symbolism

CHAPTER IX. THE PLACE OF WOMEN IN THE CLAN
ORGANIZATION 147
The Concept of a Clanswoman
Institutionalized Recognition of a Clanswoman's Status

CHAPTER X. THE SOCIAL STRUCTURE OF A SETTLE-
MENT 154
Introduction
Types of Settlement and Distribution of Population
The Stability and Continuity of a Settlement
Topographical Distinctions and the Natives' Knowledge of
Natural History
Settlement Boundaries

CONTENTS　　　　　　　　　　　　xix

The Concept of the *Tɛŋ*
The Section—*Yizug*
The Sections of Tongo
Territorial Distribution and the *Tɛŋ* in its Mystical Aspect

CHAPTER XI. LAND, LOCALITY, AND THE EARTH . 171
Definition of the Bonds between People and the Land
Farm-land and Subsistence
Productive Efficiency and the Bounds set by Nature
Striving after Security: the Ritual Background
The Social Framework of Production: Land Tenure
The Integration of the Community: Chiefship and Tɛn-
daanaship
The Tɛndaana's *Tɛŋ*

CHAPTER XII. THE LINEAGE IN THE LOCAL COM-
MUNITY 191
General Features
Analysis of a Lineage from within
The Principle of Segmentation in the Lineage
Lineage Grouping and Local Grouping
The Concept of the Lineage Home
The Influence of Lineage Localization in the Social Life
The Section
Segmentation and Equilibrium in the Sub-clan
The Local Embodiment of the Ritual Focus of the Sub-clan
Structure of the Clan Settlement among non-Namoos
Structure of Peripheral Settlements
Seniority and Authority in the Lineage

CHAPTER XIII. THE FORM OF TALE SOCIETY . 231
The Socio-geographic Region
Re-examination of the Major Cleavage: Warfare
Equilibrium and Solidarity within the Clan and Lineage
Modern Factors of Disequilibrium

POSTSCRIPT 259

INDEX 261

MAP . . . . *at end*

LIST OF ILLUSTRATIONS

The late Chief of Tongo in ceremonial dress . . . *Frontispiece*

Facing page

PLATE I. *a.* Tale settlement in the dry season. *Tɔŋgban.* *b.* Tale settlement in the rainy season 16

PLATE II. *a.* A Tale grandmother. *b.* Young girls dressed up for a visit to the market 17

PLATE III. *a.* Elders of a Maximal Lineage assemble to sacrifice to their Founder. *b.* Prayer preceding sacrifice to Clan Founder . . 56

PLATE IV. *a.* Ritual strangling of a goat for the burial of a Namoo elder. *b.* The final rite of a Namoo funeral—*Ɖma wɔyar* . . . 57

PLATE V. *a.* Elders of Zubiuŋ meet for sacrifice at the entrance to the External *Bɔyar*. *b.* Funeral rite for a Zubiuŋ tɛndaana, performed by the *sunzɔp* 80

PLATE VI. *a.* Ritual collaboration of Hill Talis in sacrifice at the External *Bɔyar*. *b.* A sacrifice at the Earth Shrine, Ɖoo, at Kpata'ar. 81

PLATE VII. *a.* The chief tɛndaanas of all Talis settlements inaugurate the Gɔlib Festival. *b.* A sacred crocodile at Zubiuŋ 160

PLATE VIII. *a.* Widows attended by their clan sisters at a funeral ceremony. *b.* Cooking beer for a funeral ceremony 161

PLATE IX. *a.* Girls stamping grain on a boulder. *b.* Women at a waterhole in the early rainy season 176

PLATE X. *a.* The Gbizug tɛndaana in ritual dress. *b.* Firing the bush at a communal hunt 177

PLATE XI. *a.* Giŋgaaŋ Puhug—the sacred dancing ground at Tongo. *b.* A miniature homestead symbolizing the ancestral home of the Maximal Lineage or Clan 224

PLATE XII. *a.* The lineage head sacrifices to the lineage *bɔyar* on his succession to the headship. *b.* Sacrifice to a *dugni bɔyar* at Zubiuŋ . 225

PLATE XIII. *a.* Yikpɛmdaana of Tongo. *b.* Lɔyani of Zubiuŋ . . 240

PLATE XIV. *a.* A Gbizug elder assists at a Zubiuŋ funeral as *sunzɔp*. *b.* Ba'ari elders assembled for the burial of the Sakpar tɛndaana . 241

PLATE XV. *a.* A mimic war parade at Ba'ari to inaugurate an elder's funeral. *b.* A vast crowd at Gɔlib Festival 256

CHAPTER I

INTRODUCTORY

The Natural Environment of the Tallensi

THE Northern Territories of the Gold Coast lie entirely within the Sudanese Zone.[1] It has been variously described as 'parkland', 'savannah', or 'orchard bush' country, terms which indicate the sparse and uniform forestation characteristic of this zone. Stretching irregularly and almost right across Africa, between the eighth and the sixteenth parallels N. latitude, it merges into the Sahara on the north and is bounded by the tropical rain forest on the south.

The traveller in West Africa who enters this region from the south is impressed by the contrast with the forest belt. According to his predilections he will view it with pleasure or dismay after the massive and gigantic gloom of the forest. Here are no great trees a hundred or two hundred feet high rooted amid thick undergrowth and enveloped in tenacious creepers. The orchard bush country is a vast plain, in some parts monotonously flat, in others gently undulating and diversified by an occasional range of hills or a steep scarp. The tracts of bush, sometimes fairly extensive, which may be encountered in the less populated areas, resemble the secondary forestation of abandoned cultivations in the rain forest. Scattered trees, no larger than our oaks and beeches, man-high grass, and scrub constitute these patches of standing bush. In the dry season the landscape appears harsh and bare, and its general drab hue is hardly relieved by the shade trees in front of the native homesteads or the remnants of vegetation along the dry watercourses. The mud walls and thatched roofs of the homesteads seem to blend indistinguishably with the dusty country-side. In the middle of the wet season, when every footpath becomes a rivulet and every depression a bog, the homesteads are hidden behind ramparts of luxuriant grain, and the whole country-side is resplendent with the green of flourishing vegetation.

The climate of the Sudanese Zone exhibits two clearly defined seasons, a dry season lasting about half the year (October to March) and a wet season lasting the remaining six or seven months (April to October). Not only are there marked variations in the mean rainfall from one area

[1] For a short account of the principal ecological and climatic features of the part of the Sudanese Zone that concerns us in this book, see Lynn, C. W., *Agriculture in North Mamprussi*, Bulletin No. 34 of the Gold Coast Department of Agriculture, 1937. Climate and vegetation are more fully discussed in Bégué, L., *Contribution à l'Étude de la Végétation Forestière de la Haute Côte d'Ivoire*, Publications du Comité d'Études Historiques et Scientifiques de l'Afrique Occidentale Française, 1937. These writers give lists of the common trees of economic value found in our area, of which the following are the best known and most frequently seen in inhabited places: Shea (*Butyrospermum parkii*); locust bean (*Parkia filicoidea*); baobab (*Adansonia digitata*); various species of acacia; the silk cotton (*Ceiba pentendra*); the tamarind (*Tamarindus indica*).

B

2   INTRODUCTORY

to another, ranging from 25 inches to 45 inches per annum, but fluctuations occur from year to year in the same area. Erratic or abnormal rains may so disturb the cycle of food production as to subject a majority of the population to severe privation. The temperature in the vicinity of 10° 30' N. latitude and 0° 30' W. longitude varies from a minimum of about 70° F. to a maximum of about 93° F. A characteristic feature of the dry season is the harmattan, a hot parching wind laden with fine dust which blows from the Sahara, so strongly at times as to obscure the landscape in a haze which limits visibility to a few hundred yards. Heavy dew and mists cause the mornings to be chilly and bracing, so much so that the natives squat shivering round fires or remain indoors until the sun is high; from the forenoon until about 4 p.m. the sun blazes relentlessly through the faint haze; sunset ushers in a cool and balmy evening; and night brings a relatively marked drop in temperature. Violent nocturnal tornadoes from the east and north-east, accompanied by lightning and thunder, introduce the rainy season, during which the prevailing wind blows from the direction of the Gulf of Guinea, to the south and south-east. During this season the temperature remains fairly stable throughout the day. Though it is never as hot as in the hottest days of the dry season, the humidity makes it at times excessively oppressive. The peak of the rains comes in August–September. It rains so heavily then that many social activities are impeded. These conditions of vegetation and climate fundamentally influence the economy and the social life of the inhabitants of the Sudanese Zone.

This book is concerned with the population of a very small section of the Sudanese Zone, a part of the region drained by the Volta river system. The head-waters of this system lie in French West Africa. About 20 miles south of the international boundary between the Gold Coast and French Ivory Coast, which has been arbitrarily fixed to coincide approximately with the eleventh parallel N. latitude, the Red Volta flows into the White Volta. Between these two rivers, on the east and south respectively, and the Sissili river on the west lies an area, arbitrarily truncated on the north by the international boundary, comprising two of the most heavily populated administrative districts of the Gold Coast. The eastern third of this area constitutes the administrative district of Zuarungu, the remaining two-thirds the district of Navrongo. The Red Volta separates Zuarungu district from another administrative unit, Kusaasi, and the White Volta forms a natural boundary between it and the Mamprusi district, to the south of which lies the territory of the Dagomba.

As the following table[1] from the census of 1931 shows, the Zuarungu district is the most densely populated part of this area; and as the population tends to be concentrated in the centre and north, the actual density of settlement exceeds the figures given. In some localities this is reflected

---

[1] See *Appendices containing Comparative Returns and General Statistics of the 1931 Census*, Gold Coast, 1932, p. 3; and Cardinall, A. W., *The Gold Coast*, 1931, Population Map, p. 156. Mr. Cardinall remarks (p. 123) that ' A majority of the census officers were of opinion that the figures collected by them are lower than they should have been by from 2 per cent. to 10 per cent.'—a contingency inevitable in a country which is for the most part still pre-literate.

INTRODUCTORY 3

in serious soil erosion due to over-cultivation and in the diminution of
uncultivated bush land, so that firewood and other sylvan products
cannot be found within six or more miles of the settlements.

District		Area	Population	Density per sq. mile
Navrongo .	.	1,551	120,870	77·96
Zuarungu .	.	781	133,981	171·55
Kusaasi* .	.	1,227	151,715	123·64
Mamprusi*	.	2,719	61,520	22·62
Dagomba*.	.	12,257	191,956	15·66

* Partly in Mandated Territory of Togoland.

In spite of the general similarity of climate and vegetation ·in the
Sudanese Zone, local variations produce significant ecological differences.
This is shown in the Northern Territories of the Gold Coast by the
differences in agriculture north and south of the Gambaga scarp. The
steep scarp marks both a geological and an ecological line of division.
South of it the rock formations are of sandstone and shale, north of it
granite, quartz, and greenstone predominate. South of the scarp a form
of shifting cultivation is customary, and yams (*Dioscorea* spp.) are grown
on a large scale side by side with millet (*Pennisetum typhoides*, var.),
guinea corn (*Sorghum vulgare*), and maize (*Zea mays*). North of it yams
will not grow easily and cereal crops form the staple food supply.[1]

The relative scarcity of population in the yam-growing districts compared with the congested areas north of the White Volta may be due to
unknown historical and cultural factors, but endemic diseases have
undoubtedly impeded population growth. While malaria, yaws, and
leprosy, to mention only the commonest enemies of native health, are
widespread throughout the Northern Territories of the Gold Coast,
sleeping-sickness is also endemic throughout the Mamprusi and Dagomba
districts. In the central sectors north of the scarp sleeping-sickness occurs
only sporadically near the rivers.

Topographical differences also appear to influence the distribution of
population. The high plateau which stretches from the White Volta
northwards is more suited for permanent habitation than the low-lying
flats which make up the greater part of Mamprusi and Dagomba. In the
wet season they turn into quagmires, in the dry season they are arid tracts
seriously short of water-supplies. North of the White Volta numerous
streams and small rivers combine with the relatively greater elevation
to drain the plateau effectively during the heavy rains; and though surface
water becomes scarce in the dry season, shallow pits generally provide
sufficient water for normal needs.

The district of Zuarungu is a typical portion of the Trans-Volta plateau.
A number of bouldery hills from 100 to 500 feet high are scattered over
its undulating surface. The most conspicuous are the Tong Hills, a small
range stretching for about four miles just north of the river. It adds an

[1] Cf. Fortes, M. and S. L., 'Food in the Domestic Economy of the Tallensi',
Africa, ix. 2, 1936; and Lynn, C. W., op. cit.

4   INTRODUCTORY

attractive touch to an otherwise uninspiring landscape. A fringe of uninhabited bush, the home of a fair amount of game, follows the course of the two Voltas. From the Tong Hills the area of close settlement and perennial cultivation spreads out like a fan to the west, north, and east. Generally speaking, settlement is relatively sparse and recent along the periphery of this area, except in the north to north-west segment, and densest and most ancient in the middle.

The Northern Territories of the Gold Coast have been under effective Government control for about twenty-five years. From the first efforts were made to develop modern communications. At the present time a main road, suitable for motor traffic, connects Bawku in Kusaasi district, the northernmost administrative station, with Tamale, the capital of the Northern Territories, 145 miles to the south, and continues from there to Kumasi in Ashanti, another 220 miles. Branches link it with the principal Government stations in the Northern Territories. This road system was maintained, until recently, only for essential services in the wet season, but was always passable in the dry season. In 1936 large-scale works were undertaken to make it a permanent highway. Head carriage and footpaths still remain the only means of local transport and communications. About 50 miles of this road system traverse the Zuarungu district, the administrative head-quarters of which is at Zuarungu (Talni, *Zuwaruŋ*) on the central road.

The people we are concerned with in this book occupy less than half of the Zuarungu district. Their country, which, for convenience of reference may be called Taleland, embraces most of the southern half of the district between the two Voltas and the western boundary. On the north it can be demarcated only by an arbitrary boundary which extends in a wavy line from Zuarungu due east to the river. A typical section of the district, Taleland includes the Tong Hills, the vicinity of which harbours the densest and oldest settlements of the country. Its total population, according to the 1931 census, numbers about 35,000. Nearly a third of it is concentrated within a radius of two or three miles of the Hills. I estimate the total area of Taleland at about 300 square miles, which would imply an average population density of approximately 100 to the square mile, though the actual density of settlement in the inhabited areas must be considerably higher. Thus Taleland is thickly populated, by African standards.

Cultural Affinities of the Tallensi

Delafosse, in his monumental survey[1] of the peoples of the western Sudan, distinguished five 'families' by ethnological and linguistic criteria. His largest division, the Voltaic family, comprises the tribes inhabiting the basin of the Volta rivers, from approximately 9° 30' to 14° N. latitude.[2] Delafosse subdivides the Voltaic family into seven branches, one of which, the Mossi group, includes all the peoples living between Ouagadougou in the French Upper Ivory Coast and Salaga in the Gold Coast.

More recent research has not invalidated Delafosse's broad classification.

[1] Delafosse, M., *Haut-Sénégal-Niger*, 3 vols., 1912.
[2] Op. cit., i, pp. 115 ff.

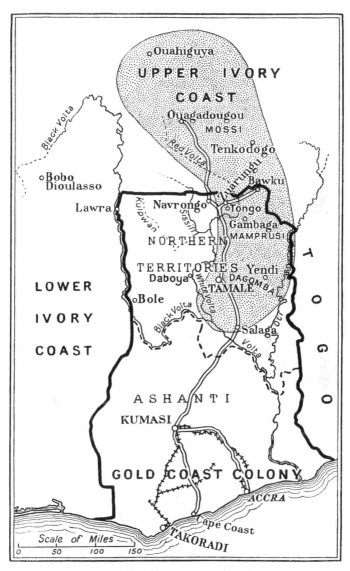

BOUNDARIES OF THE GOLD COAST
The dotted portion shows the area occupied by Mole-Dagbane speaking peoples

6   INTRODUCTORY

Westermann has shown[1] that the Voltaic tribes all speak languages belonging to the *Gur* group of Sudanic languages. The Mossi (or, more accurately, the Mole-Dagbane speaking) group all speak Mole-Dagbane dialects, which form a distinct branch of the *Gur* family. The people of Taleland speak a Dagbane dialect. From Zuarungu northwards Mole influence is linguistically predominant.

The cultural uniformity of the Voltaic region is equally strikingly shown in forms of social and economic organization, in custom, belief, and material culture. Though local variations are great and have important sociological implications, as we shall find, the common patterns and contents are obvious.[2]

Among the Voltaic peoples, the Mossi, the Dagomba, and the Mamprusi have centralized forms of political organization of the type common throughout West Africa. The aristocracies of the three nations claim to be kinsfolk descended from conquering immigrants who established themselves first in the country of the Mamprusi and spread northwards and southwards from there. The three paramount chiefs still maintain ceremonial ties accounted for by quasi-mythical traditions of kinship and migration well known in all three countries.

Between these centralized states stretches a block of tribes which seem to have no political unity. Each so-called tribe appears to be independent of and sporadically at enmity with its neighbours, and there is no overriding central authority. Nor does the tribe seem to have any internal political unity.

We owe to Rattray the discovery that these central Voltaic tribes comprise two major groups of communities. On the one side are those that claim to be the descendants of immigrants from parts of the country other than their present habitats. On the other side are communities that claim to be the autochthonous inhabitants. The two groups are found in every tribe, including the Mossi, Mamprusi, and Dagomba, living side by side and indistinguishable from one another by broad cultural or linguistic criteria. Many of the immigrant communities claim descent from forbears of the Mampuru ruling stock. Though now wholly amalgamated with the alleged aboriginal inhabitants, they have certain ritual observances and a system of chiefship similar to those of the Mamprusi. In fact the Paramount Chief of Mampurugu appoints many of their chiefs. But this is symbolical of kinship and ideological ties, not of political suzerainty. For though these communities may be regarded as the distant outliers of the Mampuru social and political structure, they are politically independent of the Mamprusi.

---

[1] Westermann, D., *Die westlichen Sudansprachen und ihre Beziehungen zum Bantu*, pp. 121 ff.; and in Rattray, R. S., *Tribes of the Ashanti Hinterland*, chap. iv.

[2] The literature on this area is scanty and of very unequal value. The following are the most informative ethnographical monographs, in order of reliability: Rattray, op. cit.; Delafosse, op. cit.; Labouret, H., *Les Tribus de Rameau Lobi*, Travaux et Mémoires de l'Institut d'Ethnologie, Paris, 1931; Tauxier, L., *Les Noirs du Soudan*, Paris, 1912; id., *Les Noirs du Yatenga*, Paris, 1917; Dim Delobsom, A. A., *L'Empire du Mogho-Naba*, Institut de Droit Comparé, Études de Sociologie et d'Ethnologie juridiques, Paris, 1932; Cardinall, A. W., *Natives of the Northern Territories of the Gold Coast*, London, 1925.

INTRODUCTORY 7

The institution distinctive of the autochthonous communities is the office of 'Custodian of the Earth'. This ritual office, involving priestly functions in connexion with the cult of the Earth, is found among many West African peoples from the Senegal to the mouth of the Niger. In the Voltaic region it is the exclusive prerogative of the autochthonous communities.

The ethnographic picture of to-day suggests that the population of the Voltaic region was, in the past, constantly being redistributed by migrations of small groups. In the absence of written records that is all we can say. The fact that such migrations have gone on in the recent past, and are still going on in the central area, suggests that these migrations were (as they are) the result rather of ecological pressures and social forces than of large-scale conquests. But marauding slave-raiders may have been a cause of migrations in some areas. Two of the most notorious, Samory and Babatu, were spreading devastation in the north-western parts of the region at the time when the French and the British were partitioning the country during the last decade of the nineteenth century.

Physically, culturally, in their economic organization, and their social and political structure, the people of Taleland are typical in every respect of the tribes of the central Volta region.

General Characteristics of the Tallensi

The people of the central Volta region are of negroid stock. They are not a notably fine physical type, but the best of them are attractive physical specimens, as may be seen from the photographs in this book. Head measurements of thirteen Tale men gave an average C.I. of 74·7. The predominant head type appears to be dolichocephalic. In skin colour they vary from black through chocolate brown to bronze, which the natives call 'red' (bon-ze'e) and regard as the most attractive bodily hue. Their hair is of the usual negroid peppercorn type. They have also the typical negroid nasal and lip forms, but the very broad, flat nose and markedly everted lips are not so common as in the tropical forest belt. Both men and women are of medium stature, the men being slightly the taller. Anybody over 5 ft. 7 or 8 in. is considered tall. Though they are mostly slight in build, all the somatic types with which we are familiar may be seen among these people: the stocky pyknic, the slim asthenic, the stalwart athletic, to use Kretschmer's terminology, are all common. Fat men or women, however, are very rare. Climatic conditions, density of population, and a primitive agricultural technique[1] all conspire to keep the average standard of nutrition low. In the best seasons the natives grow only enough cereals for their needs.[2] Their animal husbandry provides little surplus to exchange for cereals, and they have no crafts worth speaking of. The labour they supply to richer parts of the Gold Coast contributes very little return by way of foodstuffs to the home community. Like most subsistence farmers in Africa, their diet is notably deficient in animal protein.

[1] *Vide* Lynn, C. W., op. cit.
[2] This aspect of Tale economics is more fully discussed in Lynn, op. cit., and in Fortes, M. and S. L., loc. cit.

INTRODUCTORY

No biological or medical research has hitherto been carried out among the Tallensi or their nearest neighbours. Hence it is impossible to determine how far their physique, efficiency, and standard of health have been affected by their low scale of nutrition. To the lay observer they do not appear to be stunted or to show a high incidence of physical defects. They are fortunate in living outside the sleeping-sickness zone, but the common endemic diseases of the region are rife among them. The natives have no reliable remedies for these diseases, and the Government dispensary at Zuarungu, the only regular medical service provided for the district, cannot cope with more than a fraction of the sick. From the point of view of physical health the Tallensi of to-day are probably little better off than their fathers were.

Native habits of dress and personal hygiene are doubtful assets from the point of view of health. Children go stark naked till adolescence, in the case of boys, and till their first pregnancy in the case of girls. Women go naked except for the perineal band. Men always wear a loin-cloth for the sake of modesty, but it is usually grimy with accumulated dirt. In addition, a man usually wears a goatskin or sheepskin, or a ragged remnant of an old tunic or cloth slung across his back, as his working garb; clothes are worn only on special occasions.

Whether or not these customs of dress are injurious, the indifference of the Tallensi to bodily cleanliness cannot be beneficial to their health. By European or Coast African standards, the Tallensi and their neighbours are dirty people. They wash only rarely, especially in the dry season. This is due, in part, to the scarcity of water and to the fact that soap is still an expensive luxury, but also in some measure to native ideas of cleanliness. Tallensi do not object to body dirt. Only young dandies and marriageable girls take pride in a 'clean skin' as a mark of beauty and wash regularly. It is not surprising, therefore, that the most superficial wounds usually fester.

The sanitary habits of the natives are equally primitive. A homestead is usually kept fairly clean indoors, but the live-stock yard is inside the homestead, and the accumulation of manure there, as well as the refuse midden just outside the entrance, are the breeding-places of swarms of flies. Then, also, the natives defecate just outside their homesteads. The stench around a Tale homestead in the rainy season is enough to shake the hardiest anthropologist. These noisome accompaniments of home-life do not trouble the natives, who look upon animal manure and human excrement as essential fertilizers for their farms.

In spite of these hardships and hazards Tallensi set a very high value on their culture and way of life. In his workaday life the native gives an impression of being a steady, sober person with a good grip of himself. He can work hard if necessary, but he can enjoy idleness too. Wasteful and extravagant at times, especially on certain ceremonial occasions, he is normally frugal and abstemious. A keen sense of property and of the value of material goods goes with generosity to kinsfolk and friends. Though he is no stickler for the letter of custom, he attaches great importance to social rights and obligations. Respect for social and genealogical superiors is a strong point of Tale etiquette, but natives are rarely

INTRODUCTORY 9

obsequious among themselves. With all their respect for custom they are not its slaves. Individual initiative, ambition and independence of action, within the limits imposed by their social and material order, are common.

Tallensi do not question their traditional ritual values, but there is an element of what we should call rationalism in their religious attitudes. Their ancestor cult, an elaborate body of beliefs, rites, and ceremonies, is minutely woven into their everyday existence, but it does not pursue them with phantom terrors. On the contrary, it is the principal means provided by Tale culture for keeping the individual and the group on an even keel.

Stability; tolerance of physical hardship and discomfort as well as of human frailty and idiosyncrasy; a reasonable degree of conformity; a tenacious attachment to life fortified by an elaborate ancestor cult—these characteristics of Tale culture strike the observer at the outset. On the surface the Tale ideal is to have enough to eat, to be a successful parent, and to live at peace with one's fellows. Closer acquaintance, however, reveals hidden undercurrents. Beneath the overt stability and integration of the social order lie continuous tensions. Indeed the stability of Tale society can only be understood as a product of these tensions, created and maintained by the social processes that resolve them. Again, the natives' keen sense of the importance of social obligations hides a tendency to aggressive self-assertion. Tallensi are quick to anger if they feel themselves wronged, and are good haters. Their usual spirit of good-natured tolerance masks a proneness to suspicious watchfulness, and their frugality covers a spendthrift streak. These contradictions are subtly revealed in their religious practices. The strength of their ancestor cult rests not only on its predominant role as an integrating force in their social structure, but also on its profound psychological value for the individual. Tallensi react to misfortune with strong anxiety and guilt feelings from which they find a refuge in their ancestor cult.

This sketch of how the Tallensi strike a European calls for qualifications. It is couched in terms of our cultural values in order to help us to visualize these people in terms of a familiar vocabulary and automatic mental images. Objectively, from the standpoint of the people themselves, the value judgements implicit in our description lose their meaning. What we see as their poverty, dirtiness, poor health, and rudeness of culture they accept with equanimity as the normal conditions of their life. They have no grievance or shame about them. Being common to everybody, these conditions do not create rifts in their society or maladjustments in the individual as they do with us. They are in one respect simply part of the atmosphere within which the culture of the Tallensi (and their neighbours) develops its own richness and amplitude; in another, the material of significant themes in that culture.

Every aspect of Tale social life is conditioned by the fact that they are a primitive peasantry. There is no division of labour apart from that of the sexes. Censuses taken in various parts of the country show that not less than 95 per cent. of the adult males are wholly dependent on agriculture for their livelihood, and all of the odd 5 per cent. are partially dependent on the same source. Craft specialists work at their crafts only

10   INTRODUCTORY

in their spare time, and chiefly in the dry season when there is no farm work. They are exceedingly few in numbers—one or two in a settlement —and their work is of mediocre quality. The only blacksmiths in Taleland are about a dozen men of the Sakpee clan of Tɛnzugu, and only one of them derives a substantial part of his livelihood from his craft. A leather-worker or two, a potteress, a sewer of caps, may be found in almost every settlement. Some men and women who are more skilful than their neighbours at making articles of common use such as hen-coops, baskets, bows, adze-shafts, &c., are in the habit of making a few for sale every dry season. The only specialized occupation is that of the diviner, and it, also, is a part-time occupation in addition to farming, though a popular diviner, making perhaps a shilling or eighteen pence a day, may farm less land than he normally would. Diviners are numerous. There may be as many as ten or twenty in a large settlement, but only one or two of them will earn more than a few pence a day by divining.

British Rule and Contact with Western Civilization

Until the time of my first visit to Taleland the natives had been very little influenced by the agencies of British government and of European civilization that are active in these parts. The main roads skirt Taleland so that the flow of north- and south-bound traffic by-passes the largest part of the area. Nevertheless, these roads have served to open up Taleland to a wider sphere of intercourse with other parts of the Gold Coast than was possible twenty years before. Political and social conditions made it impossible for people to travel freely beyond a radius of a few miles from their own settlements in former days. To-day young men and even women go in increasing numbers every year, in the dry season, to Tamale, Kumasi, or the coast towns. Some go to visit friends or relatives, some carry fowls for sale, others go as seasonal labourers, and others go to work abroad for a term of years. In 1923 the Administration of the Northern Territories reluctantly agreed to assist in the recruitment of labour for the mines and cocoa farms of Ashanti and the colony. The experiment failed and was soon abandoned. Nowadays labour migration from the Northern Territories is entirely voluntary. It has become linked up with the normal economic life of the natives. Whereas, in former years, a young man moved out temporarily to the periphery of settlement on account of a shortage of land in his natal community, nowadays he often goes to Ashanti or the mines as a labourer. The cessation of agricultural activity in the dry season makes it easy for a young man to get away for a few months without loss to the routine of farming.

Economic incentives, which the natives sum up as 'the desire for money', therefore lie behind much labour migration in the Northern Territories. And the value of money may be gauged from the fact that a hen could be bought for 6d. to 1s., a cow in good condition for £2. 10s., and a dish of porridge enough for a satisfying meal for 1/10 of a penny in any market in 1934–7. But there are other incentives as well. Curiosity, and the desire to see the places and experience the life which those who return from a stay abroad describe to their fellows at home, stimulate many a youth to go south for a short or long period. And friction with

INTRODUCTORY

relatives may impel a young man to run away to 'Kumasi', the symbol for everything south of the Black Volta.

Thus one finds that about one man in three has at some time or other in the past two decades visited these, to the Tallensi, still foreign parts. In the settlements near the main roads the dry-season migration of young men may, according to rough estimates made in 1936–7, reach over 10 per cent. of the adult male population. Administrative officers estimate that in 1938–9 about 7 per cent. of the adult male population of Taleland were working abroad with the apparent intention of staying away for a lengthy period. These men bring back small sums of money, ranging from a few shillings to four or five pounds, as well as clothes and other miscellaneous trade goods. Money and clothes[1] are eagerly desired by the Tallensi. These are the most important new wants that have grown up recently as a result of culture contact. Foreign utensils, implements, or tools have hardly entered the productive system of the natives. The foreign ideas and exotic information brought back by the young men arouse curiosity but have made no appreciable impression on the native scheme of values and beliefs, or on their practical knowledge. Labour migrants remain strongly attached to their families and natal settlements, and it is always assumed that they will eventually return. Hitherto, among the Tallensi, very few have been lost to their natal communities; and when they do return, they resume the traditional way of life. Though they are one of the influences modifying the strict letter of custom in minor respects, they are not a disintegrating ferment

[1] Tallensi maintain that there has been a tremendous increase in the amount of clothes worn since the white man opened up the country, and especially since the last war. They point out that nowadays every small boy has a loincloth for festive occasions, whereas even twenty years ago a youth only obtained one when he began courting, at the age of 18 or 19. In those days the ordinary man rarely had a cloth or tunic. His only garb was an animal skin. Nowadays every man has at least one cloth to cover himself at night and to wear during the day when he is not working, and many have two or three garments—a cloth and a tunic, for instance—while well-to-do men have considerable wardrobes. All cotton goods are imported. The Mossi cloth used in former days is still a favourite, especially for loin-cloths and caps, and tunics for special wear. The bulk of it is still imported from French territory, but there are some Mossi weavers at Boləga and Zuarungu who add to the supply. However, quite half if not more of the cotton goods worn by Tallensi is of European origin and the demand is increasing. I once listed all the clothes worn by a number of men and women from one of the most prosperous communities of Taleland as they passed my rest house on the way to the market. The figures are instructive as an indication both of the standard of living of the Tallensi and of the degree to which acculturation in this sphere has progressed. The sample consisted of 62 men and 64 women. Of the men, 35 (56 per cent.) wore cover-cloths of European cotton print; 18 (29 per cent.) wore Mossi cloths; 9 (15 per cent.) wore skins; 8 (13 per cent.) wore khaki shorts, several of them on top of native loin-cloths; the remainder wore native loin-cloths; 19 (30 per cent.) wore some form of European head-gear; 30 (48 per cent.) wore native-made caps. Thus 85 per cent. of these men were clothed, but none of them wholly. Of the women 12 (15 per cent.) wore a piece of cotton print and one wore a Mossi cloth—a very large incidence such as would not be found in most other Tale communities. The rest were nude, except for the perineal band and back-flap. As people dress up specially for market day, these figures are not indicative of everyday habits. The greater conservatism of women suggested by these figures is due in great part to their lack of opportunities for obtaining cash incomes for personal use.

INTRODUCTORY

in the native social order. Apart from money and clothes, the material articles, habits, and ideas which they have acquired abroad soon decay from disuse, or come to serve for ostentation only, since they have no functional relevance to the economic life and social structure of the native society.

The Tallensi, in short, still preserve the culture bequeathed to them by their forefathers and the social structure of their own, homogeneous society. Their economy is a primitive, static, subsistence economy. They continue to farm by the same methods and with the same tools and the same knowledge as their forefathers had. They grow no cash crops and produce no surplus of local crops for sale outside Taleland. The introduction of British currency and the opening up of the country have accelerated local exchange and slightly mitigated the hardship of winning a living by primitive technical methods from a soil of no great fertility. They have not otherwise affected the livelihood of 99 per cent. of the people.

Literacy and Christianity had, until 1936, barely touched the Tallensi. A few children had been sent to school reluctantly in deference to the commands of the District Commissioners. Only one stayed the course and left school with a moderate command of English and the three R's. Two or three younger boys were still at school at Gambaga or Tamale. The nearest mission station to the Tallensi is that of the White Fathers at Bolǝga, outside Taleland. Up to 1936 the missionaries had made only an occasional visit of reconnaissance to the nearby Tale settlements. They had succeeded in attracting only two or three Tale youths to their school. These were the sons of two ambitious, and, from the native point of view, upstart headmen who were keen to have their sons taught the white man's skills the better to serve their own political ambitions. The only one of these youths who achieved a fair degree of literacy and accepted the Christian faith was in Government employment.

Most of the social changes that have occurred and are taking place with increasing rapidity in Taleland are due to a single powerful extraneous factor, British rule. The Tallensi, in common with other tribes of these parts, put up a truculent resistance to British rule at first, and had to be subjugated by military operations and other punitive measures. The last pocket of Tale resistance, in the Tong Hills, was finally broken by a small armed force in 1911. The people of the Hills were expelled from their ancestral homes, which were razed to the ground, and lived in exile on the plains at the foot of the hills until they were permitted to return in 1935. Judging by the scanty memoranda of the Administrative officers of the decade 1911–21, the Tallensi gave them a good deal of trouble.

These events are still vividly remembered by the natives. Their fear and suspicion of the white man was not unnatural since they had never before met him. However, their subjugation and the subsequent imposition of peace have produced in them a deep respect for the might and power of the white man. They have since learnt to have complete confidence in the justice and good intentions of the Administrative officers. They speak with gratitude of the benefits which the white man's peace

INTRODUCTORY

has brought them. But in the background there still lurk traces of fear and suspicion, a sense of the inscrutability of the white man.

The influence of British rule has naturally been most marked in Tale political life. At first it was directed towards two main ends: to maintain the peace between the Administration and the native communities as well as amongst the latter, and to ensure a sufficient supply of labour and local materials from the native population for keeping up roads and rest houses. The Administrative officers laid down boundaries, meted out justice, and backed up chiefs and headmen, mostly appointed by themselves, in the exercise of coercive powers over the mass of the people. Nothing was known about the country or the people, and the Administrative officers had to rely on their own sense of justice and their own ideas of what was in the interests of the population. The natives look back on this period with few regrets. They describe it as a time when extortion was widely practised not only by the police, the soldiers, the interpreters, and others who stood between them and the District Commissioners, but also by their newly empowered chiefs and headmen. They learnt to think of any official or unofficial servant of the white man as armed with arbitrary authority which it would be futile to resist.

The outstanding political changes due to this period were the authority given to chiefs and headmen, and the unofficial tribunals held by them. These grew up gradually out of the need to keep the peace; for the ancient method of settling disputes was by negotiation backed by armed self-help. From the native point of view the most valuable relic of this period is the embryonic legal system which grew up then. Armed self-help has disappeared, but some of the values connected with it remain. The other institutions of the native political organization retain their vigour. They function side by side with the institutions imposed by British rule, for they serve different ends and correspond to different values. It is often an uneasy partnership leading to insoluble conflicts. Most of the political troubles of the Tallensi since 1921 can be traced to the clash between interests and loyalties springing from the native political system and those created by the new political dispensation and its accompanying economic changes. For the first time in its history a few men of outstanding wealth have arisen in Taleland by extorting goods and services from their fellows on the strength of their political powers, or by exploiting opportunities due to the opening up of the country. And this has brought social friction in its train.

This period of British rule came to an end about 1931. Between 1931 and 1936 the Administration undertook a complete political reorganization of the Northern Territories of the Gold Coast. The principles of what is commonly called Indirect Rule were applied. Native Authorities were established, a graded scale of direct taxation was introduced, a policy of economic development was started, and social services were multiplied. The effects of this policy will not be discernible for some years.

Taleland is a very small portion of the Northern Territories of the Gold Coast. But in its culture and social structure, as in its geography and climate, it is typical of the whole plateau north of the Gambaga scarp.

CHAPTER II

THE MEANING OF 'TALLENSI'

Tribal Divisions

TALELAND is, as we have seen, merely a portion of a far greater, eco-logically uniform region, marked off only by an artificial boundary. The same kind of subsistence farming is practised throughout the whole region of which Taleland forms a part. The culture of its inhabitants likewise represents a far more widely spread type. Before we embark on our sociological analysis we must know what sort of a unit we are dealing with. Have the people of Taleland any form of cultural or structural unity and singularity that differentiates them from neighbouring socio-geographical areas? Or are they a fraction of a greater society arbitrarily circumscribed to suit the convenience of the field worker?

The question is not so easy to answer as might be expected. For the natives of Taleland, like the other so-called 'tribes' north of the Gambaga scarp, have no obvious political unity distinguishing them from like political units. In terms of their own political and social organization there is no single government exercising authority over all the people of Taleland, and only over them, within their own defined territory. This has been the most serious obstacle confronting British adminis-tration in this area.[1] We must approach the problem from a different angle.

In the literature and in administrative practice the inhabitants of Taleland are called the Tallensi[2] and are distinguished as a 'tribe' from neighbouring 'tribes', the Kusaasi on the east, the Namnam or Nabdam on the north, the Nankansi or Gorǝnsi (in Talni, Gɔrisi) on the west, the Mamprusi on the south of them. All these groups speak dialects of Mole-Dagbane. But Kusal, Nabte, and Gɔrni are closely akin to Mole, whereas Talni and Mampurule have closer affinities with Dagbane. These dialect areas have no strict boundaries. At the frontiers one passes through intermediate zones where the people speak intermediate dialects or are equally familiar with two contiguous dialects. But it is clearly recognized, both by the natives and by outside observers, that the tribes enumerated above have more in common with one another linguistically than any of them have with the peoples of the same cultural type farther away, such as the Woolisi (usually called the Kassena in the literature and by the

---

[1] For an outline of Tale political organization and a discussion of some of the theoretical problems raised by it, see *African Political Systems*, edited by M. Fortes and E. E. Evans-Pritchard, Oxford, 1940.

[2] *Sc.* Talense (Rattray), Talansi (Cardinall), sing. Talenga, Talanga. This form, correctly Talǝnsi, sing. Talǝŋa, is taken from the dialect of the Zuarungu district (Gorǝni, or in the dialect of the Tallensi, Gɔrni). The artificial spelling I use has been adopted to show that the Tallensi regard this phonetic form as a foreigners' version of the name by which they designate themselves. In their own dialect (Talni) they call themselves Talis, sing. Talǝŋa. Talni forms will henceforth be used for all vernacular words in the text.

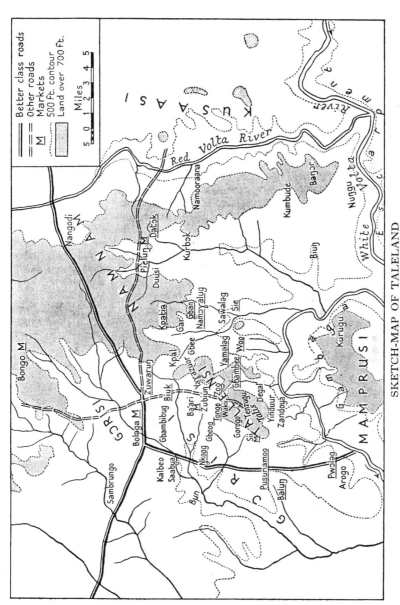

SKETCH-MAP OF TALELAND

Note: All place-names are spelt phonetically according to their Talni form.

16   THE MEANING OF 'TALLENSI'

Administration) of Navrongo or the Bulisi (Builsa) of Kanjaga district, whose tongues are not intelligible to Mole or Dagbane speakers.

In the same way it is well known that the Kusaasi, Namnam, Gorənsi, and Tallensi are more closely allied in culture *inter se* than they are with other neighbouring 'tribes'. In this part of West Africa one can often tell where a person comes from by his facial cicatrizations.[1] People of these four groups all have the same facial marks, a slashed scar (*bɛn*) running diagonally downwards from the bridge of the nose across one or both cheeks, which are, in addition, often embellished with a neat tracery of tiny incisions (*yiis*) spreading in herring-bone lines over the forehead and down to the neck. These markings are an emblem of their cultural uniformity, as compared with neighbouring groups. Mamprusi and Mossi, frankly contemptuous of their nakedness and poverty, lump them all together under the sobriquet ' Gorənsi '. Since the coming of the white man they have been called 'the Farafaras' and they are beginning to accept this appellation, which is said to be derived from one of their customary expressions of greeting, *ni i fara-fara-fara*.

There are, in short, no precise linguistic or cultural boundaries between these four groups. Nor are there precise political or structural boundaries between them. They overlap with one another in every way; and further research would, I am certain, show that the Kusaasi, Namnam, and Gorənsi also overlap to some extent with their neighbours other than the Tallensi. At the same time, each of these four groups is considered by members of the other three and by its own members to be in some way a distinct territorial, linguistic, and cultural group. It is, however, a distinction of degree, not of kind. Each group comprises a cluster of communities which have more in common among themselves, linguistically and in the details and nuances of custom, belief, and values, than any of them have with other neighbouring communities. They have closer social ties among themselves than any of them have with their other neighbours, though they have no apparent political unity and never, in the past, combined for war against external enemies or for common defence.

This largely implicit feeling of their difference from neighbouring dialect areas which prevails amongst such a cluster of communities is not based on a conception of tribal unity. Sharp distinctions of custom, belief, and values, as well as of structural relationships, are recognized within the cluster. They are, indeed, of fundamental importance for the social interrelations of the communities making up the cluster. On the same principle as before, the cluster is subdivided into smaller constellations of communities which have more in common, closer bonds, *inter se*, than any of them have with other communities. Culturally, and structurally, as we shall discover in the course of our study, society in the Volta region is built up on a segmentary principle. The degree of unity, coherence, autonomy, or singularity of a socio-geographic segment of

[1] These distinguishing facial marks were noted by the first European traveller who visited the Northern Territories of the Gold Coast, the Frenchman Binger. Cf. Binger, Capitaine, *Du Niger au Golfe de Guinée*, 1893, vol. ii, pp. 34–7. For diagrams of these markings see Armitage, C. H., *The Tribal Markings and Marks of Adornment of the Natives of the Northern Territories of the Gold Coast*, Royal Anthropological Institute, 1924, especially figs. 4, 6, 26.

PLATE I

(a) Outskirts of a Tale settlement in the late dry season. In the distance (right) a sacred grove (tɔŋgban).

(b) View of a Tale settlement about the middle of the rainy season.

PLATE II

(b) A pair of marriageable maidens dressed up for a visit to the market.

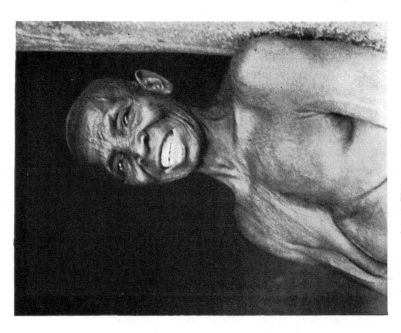

(a) A Tale grandmother.

THE MEANING OF 'TALLENSI'

society is a function of its segmentary relations to other like regions and to more inclusive regions, up to the limit of the widest frame of social reference relevant for that region. In consequence, social groups are identified in relation to one another by a technique of contraposition. This is very clearly seen among the Tallensi.

Cultural Segmentation of the Tallensi

From Zuarungu one can see the silhouette of the Tong Hills bounding the horizon seven miles to the south. That, say the people of Zuarungu, is where the Tallensi live. As a group they consider themselves to be quite distinct from the Tallensi, though many individuals have kinsmen among the latter—their own mothers' people, or more distant cognatic kinsmen, or affinal relatives. Even nowadays, when women and children can travel safely anywhere, intercourse between Zuarungu and the Tallensi is confined almost entirely to trade in the markets. In former times it was more than a Zuarungu man's life was worth to venture amongst the Tallensi unless he had kinsfolk there to protect him.

Between Zuarungu and the Tong Hills stretches an unbroken chain of settlements—Biuk, Ba'ari, Zubiuŋ, Tongo, Wakii, and Soog. The people of Biuk speak Gɔrni and consider themselves an outpost of Zuarungu. But a number of them live across the watercourse which separates their land from that of Ba'ari, side by side with Ba'ari families and farming on Ba'ari soil.[1] Such overlapping of contiguous settlements is common. The Ba'ari people are Tallensi, though a great many of them understand Gɔrni as easily as their mother tongue owing to their contiguity with Gɔris. Gɔrni forms have even crept into their vocabulary. Between them and their Gɔre neighbours there is much intermarriage; but the insistence on their distinctness remains. The picture is the same from whichever direction one enters Taleland. At Gar I was once told 'We are Namnam-Tallensi'—an accurate enough description of their linguistically and culturally intermediate position.

And yet, everywhere along the frontier the Tong Hills are pointed out as the real centre of the Tallensi. To the testimony of their neighbours may be added that of the Administration which has always regarded the Tallensi as a distinct, if amorphous, political unit.

The easiest if most superficial approach to the social structure of a society is through the nomenclature of social identification, the techniques by which people sort out their relations to one another in order to know how to conduct themselves. But nomenclature, like the conduct it tends to precipitate, is always a function of a situation, not an absolute classification.

Foreigners and their neighbours have a single label for all the Tallensi. The latter equally make no distinction in nomenclature between one Gɔraŋ and another, or one Nabt and another, no matter where he may come from, when the circumstances require no more precise specification.

This technique of identification is based on locality, direction, propinquity, and actual or alleged contrasts of language and institutions; it is a technique of contraposition arising from the segmentary structure of the society, and is the commonest method of social classification employed

[1] And Biuk is also linked to the Tallensi by clanship as we shall see (Ch. IV).

18   THE MEANING OF 'TALLENSI'

in the culture of this area. A member of one social group identifies another social group or individual by comparison or contrast with his own social identity, and in terms of the most inclusive grouping which suffices to identify the latter unambiguously. The exact identification is relative to the frame of reference common to both parties.

Wherever he may come from in Taleland, a man calls himself a Taləŋ in contrast to non-Tallensi, citing differences of speech and custom. Thus, female circumcision is practised over a large part of the Northern Territories. All the Tallensi think it a repugnant custom, and say: 'We Talis don't do that—it is a custom (lit. work) of the Gəris (*Tam Talis pu ɛt lan—Gɔris tuomər nla*).' But Tallensi from different parts of Taleland draw almost equally sharp distinctions amongst themselves, using the same technique of contraposition.

To understand this we must consider the spatial distribution of Tale settlements. For Tale social structure is inseparable from the spatial relations of social units. We shall start from Tongo (Talni, *Tɔŋ*), about a mile from the foot of the hills (see sketch-map, p. 15), one of the most thickly populated settlements in the country and regarded by the Administration as the capital of Taleland. Typically of this part of the country, Tongo and the settlements adjacent to it on all sides— Ba'ari, Zubiuŋ, Zoo, Soog, Wakii, and Gbeog—form a continuous area of habitation thickly studded with homesteads. Beyond this aggregate stretches another ring of settlements indistinguishably continuous with it at many points. On one side of Ba'ari live its Gəre neighbours, on the other is Yaɣazuor, which is separated only by small hillocks and a block of bush-farms from Kpatia, Kpal, and Gbee. The farthest homesteads of Zubiuŋ lie against a low bulge in the plain from the bouldery tip of which one looks down on Sɔk and Yaməlɔg, a mile or two away. Zoo and Gbambee merge into one another and overlook Woo. Soog, Wakii, and Gbeog encircle the slopes of the Tong Hills and are separated from Tɛnzugu, the settlement in the fertile hollow embracing almost the entire summit, only by the ridge of enormous boulders which forms the crown. Gbeog overlaps Ka'ar, which is continuous with Gorogo, Sipaat, and Sii. These settlements climb right up into the gullies and amongst the boulders of the slope of the Hills and straggle out across the broad plain to blend with Ŋkoog. The homesteads of Sii curl round the nose of the Hills to mingle with those on the outskirts of Yinduur and Zandoya, on the other side below the rim of the Hills. A mile farther along, at the foot of the Hills on their eastern side, are the more scattered homesteads of Santɛŋ, Teelɔg, Syɛk, and Wɔɣar, separated from Tɛnzugu only by the brow of the Hills.

This compact block of settlements is barely separated from a similar block five or six miles north-east of the Hills which begins at Sawalɔg. Between Zoo and Yaməlɔg lies a mile or so of stony hummocks, covered in parts with the low scrub which shows that it had been cultivated and then abandoned. This is where many people from Tongo and Zoo have their bush-farms. Yaməlɔg occupies a shallow depression between hillocks. Then comes a stretch of two or three miles of typical orchard bush before the homesteads of Sawalɔg and Sie are reached. Thence a traveller can

THE MEANING OF 'TALLENSI'

continue through Sie-Tɛndaaŋ or Namɔyalug to Gban, Gar, and Kpatia or to Buug, Duusi, Datɔk, and beyond to Pieluŋ and Nangodi with scarcely a break in the continuity of settlement.

In addition to these two main blocks of settlements—let us call them, for convenience, the Tongo district and the Sie district—there are scattered Tale settlements, separated from them and from one another by stretches of bush, between them and the Volta rivers—Namooraana, Diga'ar, Tola, Kumbude, Biuŋ, and Gbiug-on-the-river being the most important. But other settlements on the frontiers of Taleland, the inhabitants of which are not recognized as Tallensi by outsiders, also fall into the framework of their political geography.

The first puzzle a stranger must unravel, if he hopes to understand the life of our people, is the apparent contradiction between the density of residential aggregation and the cleavages underlying their social relations. He will meet it latent in simple and casual occurrences, or conspicuously overt in organized collective events such as the communal hunting and fish drives, the Great Festivals, or other ceremonial gatherings.

Taleland is thickly populated. The Tongo district alone has a population of over 12,000 according to the 1931 census. This area of ancient habitation—*tɛŋ kɔrɔg*, an old country, as the natives describe it—has supported a sedentary population for a period which cannot be less than several centuries. Sacrifices are made on graves of ancestors said to have lived ten or eleven generations ago. No one familiar with the people would doubt the authenticity of these graves; but the three centuries or so of settlement this implies must, I believe, be considered a minimum period. Centuries of intermarriage have woven a web of kinship which embraces the whole country. The patterns of institutions and ideas are uniform throughout Taleland. Yet a fundamental dogma of their collective life is that of local and sectional particularism, and of divergence within the common patterns.

The 'Real Talis'

Neither the Tongo people, nor those living in the Sie district, are considered to be real Talis; the 'real Talis' are the folk who live on and around the Tong Hills. The Great Festivals are usually cited as a decisive criterion of classification. The 'real Talis' (*Talis mɛŋa*), a Tɛnzugu elder once stated, are in the following places: Tɛnzugu, Santɛŋ, Yinduur, Sii, Gorogo, Wakii, Gbeog, and Soog, as well as the small settlements near Santɛŋ and the offshoots of Wakii at Gbambee and Woo. '*Tam tɔmɔra Talis tuntuoma, ti Gɔlib ni ti Bɔyaraam*—We perform the works of Talis, our *Gɔlib* and *Bɔyaraam* festivals.' Tongo and Zoo, Yamɔlɔg and Sie, are Namoos, he continued; and Zubiuŋ and Sɔk, Ba'ari and Yaɣazuor, belong more closely to the Namoos than to the Talis. '*Bam tɔmɔra namoorɔt*—They celebrate (lit. work) after the Namoo fashion, the *Giŋgaaŋ* and *Da'a* festivals.' There remain Sawalɔg, Sie-Tɛndaaŋ, Duusi, and the settlements close to them. '*Bam lɛbɔra Namnam sani*—They fall in with the Namnam' (whose chief festival is called *Tɛŋɔn-lɛbɔgɔt*.)[1]

---

[1] A brief account of one aspect of these festivals is given in my paper 'Ritual

THE MEANING OF 'TALLENSI'

The Zubiuŋ and Ba'ari people, however, do not accept this classification, which expresses the orientation of Tɛnzugu, without qualifications. The former admit their close territorial and political assimilation to Tongo, but they insist on their cultural distinctness, associating themselves, in this respect, with the Hill Talis. They quote in support other discriminatory indices than the Great Festivals. Firstly, like all the Talis, they do not have the avoidances of the first-born children distinctive of all Namoos (see below, Chap. V). On the contrary, all people of Zubiuŋ descent avoid eating tortoise (*pakur*), turtle (*mieŋ*), and cat (*sakoo*), the first two of which are also taboo to most of the Hill Talis. Secondly, they cite their mortuary and funeral ritual, the two points of crucial divergence being that they, like most of the Talis, dress the dead in a loin cover of sheepskin (*suona pɛhug*), whereas the Namoos use a goatskin (*suona buu*); and that to conclude a funeral they *ŋma ma'ala* with the sacrifice of many fowls, whereas the Namoos *ŋma wɔyar*—a totally different rite in which weapons and household utensils are offered to the departed spirit. Finally, Zubiuŋ people say: '*Tam dira tɛndaan, ti pu diit naam la*—We (like all Talis) have (lit. eat) the tɛndaanaship (i.e. the ritual office of Custodian of the Earth), we do not have the chiefship (like the Namoos).'

The Ba'ari people, with the added self-assurance due to their political independence of Tongo, declare themselves to be Talis on the same grounds, though their totemic avoidances differ from those of the hill folk. As a clinching argument they point out that the Great Festivals celebrated by the Talis form part of a cycle inaugurated by the senior Ba'ari tɛndaana.

Tongo shares the views of Zubiuŋ and Ba'ari about their relationship to the Talis. Very often at a Zubiuŋ funeral I could not help being amused at the behaviour of Tongo visitors. Close neighbours though they are of Zubiuŋ with which they have, individually, innumerable ties of cognatic and affinal kinship, they always adopted a posture in keeping with this structural cleavage. They would sit all together, at a little distance from the spot where the rites were in progress, punctiliously preserving an appearance of indifference, as befits outsiders. At the same time, Tongo people emphasize their specially close local and political ties with their immediate neighbours which mark the latter off from the Hill Talis in certain respects. Similar distinctions are made in the Sie district. A Tongo, Ba'ari, or Tɛnzugu man bound for Sie or Datɔk says, 'I am going to Nabrug (the country of the Namnam)', unless it is necessary to be more precise. The people of Sie and a number of the neighbouring settlements are Namoos; yet talking about farming they say: 'The Talis always sow first and then we follow'—referring thus to all the settlements south-west of Zoo. But when they are discussing war or marriage, ritual or chiefship, they distinguish between Tongo and Zoo on the one hand—*ti mabiis*, our brethren—and the real Talis on the other. At Duusi and Sie-Tɛndaaŋ dwell the senior tɛndaanas of the district, whose social and ritual status is identical with that of the tɛndaanas of the Tongo district. 'Taləŋ' in contraposition to themselves means essentially someone from the vicinity

Festivals and Social Cohesion in the Hinterland of the Gold Coast', *American Anthropologist*, vol. xxxviii, No. 4.

THE MEANING OF 'TALLENSI'

of the Tong Hills; yet 'we and the Talis are one' they maintain. In proof of this they point out that their *Tɛŋən-lɛbəgət* Festival belongs to the same cycle as *Da'a* and *Bɔyaraam*, though they have but the vaguest hearsay knowledge of the esoteric ritual of these festivals. Their neighbours at Sie and Datɔk they call Namoos.

> *Note*: For convenience of exposition we shall adopt the following convention in this book. Whenever we speak of all the inhabitants of Taleland, irrespective of their internal subdivisions, we shall use the name given to them by other outsiders and speak of them as *Tallensi*. When we wish to refer to that section of the Tallensi whom they themselves describe as the 'real Talis', we shall refer to them as *Talis*, distinguishing among them, when necessary, between the *Hill Talis*, who live on and around the Tong Hills, and the Talis of the Plain, who live nearer Tongo (i.e. Zubiuŋ, Gbizug, Ba'ari, Yayazuor).

Nomenclature and the Structural Scheme

This nomenclature reflects a structural scheme of considerable complexity. It points to institutional allegiances which segregate adjacent social units from each other and group together spatially dispersed units. The major cleavage it reveals is that between the Namoo communities, on the one hand, and the settlements of the real Talis and of those who claim to be akin to them, on the other. But it indicates, also, that there are other lines of division and bonds of union both within each major grouping and cutting across the cleavage. It is a cardinal principle of Tale social structure that every social grouping defined as a unit in one situation, or according to one principle, dissolves into an association of lesser and differentiated units in another situation or according to another principle. Variation in custom or in ideological emphasis is regarded by the natives as one of the most significant indices of group differentiation. It is also, as we shall see, an important factor of social integration.

It is therefore a topic of perennial interest to the natives to observe and comment on variations of usage and doctrine. The idea that identity of custom and belief is desirable or natural is inconceivable. Everybody adheres staunchly to the forms of social behaviour accepted in his own group without desiring to impose them on others. 'Look at the Namoos,' observed Ta'aŋ one day, 'don't they (i.e. different sections of the same clan) do different things at funeral ceremonies? But their use of a goat (in mortuary rites), that is all one. We Talis, again, using our sheep (in mortuary rites)—this is the same for all of us. But as for our ritual, we split up and do different things.' Each one with his father's ways, everyone with his ancestor's ways (*Sɔ ni u ba yɛl, sɔ ni u yaab yɛl*)—that is, every group has its distinctive ancestral customs—is a characteristic Tale aphorism. This attitude, emphasizing simultaneously community and differentiation, similarity of pattern, and divergence of detail, permeates Tale thought.

Myths of Origin

Whenever Tallensi discuss the cleavages in their society they trace

22 THE MEANING OF 'TALLENSI'

them back to differences of origin. Everyone knows that all Namoos came originally from Mampurugu, how long ago nobody can tell. The tradition of Tongo, as it was related to me on many occasions, is as follows: The ancestor who founded Tongo was Mosuor. He was the Paramount Chief (*na'ab*) of Mampurugu, but had to flee the country after being vanquished in a fight for the chiefship. When he reached Tongo the Gbizug tɛndaana, Gɛnɔt, was living there. Mosuor came to the house but found nobody there; for Tɛndaan Gɛnɔt had seen him coming and had sought refuge in the nearby hills. Now, there is a watercourse a little distance off and there he found a shallow pit beside which stood a *kiŋkaŋ* (*Ficus*) tree which was shedding its leaves. A path led from this water-hole towards the Hills and someone had been carrying water which had spilled over on to this path. 'Thereupon', to quote the version of one of my Tongo informants, 'our ancestor said, "There is someone in these hills who comes to fetch water here". So he caused the dry fig leaves to be scattered on the path and went to hide quietly. In due course he saw Tɛndaan Gɛnɔt stepping along the path, while the leaves crunched *kaɣa, kaɣa*, coming to fetch water. Thereupon our ancestor Mosuor, having seen him, caught him and asked him what he was afraid of. Why did he run away and hide? Gɛnɔt replied that he had seen him wearing a gown and that there was something on his head all red, and fear took hold of him.[1] So Mosuor brought him back and asked, "Who owns this house?" He said that it was his house, and Mosuor brought him home thither and said that he himself would settle down here and Gɛnɔt as well. He said that Gɛnɔt would be his tɛndaana to carry out the sacrifices on his behalf.'

Gbizug elders told the story of Mosuor in much the same way but omitting the trick by which Mosuor caught their ancestor, adding that it was the horses and guns of Mosuor that inspired fear in Tɛndaan Gɛnɔt. They say, also, that having accepted Mosuor as a settler and having allotted land to him close beside his own homestead, he told Mosuor what were the taboos of the country (*tɛŋɔn-kiha*), and entered into a solemn pact of blood-brotherhood with him. They *ŋma pɔlɔŋ*, cut wrists. A cut was made on the wrist of each, and each licked the blood of the other. Thus '*ba leeba mabiih, ba leeba soog*, they became brethren, they became uterine brothers' and pledged themselves and their descendants to perpetual peace. This was a unique instance of blood-brotherhood, which is not practised in Taleland to-day.

According to this tradition, Tɛndaan Gɛnɔt told Mosuor of his kinsmen, the Ba'at-Sakpar Tɛndaana, the Wakii Tɛndaana, the Degal tɛndaana, and the Ka'ar tɛndaana. These five were the original inhabitants of the country. They sprang from the Earth itself, say their descendants. At Gbizug they declare that Tɛndaan Gɛnɔt's ancestor Bumbiogta'adug sprouted from the earth (*u bulme na*), he had no father or mother (*u ka ba u ka ma*). Pressed further they say, '*u yi Naawun zug sig na*—he descended from Heaven'. Heaven and Earth are one, they contend; they have the same mystical value. At Wakii they call their first

---

[1] A red fez and a cloth tunic are the distinctive costume of chiefs of Mampuru origin. Tɛndaanas may not wear garments of cloth. They are ritually obliged to wear skins only. Chiefs and their clansmen may ride horses, tɛndaanas not.

THE MEANING OF 'TALLENSI' 23

ancestor Teŋənbuləg—Earth-begotten—and give the same myth of his origin. The people of Degal and of Ka'ar attribute a similar origin to their first ancestors. Tendaan Genət is said to have begotten Dagbeog (Bearded man) whose descendants are the Gbeog people, who are therefore a 'brother' lineage to Gbizug (=*Gbeog zug*, the upper part of Gbeog).

One of Genət's 'brothers'—the exact genealogical relationship is regarded as of no consequence, some describing him as *soog* (uterine kinsman), others as *pit* (younger brother)—was Daziug (Red man), a hunter who founded the Ba'at-Sakpar line; and another 'brother' of his founded one of the Zubiuŋ lineages. Indeed all the primordial tendaanas were 'brothers' in a more general sense, the concepts of kinship serving here consciously to identify them with one another.

These myths, meagre as they appear, are laid down with a finality of conviction that makes any question of their historical truthfulness irrelevant.

Most of the Hill Talis are also alleged to have been immigrants originally who arrived to find the Degal Tendaana living on top of the hills. But their myths of origin are as deficient in circumstantial detail as those of the primordial tendaanas. Thus candid people at Yinduuri said complacently: 'We don't know, it is said that our ancestor came from Tampoləŋ in Mampurugu, but now we have all become Talis.' People of other clans told a vague story of an ancestor wandering about the uninhabited hills, sheltering in caves, until one day he observed the smoke of a fire. Going towards it he discovered the Degal tendaana, and later settled on the Hills. Gorogo is said to have been founded thus by Woolisi immigrants, Sii by Bulisi and Mamprusi, and some of the Tenzugu lineages by Mamprusi, Kusaasi, or Gərisi. The origins thus attributed to any community symbolize special ritual relationships with the areas they are alleged to have migrated from, which are still maintained.

All these myths of origin become intelligible when it is realized that they are nothing more than formulations of the contemporary scheme of political and ceremonial relationships. The Tallensi themselves are philosophers enough to appreciate this. Many Namoos, for example, privately view the myth of the primordial tendaanas with unaffected scorn. 'They lie', declared Sayəbazaa, a shrewd and respected elder of Tongo, himself a kinsman of the present[1] Gbizug tendaana. 'A human being can't emerge sprouting out of the earth. The rain falls, and the millet comes up, trees come up, grass comes up; but we have never seen a human being sprout up.' When I tried to defend the tendaanas, he countered triumphantly: 'And if their ancestor really sprouted up, why don't they let a person sprout again?' Then, with a sudden inspiration he proposed an explanation: 'Suppose you come and settle here and your children succeed you, and their children, and their children succeed and so on, and so on. Then, one day strangers come and ask your descendants whence they have sprung. Will they not say that their ancestor was begotten of the earth? We Namoos', he concluded, 'are immigrants (*kpeeha*) here.' This acute estimation of the myths gives a clue to their

[1] The present time throughout this book refers to the years 1934–7.

24 THE MEANING OF 'TALLENSI'

ideological significance as a counterweight to the Mosuor legend and as a dogma of prior habitation.

In the Sie district the Sawaləg people, whose political and ceremonial relations with the Sie Namoos are exactly parallel to those of Gbizug with Tongo, also declare that their ancestor came into being miraculously, self-generated. In the identical phraseology of the people of Gbizug and Wakii, they say, 'Our ancestor descended from Heaven', or 'Our ancestor sprouted from the earth'. I once challenged the clan-head of Sawaləg to prove how this was possible. His answer, shrewdly rationalistic, deserves to be recorded. 'We have not heard that our ancestor came from any other land. We have no other land to return to as the Sie people (immigrant Namoos) have. If they desecrate (sayəm, lit. spoil) the land here, they return to their (original) land yonder (at Tongo). That is why we say that we have descended from Heaven'—an interpretation which coincides with that of Sayəbazaa, the Namoo.

The covenant between Mosuor and Tɛndaan Gɛnət, again, accords well with a myth which is but a projection into the unchallengeable past of the present-day relationships between Gbizug and Tongo. The amorphous and unstandardized myths of origin with which the Hill Talis are satisfied symbolize the remarkable social integration they had achieved before their subjugation by the British in 1911. For nowadays the Hill Talis are rent by factions and by an intestine struggle for power amongst the various ritual office-holders. Rival claims are validated by citing established custom, by appealing to the memories of men, or, in the last resort, by the fabrication or distortion of myths of origin. The Administration recognizes as chiefs only those clan heads whose title is derived directly or indirectly from the Paramount Chief of the Mamprusi. Hence we find the Gɔlibdaana of Tɛnzugu justifying his pretensions to recognized chiefship by concocting, for the benefit of a white inquirer, a story of how the founder of his lineage migrated thither from Mampurugu—a story which his enemies scoff at. The Sii Bɔyaraan, on the other hand, tries to strengthen his claim to precedence by alleging not only a Mampuru origin for his ancestors, but also that they were the very first to come and settle on the Hills.

These new myths are part of the defensive ideologies engendered by social conflict, but they follow the axioms of Tale thought. The Tallensi have no conception of a mythological or historical past of their society when people lived and behaved differently from to-day. The past is but an extension into the days of their forefathers of the life of to-day on the same rational plane of existence. Their history is to them not a sequence of events or a progression but a continuity. All that matters of the past, which lies beyond the span of man's recollection, lives on in the social structure, the ideology, the morality, and institutions of to-day. These are the palpable proofs of things that happened 'oh ho, ti banam ni ti yaanam ni—in the days of our forefathers and ancestors'; one can infer from them what must have been the state of society in those far-off times. Conversely, the social arrangements which prevail to-day are valid, sensible, and appropriate not only because they achieve desired ends but also because banam ni yaanam ndaa piil na—the forefathers and ancestors

THE MEANING OF 'TALLENSI'

started and transmitted them. Custom is not inviolable in its own right. It is compelling because it is the legacy of the ancestors.

These notions are perfectly explicit in the behaviour and thought of the natives, for whom they have a profound moral value. *Banam ndaa ɛŋ de, yaanam ndaa ɛŋ de*—our forefathers used to do it, our ancestors used to do it, is a recurrent formula in every ceremonial speech or ritual invocation during the Great Festivals. So the Samiitna'ab protesting his loyalty to traditional values and to the Kpata'arna'ab, in the latter's feud with the Gɔlibdaana, exclaimed: 'It is the young men who are causing the trouble. They desire their cloths and their caps; but I know only what my ancestors did (*man mi la n-yaanam ndaa ɛŋ siem*). My ancestor (*n-yaab*) wore a skin and I, too, wear a skin; my ancestor knew nothing of cloth. I know only my forefathers' path and I adhere to that (*man mi la mbanam suor, man dɔla dɛni*).'

In the same way, and because their social system engenders so strong a sense of the continuity and stability of their culture and social organization, Tallensi always stress the importance of passing on to their descendants the way of life bequeathed to them by their forefathers. At ceremonies or when disputes are argued out before a chief or a lineage head, it is not uncommon to hear the old men praise the young men who attend. 'Thus,' the old men say, 'they (the young men) will learn the customs (*yɛla*) of our ancestors.' Tallensi place an extremely high value on their social order. An individual or a particular corporate group might desire to alter his or its position in the society. A man might desire to have greater prestige or more power than his neighbours. A clan might strive to assert its supremacy over other clans, whether or not it is entitled to do so. No one would dream of trying to overthrow the whole social order or of agitating against the existing customs and values.

This does not mean that Tale customs never change, or that the Tallensi believe this to be the case, or invariably resist cultural changes. There have been many shifts in custom and usage during the past two decades. The imposition of peace and an embryonic judicial system have diminished the tensions that kept unrelated clans apart and so have made it unnecessary for them to over-emphasize the emblems and symbols of their separateness. Fifteen years ago men of a tɛndaana's clan used to observe strictly the taboo against wearing gowns and trousers, the distinctive garments of chiefs and men of chiefly (i.e. Namoo) clans. To-day the young men of tɛndaanas' clans all wear such clothes outside the territory with which they have direct ritual ties. By this simple compromise they make the best of both worlds, the old world of strictly defined local, genealogical, and politico-ritual exclusiveness and the new world of free movement, unrestricted social intercourse with all and sundry, and cheaper clothes. They wear the ancient prescribed garb of a skin and a loin-cloth on ritual occasions, especially during the Great Festivals, when they take a pride in advertising their politico-ritual status. This change of custom does not cut athwart the basic values and principles of Tale social organization. It has arisen because the young men of tɛndaanas' clans are as eager to display themselves in fine clothes as the young men of other clans, and because the wearing of clothes is economically easier to attain than formerly, and the social cleavages symbolized in this habit are no longer so drastic as before. On the other hand, when the Golibdaana, in his overweening conceit, tried to copy the dress and the court procedure of a Mampuru chief, there was wide indignation. The Chief of Tongo, with whom he thus sought to equate himself, protested with such vigour to the District Commissioner that the latter ordered the Golibdaana to stop his new practices. A man of enormous wealth and great power failed to get away with an innovation prepared with extravagant expense, because it ran counter to the politico-ritual structure of the society. He would never, incidentally, have dared to attempt this in former times, or, for that matter, have had the motive to do so. His behaviour is due to the arrogance of newly acquired wealth and power. But Tale institutions are still too strongly integrated to give way to such blatant subversion.

The notions of the continuity, persistence, and stability of their culture and social organization, so vital for the Tale outlook on life, have their roots in the lineage system. The whole social system of the Tallensi hinges on their lineage system with its religious counterpart, an elaborate ancestor cult. Unbroken continuity of descent, persistence of self-identical corporate units, stability of settlement—these are the intrinsic characteristics of the Tale lineage system. It requires the assumption, which the ancestor cult places beyond question, that the social structure of to-day is the same as it was in the past.

The Tallensi, therefore, have no history in the sense of a body of authentic records of past events. The memories and reminiscences of the old men are parts of their biographies and never contribute to the building up of a body of socially preserved history. Their myths and legends are one means of rationalizing and defining the structural relationships of group to group or the pattern of their institutions. Some of them have perhaps been built up around events which actually occurred and people who actually lived. It is, for example, quite probable that the Namoos actually came from Mampurugu originally, and that Mosuor really lived. The ancestor cult, the settled life, and the whole cultural idiom of the Tallensi lend support to such an inference, but there is no objective evidence. Tale myths and legends counterfeit history; they do not document it. They are a part of Tale social philosophy, projected into the past because the people think of their social order as continuous and persistent, handed down from generation to generation. A myth or a legend postulates a beginning for what has existed thus ever since. Even in our civilization naïve philosophers try to understand their society by similar devices. In the elaborately differentiated structure of Tale society there are regions of high tension where groups are coupled together in polar opposition and regions of low tension where the units of structure are articulated in complementary relations to one another. The myths epitomize the factors which differentiate one group from another. The greater the differentiation at any point the more elaborate is the legend. Hence we find the most definitive and conspicuous legend, that of Mosuor, associated with the relationship of greatest tension, that of the Namoos to the Talis. We find, also, that the emphasis of a myth is on the relationships which most precisely define the structural position

THE MEANING OF 'TALLENSI'

of the group to which it refers. Owing to the balanced distribution of political and ceremonial functions between units of structure, the members of a group always overrate their own relative significance while non-members underrate its importance. These, sometimes contradictory, valuations find expression, also, in the way myths are presented. It is the technique of contraposition coming to the surface again. When, therefore, in these days new tensions develop, erupting sometimes into open conflict, they are inevitably reflected in the cast given to their myths of origin by interested parties.

The Major Cleavage in Tale Society

Our reconnaissance of the cultural landscape of the Tallensi has left us with a tangle of facts which do not fall into an obvious pattern. The reader may rest assured that his perplexity bears no comparison to that of an ethnographer seeking, for the first time, to understand Tale culture and social organization. The perspective changes as the investigator shifts his vantage point. The greatest puzzle of all is why there is so little apparent unity and coherence in an area of such dense and close habitation, carrying a population that has been sedentary for a long time, has a more or less homogeneous culture, and a strong sense of the continuity and stability of its social order. Leaving aside this puzzle, for the present, let us see what are the positive conclusions to which our survey leads.

The point of primary importance is that a major cleavage runs through the whole of Tale society. On the one side stand communities or parts of communities the members of which are generally agreed to be the descendants of immigrant Mamprusi. These are the Namoos. On the other side stand similar social groups who claim to be and are accepted as the descendants of the aboriginal inhabitants of the country and earlier immigrants whom they absorbed. This cleavage is given a symbolic formulation in myths of origin the historicity of which need not concern us.

This cleavage is so fundamental that it permeates the whole social outlook of the people. One sees it most vividly in the martial choruses chanted at important funerals. One of the high lights at the opening ceremonies of the funeral of an important person is a grand mimic war march (*dee*) of the men of the clan. In their finest clothes, weapons in hand, plumed helms on their heads, blowing whistles and accompanied by drummers, the men gather in lineage squadrons to march round the settlement, and eventually mass at the house of the funeral. They march irregularly in an unorganized mob with excited children trailing behind and women dancing on the flanks trilling the shrill *kpɛlɔmɔt* cry of elation. And as they march, especially as they approach the funeral house, they chant defiant challenges against their traditional enemies in the wars of former days. 'Yo ho!' they chant, 'we might rise one day at break of dawn to sally forth against certain people.' 'Is it not because of us', the Namoos chant taunting the Talis, 'that you have water to drink?' And again, 'Do you not mock at them, do you not laugh at them?' And now and then a man leaps forward, crouches scowling, pretends to shoot off an arrow, and cries scornfully, 'If it were not for the white man, by now we would be meeting them in battle'. It is all play-acting, but there is an

28 THE MEANING OF 'TALLENSI'

undercurrent of passion and tension. When a *dee* parade reaches the border between adjacent Namoo and Talis settlements, there is a danger of a hostile demonstration from the other side and the older men have to be very watchful. In 1936 a Tongo *dee* parade was attacked by a group of Gbeog men who were simply swept off their feet by the sight and sound of the armed mob of their traditional enemies.

One is constantly reminded of the cleavage between Namoos and non-Namoos in less dramatic ways, too, for they are for ever contrasting themselves. The Namoos scoff in private at the esoteric ritual practices of the Talis, the non-Namoos everywhere vaunt their superiority, as the true 'owners of the land', to the immigrant Namoos. And, at the same time, the politico-ritual leaders of each group keep jealous watch on those of the other to see that their mutual bonds of politico-ritual collaboration are maintained. The most serious obstruction I had to overcome in my field work was the passive resistance of the Talis inspired by my initial association with the Tongo Namoos.

This cleavage comes to the fore in different ways in different parts of Taleland. It is most precisely worked out in the Tongo district, where it dominates the politico-ritual relations of group to group. It is justifiable, moreover, to see a connexion between this and the fact that the Tong Hills, the most conspicuous landmark in the country, are universally accepted as the centre of the 'real Talis'. Though many Hill Talis clans claim to be of immigrant descent, they are socially alined with the alleged aboriginal clans. This in itself would suggest that the cleavage between Namoos and non-Namoos is not an artifact of history but the expression of a deep-lying principle of social organization in Tale society.

Furthermore, it is evident that the natives visualize their society as composed of three major regions, the region of the 'real Talis', the region of Tongo and the clans adjacent to it, and the region of the clans adjacent to the Namnam. These regions are not, however, precisely defined socio-geographic territories. They overlap one another and merge into one another. They also overlap adjacent regions of non-Tale clans; but the Tallensi lay no stress on this, for they are differentiated by the index of the Great Festivals. Each region has its particular form of Harvest Festival, but the Great Festivals of the Tallensi constitute a single cycle. The festivals specific to the different regions follow a fixed sequence in relation to one another, and this is a matter of ritual obligation, not merely of convenience. Thus the very index which in certain perspectives and certain situations serves to differentiate the three regions of Tale society, in other perspectives and other situations serves to demonstrate their interdependence and overlapping.

In addition, the cycle of Great Festivals embraces clans of Gɔris, Namnam, and Mamprusi on the frontiers of Taleland. These clans take the cue for the date of their particular Harvest Festivals from neighbouring Tale clans, and in turn pass on the signal to other non-Tale clans, though they themselves fall outside the normal frame of social reference of the 'real Talis', upon whom the cycle pivots. The best example of this is Nuŋ, a tiny settlement between Biuŋ and the White Volta. Politically and ritually the people of Nuŋ are Mamprusi. The head of the settlement

THE MEANING OF 'TALLENSI'

holds an important ritual office connected with the paramount chiefship of Mampurugu. But, as befits their interstitial socio-geographic position between the Mamprusi and the Tallensi, their Harvest Festival belongs to the Tale cycle and is, in fact, the last of one of the series constituting the cycle.

The differentiation of Taleland into lesser regions follows the same general principle as the differentiation of the Mole-Dagbane-speaking peoples into 'tribes'. A region is a socio-geographic segment of the society in which the communities that constitute it have a greater degree of interdependence and cohesion with one another than any of them have with other neighbouring communities. And this interdependence and cohesion is a function of the common interests symbolized in the Great Festivals. The regions overlap in so far as the communities belonging to one region have other interests in common with and other loyalties towards communities belonging to a neighbouring region.

This is the façade of Tale society. Behind it lie the bricks and mortar of the social structure. It is at that level of Tale social life that we must look for the foundations of the principles of social organization whose superficial action we have met with in this chapter.

CHAPTER III

PARADIGM OF THE LINEAGE SYSTEM

TALE society is built up round the lineage system. It is no exaggeration to say that every sociological problem presented by the Tallensi hinges on the lineage system. It is the skeleton of their social structure, the bony framework which shapes their body politic; it guides their economic life and moulds their ritual ideas and values. The social life of the Tallensi cannot be understood without a knowledge of the principles that govern their lineage organization.

These principles will be briefly and formally stated in the present chapter. This will give us a paradigm by which to orient our analysis. Something of this sort, though less systematic and abstract, is in the mind's eye of every well-informed native when he discusses the structure of his society or takes his part in public affairs. The schematic analysis given here will be amplified in later chapters and some repetition is therefore unavoidable. In studying a society of this type we cannot avoid traversing the same ground repeatedly from different directions. For the same basic units, relations, and principles of structure lie behind all forms of association and all organized social activities.

A preliminary bird's-eye view of the lineage system is important, also, in another respect. A lineage always functions as a whole. Whenever a lineage emerges in social action it does so as a product of its component parts and of the relations between them; when a part of a lineage emerges in social action it does so relatively to other parts of it and to the whole. Anyone wishing to understand the way a Tale lineage functions must think of it as a field system, in which the behaviour of the part is regulated by its relation to the whole and the behaviour of the whole is a product of the relations of the parts.

From the Tale point of view a lineage is an association of people of both sexes comprising all the known descendants by a known genealogy of a single known and named ancestor in an unbroken male line. From the sociologist's point of view it is an association of people of both sexes comprising all the recognized descendants by an accepted genealogy of a single named ancestor in a putatively continuous male line. It is, in other words, a strictly unilineal, agnatic descent group.

Lineages vary in *span* proportionately to the number of generations accepted as having intervened between their living members and the founding ancestor from whom they trace their descent. The lineage of minimum span, which we shall call the minimal lineage, consists of the children of one father. The lineage of maximum span, which we shall call the maximal lineage, is the lineage of widest span to which any of its members belongs. It consists of all the descendants in the male line of the remotest common patrilineal ancestor known to the members of the lineage. Whenever we speak of a lineage without qualification to indicate its span, we use the term in the generalized sense of a lineage of any span

PARADIGM OF THE LINEAGE SYSTEM

and any order of segmentation. What is meant by *order of segmentation* is defined below.

The number of antecedent generations reckoned to the point of convergent ascent varies slightly from one maximal lineage to another in Taleland. It is, as will be clearer later, proportional to, and an index of, the range of segmentary differentiation in the existing maximal lineage. Eight to ten ascendant generations are usually reckoned between contemporary minimal lineages and the founding ancestor of the maximal lineage of which they are part. Genealogies are not remembered for their own sake by the Tallensi. They are relevant, primarily, as the mnemonics of the lineage system. They are bound up with the institutions which demonstrate and make overt the formal unity, or the internal differentiation of a lineage. Among the social events in which this occurs most conspicuously and frequently are sacrifices to ancestor spirits and mortuary and funeral ceremonies. The latter, especially, epitomize the entire social structure and enable one to see precisely how the lineage system is constituted.

All Tale lineages are hierarchically organized between the limits of the minimum span, i.e. the minimal lineage, on the one hand, and the maximum span, i.e. the maximal lineage, on the other. Thus every minimal lineage is a segment of a more inclusive lineage defined by reference to a common grandfather, and this, in turn, is a segment of a still wider lineage defined by reference to a common great-grandfather; and so on, until the limit is reached—the maximal lineage, defined by reference to the remotest agnatic ancestor of the group. But a minimal lineage crystallizes out, as we shall see, only on the death of its founder. Until then it is submerged in a wider lineage.

Within a lineage of whatever span each grade of segmentation is functionally significant. Each segment has its focus of unity, and an index of its corporate identity, in the ancestor by reference to whom it is differentiated from other segments of the same order in the hierarchically organized set of lineages. Sacrifices to the shrine of this ancestor require the presence of representatives of every segment of the next lower order; and this rule applies to all corporate action of a ceremonial or jural kind of any lineage. This is the fundamental rule of the lineage organization.

The solidarity of a lineage is a function of the co-operation of its major segments, i.e. the segments of the highest order. In matters that concern the lineage as a whole, and in situations which express its corporate unity, members of the lineage co-operate as representatives of its major segments. The lesser segments constituting each major segment receive explicit recognition only in relation to the major segment. They emerge, then, as major segments of a major segment, and their segments, again, emerge only in relation to them; and so on down to the minimal segments. In these affairs of common concern, rights and duties, privileges and obligations are distributed equally amongst the major segments of a lineage. This emphasizes their equality of status.

A lineage of any span emerges in any of its activities as a system of aliquot parts, not as a mere collection of individuals of common ancestry. It represents an equilibrium, maintained by the relations between its

PARADIGM OF THE LINEAGE SYSTEM

constituent parts. The simplest way of achieving this is for its internal differentiation into segments to be of a limited and balanced kind. That is why only the first order of segmentation, a division into major segments, is recognized in the corporate activities of a lineage. In Tale theory the source of this primary segmentation of the lineage is the minimal lineage, in which a group of brothers (two or more) are differentiated from one another as individuals each of whom is the potential founder of a new lineage, but are united through their common father. A pair of brothers by the same father (*sunzɔp*, sing. *sunzɔ*) are the potential originators of a pair of major segments of the lineage deriving from their father. So all major segments of a lineage of any span are visualized as being derived from brothers, sons of the lineage founder, and are described as *sunzɔp* to one another. Their lineage ties, summed up in the concept *sunzɔt* (brotherhood), are thought of as being founded on, and derived from, the ties that hold between brothers. By the rule of exogamy women members marry out of the lineage, so they do not contribute to its perpetuation and do not affect its organization.

The growing-point of the lineage, it will be seen, is the family. It is always patrilocal; ideally, it is also polygynous. Thus children of the same man are differentiated from one another as children of different mothers. This provides a further criterion of differentiation within the lineage. Like the sons of different mothers and the same father, segments of a lineage may, in certain situations, be distinguished from one another by reference to their different progenitrices. In other situations, like the sons of one mother, segments of a lineage may be grouped together by reference to a common progenitrix.

A maximal lineage cannot, by definition, have any *sunzɔp* identified strictly in terms of common agnatic descent. If it had it would be a segment of a more inclusive lineage. The ancestor who founded it must be unique, in retrospect. As we have seen, he may be accounted for by a myth; but his unique place in the genealogical tree can sometimes be naturalistically explained. If the formation of recent lineage segments is studied, it can be seen that segments sometimes disappear, owing to the extinction of a branch of the lineage. When this happens, the surviving segments reach a new equilibrium. The defunct collateral line is forgotten in due course, together with its genealogy; for this no longer has any structural significance. Thus an existing maximal lineage may be merely the surviving segment of what might have been a wider maximal lineage.

It is characteristic of Tale social organization, however, that maximal lineages do often have *sunzɔp*, either through ties of clanship, or by incorporating, or being joined to, lineages not strictly of the same agnatic descent.

A lineage is a temporal system. Continuity in time is its fundamental quality. Its constitution and dimensions at a given time represent a phase of a process which, as the natives see it, has been going on in exactly the same way from the beginning of their social order and is continuing into the future. The contemporary phase of a lineage is more than a product of its past; it embodies all the significant changes that have occurred in it

PARADIGM OF THE LINEAGE SYSTEM

throughout its past; and it is, at the same time, the embryo of its future organization. A Tale lineage cannot be dissociated from its temporal extension.

A maximal lineage is fixed with reference to its founding ancestor, who is the focus of its unity and the symbol of its corporate identity. From time to time its unity and identity become explicit in the common cult of this ancestor and in the regulation of intra-lineage relations which hinges on it. The ancestor cult is the calculus of the lineage system, the mechanism by means of which the progressive internal differentiation of a lineage is ordered and is fitted into the existing structure. It is also the principal ideological bulwark of the lineage organization.

Every maximal lineage is continually expanding and proliferating through the fission of its minor segments. But though its span is thus constantly increasing, its form does not alter. It has a fixed centre and a fixed locus we might say. In theory it always remains the same lineage, and new maximal lineages cannot arise through the splitting up of an existing maximal lineage. It is a unit of common agnatic descent, and no branch of it can ever repudiate this. In theory ties of descent can never lapse. A maximal lineage is also an exogamous unit, and no branch of it can contract out of this bond.

To the contemporary observer the Tale lineage system appears as a stable and finally established factor of the constituted social structure, the ground plan of which was laid down in the distant past by processes which are still going on. In any maximal lineage, therefore, the fission of minor segments does not alter the equilibrium of the major segments at any given time. Changes in minimal lineages, in fact, cannot alter the equilibrium of any segment greater than the minimal. This is reflected in the naming of lineages and their segments. Every lineage is named after its founder, and as long as a lineage persists it bears the same name. Thus the names of segments greater than the minimal may be regarded as fixed once for all. A lineage is called the 'children (biis) of so-and-so' or 'the house (yir) or people of the house (yidɛm) of so-and-so'. These ways of denoting a lineage are interchangeable. A lineage may also be described as a 'room' (dug) of a superordinate lineage. This indicates that it is being thought of as a segment of the latter.

This formal analysis will be more easily understood from the diagram which follows. It shows, in a simplified way, the structure of a major segment of a maximal lineage which is assumed to have only two major segments. The major segment not included must be homologous with the major segment shown here since a lineage necessarily divides into segments of equal order. Similarly, the relations of the two major segments of our hypothetical maximal lineage to each other are repeated, at a lower order of segmentation, in the relations of the major segments of each major segment to one another. In the diagram the relations of subsegments X and Y to each other, within the framework of Major Segment I, are identical in form with those of Major Segment I and its brother (sunzɔ) segment, Major Segment II, and this rule holds for every subsequent order of segmentation. We shall later on study the interests, rights, and obligations associated with such an ordered series

D

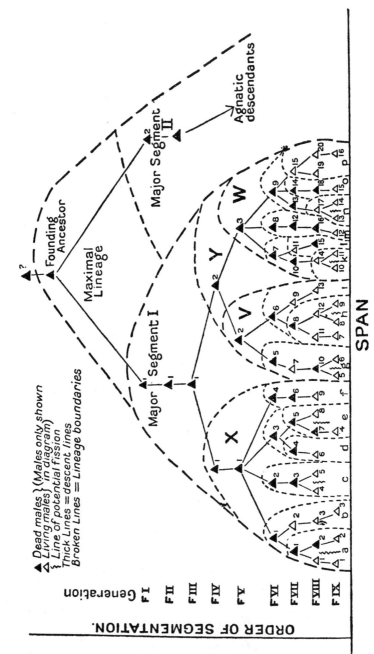

Diagram illustrating the Paradigm of the Lineage System

PARADIGM OF THE LINEAGE SYSTEM

of homologous inter-segment relations, and see, then, how they vary in kind and are graded in precision.

If we describe a major segment of a maximal lineage as a primary segment, then segments of the order of X and Y in the diagram can be called secondary segments, and Y is split into two subsegments (tertiary segments) of the next lower order V and W. These have, respectively, two (g and $h+i$) and three ($k+l$, m, and $n+o+p$) segments of still lower order; and some of these consist, as the diagram shows, of subordinate segments of the lowest order, i.e. minimal segments. X has no segments co-ordinate with V and W, but has four segments of the next lower order ($a+b$, c, $d+e$, and f), some of which are subdivided into minimal segments.

These are all various ways of grouping the same thirty-five males in a set of lineages of common agnatic descent. Women members are excluded from the diagram for the reason previously stated. In some situations each grouping emerges as a lineage in its own right; in others it acts as a segment of a lineage of higher order. When, for example, the 'house' (*yir*) of F.VI.1 (i.e. $a+b$) assembles to sacrifice to his spirit, it acts as a self-contained corporate unit, a lineage. Both its segments, a and b, must be represented and the animal sacrificed is divided equally between them. The portion given to a is then equally shared, again, between F.VIII.1 and his brother's son F.IX.2—i.e. the two nascent segments of the house of F.VII.1. Actually, during the lifetime of F.VII.2, the head of the house of F.VI.1, a remains only a potential lineage, submerged in $a+b$.

The same rule holds for the higher orders of segmentation. The house of F.VI.1 is a segment—a 'room' (*dug*)—of the house of F.V.1—i.e. of the lineage X. When sacrifice is made to F.V.1, all the four segments of X must be represented and the animal slaughtered is divided equally amongst them, to be redistributed by each segment amongst its sub-segments. F.VII.2 is head of lineage $a+b$ and sacrifices on their behalf to their immediate founder F.VI.1. He is also head of X sacrificing, on behalf of all its four segments, to F.V.1 and F.IV.1.

The minimum differentiation of X requires the recognition of the same four segments of equal status, whether F.IV.1 or F.V.1 be considered as the focus of the lineage, since there are no intermediate segments derived from F.IV.1. Contrast lineage Y, the minimal differentiation of which recognizes two segments of a higher order than the four which constitute X—i.e. of an intermediate order between the segments derived from F.III.1 (X and Y) and those derived from F.V.1, 2, and 3. The constitution of lineage X has the same form as that of the whole lineage, the agnatic posterity of F.III.1, of which it is a major segment.

In lineages thus constituted an ancestor who has no significance as a focus of differentiation from other co-ordinate lineages loses his structural relevance and has no distinct ancestor-shrine. He is merged with a predecessor who still symbolizes the focus of differentiation of the lineage, and often no doubt fades into oblivion. In this way genealogies get telescoped and the ranking of structurally insignificant ancestors gets confused. Thus Major Segment I would probably be named the house of F.I.1 after the ancestor who symbolizes their differentiation from the co-ordinate major segment derived from his 'brother', F.I.2. The

36 PARADIGM OF THE LINEAGE SYSTEM

tendency is to retain the ancestor to whose generation the fission of the segments can be most appropriately attributed. The naming, here, would fit in with the relations of the two major segments as representing the primary differentiation of the maximal lineage one generation nearer than the founding ancestor. Though F.II.1 and F.III.1 are still invoked in sacrifices, their order of succession tends to be confused. F.II.1 will lapse more easily than F.III.1, who will be remembered as the actual father of F.IV.1 and F.IV.2.

Similarly, lineage X will be described as the house of F.IV.1 when its status as a major segment of the house of F.I.1, co-ordinate with Y, is the main issue. But members of its constituent segments might also describe themselves collectively as the house of F.V.1, after the most recent ancestor from whom their lines of descent diverge, when stressing their connexion as 'rooms' of a single lineage. Which nomenclature is used depends on the situation and on the range of the lineage concerned in it.

These usages illustrate again the natives' inveterate habit of naming social units by contraposition. They explain, also, why no historical validity can be attached to their genealogies, beyond the time of their great-grandfathers. A genealogy maps out a particular set of lineage relations; it is not a true record. Thus it is impossible to ascertain, as it is from the Tale point of view irrelevant to ask, whether or not any ancestors intervened between the founder of a maximal lineage such as is here sketched and the originators of its existing major segments. If there were any, it is quite possible that they have been dropped from the genealogy because they are redundant, in terms of the structure of the lineage. Similarly, the ancestor whose name is preserved as the founder of the maximal lineage may have been preceded by others whose names have lapsed from tradition for the same reason.

Lineages of the same order of segmentation are not all of equal span. Though lineage span and order of segmentation overlap, they are not interchangeable categories. Lineage c—the house of F.VI.2—is co-ordinate with (i.e. of the same order of segmentation as) lineage $a + b$— the house of F.VI.1—but of a lesser span. Lineage X, similarly, has a lesser span than lineage Y. The span of a lineage is a measure of its internal differentiation, whereas its order of segmentation defines its relations, as a corporate unit, with other units of a like sort.

The distinction is important in the conduct of lineage and community affairs. Co-ordinate segments are brothers (*sunzɔp*) to one another, irrespective of span; but a lineage of small span is more closely integrated than one of large span. Thus the major segments of our diagrammatic maximal lineage are *sunzɔp*, being descended, as it is thought, from a pair of brothers by the same father; so are X and Y; so are V and W; so are the four constituent segments of X, the two constituent segments of V, and the three constituent segments of W; and the same rule holds for the lesser lineages down to a pair of brothers, like lineage c, who are also *sunzɔp*.

It is evident that brothers (*sunzɔp*) can be graded according to their genealogical distance from one another. The natives say '*ti a ba yɛni*

PARADIGM OF THE LINEAGE SYSTEM

biis—we are the children of one father', when they want to stress recent common ancestry, or '*ti a yaab yɩni biis*—we are the children of one ancestor', whenever they emphasize remote common ancestry. The same contrast is expressed in the appellations *dug* (room) and *yir* (house). Members of lineage V, for example, will speak of themselves as *dugdɛm* (members of one room) by contrast with members of lineage W, whom they would describe as *ti yidɛm* (people of our house). Members of X will say 'We, the children of so and so (F.IV.1), are four rooms', but they will speak of themselves as *dugdɛm* in contrast to Y, who would be called their *yidɛm*, e.g. at funeral ceremonies. Thus the segments of X or of Y are closer *sunzɔp* than are X and Y, which, again, are closer *sunzɔp* than are the major segments of the maximal lineage. A specially close tie is acknowledged also between lineages of common agnatic ancestry which have a common ancestress. Thus, if F.V.1 had three wives, from whom have sprung, respectively, segments *a+b* and *c*, *d+e*, and *f*, then the first two segments regard each other as closer *sunzɔp* than either of the other two.

Genealogical distance and the tie of brotherhood (*sunzɔt*) are most palpable in situations which bring out the structural equilibrium of the set of lineages. When, for instance, a funeral occurs in lineage *g*, contributions of cooked food will be made by the *sunzɔp* as follows: by the head of *h+i*, the closest *sunzɔ* segment, on behalf of that segment; by the head of W on behalf of the whole lineage, not by its constituent segments, the contribution being given to its *sunzɔ* V, not to the segment *g*; and by the head of X, if it is the funeral of an elder, on behalf of the whole of X, when the recipient unit is considered to be Y, not *g*. If the other half of the maximal lineage, Major Segment II, sends a contribution, it will be given by the head of the segment on behalf of the whole unit as an obligation owed to the *sunzɔ* segment, the house of F.I.1. Cooked food, beer, and the meat of ceremonially slaughtered animals are distributed according to the same scale of genealogical distance, and the allocation of ritual duties, though less strictly regulated, depends on it, too. Hence any members of W who may be present at the funeral are regarded as representing W, however many segments of W they may individually represent. They are entitled only to those portions of food, beer, and meat which are the due share of W. An identical share can be claimed by members of X who may be present, whether they come from one of its segments or from all; and the same holds for the major segments of the maximal lineage. *Sunzɔt* here implies duties and privileges vested in the lineage as a corporate unit and exercised on its behalf by any representatives of that unit in relation to other units of a like sort.

There are many other institutions and situations in which the tie of *sunzɔt* operates in the same way and receives precise and formal recognition according to the same rules. It operates thus in all corporate actions and in relation to all corporate interests of a lineage. It dictates the manner in which every activity associating people in groups is organized. Hoeing and building teams organize their work broadly along the lines of the lineage structure and distribute the food they receive in reward in accordance with it. In a hunting party lineage *sunzɔp* have the right to

38 PARADIGM OF THE LINEAGE SYSTEM

'pull out' (*fɔ*) a foreleg of any animal killed by a member of a *sunzɔ* lineage. But for the present we are concerned only with the paradigm of the lineage system, a mere definition, though necessarily a somewhat lengthy one, of the fundamental concept of Tale social organization. The principal interests which direct the life and activities of a lineage, the critical jural norms which regulate the relations of its members and subdivisions to one another, the chief doctrines, myths, ceremonial usages, and ritual observances in which its structure is conceptualized and its existence and coherence invested with value for its members, will be considered at later stages of our inquiry.

CHAPTER IV

CLANSHIP: THE NAMOOS

The Dispersion of Mosuor biis

FOR the Namoos of Tongo[1] history begins with Mosuor. Of his Mampuru forbears nothing is known. When a Namoo piously invokes the names of Toohug and Gbamwaa, the mythical founders of the Mampuru State, these are to him mystical words. Dominated in his moral and mystical thought by the ancestor cult, he is ready to infer that they were probably remote ancestors of the Mampuru stock; but no one in Taleland knows the myths which the Mamprusi relate about them. There is at the present time constant intercourse between the Tallensi and the Mamprusi, especially between the Tale chiefs and the court of the Paramount Chief of Mampurugu (*Mampurugna'ab*); but the myth of Toohug and Gbamwaa has not diffused to the Tallensi, for it has no relevance to their internal social structure, and the names alone suffice to symbolize the bond of common stock with the Mamprusi.

Mosuor died at Tongo. His grave indicates where his homestead stood, a stone's throw from the sacred dancing-ground, Giŋgaaŋ Puhug, which was the site of Tɛndaan Gɛnɔt's homestead. After Mosuor's death, it is related, his eldest son, Naŋkamuŋ, wished to assume the chiefship at once; but a younger son, Sɛyahɔg, insisted that his father's death should be ceremonially reported to the Mampurugna'ab, the fountain-head of their chiefship (na'am). He went secretly to do so, and was invested with his father's chiefship by the Chief of the Mamprusi in return for a payment of 100 cattle. Naŋkamuŋ, resenting his younger brother's guile in robbing him of his patrimony, thereupon seceded and settled at Yamɔlɔg beside the people of Sɔk and their tɛndaana. This place, it is related, came to be called so because Naŋkamuŋ declared that he would go and settle just nearby (*yama yama*), where he could keep in touch with his kinsfolk at Tongo.

Sie, which the Namoos say means beside (*sie*, side) Yamɔlɔg, was founded by another 'son' of Mosuor, Kuŋkye. Sie people claim to have been the first settlers in the area. On the other hand, with characteristic emphasis on their own priority, Sawalɔg people assert that Kuŋkye was received by their ancestor the Sawalɔg tɛndaana, who had 'sprouted from the earth'. The tɛndaana allowed him to settle there beside (*sie*) himself, after having presented him ritually to the Earth shrines. This myth is a replica of that told by the Gbizug people, and symbolizes a structural and ideological relationship of the same order as that which exists between Gbizug and Tongo.

Yet another 'son' of Mosuor—the exact genealogy is obscure, since *bii*, child, can be used to refer to any descendant—migrated to Biuk, where his descendants adopted the speech and customs of the Gɔris.

[1] The correct vernacular form is Tɔŋo, but we shall keep the more familiar English form throughout this book.

The Chain of Sub-clans

Thus came into being this chain of four patrilineal sub-clans (Tongo, Yamələg, Sie, and Biuk), each the skeleton of a community. From these primary nuclei colonies have continually hived off to settle in neighbouring areas, particularly at Gbambee, Gorogo, Ba'ari, Woo, and Datɔk. Each sub-clan is itself a composite system of lineages: authentic lineages constituted by the direct line of agnatic descent from the clan founder, Mosuor; attached lineages, linked to these usually by the dogma of sister-descent; and assimilated lineages. The attached lineages are identified as *ti tau biis*—our sister's children—descendants in the direct male line of a female member of one of the authentic lineages. The stereotyped formula attributes the origin of such a lineage either to a sister's son (*ahəŋ*) who came to live in his mother's brother's (*ahəb*)

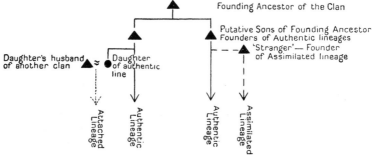

Diagram showing Relationship of Accessory Lineages to Authentic Line

community, or to a sister who was divorced by her husband by the irrevocable procedure of blowing ash on her (*pɛbh*), and returned to the shelter of her parental home with her children. By this form of divorce a man renounces his rights in his children, who henceforth become members of their maternal lineage, as if they had been illegitimately begotten by a lover. The agnatic posterity of such children, as of any spinster's son, becomes a lineage attached to that of their ancestor's mother.

We shall call these 'attached lineages' because they are linked to the authentic lineages by actual or putative cognatic ties. An attached lineage maintains its continuity and distinctness, like any other lineage, even if its patrilineal progenitor is alleged to have repudiated its ancestress and his own progeny.

The existence of the assimilated lineages is often traced to an ancestor who was a 'kinsman' (*mabii*) accompanying the founder of the authentic lineage when he first arrived. Of some such lineages, however, it is whispered that they sprang from slaves of the authentic lineage with which they are connected, or from foreign refugees who sought their protection. The term used for these lineages is intended to convey that they are incorporated in the sub-clan by virtue of their dependence on and participation in the life of an authentic lineage. We shall also describe these two kinds of lineages collectively as accessory lineages.

CLANSHIP: THE NAMOOS 41

This summary statement follows closely the formulations of the Tallensi themselves. They normally think of a lineage, a set of lineages, or a community, as a unit in relation to other units of a like sort, irrespective of its internal differentiation. Thus, Tongo people say: '*Tam ni Yaməlǝgdɛm ni Siedɛm ni Biukdɛm a la yaab yɛni biis*—We and the people of Yaməlǝg, and the people of Sie and the people of Biuk are the children of one ancestor.' The place-name serves to designate the social group. Once, at Sie, some young men from Tongo, members of an assimilated lineage, called on me. 'We've only come on a visit', they said, '*daya ti mabiis n a Siedɛm?*—Are not these people of Sie our kinsfolk?'

Such intercourse is constant amongst the three Talni-speaking branches of Mosuor's posterity (*tu'u*). Biuk, both because of its fusion with the Gǝris and its geographical location, is somewhat isolated from regular contact with its Talni-speaking clansmen. But the ties which control this voluntary fraternization emerge more precisely in a number of critical norms and institutions.

The Critical Norms of Clanship

Most important of these is the rule of exogamy. Marriage is unconditionally prohibited between the four branches of Mosuor's posterity— i.e. between members of the authentic lineages of Tongo, Yaməlǝg, Sie, and Biuk. The prohibition extends to the assimilated lineages as well, but not to all attached lineages, though the natives state it as if it applied to the entire sub-clan. They regard it as the inevitable corollary of their common ancestry. It is, therefore, the widest extension of the rule which prohibits marriage within the agnatic lineage. I discovered only one instance of the transgression of this rule at Tongo, and this occurred in abnormal circumstances.

A second critical norm always cited is: '*ti diit taaba pakoya*—We marry one another's widows.' A Tongo man has the right to seek the hand of the widow of a Yaməlǝg, a Sie, or a Biuk man; but in actual practice remarriage of widows is restricted by so many other conditions that this leviratic right is mainly significant as an ideological index of clanship. It is the correlative of the rule of exogamy and, like it, the widest extension of a right which holds primarily within the lineage. Occasionally this right is exercised in its widest sense. The Chief of Tongo, for example, has availed himself of it to solve the problem of accommodation for himself and his retinue when he is compelled to visit the Administrative Headquarters at Zuarungu. An elderly widow at Biuk is nominally his wife and he may therefore stay in her house without embarrassment. In another case a middle-aged Yaməlǝg widow elected to marry a stalwart young man from Tongo in preference to any of her dead husband's closer kinsmen. It is extremely unlikely that either woman would have been permitted to marry so distant an agnate of her dead husband if she were still capable of child-bearing. Nevertheless, it is an essential consequence of the leviratic right that if a man from one of the sub-clans should succeed in marrying a young widow of a member of another, no reprisals could be publicly undertaken against him, whereas anyone outside the range of clanship would be courting armed vengeance by such an act.

42 CLANSHIP: THE NAMOOS

When, some forty years ago, a Tongo man married a Zoo widow and his son was shot dead in revenge by a Zoo man, the Chief of Tongo forbade a raid of retaliation. It was, my informants said, a just vengeance since 'we don't marry the widows of Zoo people'.

Again, it would be a serious breach of solidarity for a member of one of the sub-clans to abduct the wife of a member of any other, and I have never heard of such a case. Warfare between them is inconceivable, so the injured group would have to rely upon moral pressure through the chief and elders of the offender's community. But these measures would undoubtedly succeed, even in these days when rebellious young men can flee to foreign lands.

This is likewise the widest extension of a restriction which holds with greatest force for the segments of a maximal lineage belonging to the same sub-clan, e.g. for the segments of Tongo *inter se*. In a lesser degree it applies also to ex-wives. A man who marries the former wife of another, even if the marriage was severed for just and accepted reasons, incurs the hostility of the first husband's entire lineage both towards himself personally and towards his clansmen as a group. Reprisals will be taken when an opportunity occurs. When the parties are clansmen, feelings about such acts become very bitter, and the more so the closer the tie. Marriages of this kind take place from time to time, producing conflicts and reprisals but not disruption of clanship ties.

Another proof of kinship (*mabiirɔt*) usually cited by the natives is that warfare between the four sub-clans was forbidden. They were allies in war in the old days. They did not all come to one another's help, nor were they each other's sole allies. But they could call upon one another's assistance in the name of kinship. The recollections of the oldest men go back no farther than the time of their grandparents, four or five generations ago. They tell of ancient fights in which Tongo, Sie, and Yamaləg supported one another; but Biuk, it seems, maintained an isolationist policy in the wars and feuds of its Tale kinsmen. The greatest war still remembered in tale and anecdote occurred forty or fifty years ago. Yamaləg became involved in it; and when Ba'ari raised the war-cry against Yamaləg, Sie and Tongo attacked Ba'ari on the flanks.

Mosuor biis: a Maximal Lineage

These four branches of Mosuor's agnatic posterity (*tu'u*) constitute what appears to be a single, dispersed clan—the only clan of this type in Taleland; more accurately, it is a maximal lineage—the most inclusive agnatic lineage to which any descendant of Mosuor in the male line (i.e. any member of the four branches) can belong. In the eyes of the natives an important qualification is that the four branches are of equal status though graded in seniority. Tongo is the most senior because it remained in possession of the original home of the clan—'*ti waabi daboog*, the ancient home-site of all of us', they say—and has retained the custody of Mosuor's grave and *bɔyar*, the shrine which symbolizes the perpetuity, identity, and common ancestry of the entire maximal lineage. Yamaləg, Sie, and Biuk follow in that order; but they no longer participate in sacrifices to Mosuor. Each of them has its own ancestral *bɔyar*, enshrining

CLANSHIP: THE NAMOOS 43

its founding ancestors and its own differential line of agnatic descent. Each sub-clan sacrifices separately to its own founding ancestor. Mosuor is regarded as the common ancestor of all the sub-clans, but the cult of his shrine is the sole prerogative and duty of the Tongo branch of his posterity. According to Tale interpretation, a long period of territorial separation, bringing about political independence of one another, has inevitably resulted in the corresponding religious autonomy of each unit. A *bɔyar* cannot be separated from the grave and the home-site (*daboog*) of the ancestor it enshrines. Though the custody and cult of Mosuor's *bɔyar* are the exclusive province of the Tongo branch of the clan, because residence, lineage, and ancestor cult must have a concurrent continuity, these rights and duties are held to be exercised on behalf of the whole clan.

An unusual incident showed how the cult of Mosuor's *bɔyar* is related to the constitution of the clan. It was on the occasion of the great sacrifice to Mosuor and the other early ancestors of Tongo described below (pp. 53–4). When the beer was being distributed, a man called out that there was a young man from Yamɔlɔg present. This was quite unprecedented. The elders began to discuss the situation vigorously. The people of Yamɔlɔg had no right to attend such a sacrifice; but they were Mosuor's agnatic descendants, and if one of them turned up by chance, could he be excluded? 'Is not Mosuor their ancestor as well as ours?' At this point the Yamɔlɔg man stepped forward. He said that the question was of no importance; he was not a complete outsider intruding on the ritual of people not connected with him, neither was he there as a representative of Yamɔlɔg; he had come solely in his personal capacity, to 'scrounge' some of the beer and meat, and not to take part in the sacrifice. In short, though he could not be turned away from the sacrifice (as, say, a Zubiuŋ or Zoo man would have been) without offence to the clan ancestors, his presence there did not signify a claim by Yamɔlɔg to be represented at such rites, nor would it establish a precedent for the future. On this understanding, so amicably reached, he was given a courtesy portion of beer and meat.

As with the ancestor cult, so with the chiefship. Each sub-clan has its own chiefship (*na'am*), in keeping with its territorial and political autonomy, but the prototypical chiefship is that of Tongo, since it was established by Mosuor. Just as the four sub-clans are 'brothers' (*sunzɔp*) to one another, so their chiefs are 'brothers' (*sunzɔp*) equal in status but graded in seniority of rank, Tongo being the most senior and Biuk the most junior.

The equality of status of the four sub-clans is paralleled in the structure of the maximal lineage which they constitute. In their relations of clanship they are distant 'brothers' (*sunzɔp*), treating one another as relatively autonomous lineages. A Tongo man, when his conduct is determined by the norms of clanship, thinks of Yamɔlɔg, Sie, or Biuk as a corporate unit. Its internal structure is of no relevance to him. At any of these places, in any relations of clanship, he represents Tongo, taken as a unit, irrespective of his position in its internal structure.

The children of Mosuor think of their maximal lineage as finally and

44 CLANSHIP: THE NAMOOS

immutably established. The colonies which have budded off since the foundation of the four primary sub-clans rank only as minor segments of the sub-clans from which they come. Bɔləgraanyidɛm at Woo, Puliebər-yidɛm at Gorogo, Doohyidɛm at Ba'ari, all count as minor segments of their paternal sub-clan, Tongo.

The Lineage Principle in the Structure of the Clan

Distant *sunzɔp* do not regularly attend funeral celebrations, but when an important person dies they occasionally come to pay their respects, though they do not bring contributions. Yamələg people used to be frequent visitors at big Tongo funerals before their present chief quarrelled with the Chief of Tongo (Tɔŋraana). Sie has a closer tie with one of the segments of Tongo (the house of Kabuu) through their founder's mother than with the others, hence a Sie party would be very likely to turn up for the funeral of a Kabuu-yir elder. Biuk has a similar link with Nɔŋsuur-yir at Tongo, and when Saɣəbazaa, the head of that lineage, died in 1936, a party of mourners from Biuk came to the funeral. *Sunzɔ* lineages, as we have seen, are entitled to particular portions of animals slaughtered as offerings to the dead, of beer, and of the food contributions. Whatever the motives which bring a party, or even an individual, from Sie or Yamələg or Biuk to a funeral at Tongo, the prescribed share (*tɔrəg*) is given to them; a hind leg to the most senior of the three sub-clans which may be present, a foreleg to any of the others.

Each sub-clan behaves and is treated as a major segment of the maximal lineage in such a case; Tongo, the host segment, being regarded as a unit in contraposition to the guest segments and other more distant *sunzɔp*. If the other sub-clans are not represented, the major segments of Tongo emerge as the relatively autonomous units of the highest order, the one celebrating the funeral being the host segment. The host segment retains one hind leg of the beast slaughtered—the share of greatest distinction— and the other hind leg is the rightful share of the *sunzɔ* segment of equal status and grade in the lineage system. The forelegs, the shares of lesser distinction, go to *sunzɔ* segments which are more distant genealogi-cally. The situation is always organized as an equilibrium of aliquot parts.

Thus, when the party from Biuk came to Saɣəbazaa's funeral they received a hind leg of the cow which was slaughtered, since neither Yamələg nor Sie was represented. Tongo people have the same rights at the other places. In such situations, in conformity with the principle of unit representation, any member (or members) of the unit who happens to be present exercises the prerogatives or carries out the duties appro-priate to that unit. When the meat or beer is being apportioned at a Tongo funeral and Yamələg or Sie people are known to be present, the man in charge of affairs—who is acting also as representative of a unit, his segment of the sub-clan—calls out, 'Are any Yamələgdɛm here?' and hands them their share; and so on for the others. I once saw this principle pushed to an absurd point. A Mampuru tramp followed me to a funeral ceremony in the hope of begging some money from me. When his

CLANSHIP: THE NAMOOS 45

presence was discovered, some were for driving him away immediately, others maintained that as he had followed me he should share my portion of the beer; but one elder demanded that he should be treated with special courtesy. '*U a Mampurug na'ab bii*—he is the child (i.e. subject) of the Chief of Mampurugu', the old man solemnly insisted, and he proceeded to welcome the ragged tramp respectfully. So a pot of beer was offered to him, somewhat grudgingly, as a scion of the Mamprusi, the ancestral stock of the Tongo Namoos, whom he was here regarded as representing. It was the logic of the situation which caused the intruder to be assigned a specific place in the structural scheme. When we dispersed nobody took any more notice of him.

We describe the four units we have been dealing with as sub-clans together constituting a single clan, for convenience of reference; for the Tallensi have no terminology corresponding to this. People of the four sub-clans say, '*Mosuor ndɔya ti waabi*—Mosuor begot us all'; or '*ti dɔyam a bukɔ'la*—our birth is one', i.e. 'our line of descent is single'; or they describe themselves simply as Mosuor biis, the children (i.e. descendants) of Mosuor. Such expressions indicate the fundamental canon of clanship, that of descent from a common ancestor in the male line. This equates the clan with the agnatic maximal lineage. Having stated this dogma, a man may add, '*ti a bim bukɔ'la*—we are of one kind', or '*ti buurət a dekɔ'la*—our stock is one'; but neither *bim* nor *buurət* is equivalent to the concept 'clan'. They are used for classes of plants, animals, and inanimate objects as well as for social groups; *buurət* is most commonly heard in the sense of 'seed', its primary meaning, e.g. *naarbuura*, seed of early millet. '*Toog kama a bim bukɔ'la*—All sickness is of one kind', I was once told. The segments of a maximal lineage may be referred to as *ti bim, ti bim*, each of our kind, when their relative autonomy rather than their unity is emphasized.

Tale clanship, however, involves a wider nexus than the lineage system from which it derives. Clanship operates on the same level of relations as the lineage system, within the limits of common agnatic descent. It implies the notion of convergent patrilineal ascent; but in actual fact its range is extended by modifications of the strict rule of patriliny. The lineage system is the core of clanship, but not the whole of it. Lineally discrete groups are linked together by ties of clanship, so that the clan organization as a whole consists of a series of interlocked chains of linked maximal lineages.

The Internal Differentiation of the Clan: (A) Sie

The canon of agnatic descent from Mosuor, strictly applied, defines a range of membership—which could be measured by a count of heads—embracing the four settlements we have mentioned and their offshoots. At Sie those who fall within this range comprise the three major segments of the sub-clan: (A) Baɣana yidɛm; (B) Sa-tɛŋɔrdɛm; (C) Wooŋ yidɛm. These are all the agnatic posterity of Kuŋkye, the founder of the settlement of Sie, and can best be described as Kuŋkye biis, the children of Kuŋkye. They are the people of Sie proper.

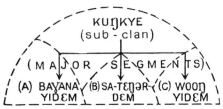

But Sie also includes a pair of accessory lineages, (D) Daaŋ yidɛm and (E) Kalǝŋkaa yidɛm, which are locally and structurally combined to form a single section known as Sie-datɔk.

SIE—the settlement

Sie proper	Sie-datɔk
Kuŋkye biis true sub-clan of Mosuor biis	Two accessory lineages: Daaŋ yidem and Kalǝŋkaa yidɛm

SIEDEM
'The people of Sie'

Their original patrilineal ancestors are said to have come from Kurugu in Mampurugu, long after the foundation of the settlement by Mosuor's 'son' Kuŋkye. As in very many of these traditions of an ancestor who migrated from elsewhere, the motives attributed to him are the same as those which frequently prompt young men to move out to the periphery of settlement nowadays—the temptation of ample land when there is a shortage of farm-land at home, or the desire for independence. The Sie-datɔk lineages are, therefore, considered to be of the same Mampuru stock (*buurǝt*) as the other Namoos. They have the same funeral ritual and totemic observances as all Namoos—a fact which is the most palpable proof to the natives that they are Namoos.

As with the myth of Mosuor, there is no means of verifying this tradition. The Sie-datɔkdɛm advance as evidence the fact that they still maintain political and social contacts with Kurugu; but other Namoo clans and lineages have similar relations with the people of Kurugu and do not, on those grounds, claim kinship (*mabiirǝt*) with them, except in so far as all Namoos speak of themselves as the kin (*mabiis*), in the widest sense, of the Mamprusi. The Tallensi, as we have already observed, do not make these critical comparisons. Their tradition accounts satisfactorily, in their view, to the Sie-datɔk lineages—and also to the people of Sie proper—for their being Namoos, and for their relations with the authentic lineage of Mosuor biis at Sie.

In relation to each other the two lineages of Sie-datɔk act as the major segments of an inclusive maximal lineage, though they do not claim to have a single common ancestor. This assimilation is rationalized by the dogma that their ancestors were kinsmen (*mabiis*), though of what degree they do not profess to know, nor do they consider it relevant. This dogma, like their tradition of origin, is validated by the existing structural relations which it subsumes under the canon of agnatic descent. The two lineages co-operate in ritual and secular affairs like lineages which are close *sunzɔp* to one another. Each lineage, for example, sends through its principal elder the formal contributions due from a brother (*sunzɔ*) lineage to funerals of the other and is entitled to receive the share of meat, beer, and other ceremonial gifts due to a *sunzɔ* lineage. Marriage between members of the two lineages is, of course, prohibited; widows of members of both may be inherited by members of either; and, though they have no common ancestral *bɔyar*, when either sacrifices to its ancestral *bɔyar* representatives of the other may attend and will be given a courtesy portion of the meat of the sacrifice.

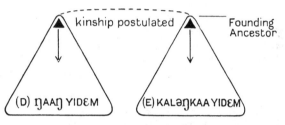

In the political, economic, and ceremonial affairs of the community Sie-datɔk acts as a single section (*yizug*). We shall go more fully into the significance of this term later. Here it is enough to say that it implies corporate action as a local and lineage segment of the larger unit which also includes Sie proper. But the two component lineages of Sie-datɔk are separately incorporated into the structure of the sub-clan. (D) Ŋaaŋ yidɛm is an attached lineage of (A) Baγana yidɛm and has the same reciprocal ties of clanship with it as it has with its other *sunzɔ* lineage (E) Kalǝŋkaa yidɛm of Sie-datɔk. (D) Ŋaaŋ yidɛm and (A) Baγana yidɛm do not intermarry; the injunction against abducting one another's wives is rigorously maintained; they have joint leviratic rights; and the bond of reciprocity of services, contributions, and claims in ritual and ceremonial situations holds. (D) Ŋaaŋ yidɛm participate in sacrifices to the lineage ancestor of (A) Baγana yidɛm, but not on an equal footing with the latter. The portion of the sacrificial meat they receive is what is due to an attached lineage, not to a lineage of the true agnatic line. For their relation to (A) Baγana yidɛm is explained by the usual dogma of descent from a 'sister's son' (*tau bii*). (E) Kalǝŋkaa yidɛm are attached in the same way to (B) Sa-tɛnɔrdɛm whose 'sister's' descendants they are said to be. The symmetry of this arrangement, and of the formulas by which it is rationalized, should be noted. It is an instance of the working of a principle we shall constantly meet with in the analysis of Tale social structure: the tendency of every field of structural relations to take the form of an equilibrium of ties and cleavages.

If we analyse the lineage structure of Sie more fully, we can see that the ties which bind the two lineages of Sie-datɔk are of the same type as those which bind the three segments of Sie proper, and spring from the same central notion of unilineal, agnatic descent or of presumptive convergent ascent in the male line which takes its place where common patrilineal ancestry is not self-evident. The differential incidence of these ties, which is correlated with local distribution, creates cleavages which demarcate Sie-datɔk and Sie proper as relatively autonomous corporate units. But a further differentiation in the distribution of these ties within the same field of relations counterbalances these cleavages by binding each segment of Sie-datɔk to a segment of the counterposed corporate unit of Sie proper, and the canon of agnatic descent is once again modified to subsume these ties.

A significant feature of this constellation of ties and cleavages is that the two Sie-datɔk lineages each have ties of clanship with only one major segment of Sie proper and not with the others, or with the other branches of Mosuor biis. Between (D) Daaŋ yidɛm on the one hand and (B) Sa-tɛŋərdɛm and (C) Wooŋ yidɛm on the other, there are no reciprocal rights and duties, nor are they prohibited from intermarrying; and the same rules apply to the relations of (E) Kaləŋkaa yidɛm with the two Sie lineages which have no clanship ties with it. Tongo, Yaməlag, and Biuk lie completely outside the range of the clanship ties of either lineage.

The three segments of Sie proper, having a common agnatic ancestry, are major segments of a single lineage. Each has the rights and duties of *sunzɔp* to both of the others. They sacrifice together to their common ancestor's *bɔyar*, as equal partners. As a corporate unit they have a bond of supreme importance in their chiefship and in their cult of their common ancestral *bɔyar*. Common agnatic descent, the chiefship, and the cult of one ancestral *bɔyar* are functions of one another. They establish equality and reciprocity in the rights and duties of the three segments towards one another and they mark off Sie proper uniquely as a corporate unit. Neither of the Sie-datɔk lineages has the right to hold the chiefship or to participate in sacrifices to the founding ancestor of Sie.

The spatial grouping of these five lineages parallels closely their structural relations. Taken together they form a continuous local aggregate. But each unit occupies its own more or less distinct quarter of the community. The spatial and social concatenation of Sie proper and Sie-datɔk can be represented in a diagrammatic way thus:

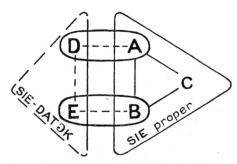

Solid lines represent ties of clanship based on accepted common ancestry; heavy broken lines, ties of clanship based on fictitious common ancestry; thin broken lines, ties of clanship based on lineage attachment through the dogma of cognatic linkage

CLANSHIP: THE NAMOOS   49

Spatially and structurally Sie-datɔk is closer to (A) Baɣana yidɛm and (B) Sa-tɛŋərdɛm than to (C) Wooŋ yidɛm. The coincidence of spatial and social affiliation is a regular feature of Tale social structure.

There are also at Sie proper one or two accessory lineages which are said to be of recent origin in terms of generations. Though their members may not hold the chiefship or take part in sacrifices to the ancestral *bɔyar*, they are more intimately incorporated into the major segments to which they are attached than are the lineages of Sie-datɔk. One at least is said to be of slave descent.

To outsiders, to neighbouring settlements, and even to the other branches of Mosuor biis, Sie and Sie-datɔk together form a single community, which will act as a unit in a matter of common interest, such as the abduction of a wife, whichever one of the five lineage segments is directly involved. But looked at from within, this unit resolves itself into a number of differentiated parts of identical form, which are so articulated with one another that each of them has unique ties with some of the rest, and no such ties with others. A social event occurring in one of these component lineages of the sub-clan of Sie mobilizes a different set of lineages from that which would be mobilized by the same event in any other of the lineages, even in a lineage linked to it by clanship. Thus, in a funeral of a member of (C) Wooŋ yidɛm, only the three major segments of Sie proper are directly concerned. Only they are bound to render ceremonial services, duties, and contributions, and only they have the corresponding rights and privileges of *sunzɔp*. A funeral of a member of (A) Baɣana yidɛm brings (D) Daaŋ yidɛm also into active and obligatory co-operation; and this co-operation unites, for a time and with reference to a common bond which cancels out the lineage cleavages, three segments which are not linked by clanship. The structure of the sub-clan, on the plane of clanship, is such that there can never be an irreconcilable conflict between any of its segments or between any combination of segments and any other combination of segments. There will always be a segment linked by ties of clanship to both parties to hold the balance between them and to work for reconciliation. Just as the stability of a tent is the product of a number of guy ropes pulling with equal force in opposed directions from a single centre, so the cohesion of Sie is a function of the balance attained between the ties and cleavages that link and differentiate the component segments. This is a characteristic feature of Tale clanship.

The Internal Differentiation of the Clan: (B) *Tongo and the Status of Accessory Lineages*

Sie is typical of Tale clan organization in that it is not an exclusive, closed genealogical unit, or part of such a unit. Sie proper, as we know, is a branch of Mosuor biis. Its three *sunzɔ* sub-clans vary slightly in structure from it and from one another, but the basic plan is the same; only the details vary in their interrelations and complexity.

At Tongo there are, formally, two major segments, but one of them has split into three lesser segments which function as major segments in the affairs of the sub-clan. This is an adjustment to maintain the internal equilibrium of the sub-clan. Each major segment consists of several

E

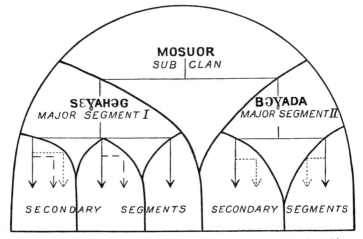

Diagram showing the major segments of Tongo by descent

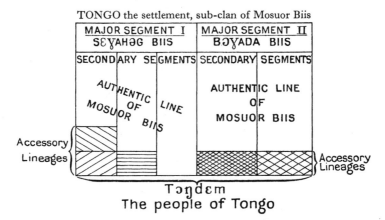

Diagram showing general structure of Tongo

secondary segments of authentic agnatic descent from Mosuor, together with one or more accessory lineages. Thus there are three attached lineages, said to have sprung in the male line from 'sisters' sons' (*tau bii*, pl. *tab biis*) of the authentic lineages to which they are attached. They are incorporated into, and live in close proximity to, the branches of the two major segments to which they are respectively attached. Being scattered thus they have no organization *inter se* like that of Sie-datɔk to give them a unity and solidarity counterbalancing that of the authentic lineages, which are united by their common patrilineal descent. They have, in consequence, become almost completely submerged in the authentic lineages. Only one attached lineage (Zɔŋ yidɛm) still intermarries with other members of the sub-clan, provided they belong to a different major segment from that to which Zɔŋ yidɛm are attached, and these marriages are not encouraged. At Sie, by contrast, 15 out of the 43 wives of Sie-datɔk are members of Wooŋ yidɛm or other branches of Mosuor biis not related to them by clanship ties.

The attached lineages at Tongo are accounted for by the stereotyped tradition which is found, in similar circumstances, all over Taleland. The story is that a woman of the authentic lineage concerned (e.g. Lɛbhtiis yidɛm)—a 'sister' in the classificatory sense—married a member of one of the Hill Talis clans and bore children to him. Later, however, her husband divorced her by the rite of 'blowing' (pɛbh), by which he not only banished her from his home but disowned the children she had borne to him. She returned to live at her parental home, where her children grew up and settled, and where one son gave rise to the lineage attached to his mother's brother's lineage. Because of their founding ancestors' paternity, which even the act of formal repudiation of wife and child could not extinguish, two of the attached lineages preserve the totemic taboos and some of the funeral customs of the Hill Talis. It is a religious duty which they say could not be abandoned without the greatest peril.

Apart from this mark of distinction and the disabilities which will be mentioned later and which apply to all accessory lineages, they participate in social events as ordinary segments of the lineages to which they are attached. They can even represent these lineages in relation to other groups.

An attached lineage is said, sometimes, to have sprung from an un-married girl's son (yiyeembii). His paternity never having been socially recognized, it has no influence on his social role or on that of the lineage which originates from him. Thus, such a lineage has all the customs and observances of its maternal lineage—the lineage, that is, of its founder's mother, to which her son is reckoned as belonging. The third attached lineage at Tongo is said to be descended from an unmarried 'sister's' son and their ritual observances confirm this view.

Tongo also includes several assimilated lineages. These are indis-tinguishable, at first sight, from the authentic lineages either by the criterion of differences in custom or from their manner of participation in the social events which mobilize structural relations. Whatever their real origin may be alleged to be, they are linked to the constellation of authentic lineages by the fiction of direct agnatic descent from the founder of the whole sub-clan, Mosuor himself. They are, as this implies, more closely welded into the sub-clan than are the attached lineages. It would be inconceivable, for example, for a member of an assimilated lineage to marry any other member of the sub-clan.

Attached lineages, everywhere, are incorporated into a lineage of authentic descent by an indirect route, as it were. They are hinged on to the true agnatic line by a compromise, as descendants of a woman of the true agnatic line. This introduces a clear distinction by the canon

52 CLANSHIP: THE NAMOOS

of descent. The status of an attached lineage is always somewhat ambiguous. On the one hand, there is nothing derogatory, by native standards, in the link through a woman, as will be more fully appreciated when we come to the domestic side of Tale social structure.[1] It is but an accident of birth, argue the natives, which made their ancestress a woman instead of a man; otherwise they might have been as much members of the unbroken patrilineal line as the authentic lineages. This explains why attached lineages do not hesitate to advertise their identity by holding to distinctive ritual usages and traditions of origin, and why they may, as at Sie, have a place in the social structure which makes use of their genealogical position. The 'accident of birth' is capitalized as a factor of social organization. On the other hand, there is no escaping the fact that it bars the attached lineage from complete absorption by the authentic line. Its members are debarred from the privileges which are indefeasibly bound up with the unbroken agnatic line and symbolize the uniqueness of this line. They could not at Tongo, for example, participate in sacrifices to Mosuor until recently (see below, pp. 54–5), and they cannot succeed to the custody of his *bɔyar*. They can join in sacrifices to the founding ancestor of the authentic lineage-segment to which they are directly attached; but they cannot hold the custody of his *bɔyar*. The Tongo chiefship is of course rigorously closed to them. All these are crucial values, and to be excluded from the rights and privileges associated with them is a distinct disability. The rights which an attached lineage has in the sub-clan are in part a concession. Thus, though its status need never be glossed over, it cannot be vaunted.

Assimilated lineages, by contrast, cannot be discriminated by means of an explicitly accepted modification in the canon of agnatic descent, since they are always regarded as having sprung from 'strangers' (*saan*, pl. *saam*), slaves or refugees. To incorporate them in the lineage structure of the sub-clan there is no alternative but to assimilate them by a fiction. A male slave is thus incorporated into his master's family and a refugee into that of his protector. Homeless and kinless, they must be endowed with a new social personality and given a definite place in the community. But the bond of actual paternity cannot be fabricated; the fiction is a makeshift and always remains so. A slave or a refugee can never acquire the one right which is conferred exclusively by the tie of blood, or as the Tallensi say, of begetting (*dɔyam*), the right to offer sacrifice directly, as the owner (*daana*) of his shrine (*bayɔr*)[2] to the spirit of the patron whom he has described in his lifetime as his father (*ba*). In this respect they have no advantage over matrilateral kin, for a man's spirit can receive direct sacrifice only from his agnatic posterity. Like matrilateral kin, also, an adopted slave is barred from rights of inheritance and succession that are confined to the agnatic line, even though he is for all practical purposes the child (*bii*) of his patron in a way that a matrilateral kinsman could never be.

---

[1] This is dealt with in the second part of this study, *The Web of Kinship among the Tallensi.*

[2] *Bayɔr* (pl. *baɣa*) is the generic term for any ancestor or medicine shrine; *bɔyar* (pl. *bɔɣa*) is the special shrine dedicated to the founding ancestor of a lineage.

CLANSHIP: THE NAMOOS

Assimilated lineages, therefore, all over Taleland, though thoroughly absorbed into the structure of the sub-clan or clan, suffer the same disabilities as the more precisely differentiated attached lineages; they cannot, however, make a virtue of this, as the latter sometimes can; they cannot explain away their status. To tax a person, openly or explicitly, with being the descendant of a slave (*da'abɔr bii*) is one of the deadliest insults, however remote his slave ancestry may be. This is more than a matter of etiquette. It amounts, in certain circumstances, to blasphemy against the spirit of the man who originally adopted this slave ancestor. Thus, under this rule of courtesy to clansmen and respect for ancestors, the status of an assimilated lineage is never commented on publicly unless a serious issue hangs on it or a severe quarrel is involved. This exceptional circumspection about assimilated lineages shows better than anything else their ambiguous position in the clan.

Such elements of the social structure as these are not apparent at first glance. I did not discover the existence of assimilated lineages at Tongo until the end of my first year in the field. To do so it was essential to have a very thorough understanding of the way the lineage system works and of the internal structure of the Tale community. I was able then to notice and to be puzzled by the absence, or self-effacement, of certain people in situations where they would normally be representing their lineage segments. It was not the behaviour to be expected of them if their segments were of equal status with the authentic segments of Mosuor biis. Veiled hints began to have a meaning which confidential informants confirmed.

One of my earliest friends and frankest informants at Tongo was Saɣɔbazaa, an elder in whom the chief had the greatest confidence and who was universally esteemed for his industry and probity. Saɣɔbazaa was the head (*kpeem*) of Nɔŋsuur yidɛm, a major segment of one of the major segments of Tongo. One of its members held an important and confidential office under the chief. Nɔŋsuur yidɛm appeared to be of the true agnatic line of Mosuor. I took this for granted the more readily because, when the Great Festival season came round and all the elders of Tongo were summoned to the chief's house so that a diviner could be consulted, it was Saɣɔbazaa who consulted the diviner on behalf of the chief and the whole of Tongo, in order to ascertain what offerings must be given to Mosuor and the chiefly ancestors.

Nevertheless, Nɔŋsuur yidɛm is an assimilated lineage whose founding ancestor is vaguely said to have arrived with Mosuor. Though almost completely absorbed by the authentic line of Mosuor biis, a last barrier remains, which I discovered only through one of the most striking of the events which revealed the existence and status of accessory lineages at Tongo. It showed also how there is a continuous process of adjustment going on in every sector of the social structure, resolving the tensions and contradictions latent in it.

It was an occasion of historic importance marking the climax of one phase in the absorption of the accessory lineages by the authentic lineages of Tongo. The occasion was that of the great thanksgiving sacrifice to the founding ancestors of Tongo, Mosuor and his son Sɛɣahɔg, which took place in 1936. Beer and animals were contributed by the chief, who gave

54 CLANSHIP: THE NAMOOS

a cow, and by all the segments of the sub-clan—the heads bringing a sheep each, the elders next in seniority in each segment a goat each, and the junior elders bringing fowls. It was noticeable that assimilated and attached lineages also brought contributions of fowls, by express command of the chief. Never before in the memory of the oldest men had so many animals been slaughtered in sacrifice to the ancient ancestors (*yaabkɔrɔg*, pl. *yaakɔrɔb*) of the sub-clan on one day; and a great concourse of men of all ages, such as had never in living memory gathered for such a sacrifice, assembled for the occasion. Among them were several members of assimilated and attached lineages, but, surprisingly, none of the senior elders of these lineages. The authentic segments were there in full force, their senior elders acting as their formal representatives and taking the lead in the rites. In the days of their youth, some of the old men murmured with disapproval, only the heads of the authentic lineages used to be present at sacrifices to Mosuor. A noisy crowd of men of all ages would have been considered altogether out of keeping with so sacred and esoteric a *bɔyar* as that of the founding ancestor. But times have changed; these are the chief's orders; and if it is obligatory for every authentic lineage to be represented at such a sacrifice, it is also the right of any of their male members to participate if they wish. There were whispers, also, about 'strangers' (*saam*) being present, and I thought, at first, that they must be referring to me.

The ceremony proceeded with the usual alternation of reverential solemnity and conviviality and lasted far into the night. But for two incidents one might have forgotten the presence of those men who by the strict canon of agnatic descent were intruders. There was a long delay at the outset while the elders of the segment which has the custody of the graves and shrines of the clan founders (Lɛbhtiis yidɛm) held a private conference at the house of their lineage head. This aroused the suspicion of some of the better informed men amongst the crowd waiting impatiently for their arrival. Next day we learnt that these suspicions were justified. Lɛbhtiis yidɛm had been debating with some acrimony, though inconclusively, what was the right line to take about the presence of members of accessory lineages.

Later, there was another hitch just before the culminating rite, the actual sacrifice to Mosuor's *bɔyar*. There were whispered consultations. An impetuous member of Lɛbhtiis yidɛm protested that the intruders should be shut out, but he was overruled by an elder who counselled moderation in view of the chief's wishes.

Next day these incidents were threshed out by the chief when all the elders met to congratulate him on the success of the sacrifices. He rated Lɛbhtiis yidɛm scathingly for their reactionary conduct. 'Times have changed', he said in the course of a long harangue, 'and you must disregard those old tales. Anyhow, you are only my deputies. It is I who really own Mosuor's *bɔyar*, and it is I who will suffer the penalties if Mosuor is offended by what I am doing. And what if some people are of slave descent? They won't steal the *bɔyar* from you. If a man has a slave he calls him to come and join in sacrifices to his ancestors; his slave is like his son. Mosuor established (*naam*, lit. created) all of us, he owns

CLANSHIP: THE NAMOOS   55

all of us (i.e. those of alleged slave descent as well). Who are you to decide who is or is not to be allowed to take part in sacrifices to him?'

Crest-fallen, the supporters of the *status quo ante* begged the chief's pardon. It was a victory for the forces of community integration and a personal triumph for the chief over the cleavages due to the strict application of the canon of agnatic descent.

One of the chief's most intimate and influential elders commented to me afterwards, cautiously but with a hint of regret, that soon it would become impossible to withhold the chiefship from the accessory lineages now that they had practically won the right to participate in the most esoteric ritual cult of the true agnatic sodality. But the battle for consolidation is not yet over. The presence of some members of accessory lineages at the sacrifices was not part of a deliberate scheme to gain equality of status but was an unthinking reaction to the whole situation— the unusual publicity of the ceremony, its emphasis on an all-embracing solidarity of the whole sub-clan, and the chief's insistence on interpreting this to mean all the people of Tongo and not only those of true agnatic descent from Mosuor. Some elders of the accessory lineages were as dubious about the affair as some of the elders of authentic lineages. To take part in sacrifices from which one's fathers and grandfathers (*banam ni yaanam*) had been rigidly excluded might well be an offence against one's own ancestors, even though the chief had taken the responsibility on himself. Members of accessory lineages do not resent their disfranchisement as a disability to be fought against, but accept it as part of the fixed order of society validated by the whole religious system.

Thus these elders of the accessory lineages will not take it for granted that they now have the same rights as the authentic lineages. They are aware, also, that the occurrence has left behind a good deal of hidden resentment which may, at some future crisis, precipitate a violent reaction against the inclusion of accessory lineages in the ritual brotherhood of Mosuor biis. The forces of integration are strong at Tongo; but the genealogical cleavages in its lineage structure are so fundamental that this historic sacrifice may yet prove to be a warning against their abrogation rather than a precedent for it.

This episode brought out more vividly than anything I had previously encountered the significance of the ancestral graves and shrines, in particular of Mosuor's *bɔyar*, as the focus of the sub-clan's unity and the symbol of its corporate identity; for it was obvious that until they were able to participate on equal terms in sacrifices to this *bɔyar*, the accessory lineages would not be regarded as, or feel themselves to be, completely absorbed by the authentic lineages.

Tongo, we may conclude, though it is more closely knit than Sie, is also an open system in its lineage structure; and this is equally true of Yamɔlɔg and Biuk. This peculiarity of the clan organization is more precisely apparent in the asymmetrical linkages of the component lineages of the different sub-clans of Mosuor biis. It is evident from our analysis that the ties of clanship summarily posited by the natives as linking *all* of Tongo with *all* of Sie, *all* of Yamɔlɔg, and *all* of Biuk, measured by the strict canon of agnatic descent as well as by the critical norms of clanship,

56   CLANSHIP: THE NAMOOS

really hold only for the authentic lineages and, through them, for the assimilated lineages. The natives ignore this qualification when they make general statements about their clan organization—not because they reason obliquely, but on sound sociological grounds; for in their corporate relations with one another the four sub-clans treat one another as units irrespective of what the internal structure of each may be. Members of accessory lineages can represent the whole sub-clan in relation to one of the other sub-clans.

The Nexus of Clanship Ties

Let us go back to Sie. The two lineages of Sie-datɔk have no ties of clanship with the distant *sunzɔp* of the Sie proper lineages to which they are attached by ties of clanship—that is, with Tongo, Yamələg, or Biuk. But to balance this they are linked by ties of clanship to other units with which the authentic lineages of Sie have no such ties.

Gban is a Namoo community adjacent to Sie. The people of Gban (Gbandɛm) comprise three maximal lineages: (F) Dabierugyayardɛm; (G) Gbandaan yidɛm; and (H) Buŋwari yidɛm. Taken together these three units form a local clan; they are linked by all the ties of clanship, but they do not claim to have a single common ancestor or postulate the convergence of their lines of ascent as do the Sie-datɔkdɛm. (F) Dabierugyayardɛm claim to have been the first to settle there, as their ancestor came there from Kurugu—like the ancestors of Sie-datɔkdɛm, it will be remembered—before the founders of the other two maximal lineages arrived. But now they have all become *dɔyam bukɔ'la*—one consanguineous kin.

Sie-datɔk and Gban are linked by ties of clanship exactly in the same way as the component lineages of each are linked *inter se*, and as the two lineages of Sie-datɔk are linked to the authentic lineages of Sie to which they are attached, or as Sie and Tongo are related to each other.

Just as Sie proper has a closer bond with the segment of Kabuu yidɛm at Tongo than with the other Tongo lineages, so the senior lineage of Sie-datɔk, (D) Daaŋ yidɛm, has a special tie with the senior segment (Tasoo yidɛm) of (F) Dabierugyayardɛm at Gban. Their respective ancestors are said to have been kin (*mabiis*) whose common home was Kurugu. Hence these two lineages attend each others' sacrifices to their respective founding ancestors and are entitled to the portion of the sacrificial animal due to close *sunzɔp*, a hind leg (*gbɛr*). If there is a funeral among (D) Daaŋ yidɛm, representatives of (F) Dabierugyayardɛm will be sure to attend and assist as a matter both of loyalty and of duty; representatives of the other two Gban lineages may or may not turn up, as they please. It is not an obligation to do so, though they have clanship ties with Sie-datɔk. It is as if the primary tie of clanship between Gban and Sie-datɔk is that which links (F) Dabierugyayardɛm to (D) Daaŋ yidɛm and that this tie is merely extended to the other component lineages of the two units, through the effect of their bonds with the two lineages primarily interlinked. The relation is similar to that which obtains between any of the assimilated lineages of Tongo and the authentic

PLATE III

(a) Elders of a Maximal Lineage assemble to sacrifice to their Founder.

The Maximal Lineage is a corporate unit: The elders of a maximal lineage, representing all its component segments, assemble to perform a sacrifice on the grave of one of their founding ancestors. Note that (a) only men are present; (b) the members of each segment sit together; (c) the close-packed form of the group, an index of the strong sense of lineage solidarity in such situations.

(b) Prayer preceding Sacrifice to Clan Founder.

An episode in the great sacrifice to Mosuor and the other founding ancestors, at Tongo, in 1936. Men of the sub-clan assembled at Mosuor's grave (stones in foreground) and tree shrine (baobab tree). The photograph was taken as the prayer preceding the sacrifice was being offered.

PLATE IV

(a) Ritual strangling of a goat to provide the loin cover for a Namoo elder's burial.

(b) Ŋma wɔyar, the final rite of a Namoo funeral, is peculiar to Namoos.

lineages of Sie. There are gradations in the operation of clanship ties in this case.

Gbandɛm have no ties of clanship with Sie proper or with the other branches of Mosuor biis, with all of whom they intermarry freely. Their only connexion with one another is that they are all Namoos.

To complete the picture let us look again at the Tongo end of this chain of clan linkages. There the attached lineages should, by formal reckoning, have ties of clanship with the communities of Talis from whom they are

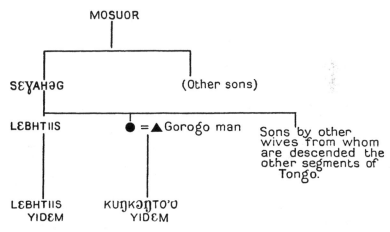

Diagram showing the genealogical tie between an attached lineage, Kuŋkɔŋto'o yidɛm, and the authentic lineage, Lɛbhtiis yidɛm, to which it is attached.

said to have sprung on the male side. But these ties are now purely nominal owing to the advanced stage of fusion with the authentic lineages of Tongo which these attached lineages have reached. Gorogo people never come to funerals celebrated by Kuŋkɔŋto'o yidɛm of Tongo, the attached lineage which is said to have originated from a 'sister's son' of Lɛbhtiis yidɛm begotten by a Gorogo man who later divorced his wife (see diagram above). Yet Kuŋkɔŋto'o yidɛm retain most of the funeral ritual and the totemic taboos of the Talis. They account for this on the grounds that their founding ancestor was initiated by his Gorogo father into the *Bɔyar* cult of the Talis[1] before being disowned by him. They are bound therefore, through the principle of lineage continuity, to maintain his ritual observances. What is more significant, Kuŋkɔŋto'o yidɛm freely marry Gorogo women. They argue in defence of this—following exactly the logic of the lineage system and the principles of kinship—that they no longer know which of the component lineages of Gorogo is their *dɔyam* (consanguineous kin) and therefore forbidden in marriage to them, and which of them are not *dɔyam* and therefore marriageable. The criterion of exogamy has lapsed; and one reason for this, without a doubt, is that Tongo and Gorogo are on opposite sides of the great cleavage between

[1] Cf. pp. 103 ff. below.

58 CLANSHIP: THE NAMOOS

Namoos and Talis. Kuŋkɔŋto'o yidɛm could maintain ties of clanship with Gorogo only if they had the necessary degree of corporate autonomy within the lineage structure of Tongo. But they are so thoroughly incorporated into this lineage structure as to count merely as a segment of the third or fourth order. They are completely identified with Tongo, and the conflict of loyalties would be too great if they had ties of clanship also with Gorogo. Abandoning these entirely, Kuŋkɔŋto'o yidɛm regard Gorogo as a single unit, any member of which they may marry. In such cases the Tallensi choose the course of least restriction and most advantage.

The two lineages of Sie-datɔk are intercalary between Gban and Sie proper; (A) Baɣana yidɛm of Sie are an intercalary lineage linking Sie proper with Sie-datɔk and so are (B) Sa-tɛŋɔrdɛm; but Kuŋkɔŋto'o yidɛm of Tongo are not an intercalary lineage.

There is, however, one intercalary lineage at Tongo the status and structural ties of which introduce a factor of clanship which is obscured elsewhere by the convention of always subsuming clanship ties under the dogma of common ancestry. Ligɔr yidɛm are an assimilated lineage whose founding ancestor is believed to have been a refugee from afar, a Gɔrɔŋ. Their homesteads merge with those of Gbizug on one side and those of the authentic lineage of Tongo to which they are assimilated on the other. Ligɔr yidɛm have ties of clanship with Gbizug, though only the minimal ties of mutual exogamy and fraternity; the right to inherit one another's widows would never be exercised though it is formally presumed to exist; and there are between them no ties of a cult of a common ancestor or even of attending one another's sacrifices to lineage ancestors. No other Tongo lineages—the *sunzɔp* of Ligɔr yidɛm—have ties of clanship with Gbizug, and Ligɔr yidɛm have no ties of clanship with the lineages of Gbeog, Ba'ari, and other adjacent communities who are the *sunzɔp* of Gbizug (cf. p. 82).

This linkage, which so much resembles those of the intercalary lineages at Sie, is particularly illuminating. Ligɔr yidɛm, as a Tongo lineage, are Namoos, sharply separated from the Gbizugdɛm who are Talis, in ritual observances and in their political allegiance. This enhances their ties with Tongo, and explains why their clanship ties with Gbizug are no more than minimal. The stronger pull is that of Tongo. When there is a death among Ligɔr yidɛm both their Tongo *sunzɔp* and their Gbizug *sunzɔp* send representatives and contributions to the mortuary and funeral ceremonies, and it is interesting to see how the different significance of the two sets of ties comes out then. In the esoteric phases of the ceremonies Gbizugdɛm play no part and bring no contributions; but in the non-ritual formalities they have as prominent a role as the Tongo *sunzɔp*. Ligɔr yidɛm act reciprocally whenever there is a funeral at Gbizug.

In this instance a bond of common ancestry between Gbizug and Ligɔr yidɛm is not invoked. Gbizug elders say that Ligɔr yidɛm are their 'kin' (*mabiis*) because the Gɔrɔŋ from whom the latter are descended first sought the protection of the Gbizug tɛndaana of that time, though they do not know which of their tɛndaana ancestors this was. Upon inquiry it appeared that the stranger came from a community of Namoos, having the same funeral ritual and totemic avoidances as the Tale Namoos.

CLANSHIP: THE NAMOOS

So the tendaana sent him to the Chief of Tongo, but, having already accepted him hospitably, he also gave the homeless man land to build on and to farm near his own homestead. There the stranger's posterity (*tu'u*) have remained ever since 'sitting down together with' (*kab ziin ni*) Gbizugdɛm but assimilated to Tongo. For this reason, say Gbizug elders, '*tam nso Ligər yidɛm*—we own (in the sense of being *in loco parentis* to) Ligər yidɛm'. Ligər, which means Darkness, was the name given to this stranger because he came in the darkness of night, crouching against the wall of the homestead for safety, to implore protection and hospitality. The name enshrines the myth. But the important point is that the local situation of Ligər yidɛm, between the homesteads of their Tongo *sunzɔp* and those of their Gbizug *sunzɔp*, corresponds exactly to their structural articulation and to the way this is represented in the symbolism of the myth. We shall find other instances later confirming the surmise that clanship ties, here, are a function of local ties.

That does not mean that local ties, however close they may be, always imply corresponding ties of clanship. All social ties between corporate units in Taleland, whether they are based on actual or putative genea- logical links, on local contiguity, on ritual collaboration and interdepen- dence, or on political connexions, tend to be assimilated to clanship. Whenever and wherever such ties operate, they reflect common or mutual interests which find expression in relations of amity and co-operation modelled on those that hold between corporate units linked by ties of clanship. But these relations of clanship are modified in numerous ways according to the structural context of the particular ties they express.

A number of Tale clans have accessory lineages with intercalary rela- tions exactly like those of Ligər yidɛm at Tongo; yet Tongo itself affords an instance of a lineage which is locally intercalary but not bilaterally linked by ties of clanship to the units on either side of it. Nɔŋsuur yidɛm, who have been previously mentioned, live between the authentic lineage of Tongo to which they are primarily assimilated (Siiyɛŋ biis) and Zubiuŋ, the genealogically independent clan of Talis who are close neighbours of Tongo. Nɔŋsuur yidɛm were the first people of Tongo to come and live in that part of the settlement, according to their traditions. It is said that their ancestor who first built his homestead there was a 'sister's son' (*ahəŋ*) of Zubiuŋ and was therefore given land to build on and farm by the then Zubiuŋ tendaana. Thus Nɔŋsuur yidɛm live on Zubiuŋ land; they have cordial and intimate relations of neighbourliness with the people of Zubiuŋ; they speak of themselves in some situations as 'sister's sons' (*ahəs*) of Zubiuŋ in virtue of the kinship tie which their ancestor had with the latter; but they have no ties of clanship with Zubiuŋ. They always take part in important Zubiuŋ funerals, but as neighbours (*yi-kpeedɛm*) and as classificatory *ahəs*, contributing, through their lineage head (*kpeem*), the donations due from *ahəs* and receiving the shares of meat, beer, and food- stuffs due to *ahəs*. Ligər yidɛm, despite their ties of clanship with Gbizug, do not participate in sacrifices given by the latter to their lineage *bɔyar*; Nɔŋsuur yidɛm are generally represented at important sacrifices made by any of the Zubiuŋ maximal lineages to their lineage *bɔyar*, but, again, in their role of classificatory *ahəs*. The pull of Tongo is the decisive factor.

CLANSHIP: THE NAMOOS

The Gbizug legend of how Ligər yidɛm came to dwell at Tongo is well known to Tongo elders who are versed in such matters, and is regarded by them as true. It would never, of course, be brought up in public, especially if any Ligər yidɛm were present. The elders of Ligər yidɛm accept this story, but they would be indignant at any suggestion that it is in any way derogatory. The assimilated lineages at Tongo stand in a marginal relation to the authentic posterity of Mosuor, and this is reflected in the general attitude of tacit discretion about their presumed origins and the disabilities these entail. These cannot be covered up, and no upright person would wish to do so; but they are not matters of which a public display is made unless there is a really serious issue at stake.

It is unnecessary to describe at length the lineage structure of Yamələg and Biuk, both of which closely resemble Tongo. At Biuk we enter the country of the Gərisi. Not only do the people of Biuk, though linked by ties of clanship with Mosuor biis, speak Gərni and practise some Gəre customs not found among the Tallensi, but they are also linked by clanship ties, through intercalary lineages, with the Gərisi of Zuarungu. These clan linkages of the people of Biuk with Gərisi are not known to the people of Tongo, Yamələg, and Sie, nor are they of any interest to them. Biuk marks the limit of their frame of social reference, though the chain of clanship ties which links them to one another extends beyond it, across the frontier of linguistic and cultural variation.

Our analysis of the clan structure of Mosuor biis and their clanship ties with other units may be summed up in the following table and diagram. For the sake of simplicity Yamələg and Biuk are omitted, since they constitute only a wider ramification of the structural arrangements represented in the table.

TONGO

Authentic lineages (grouped in four major segments of the sub-clan)	have ties of clanship with	All Yamələg / All Sie / All Biuk
Accessory lineages (distributed amongst the four major segments; no corporate organization *inter se*)	have ties of clanship, extended from those of the authentic lineages with	All Yamələg / All Sie / All Biuk
One assimilated lineage (Ligər yidɛm)	has, in addition, ties of clanship with	Gbizug (Talis)

SIE PROPER

Authentic lineages (forming three major segments)	have ties of clanship with	All Tongo / All Yamələg / All Biuk

These ties of clanship extended to the accessory lineages at Sie.

Authentic lineage (A) (Baɣana yidɛm)	has ties of clanship with	Lineage (D) (Ɖaaŋ yidɛm) of Sie-datɔk
Authentic lineage (B) (Sa-tɛŋərdɛm)	has ties of clanship with	Lineage (E) (Kaləŋkaa yidɛm) of Sie-datɔk

CLANSHIP: THE NAMOOS

SIE-DATƆK

Two maximal lineages constituting a relatively autonomous corporate unit	each has ties of clanship with	one authentic lineage of Sie, but not with the others
	no ties of clanship with	the other three branches of Mosuor biis
One lineage (D) (Ɖaaŋ yidɛm)	has ties of clanship with	one lineage (F) Dabierugyaɣardɛm of Gban

By extension of the clanship ties between Ɖaaŋ yidɛm (D) of Sie-datɔk and Dabierugyaɣardɛm (F) of Gban, both lineages of Sie-datɔk have ties of clanship with all Gban.

GBAN

| Three maximal lineages not claiming convergent ascent. (A composite local clan) | have ties of clanship with | Sie-datɔk |
| | but no ties of clanship with | Mosuor biis. |

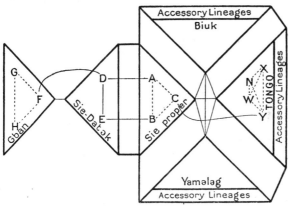

Diagram showing the Nexus of Clanship Ties from Gban to Tongo
Clanship Ties are shown thus: ———
A. etc. = Major segments of clan or sub-clan.

The Field of Clanship

To avoid circumlocution we may speak of this system of linked lineages as a clan organization. We can describe Mosuor biis collectively as a clan, and each of the four locally distinct branches of this agnatically defined grouping as a sub-clan—overlooking, for the sake of simplicity, the peculiar association of accessory lineages within each sub-clan. We can, more appropriately, subsume the principles which determine the connexion between lineage and lineage in the chain, both within the clan or sub-clan and across clans, under the concept of clanship. This would be isolating a special sense of the associated Tale concepts *mabiirɔt* (kin), *dɔɣam* (consanguinity), and *sunzɔt* (brotherhood), which emerges quite clearly when these terms of wider meaning are applied to relations

62   CLANSHIP: THE NAMOOS

between corporate units. We may define a clan, then, as a set of locally united lineages, each of which is linked with all or most of the others by ties of clanship, which act together in the service of certain common interests indicated by the bond of exogamy, by reciprocal rights and duties in events such as the funeral of a member of any one of them, and by the ban on intestine war or feud; and which act as a corporate unit in respect of these common interests in relation to other such units. We must stress the point that the clan, as here defined, is a local unit, occupying a specified locality from which it takes its name.

This definition applies to the ideal type of the Tale local clan. It does not exhaust all the attributes of social relations based on clanship ties among the Tallensi. In the case of Mosuor biis, we should substitute 'sub-clan' for 'clan' in this definition, though the natives would contend that it is merely a matter of degree. They would say that the four branches of Mosuor biis represent a particularly wide dispersal of what is really a single local clan of the more usual kind. Many other Tale clans have colonial offshoots, but as they are not so well differentiated, either genealogically or spatially, as Mosuor biis they are not reckoned as separate units of clan organization. Again, there is a difference between a sub-clan like Tongo, all the component lineages of which are segments of a single inclusive lineage and have a common founding ancestor, and a clan like Gban, the component lineages of which are genealogically independent maximal lineages. Gban is an example of what might be called a composite clan. Lastly there are units such as Sie-datɔk, which has the corporate structure of a composite clan, but with so much less local and lineage autonomy than is characteristic of a clan that it is regarded by the natives as an appendage of Sie.

Tale clans, as these few examples show, are very varied in their constitution. But the ground-plan of all is the same. The core of every clan is a maximal lineage. In the special case of Mosuor biis, a major segment of the maximal lineage is the foundation of each sub-clan, but these major segments are functionally homologous with the maximal lineages of composite clans. The maximal lineage, everywhere, is a clearly defined structural unit. It is the only irreducible unit of the clan organization.

Tale clan organization can best be understood if we realize that every maximal lineage is the centre of a field of specific social relations marked out by the ties and cleavages established by the principles of clanship. The dimensions of the field of clanship of a lineage, in the narrow sense, are determined by the fundamental principle of clanship, the canon of agnatic descent, applied directly, fictionally, or by a compromise through the assumption of a cognatic link. Even clanship ties which seem to be rooted in local contiguity are translated so as to fit in with this principle. It is the organizing principle of social relations on the plane of clanship. All corporate units tend to be modelled on the agnatic lineage; all social ties and cleavages between corporate units tend to operate in accordance with the norms premised by the patrilineal principle.

Clanship ties and cleavages mark out, for each lineage, one or more other lineages in relation to whose members its own members are automatically subject to the rule of exogamy, and have, in theory, the unconditional right to inherit widows. This is the minimum definition of the field of clanship of a lineage. It is equally important, from the Tale point of view, that a lineage is, in its corporate capacity, vested with specific rights and duties in relation to other lineages in its field of clanship; and these rights and duties may be exercised by any of the male members of a lineage on its behalf. Clanship, as thus defined, is the basis of Tale political organization.

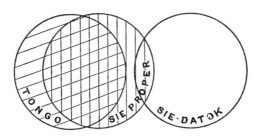

Diagram illustrating the overlapping of fields of Clanship.

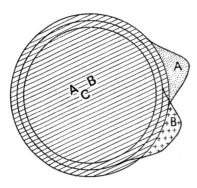

Diagram showing congruence & differentiation in the Field of Clanship for the three Major Segments of Sie.

⫽ Field of clanship common to all three segments

▓ Portion of Segment A's field of clanship specific to it.

⁺⁺⁺ Portion of Segment B's field of clanship specific to it.

It is clear that lineages belonging to the same clan, or to a series of linked clans such as we have been describing, do not have completely congruent fields of clanship. Here again it is the canon of agnatic descent that principally determines the degree of coincidence of the fields of clanship of any two lineages. There is a field of clanship common to all the authentic segments of Mosuor biis, the region—to use a spatial analogy—where the particular fields of clanship of all these segments overlap. But the fields of clanship of all the segments do not overlap completely; each has a region of clanship specific to itself. This is especially well illustrated by the component lineages of Sie-datɔk. Stated in these terms a clan is the region where the fields of clanship of two or more lineages have the maximum overlap, and a chain of linked clans can be resolved into a series of overlapping fields of clanship of varying

64 CLANSHIP: THE NAMOOS

dimensions. The clan is also the region where a lineage's clanship ties
have the maximum force; for, as we have seen, there are differences in
the range and precision of the rights, obligations, and participation in the
secular and ceremonial matters of common interest implied by the ties
of clanship which a lineage has with other lineages.

A lineage's field of clanship is not homogeneous. As will become
clearer when we have analysed one or two more chains of linked lineages,
spatial distance and genealogical distance are the main factors upon which
the incidence and variation of the rights and duties of clanship depend.
The farther away a lineage lives from another with which it has ties of
clanship, the less intercourse is there between their members and the
less likely are they to co-operate in those situations and events which
mobilize these ties. Again, the closer the genealogical links, actual,
putative, or fictional, between two linked lineages the more regularly will
they co-operate and the more effectively assert the rights and perform
the duties of clanship.

The principles so far elicited have a general application throughout
Taleland. But the clan of Mosuor biis is unique. The typical clan in
Taleland is a single local unit of the composite kind. Mosuor biis are
certainly the most numerous patrilineal descent group in Taleland.[1]
It must not be forgotten that in addition to the four localized branches of
the clan which form its recognized major subdivisions, there are the
minor colonial offshoots.

The natives see no difficulty in explaining the numerical preponderance
of Mosuor biis. It is, in their eyes, due simply to a fecundity greater than
that of other lineages. Members of Mosuor biis themselves give this a
mystical rationalization. They say that they are prolific because they all
have but one religious cult, that of their ancestors, which binds them to
one another in mutual amity and solidarity. In their cult of their ancestors
each branch of Mosuor biis seeks not only its own increase and prosperity
but the increase and prosperity of all its clan brethren as well. To do
otherwise would be a sin inviting the wrath of the common ancestors of
the whole clan. But in composite clans, they say, each component lineage
has its own independent ancestral and other ritual cults. It is jealously
concerned with its own increase and prosperity, even regarding it as an
advantage if other maximal lineages of the same clan are diminished.
Such an attitude brings down mystical retribution; for those who seek
the ill of their fellow men are bound to suffer ill themselves.

These views are not accepted among members of composite clans, who
consider their own cults to be no less founded on, and instrumental in

---

[1] To take a complete census of the members of Mosuor biis, even of the male
members only, would be impossibly laborious and time-consuming for an
anthropological field-worker limited to a short stay in the country. Sample
censuses were made at Tongo and Sie. Going by these and by recent counts
made throughout Taleland by the Administration of the taxable male population, I should estimate the male members of Mosuor biis (including accessory
lineages) as not less than 2,000. The women are so scattered, owing to patrilocal marriage, that it is impossible to estimate their numbers. No other clan
in Taleland can, I should judge, reckon more than half this number of male
members.

CLANSHIP: THE NAMOOS 65

maintaining, amity and solidarity in the clan, and no less efficacious in promoting their increase and prosperity than the ancestral cult of Mosuor biis. Such mystical interpretations are, in fact, a reflex of the social structure. They throw no light on the problem of the numbers of Mosuor's posterity. Without historical documents we must accept it as one of the given facts of Tale society.

Here a point of particular interest may be noted. Though they are held, in common with other Namoo clans in Taleland, to be an intrusive group by origin, the clan of Mosuor biis forms the backbone of Tale political organization. They place their founding ancestor some eight to ten generations back counting from the heads of existing minimal lineages. But the clans which claim to be autochthonous and to have ante-dated all the Namoos of Taleland in their occupation of the country give pedigrees of about the same chronological extension. It is obvious there-fore that no means of estimating the relative lengths of time during which Namoos and non-Namoos have been settled in Taleland are provided by their genealogies. Like their myths of origin, the chronological retrospect implied in Tale clan or lineage genealogies has no historical value. The chronological depth of their genealogies and the fact that they preserve the graves of significant ancestors seem to justify the inference that the Tale Namoos have occupied their present settlements for not less than two and possibly for three centuries. The Tallensi, however, do not evaluate their genealogies in this way. Genealogies are significant to them as one of the principal instruments for organizing their present social relations. They are kept alive only in so far as they serve this end, and have no value, therefore, as a measure of the time during which a clan or lineage has been in existence. The uniform genealogical retrospect of Namoo and non-Namoo clans in Taleland is a reflex of the stability and coherence of their social and political relations. The only historical inference one can justifiably make is that their present social order has been in existence for a greater length of time than the memories of the oldest living natives can compass. This is the essence of the statement 'It has been thus since the days of our fathers and forefathers', which the natives regard as a sufficient explanation of the origin of most of their institutions.

F

CHAPTER V

THE DISTRIBUTION OF THE NAMOOS

The Distinctive Ritual Observances of the Namoos

CLUSTERED about the chain of sub-clans that makes up the clan of Mosuor biis are a number of other Namoo communities. None of them has ties of clanship with Mosuor biis; yet the latter speak of them as *ti buurət*, our stock, or *ti mabiis*, our kin. The emphasis here is on the common Mampuru origin claimed for all Namoos. It is widely known among the Tallensi that groups of people claiming to be of Mampuru origin are found scattered throughout the Northern Territories and the adjacent parts of the French Haute Volta. Though they have no political or social ties with them, Tale Namoos assert that they are of the same stock (*buurət*) as the Mossi in French territory, the Dagomba in British territory, and the various clans claiming Mampuru origin among the Gərisi, the Namnam, the Kusaasi, the Bulisi, and other neighbouring groups.

Whether or no these people reached their present locations by migration from Mampurugu, it is a fact that they all have certain ritual observances in common, and most of them keep up quasi-political or ceremonial ties with the dominant section of the Mamprusi, who share these distinctive ritual observances. In all these groups of people a man's first-born son and first-born daughter may not eat the domestic fowl, are forbidden, during their father's lifetime, to wear any of his garments or his quiver and to enter or even look into his granary. Amongst all of them a man's corpse is girded with a goatskin loin-cover (*ba suona buu*) ritually decorated with three cowrie shells; and one of their most solemn oaths is to swear by 'my father and his goatskin and his three cowrie shells (*mba ni u buu ni u ligəri ata*)'—a reference to this burial custom.

These are infallible tests. A number of other ritual observances and doctrines mostly connected with mortuary and funeral ceremonies are also distinctive of Namoos. Thus, if a man is survived by his first-born son and daughter, or by either, special rites are performed to release them from the taboo on using their father's garments, weapons, and granary; and the concluding rites of a Namoo funeral are also distinctive. But these ritual observances and the notions connected with them vary in detail and nuance from clan to clan and even between segments of a single clan. Some Namoo clans and clan segments have discriminative totems similar to those of non-Namoo clans in addition to the first-born child's avoidances. They may be totems associated with the locality in which they have settled, as for instance the leopard avoidance of the people of Ŋkoog (Winkogo); or they may be totems symbolizing the mythical event to which the clan or lineage in question attributes its original differentiation from other like units, as, for instance, the avoidance of the crocodile (*baŋ*) by one major segment of Baɣana yidɛm at Sie. Special myths often validate these avoidances, which serve thus to distinguish a particular clan or lineage from other Namoos in Taleland.

THE DISTRIBUTION OF THE NAMOOS 67

We have noted that Tale culture is homogeneous. Thus the totemic taboos of the Tale Namoos and their characteristic funeral rites, distinctive as they are, are homologous in form and function with the totemic observances and funeral rites of non-Namoos. We shall see the evidence for this when we examine the more elaborate differentiation of Talis and other non-Namoo clans and lineages by totemic and other ritual observances. Tallensi know this and take it for granted, as they also take for granted variations in the ritual observances of different communities which are presumed to have identical ritual forms. They attribute such variations to the influence of neighbouring communities. In fact the homologous usages of neighbouring communities have features in common which do not occur among more widely separated clans with the same practices.

But the taboos of the first-born and the goatskin loin-cover of the dead are fixed and unalterable. All Tallensi know that these are the distinguishing *kiha* (sing. *kihər*)—literally, forbidden things, but meaning ritual injunctions as well as prohibitions—of all Namoos, 'from Dagbɔŋ to Mooga', as the natives say.

Namoos say that they observe these *kiha* 'because it is the custom of our ancestors (*ti yaab yɛl nla*)'. They require no other explanation, but accept such ritual observances as facts of immemorial antiquity and part of the fixed order of society. The taboo of the fowl is the only one of these observances for which a myth of origin exists, and this is typical of the Tale myths purporting to account for the origins of totemic avoidances, being apparently trivial in content and neutral in emotional tone. Considering the fluid form and content of such myths and the fact that they are never deliberately taught, this myth is remarkably consistent in outline among Namoo clans in Taleland.[1] Tallensi display no interest in the private myths of any social group other than their own, and therefore make no secret of these myths. Knowledge of them is not deemed to be a necessary condition of adherence to the tenets they enshrine. Most young Namoos and many older men, even those who have themselves to observe the fowl taboo—an onerous enough restriction in a society whose chief sacrificial animal is the fowl—are ignorant of or but hazily acquainted with the myth. The men who know it tell it without reticence.

Significance of the Totemic Taboos of the Namoos

The fowl taboo, Namoos say, came about because 'a fowl did a great service to our ancestor'. He had a wife, and people came to her with slander of her husband, trying thus to persuade her to leave him. This made her very unhappy. But one day a broody hen sitting in the woman's grinding room told her not to weep. When her husband returns from the farm she must prepare a drink of flour-water for him, said the fowl, and it would fly up and dash the calabash from his hand. If he then killed the fowl in anger the woman would know that he was a wicked man, and if he spared it she would know that people were slandering him maliciously. When the man came home, the plan was carried out. Far from injuring

[1] Different versions of the myth are found among Namoos outside Taleland, but the central theme is the same. All versions stress the point that the intervention of a fowl was responsible for the birth of the clan.

68 THE DISTRIBUTION OF THE NAMOOS

the fowl, the man merely said, 'The fowl is thirsty'. Thus his wife knew that people had been deceiving her and she remained with him. Afterwards she bore a daughter, and vowed solemnly that her child should never eat fowl. Later a son followed, and the man declared that the boy too must refrain from eating fowl. That is why the first-born son and first-born daughter of all Namoos have the fowl avoidance; but later children may eat it, for if they, too, were prohibited, who would consume the fowls which men sacrifice to their ancestors?

If we bear in mind the enormous importance Tallensi attach to marriage and progeny, we can sympathize with the respect they pay to the common domestic fowl in return for this apparently trivial benefit conferred on their ancestor. Of course nobody knows or cares who this ancestor was, but it would not occur to anybody to doubt the truth of this tale. Every day some animal, domestic or wild, becomes a shrine (bayǝr), the symbol and medium of contact with the ancestor spirits, to some person or another in every Tale settlement; and the occasion of this ritual transformation of a commonplace creature is always a piece of good or ill fortune associated with it. Nor would the fact, admittedly contrary to ordinary experience, that a fowl broke into speech, disconcert the natives. They see no need for explaining away such incongruities, either by invoking the supernatural or by referring it to a fabulous age when animals possessed the power of speech. 'That is the story', they declare, and that is enough for them; as we might say, it fits in with the logic of the myth.

This casual attitude to the myth is due to the fact that the natives attach little importance to it in comparison with the observance it seeks to explain. For the myth is simply a formulation of the idea that the fowl taboo is the fundamental symbol of the social definition of Namoos. Everywhere within the social ambit of the Tallensi, and at all times, Namoos are those who are subject to distinctive ritual and moral restrictions in virtue of their agnatic descent; and amongst these the fowl taboo is crucial. That is how others think of Namoos, and that is how they themselves visualize their social identity. Through these observances the individual identifies himself in thought and feeling with the fraternity of clans of which his own is a part and, what is of equal significance, with the dead but still regnant forebears.

The anonymity of the ancestor in the myth shows that he stands for the prototype of all the ancestors who must necessarily have gone before in order that the present generation of men should exist, and to whom the living owe their whole social order. It is a notion entirely in keeping with the ideas underlying the kinship system of the Tallensi. But for the intervention of the fowl, says the myth, the Namoo stock might never have come into existence; and the taboo which commemorates that event came into being with the birth of their stock, which was at the same time the birth of their role in society. All Namoos, it must be remembered, are concerned with their totemic observances; for those who are themselves exempt from them have this privilege only because they are the brothers or sisters of individuals who are compelled to observe them.

The fowl taboo and the ritual observances associated with it symbolize

THE DISTRIBUTION OF THE NAMOOS 69

the paramount moral values of the Namoos. The oath a Namoo swears by his father and his goatskin and his three cowrie shells to rebut an accusation or assert his honesty is evidence of this.

The natives think of these rules as coeval with their social order. They are axioms of conduct, which men accept without questioning as they accept the fact that one is born a Namoo. Since they are binding on and restricted to the patrilineal line of descent, these avoidances serve to express the ultimate and unconditional validity of agnatic descent, through which the individual's place in a corporate unit is irrevocably fixed at birth, and by which his whole social and spiritual destiny is largely controlled. Through ignorance or stupidity, irreverence or lack of self-control, individuals sometimes, though very rarely, break these taboos. Such lapses will bring down mystical retribution on the sinner's head; that is his affair. They cannot impair the intrinsic validity of these rules or undermine their obligatory character.

It would be inconceivable for a Namoo to flout the taboo of the goatskin loin-cover for the dead. To do so would be a sacrilege so gratui- tous and so lunatic as to lie beyond the bounds of sane human behaviour. Actually a situation in which such a sacrilege would be possible would never occur, for the simple reason that a death is an affair of the clan. The clan elders conduct all mortuary and funeral ceremonies, and the inviolability of the prescribed ritual is thus safeguarded by the mechanics of its performance.

It is otherwise with the fowl taboo. This too the natives consider to be something so fundamental and axiomatic that it requires no sanction against possible breach except by accident. The danger of a breach occurs only with children. The first-born child who eats a fowl or even a hen's egg, either through inadvertence, through greed, or through childish recklessness, may sink into a decline (*u burəmrəme*), or at the least will break out in a rash on the head (*u zug koorəme*). But such a transgression by a child is venial, and the antidote is simple. The child is given an infusion of fowl droppings in water to drink which makes him vomit and so purges him.

Observation and questioning show that breaches of this taboo are as rare as the natives assert them to be. I have often seen a first-born man (*nɔ-kihir*, pl. *-kihib*, one who taboos the fowl) sacrificing fowls to his ancestor spirits and leaving them to others to consume. After such a rite a *nɔ-kihir* always washes his hands carefully lest he contaminate his food at the next meal with the blood of the fowl. Not only do parents, siblings, and other relatives take care to prevent children from breaking the taboo, but the children who have to observe it have a horror of doing so. By the time they are five or six years old children will tell an inquirer with great emphasis, 'I am an eldest child, and I don't eat fowl'. Though they do not know the myth that accounts for the taboo, they appreciate its obligatory character.

We have spoken of these taboos as symbols of moral values because, though binding on all Namoos, they do not imply specific ties either political or ceremonial, and are obligatory on individuals. Their observ- ance is in the last resort a matter of conscience and belief. In the widest

THE DISTRIBUTION OF THE NAMOOS

social setting they identify Namoo communities by contraposition with non-Namoo neighbours. The phrase 'we of the Mampuru stock' merely labels a category of clans. It becomes a coefficient of conduct for the individual within the context of clanship, local, and community ties.

The dispute over the succession to the custody of the shrine (bɔyar) of the founding ancestor of Bɔyada biis at Tongo was a case in point. Saŋgbɔŋ, the son of the deceased custodian, who had been head of Yiyaam biis, one major segment of the lineage, refused to hand the shrine over to Tinta'alɔm, the oldest living member of the whole lineage. He alleged that the latter's segment (Yidaan biis) were 'sister's children', that is, an attached lineage descended from a Sii man. All the men of Yidaan biis rallied unanimously around Tinta'alɔm, angry and resentful at this slur on their status. 'If we don't get the bɔyar', they explained, 'people will scoff at us, saying that we are the descendants of a slave' (i.e. not the authentic progeny of Mosuor).

The case was argued, with an acrimony which was hard to conceal, before the chief. Saŋgbɔŋ contended that Yidaan biis could not be debarred from taking part in sacrifices to the shrine of Bɔyada, but, as an attached lineage, they had no right to its custody. Tinta'alɔm, speaking for the whole segment of Yidaan biis, denied this story as a pack of lies, but his opponent refused to abandon his position. At length the chief put the decisive question to the elders who were present. 'What', he asked, 'do the people of Sii taboo?' 'The tortoise (pakur), the water tortoise (mieŋ), and the crocodile (baŋ)', said one of the elders, 'and they dress their dead in a sheepskin loin-cover (ba suona pɛhug), and do not taboo the fowl.' 'And what about you Namoos?' queried the chief. 'Do you avoid the fowl, or do you not? Do you put a sheepskin loin-cover on the dead?' The elders answered this rhetorical question, 'Of course we taboo the fowl! And we use a goatskin for the dead. When Talis slaughter the sheep to gird their dead we would not even touch the meat.' 'Now,' continued the chief, 'if Yidaan had come to live here with his mother's brother as an acknowledged son of a Sii man, would he have discarded his forefathers' taboos?' 'Neither he nor his descendants', exclaimed the elders with one voice; 'if they had done so they would suffer for it, they would all die out.' And an attached lineage which Saŋgbɔŋ had adduced in support of his case was quoted in proof; for they still retain the taboos of the Talis because their founder had been legitimately and ritually a member of a Talis clan. Moreover, there was the case of Puliebɔr yidɛm, the Tongo lineage living at Gorogo, who keep their Namoo taboos. There was a time when they lost many members through death in quick succession, and diviners revealed that this was a retribution for trying to participate in the initiation cult of their Talis kin. The tone and attitude of the elders showed impressively the moral importance to the natives of these taboos. It was common knowledge, they said, that Tinta'alɔm and all the members of his segment observe the Namoo taboos. Saŋgbɔŋ's story was palpably false. However, to make the decision conclusive and to save it from rankling it was left to an oracle. A fowl was slaughtered with an invocation to the ancestors and the posture in which it died showed which of the disputants was in the right.

THE DISTRIBUTION OF THE NAMOOS 71

No one was surprised when Tinta'aləm gained the verdict. Thus the ancestors themselves vouched for the legitimate status of Yidaan biis.

Other Namoo Clans

The most important of the Namoo clans that come within the political orbit of Tongo, though not related to it by ties of clanship, is the contiguous clan of Zoo. A number of Tongo families live on Zoo land, which was not so densely populated as Tongo 50 or 60 years ago and could therefore accommodate some of its overflow population. In the same way, a number of Zoo families have overflowed into the neighbouring locality of Gbambee, where they live among Tongo people. These ecological adjustments are facilitated, though not solely determined, by the structural ties between Zoo and Tongo, and by the fact that both are Namoo settlements. Ten out of the thirty-nine homesteads at Zoo belong to Tongo people, and they are members of all but one of the major segments of Tongo. By contrast, Tongo people are reluctant to move out to vacant parts of Zubiuŋ, where the people, though their neighbours and cognatic kinsfolk, are Talis in their ritual beliefs and practices. In recent years only one Tongo man has done this as a temporary measure.

The people of Zoo (Zoodɛm) comprise two maximal lineages. One of these, Zoo proper, is a maximal lineage of three segments, to one of which is attached a 'sister's son's' lineage. Their founding ancestor, Yikpɛmdaan, is said to have been a kinsman (mabii) of Mosuor, whom he accompanied from Mampurugu. As Zoodɛm marry any of the descendants of Mosuor, the fiction of original kinship (mabiirət) here emphasizes the cultural and political solidarity of the two groups, not a genealogical connexion.

Living side by side with Zoodɛm proper (Yikpɛmdaan biis) is another maximal lineage known as Zoo-Yiraaŋdɛm. These two maximal lineages exclude one another from the cults of their respective founding ancestors and from the ritual observances connected with them. Indeed, Zoo-Yiraaŋdɛm are affiliated to the Talis by ritual observance and cult. Nevertheless, Zoodɛm proper and Zoo-Yiraaŋdɛm have all the ties of clanship that hold between constituent lineages of the same clan who consider themselves to be sunzɔp. The explanation they give is that 'it is because we live together side by side (tin kab ziin ni taaba la zugu)'. Here clanship is attributed to local coalescence. These clanship ties are shown in all ceremonial matters that concern either of the lineages as well as in their co-operative enterprises. Though they do not take part in the esoteric ritual of one another's funeral ceremonies, they act as sunzɔp to one another in the public and exoteric phases of the ceremonies. If a party of Zoodɛm proper set out to pay their respects to a deceased relative-in-law, they will always be supported by some young men from Zoo-Yiraaŋdɛm; and if a Zoo-Yiraaŋ man is summoned to take a working party to help his father-in-law, he will always be accompanied by a few young men of the other lineage.

Zoo-Yiraaŋ is linked by ties of clanship to one of the component maximal lineages of Zubiuŋ.[1] Zoodɛm proper have no ties of clanship with Zubiuŋ or with any other clan. Yet they are often described as 'our

[1] See ch. VI.

sunzɔp' by Tongo people, and they take the part of distant *sunzɔp* in their corporate relations with Tongo. Thus, an important funeral at Tongo always attracts a large contingent of Zoo people, and vice versa. When Doohraan, one of the senior elders of Tongo, died, Zoo turned out in full force to join in the celebrations that inaugurated the funeral. A cow was slaughtered as an offering to the departed, and when it was divided up the Zoodɛm proper received half a foreleg, as distant *sunzɔp*, the other half going to Zubiuŋ, as the closest unrelated neighbours of the Tongo lineage which was celebrating the funeral. On this occasion Zoo-Yiraaŋ sent a number of young men to swell the ranks of their *sunzɔp*, the Zoodɛm proper, so that they could make as grand a display as possible. They themselves cannot take part in a Tongo funeral as an independent unit.

At the same time it is explicitly recognized that Zoodɛm proper are the *sunzɔp* of Tongo only by courtesy. They do not have the rights and duties of true clan *sunzɔp*. Tale social structure, highly determinate as it is, is flexible, and allows of such extensions of its basic principles. It allows the translation into the idiom of kinship and clanship of the ties of contiguity or of ceremonial or political solidarity. For the ties of clanship-by-courtesy recognized between Zoo and Tongo rest upon their spatial contiguity and political interdependence. The maximal lineage of Zoo proper has the custody of a special shrine connected with the chiefship of Tongo. According to their myth of origin, their founding ancestor performed the ritual services associated with this shrine for Mosuor when he was Chief of the Mamprusi and followed him to Tongo. These ritual services still vested in Zoodɛm proper form a strong bond between them and Tongo.

On the other hand, the fact that both groups are Namoos is an essential factor of their clanship-by-courtesy. By contrast the people of Zubiuŋ, who are as closely associated with Tongo spatially, politically, and by reciprocal ritual services, and, like the people of Zoo, always fought on the side of Tongo in the old days, are Talis, properly speaking; thus there is a stricter social separation between them and Tongo. They are not regarded as *sunzɔp*-by-courtesy by the latter; they refrain from the ritual or ceremonial activities of the people of Tongo in which Zoodɛm proper can and do take a part greater than that of mere spectators.

At the same time the genealogical and corporate independence of the people of Zoo proper, in relation to Tongo, is precisely marked. Neither group takes part in the cult of the lineage ancestors of the other; and if, for instance, in a funeral ceremony men of Zoo proper perform ritual services for a Tongo lineage, or vice versa, they do so because true clan *sunzɔp* are not present.

One infallible test of their differentiation from the clan of Mosuor biis is the fact that the two groups intermarry. Another is the rule about raiding. A generation ago, before the white man imposed the rule of his law, raiding (*ŋɔk*) was a common method of self-help in Taleland. It was the final resource of a man who wished to retrieve a debt owed to him by a member of another clan. If, for instance, a Tongo man owed a Wakii man cattle for a marriage he had contracted, and withheld payment unduly long or in bad faith, the latter would resort to self-help.

THE DISTRIBUTION OF THE NAMOOS

He would set out one day with some of his close agnates, fully armed, and they would try to seize by stealth and drive off as many cattle and sheep belonging to any clansman of their debtor as they could lay their hands on. Thus they could seize live-stock belonging to any Tongo man. Or if the chance presented itself they could seize live-stock belonging to people of Yaməlɔg or Sie, and would answer protests by 'pointing to' (*paal*) their Tongo debtor. This was legitimate, but they could not legitimately seize cattle belonging to a Zoo man in settlement of a debt due to them from a Tongo man. The Zoo people would be entitled to take severe reprisals, for Zoo and Tongo have no ties of clanship. They 'marry one another's children (*ba diit taaba biis*)'. Men who were youths in those days, and who themselves took part in such adventures, usually cite these rules of *ŋɔk* when they are explaining the nature and ramifications of clanship ties.

The people of Zoo proper have not the same local, political, and ceremonial ties with Yaməlɔg or Sie, and are not regarded as *sunzɔp*-by-courtesy of these two communities. But Yaməlɔg and Sie feel more closely akin to Zoo than to their non-Namoo neighbours.

The ties between Tongo and Zoo influence their relations in innumerable ways. A census of Zoo shows that every Zoo family (including Zoo-Yiraaŋ) is related to Tongo either by cognatic or by affinal ties. Zoo men show a preference in marriage for women from Tongo, Yaməlɔg, or Sie, rather than women from other equally near settlements. Thirty-five (29 per cent.) of a large and representative sample (120) of Zoo wives are Tongo women; and if the Yaməlɔg and Sie women are added they make up together 56 (47 per cent.) of Zoo wives. I once heard a group of elders discuss this fact, of which the people of Zoo and Tongo are well aware. A Zoo man said, 'Tongo girls like marrying us because we are such diligent farmers and always have plenty of food'. The Tongo elders denied this, and protested that they gave their daughters to Zoo rather than to men of Wakii or Tɛnzugu because of the bonds between them. 'Would we not rather', said one of them, 'marry our daughters to you, or even to Zubiuŋ, or the more distant places that used to fight on our side, than to nearer settlements which were our enemies?' Because of these ties, too, it is a grave affront for a Zoo man to abduct a Tongo man's wife or vice versa, or for a member of one clan to marry the former wife of a man of the other.

Again, the people of Zoo proper through their political head, the Chief of Biuŋ, control the great annual hunt in the Kparɔg bush. They are less strict in enforcing their rights to animals which fall to the weapon of a Tongo, Yaməlɔg, or Sie man, than to those killed by men from other places. There is greater co-operation and camaraderie between hunting parties from Zoo, Tongo, Yaməlɔg, and Sie than between any of them and parties from other settlements. When the Chief of Biuŋ sends round to announce the hunt, his messengers go to all the other Namoo chiefs in Taleland, who pronounce a blessing on the enterprise and send back fowls as a contribution to the sacrifices that will have to be made. Among them the blessing and contribution of the Chief of Tongo are regarded as the most important.

These relations between Tongo and Zoo are always a matter of degree

74 THE DISTRIBUTION OF THE NAMOOS

and depend on the particular situation. To quote the Kparɔg hunt again, if a man from Zoo proper kills an animal and a Zoo-Yiraaŋ man is present, he is entitled to take (*fɔ*, lit. pull out) a foreleg; but if a Tongo man arrives on the scene first he will claim the *sunzɔ*'s foreleg; and if the only people who happen to be near are a Tɛnzugu party they will do the same. But if a number of other hunters are present, then a Zoo-Yiraaŋ man takes precedence over a Tongo, Yamɔlɔg, or Sie man, and any of these take precedence over Talis or others. A final example of the influence of the ties and sense of solidarity holding between Zoo proper and the posterity of Mosuor may be mentioned here. Three or four generations ago Biuŋ was colonized by the Zoo family which then held the chiefship of that place. Now reduced to about a dozen homesteads, Biuŋ was a flourishing settlement two or three decades ago, to which people had flocked from all parts of Taleland and even farther afield. But the greatest number of settlers, except those from Zoo, came from Tongo. It was regarded as the natural, temporary outlet for young men who were short of land at Tongo. By contrast Tongo men rarely went to Datɔk as temporary colonists, though it is reputed to be equally if not more fertile than the lands of Biuŋ, and had much more room for settlers.

The lineage structure of Zoo is analogous to that of Gban. Both are examples of the commonest type of clan found in Taleland, the composite clan consisting of a single local community made up of two or more maximal lineages united by ties of clanship, either or all of which are again, as a rule, linked by similar ties of clanship to component maximal lineages of other clans.

At Sɛk, right among the Hill Talis, is another small Namoo group similar in structure to Zoo and connected with Tongo by the same fiction of kinship (*mabiirɔt*). Similar ties also connect Tongo with Ŋkoog (Winkogo), a large and thickly populated settlement comprising one maximal lineage and an attached lineage which is intercalary between it and Wakii. Like Zoo, both these groups marry the descendants of Mosuor; but distance and their separation from Tongo by a belt of Talis impede intercourse between them. Both groups have, in addition, a political tie with Tongo, in that their chiefs are appointed by the Chief of Tongo. In fact the people of Ŋkoog claim that their founding ancestor was a relative—some say a son—of Mosuor, who migrated to Ŋkoog from Tongo. Undisturbed by the contradiction between this claim and the absence of a bond of exogamy with Tongo, they explain this by their spatial and social separation from Tongo. For the people of Ŋkoog speak Gɔrni and have a greater affinity with their Gɔrisi neighbours in some of their customs than with the Tallensi. This, however, they regard as irrelevant, and they staunchly uphold their connexion with Tongo as their most important tie of political and social affiliation.

Neither the people of Sɛk nor the people of Ŋkoog are regarded as *sunzɔp* of Tongo. On account of their political ties with Tongo and the ceremonial relations these entail, they are sometimes figuratively described as the children (*biis*) of the Chief of Tongo. They are not, for example, represented as corporate units at Tongo funerals. On the other hand, in the matter of wives, their quasi-clanship ties with Tongo are strictly

THE DISTRIBUTION OF THE NAMOOS 75

upheld. I have heard the Chief of Tongo upbraid a young man of his own segment of the sub-clan for abducting the wife of a Sɛk man. The chief denounced this breach of *mabiirət* as a depravity possible only since the coming of the white man, and ordered the girl to be sent back.

Other Namoo communities are found at Pusunamoo, Baluŋ, and Kpɔləg (or Pwɔləg), beyond Ŋkoog. For practical purposes these Namoo groups are almost entirely cut off from Tongo. Culturally they are Gɔrisi, but Tongo people describe them as 'our kinsfolk (*ti mabiis*)'; and there is even a myth to the effect that Pusunamoo was founded by a kinsman of Mosuor who accompanied him on his flight from Mampurugu but parted company from him before he reached Tongo. As, however, these places lie beyond the horizon of the regular social relations of Tongo, their 'kinship' with Tongo becomes effective only by chance. They have no ceremonial relationship with Tongo. They do not attend Tongo funerals except as individuals drawn thither by personal cognatic ties, and they would not easily obtain redress if one of their wives were abducted by a Tongo man. Nevertheless, their 'kinship' with Tongo, nominal though it seems to be, forms an essential element, in all the Namoo communities mentioned, of the natives' view of their society and its structure. To some extent also the chain principle holds. Pusunamoo and Baluŋ have a good deal of social intercourse and regular social relations with Ŋkoog, and the latter serves as a link between them and Tongo. They are thus linked with Tongo loosely and by a relay, but more substantially than merely by a fiction, and through Tongo with the other branches of Mosuor's descendants.

In the Sie district, as we have seen, of the Namoo clans not held to be connected by origin with the children of Mosuor, Gban has the closest links with the latter. In the social perspective of a Tongo man, however, its identity tends to be masked by Sie. Gban is thought of as a satellite clan of Sie, in the same way as Zoo is regarded as a satellite clan of Tongo by the people of the Sie district. Spatial and political relations give rise to this point of view, and the habit of classifying social groups by contraposition gives it ready expression. This is the case also with Naməyalug and Gar, which are connected with Sie in much the same way as Zoo is with Tongo. There are other Namoo clans or Namoo segments of composite clans in this district which fall within the political orbit of Gbee. Some are linked by ties of clanship to adjacent settlements of Gɔrisi or Namnam. Some have so far assimilated the customs and dialectal peculiarities of their Gɔrisi or Namnam neighbours that people from the centre of Taleland hardly consider them to be Tallensi, though they themselves claim to have closer social affinities with the Tallensi than with the Gɔrisi or Namnam. In this interstitial area the mosaic of micro-cultural variations and the pattern of clan organization, though similar in principle to what is found in the vicinity of Tongo, are very intricate.

Namoos from this area marry extensively with Sie and Yamələg and more frequently with Tongo than the peripheral Namoo communities on the other side, viz. Pusunamoo, Baluŋ, and Kpɔləg. Thus, any Tongo man is far more likely to have cognatic ties with a place like Naməyalug

76   THE DISTRIBUTION OF THE NAMOOS

or Kpatia than with Baluŋ. He has more frequent social contact and closer economic relations with the former places than with the inhabitants of the latter. In the past the people of Sie sometimes took up arms to aid Gbee or Kpatia, and Tongo people might have been drawn in to aid Sie. A Tongo man therefore thinks of Gbee and Kpatia (and this applies to the other Namoo communities in their vicinity as well) as potential war allies of his clan in former times. He never thinks of Pusunamoo, Baluŋ, or Kpɔlɔg in this way. In spite of this, Tongo people insist that the people of Pusunamoo, at any rate, are closer kin to them than, say, the Namoos of Gbee or Kpatia, since their founding ancestor was a relative of Mosuor himself. There seems to be a contradiction between the actualities of social relations and the formal ties of putative genealogy. Other things being equal spatial proximity exercises a stronger pull than assumed genealogical proximity. This principle has a general application in Tale social structure.

The Meaning of 'Namoo'

The meaning of the appellation 'Namoo' in the social structure of the Tallensi has now become clear. We have examined it from the vantage point of Tongo. Had we elected to start from Gbee, for example, we should have obtained a picture built on the same principles but with a different perspective. Gɔrni-speaking Namoos beyond Kpatia, who have so remote and occasional a relevance for the normal life of Tongo that even nowadays hardly anything is known of them, are a significant element in the social frame of reference of the people of Gbee. Their community of stock and of distinctive custom which all Namoos in Taleland and the adjacent areas recognize, is not thought of as confined within territorial or political boundaries. But for every maximal lineage and clan their fellow Namoos are distributed on a graded scale of relevance according to their structural ties with them. Several factors affect the relevance of one Namoo group for another: ties of clanship; political ties; the ties of spatial contiguity or proximity; the belief in a special tie, closer than that of general kinship (*mabiirɔt*), by which Namoos are grouped together, and which, though assimilated to the tie of clanship on mythical grounds, is not so close as true clanship ties. All these, taken together, map out the main structural ties of any Namoo maximal lineage. These ties fall in a series of concentric zones, as it were, by which all the Namoo communities are arranged on a scale of diminishing social relevance for the unit that forms the centre of the given network of structural relations. Theoretically they extend 'from the land of the Dagomba (Dagbɔŋ) to the land of the Mossi (Mooga)', but the greater their distance in space from the central unit, the less likely are they to be actualized in the ordinary life of any of its members. In fact, outside a geographical radius of some five or six miles the farther zones of Namoo connexions have hardly any relevance for the central unit.

The pattern of social relations arising out of clanship ties in the narrow sense holds for other structural ties assimilated to them in form but founded on different factors. In respect of these ties, too, every Namoo clan or maximal lineage may be regarded as the centre of a field of effective structural relations with other Namoo clans and lineages. The fields of neighbouring clans and lineages overlap one another in series, cutting across the blurred boundaries of dialect and of variations in custom. Thus Tongo's field of effective structural relations includes Biuk and Ŋkoog. These units lie in the Gɔrni-speaking area and have

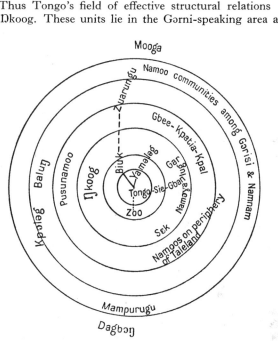

Diagram showing the Field of Clanship Relations of the Namoos of Tongo

effective structural relations with Gɔrisi who are only of peripheral relevance for Tongo. Tongo's field of effective structural relations overlaps that of Ŋkoog and that of Biuk. The latter includes the Namoos of Zuarungu, who are Gɔrisi, and whose field of effective structural relations overlaps that of Kumbahug. So one could trace out a series of overlapping fields of structural relations right across the country 'from Dagbɔŋ to Mooga', and running in every direction from any chosen starting-point. This constitutes the apparently limitless social ambit that corresponds to the notion of the common stock of all Namoos.

CHAPTER VI

THE STRUCTURAL RELATIONS OF THE TALIS

A General Point

A NUMERICAL estimate of the Namoos in Taleland cannot be made from the published census figures. In the Tongo district alone they would include, on a rough reckoning, over a third of the population; the rest are the Talis.

The Talis, as we have seen, are distinguished by name and by myths of origin from the Namoos. Close neighbours though they are, Talis and Namoos are distinctly segregated from one another by locality, and this is associated with clear-cut structural cleavages. It is necessary, however, to emphasize that Talis and Namoos are also inseparably bound to one another by ceremonial and politico-ritual ties. In addition, all Talis and all Namoos are connected with one another as individuals by an elaborate network of cognatic and affinal ties. In the present chapter we are concerned with the constituted social relations of the Talis amongst themselves, treated in isolation from the background of their social relations with the Namoos, but this background must be borne in mind.

The Clan Structure of Zubiuŋ

The clans and lineages of the Talis form corporate units of the same kind as those of the Namoos. They are connected with one another by a network of constituted ties of the same type as those that link Namoo clans and lineages in a chain system, but more elaborately distributed and articulated. Again, the paradigm applies generally, but the perspective of each clan and lineage is peculiar to itself. To keep the parallel with the Namoos we shall take as our starting-point the group of Talis most intimately associated with Tongo, the people of Zubiuŋ (Zubiuŋdɛm).[1]

As we have previously mentioned, the people of Zubiuŋ live in such close contiguity with the Tongo Namoos that anyone ignorant of the structure of the community would be unable to draw a line between the homesteads of one group and those of the other. Investigation shows that Zubiuŋ homesteads form an irregular but continuous aggregate, quite distinct, spatially, from Tongo. The nearest Tongo neighbours of Zubiuŋ are the accessory Tongo lineage of Nɔŋsuur yidɛm. Consistently with the basic principles of Tale clanship, Nɔŋsuur yidɛm have an intercalary status between Tongo and Zubiuŋ. The legend which relates that the ancestor of Nɔŋsuur yidɛm was a sororal nephew (ahaŋ) of Zubiuŋ is the rationalization of their intercalary role. But though they mediate between Tongo and Zubiuŋ in political matters, for example, they have no ties of clanship with the latter, as we have previously seen.

Zubiuŋ consists of three maximal lineages, residentially distributed in a way that exactly parallels their structural relations. The homesteads of

[1] Total male members, at home and abroad, about 250.

THE STRUCTURAL RELATIONS OF THE TALIS 79

the Yakɔradɛm ('the people of the old homes') mingle with those of their Tongo neighbours and spread out irregularly into what is properly Ba'ari. The next block of homesteads, separated from them by a stone's throw and known as the Kpaγara-yaγardɛm ('the people of the Kpaγara side'), so named after a sacred pool in their midst, abuts on the fields of other Tongo neighbours and straggles over into the part occupied by the third maximal lineage. These, the Yapaasdɛm ('the people of the new homesteads'), have Zoo homesteads as their neighbours on one side and somewhat more distantly Ba'ari neighbours on the other. By the criteria of clanship with which we have become familiar, Zubiuŋ forms a single clan; the three maximal lineages act together as a unit in all secular and religious affairs of common interest.

Outsiders regard Zubiuŋ as a single unit, like Tongo or Zoo, and the relations of its constituent maximal lineages to one another are organized on the plan of a single maximal lineage of three segments. Thus, the mortuary rites or funeral ceremonies of an important member of any one of these lineages cannot be carried out without the presence and collaboration of representatives of the other two lineages. They have the reciprocal privileges and obligations of close clan *sunzɔp* in relation to one another. They speak of one another as kinsmen by consanguinity (*dɔγam*).

Nevertheless, it is generally known that the three segments of Zubiuŋ are of diverse origin. The Yakɔradɛm have a status senior to the others. According to the myth, which has already been recorded, their founding ancestor (*yaab*) was a 'brother' of the primordial Gbizug tɛndaana. They were the first to settle at Zubiuŋ. The Kpaγara-yaγardɛm, who are next in order of seniority, claim that their line was founded by immigrants who accompanied Mosuor as his Gbandaat—a ceremonial office which is still their exclusive prerogative in relation to the Chief of Tongo. The Yapaasdɛm are said to be offshoots of the other two lineages, and are therefore the most junior. The relative status of the three lineages is shown in all their corporate activities. Thus, if they make a joint sacrifice and the sacrificial animal is provided by either of the senior lineages, the Yapaasdɛm receive only a shoulder (that is, a junior portion) as their rightful share, whereas the other lineages receive the legs (the senior portions). The two senior lineages are relatively equal in status compared with Yapaas.

Overlooking this diversity of origin, the people of Zubiuŋ say: 'We have become consanguineous kin (*ti leeba dɔγam*).' One focus of their unity and corporate identity as a clan is their External (*yɛŋha*) *Bɔγar*, Duunkpaləg, a sacred grove whose mystical powers are renowned and respected far beyond the borders of Taleland. Duunkpaləg is the shrine of all the ancestors of all three maximal lineages. 'All our ancestors are there (*ti yaanam waabi be nɛŋha*)', is the formula used by the natives to define this shrine. Any ritual event which involves a sacrifice at Duunkpaləg requires the presence of all three lineages, each represented by its head (*kpeem*), and he should be accompanied by the head of each constituent segment of his lineage and by any other of its mature male members who are able to come. The ideological dominance of

80 THE STRUCTURAL RELATIONS OF THE TALIS

Duunkpaləg in the corporate life of Zubiuŋ can be judged from the frequency of the personal name Duun. This name is given to every child placed under the spiritual guardianship of this *Bɔyar*. There is not a single family in Zubiuŋ without at least one child named Duun.

All the reciprocal duties and privileges of the three maximal lineages testify to the unity of Zubiuŋ as a clan. To cite funerals again, when a death occurs in one of the lineages it is the duty of the representatives of the other two to conduct the main rites and to give general help and supervision, according to the maxim '*sunzɔp m-maan yɛla*—brother-lineages look after one's (ceremonial) affairs'. At the funeral ceremonies of the head of one of the maximal lineages it is obligatory for the other two maximal lineages to be represented by their heads, through whom they must send the prescribed food contributions. In return for their services and support these two maximal lineages are entitled to receive prescribed portions of the animals slaughtered in honour of the deceased, and of the beer and cooked food distributed at the funeral.

Ritual Differentiation and Integration of Zubiuŋ

At the same time, each maximal lineage has a large and jealously guarded measure of autonomy relative to its two *sunzɔ* lineages. This is most conspicuously embodied in the ritual office of tɛndaana (Master, or Custodian, of the Earth). Each of the three lineages has its own tɛndaana-ship, held by the head (*kpeem*) of the lineage. This office is primarily associated with the cult of the Earth (*tɛŋ*) in its mystical aspect, whose shrines (*tɔŋgbana*) are the sacred spots found in profusion throughout the Mole-Dagbane culture area. An Earth shrine (*tɔŋgban*) may be a grove of trees, a pool, a stream, a pile of boulders, a single tree, or merely a small bare patch in the midst of cultivated fields. In the settled parts of Taleland half a mile's walk along any foot-path takes one past two or three *tɔŋgbana*, so numerous are they.

Tɔŋgbana do not all rank equally, though all are equally the shrines of the Earth. At Zubiuŋ the most important *tɔŋgbana* come under the joint custody of all three maximal lineages. On important ceremonial occasions in which the clan acts as a corporate unit, such as the installation of a new tɛndaana, all three tɛndaanas and their elders assemble to perform sacrifices at these *tɔŋgbana*. One of these, Zukɔk, is supreme over all the Earth shrines of Zubiuŋ. It symbolizes the Land of Zubiuŋ (*Zubiuŋ tɛŋ*), the local subdivision of the Earth-as-a-whole in its mystical aspect, with which Zubiuŋ is directly connected. This is another focus of clan unity.

We shall later elucidate more fully the complex relationship of these two religious foci of clan unity among the Talis. It must suffice to say that, at Zubiuŋ, Duunkpaləg, the *Bɔyar*, and Zukɔk, symbolizing the Earth, are mystically coupled together but not identical. In doctrine and in rite they form the polar principles of a single religious system. Together they constitute the axis, as it were, around which the religious ideas and values of the natives are constructed. In relation to the structure of lineage and clan *Bɔyar* and *tɛŋ* work as complementary values and sanctions. When either is the centre of a rite or ceremony, homage is paid to the other as well. In all corporate ceremonies, such as those accompany-

PLATE V

(a) Clanship at Zubiuŋ: Elders of Kpaɣara yaɣar awaiting the representatives of the other two maximal lineages at the entrance to the External *Bɔyar* Duunkpaləg, in order to perform a sacrifice.

(b) The duties of *sunzɔp*, at Zubiuŋ: The rite of 'sowing a field' for the dead during a tɛndaana's funeral. One representative of each maximal lineage of the clan has to take part.

PLATE VI

(a) Ritual collaboration among the Hill Talis: A sacrifice at the External Bɔyar of which Kpata'ardɛm are the principal custodians. Representatives of Gundaat, Samiit, Sakpee are present while the head of Kpata'ar performs the sacrifice.

(b) A sacrifice at the Earth Shrine, Doo, of which Kpata'ardɛm are the principal custodians. Representatives of Kpata'ar, Tamboog, Degal, and Bunkiuk are present on this occasion.

THE STRUCTURAL RELATIONS OF THE TALIS 81

ing the installation or the funeral of a tɛndaana, both receive sacrifices. But the Bɔyar, like its homologue among the Namoos, is more precisely a symbol of the continuity and perpetuity of the clan and its constituent lineages. It is more explicitly a focus of that solidarity of the clan or the lineage which is deemed to follow automatically from the fact of their common agnatic descent. The Earth, on the other hand, though its cult is also intrinsically bound up with the agnatic line, stands rather for the common interests and common values embodied in the customary norms and sanctions of collective life.

It is significant, however, that the Bɔyar cult and the Earth cult, both of which serve to express the unity and solidarity of the clan, also serve to emphasize the relative autonomy of its constituent maximal lineages. Each maximal lineage has its private lineage bɔyar (*dugni bɔyar*), the shrine of its particular lineage ancestors, worshipped only by members of that lineage, and the *dugni bɔyar* is conceived as itself a part of, or a derivative of, the clan Bɔyar (Duunkpalɔg). It is, so to speak, the domestic incarnation of the great External Bɔyar. In the same way each maximal lineage has its private Earth shrine, associated specifically with that part of Zubiuŋ which it occupies, and under the sole custody of its own tɛndaana. Both in relation to the Bɔyar cult and to the Earth cult, the tɛndaana of each maximal lineage represents the entire lineage. It is through him that these mystical powers are mobilized on behalf of the lineage, and through the joint action of all three tɛndaanas that they are mobilized for the good of the clan.

The integration of the clan on the religious plane is characteristic of its corporate solidarity in all matters of common interest. Every corporate activity presumes the relative autonomy of the three maximal lineages in relation to one another. The unity of the clan is built up on the relative mutual independence of its segments. Common interests emerge as a balance of divergent emphases, and conversely the autonomous interests of the three constituent maximal lineages of the clan are aspects of the common interests of the whole clan. Thus the rights and duties, privileges and obligations, vested in each maximal lineage, through the mutual adjustment and articulation of which corporate action occurs and clan unity emerges, are jealously guarded by each lineage.

Many incidents could be quoted to substantiate this analysis, but one will suffice. When the final rites of installation for the new Kpaɣara-yaɣar tɛndaana were being carried out I accompanied him and his lineage elders to Duunkpalɔg, where the most important rite of the series was to be performed. We were soon joined by the Yakɔra representatives. The Yapaasdɛm did not come for another hour or so. Indignant comments were made about their tardiness. It was said to be a chronic fault of theirs, and they were criticized also for neglecting their duty as junior *sunzɔp* who should have come to escort the tɛndaana-elect to Duunkpalɔg. The Yapaasdɛm, said one of the elders, were going the way of all things to-day, scorning established custom and taking the course they found most convenient to themselves. 'In a little while', he stormed, 'we shall all (that is, each maximal lineage) be sacrificing separately.' The other elders protested in a chorus at this, exclaiming, 'Oh no, we won't abandon our

G

82 THE STRUCTURAL RELATIONS OF THE TALIS

forefathers in that way (*ti ku zaŋ ti banam bah ŋwala*)'. Some of the younger men of Yapaas were merely being tiresome. 'You'll see', countered the man who had spoken earlier, sceptically, 'some day there will be a quarrel over something, the division of meat at a sacrifice, or the inheritance of a widow, or something of that sort, and then you people of Zubiuŋ will split up.'

Meanwhile, we continued to wait for the Yapaasdɛm, for the ritual could not be performed without the presence of their representatives. In due course they arrived. Far from expressing contrition, they excused themselves by accusing the others of having bungled the sequence of the rites. A violent argument followed, but one of the elders cut it short. No doubt, he said, the Yapaasdɛm preferred a different order of the rites. That was their affair. The senior lineages had no intention of copying them. To-day the ceremonies were *their* concern, and now that all the lineages were properly assembled they might as well get on with the business.

Linked Maximal Lineages and the Field of Clanship

Corresponding to this structural differentiation within the clan, each maximal lineage has its distinct field of clanship. One segment of Yakɔradɛm, known as Pulien biis, is an attached lineage descended from a 'sister's son' of the authentic lineage. Another segment (Zaŋgɔbɔg yidɛm) is an assimilated lineage, said to be of slave descent. Members of this segment are debarred from holding the tɛndaana-ship. Pulien biis have the right to hold the office, but mainly in a titular capacity, for they are barred from its most essential responsibilities. In other respects these accessory lineages have been fully absorbed by the authentic line of Yakɔradɛm, and participate in all the corporate activities of the latter.

The Yakɔradɛm have ties of clanship with Gbizug, which counts as the senior segment of Gbeog, and is bound to Gbeog proper by the usual ties of clanship. But there are no ties of clanship between Zubiuŋ-Yakɔra and Gbeog proper. They may not marry a daughter of Gbizug; they may and do marry Gbeog women, who would of course be barred by the rule of exogamy from marrying into Gbizug. Zubiuŋ-Yakɔra also have ties of clanship with Ba'at-Sakpar, one of the major segments of the clan of Ba'ari; but they have no ties of clanship with any of the other Ba'ari maximal lineages. Similarly, they have ties of clanship with Zoo-Yiraaŋ, but not with the Namoo lineage of Zoodɛm proper. The other two component maximal lineages of Zubiuŋ are excluded from this field of clanship. For instance, they can and do marry Gbizug, Ba'at-Sakpar, and Zoo-Yiraaŋ women.

These extra-clan ties of clanship are rationalized in various ways. Gbizug and Ba'at-Sakpar claim to be the consanguineous kin (*dɔyam*) of Zubiuŋ-Yakɔra, because, as the myth of the primordial tɛndaanas relate, the founding ancestors of all three lineages were 'brothers'. The Zoo-Yiraaŋdɛm are claimed as kin (*dɔyam*) of the latter because their founding ancestor is said to have been a 'sister's son' of Zubiuŋ-Yakɔra. It should be noted that such a remote cognatic link does not in every case establish ties of clanship. The same fiction is used to account for the existence of

THE STRUCTURAL RELATIONS OF THE TALIS 83

attached lineages, as well as for certain ritual and political ties between some groups. Thus, one segment of Tongo has a special ritual role as intermediary in the politico-ritual relations of Tongo and Zoo, and this is rationalized by the same fiction; but it does not involve ties of clanship with Zoo.

There is a close parallelism between the inter-clan linkages we have described and the spatial relations of the groups concerned. Gbizugdɛm are the nearest non-Namoo neighbours of Zubiuŋ-Yakɔra on one side; Ba'ari is contiguous with them on the other side; and Zoo-Yiraaŋ live side by side with their clansfolk at Zubiuŋ-Yapaas. There is an asymmetry in these clanship ties which appears to be mirrored in the fictions accounting for them. Gbizug and Ba'at-Sakpar are linked by clanship ties in exactly the same way as they are linked with Zubiuŋ-Yakɔra, but neither has ties of clanship with Zoo-Yiraaŋ.

Zubiuŋ-Yakɔra has more frequent and closer relations and a stronger sense of fraternity with Gbizug than with its other two linked maximal lineages at Zoo and at Ba'ari. This is fostered by proximity and by the belief enshrined in their myth of origin. Thus, when a Zubiuŋ-Yakɔra tɛndaana dies and his funeral ceremonies are performed, the heads of all three linked maximal lineages have to send an obligatory contribution of porridge, specially prepared 'to set out for the dead (*zien kpiim la*)'. They act, then, in the same way as the other two Zubiuŋ lineages, which are also obliged to send this contribution. But Gbizugdɛm do more than make a merely formal acknowledgement of their ties with the dead man's lineage; they take part in the funeral to a much greater extent than Ba'at-Sakpar or Zoo-Yiraaŋ. Their representatives never fail to attend all the important ritual events of the funeral, whereas the representatives of the other two linked maximal lineages appear only at the exoteric public ceremonies, such as the final divination when the beer is distributed. The social relations of Gbizug with Zubiuŋ-Yakɔra give them a place, as it were, half-way between the other Zubiuŋ maximal lineages and the other two linked maximal lineages in point of intimacy and corporate cohesion. Every Yakɔra man knows the wives of the men of Gbizug almost as well as the wives of his own clansmen. He speaks of them all as his 'wives', for he has a right to inherit any of them if they remain widows. If he meets one of them by chance he will chaff her, as if she were a Zubiuŋ wife. Most of the wives of the men of Ba'at-Sakpar or Zoo-Yiraaŋ are quite unknown to him, though formally he has the same rights in respect of them.

The Gradation of Clanship Ties

What distinguishes the bonds of Zubiuŋ-Yakɔra with Gbizug from their apparently identical bonds with their clansmen of Zubiuŋ is this: the latter are bound to perform all the duties of close *sunzɔp*, the former are under the much more limited obligation of giving expression to their ties of clanship through one or two formal acts. The latter, for example, are obliged to attend and to conduct all the important rites of a Yakɔra tɛndaana's funeral, whereas Gbizugdɛm come voluntarily, and if they undertake any task do so out of courtesy and friendliness. Similarly, the

84 THE STRUCTURAL RELATIONS OF THE TALIS

privileges of clanship have the force of rights in the case of *sunzɔp* belonging to the same clan, but are subject to a wider margin of flexibility and voluntary adjustment in the case of extra-clan *sunzɔp*. Some privileges which the former can claim are not held by the latter.

In short, here, as with the Namoos, clanship, or more specifically the ties of clan brotherhood (*sunzɔt*) between lineages, is a matter of degree. An illustration will show how it works. We shall take again the example of a distribution made at a funeral ceremony, but the same rules apply in all other aspects of clan relationships. A food distribution of minor importance, usually managed by the younger men, with an accompaniment of considerable hilarity, occurs on the evening of *Kogbeda'ar*, about the middle of the funeral ceremony. It is an occasion on which one usually hears the claims and counter-claims of the different groups represented argued out with great fervour. On *Kogbeda'ar* of the late Zubiuŋ-Yakɔra tɛndaana's funeral the meat of the animals contributed was divided out among the *sunzɔp* lineages as follows: Kpaɣara-yaɣardɛm, as the closest *sunzɔp*, received the share of greatest distinction, the hind leg of a sheep; Yapaasdɛm, the next closest *sunzɔp*, received the shoulder of a sheep; Gbizugdɛm, next in order of closeness, received the hind leg of a goat (for the Tallensi, unlike ourselves, regard the sheep as a nobler animal than the goat). Lastly came the Zoo-Yiraaŋdɛm, whose share was the foreleg of a goat. Ba'at-Sakpardɛm were not present on this occasion; had they been they would have been entitled to a portion equivalent to the hind leg of a goat. The closest ties of clanship are those which entail the most definite and strict obligations and carry in compensation the most definite rights and superior privileges. These are the ties that bind the lineage to the other lineages which, with it, make up a single composite clan.

The attached lineage of Pulien biis shares the extra-clan ties of clanship of the authentic lineage of the Yakɔradɛm, but it has in addition a tie of clanship independent of the authentic lineage. This links it to one of the segments of Sakpee, a Tɛnzugu clan. According to their tradition, their ancestor Pulien was begotten by a Sakpee man, who later divorced his wife, Pulien's mother, by blowing ashes on her. The recent history of this relationship throws an interesting light on the factors which keep alive the ties of clanship between linked maximal lineages, and on their dynamic characteristics.

About a generation ago a Sakpee man married a daughter of Pulien biis in defiance of the exogamic ban. The protests of the elders of both lineages were fruitless. The drastic sanctions which might have been resorted to were out of the question; in theory, because the two lineages were related by ties of clanship; in practice, no doubt, because they were extremely difficult to apply on account of the political barriers between Zubiuŋ and Tɛnzugu. So the matter was allowed to slide, and left to the arbitrament of the ancestor spirits. The marriage, said the elders, would be sterile, or all the children would die. In the end, however, the offending couple reared a large and successful family; so apparently this breach of kinship (*dɔyam*) was not a sin after all.

In spite of this, Pulien biis continued to maintain their ties of clanship

THE STRUCTURAL RELATIONS OF THE TALIS   85

with Sakpee. The innovation made by one couple was not regarded as a precedent. Their transgression was at length accepted with equanimity (the Tallensi are a practical-minded people), but not allowed to undermine the established norms. Then, four or five years ago, a young man of Pulien biis wanted to marry a Sakpee girl. When the elders of both lineages forbade it, he invoked this precedent, but to no avail. Taking advantage of the liberty of movement which people now have, the young couple eloped to Kumasi. The girl's father was faced with a *fait accompli*. He had no alternative but to accept the placation gifts and part of the bride-price necessary to make it a legitimate marriage, though he did so very reluctantly. Soon afterwards came the funeral of the late Yakɔra tɛndaana,who had been a member of Pulien biis. And for the first time in living memory their linked lineage at Sakpee omitted to send their contribution of porridge or to attend even the public phases of the ceremonies. When the beer was being distributed to all the *sunzɔp* lineages, someone remarked that the name of Sakpee had not been formally called. This provoked a discussion about the relationship of Sakpee to Pulien biis. 'You are no longer *sunzɔp*', one Zubiuŋ elder maintained, 'you have intermarried and become relatives-in-law.' The elders of Pulien biis unanimously denied this, and tried to find excuses for the Sakpeedɛm. They claimed that people can be *sunzɔp* to one another and yet marry, as is done in Tongo and Zoo. This quibble was debated with vociferous good humour. Eventually one of the elders settled the matter in a typical spirit of compromise. 'Listen,' he said, 'we and Sakpee have now become *sunzɔp*; but we used to be *yidɛm* (that is, branches of the same lineage). Marriages have caused that.'

The process[1] is incomplete; but it looks as if there is sure to be a realinement of the structural ties between Zubiuŋ-Pulien biis and Sakpee in the course of time. This change is a response to a conflict of loyalties—those arising from the ties of clanship, and those of opposite value arising out of the divergent ties of locality and of politico-ritual dependence between Zubiuŋ and Tongo, and between Sakpee and the other clans of Tɛnzugu. The other two Zubiuŋ maximal lineages have ties of clanship with two other major segments of Ba'ari, but with no other clans. Kpaɣara yaɣar have clanship ties with the section of Lakum yidɛm, and Yapaas with the section Guŋdɛm at Ba'ari. These ties operate in the same way as the extra-clan ties of Yakɔra with Gbizug, though less regularly. Thus Zubiuŋ and Ba'ari are interlinked by three mutually independent sets of ties of the same order, each Zubiuŋ maximal lineage having clanship ties with one Ba'ari lineage and not with the others.

The Pattern of Clanship among the Talis

This is the common pattern of clanship among the Talis. The clan is a local unit comprising two or more relatively autonomous maximal lineages, which regard themselves and are regarded by others as together forming a single unit. It is not a closed unit, but its constituent maximal lineages look upon one another as the closest clan *sunzɔp* in their entire

[1] A similar process in the distant past may explain the absence of exogamic ties between Tongo and Ɖ-Koog and other instances of this sort.

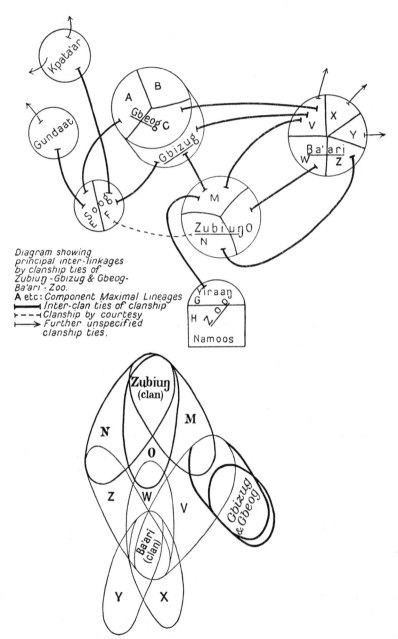

Diagram showing principal inter-linkages by clanship ties of Zubiuŋ-Gbizug & Gbeog-Ba'ari-Zoo.
A etc: Component Maximal Lineages
├──┤ Inter-clan ties of clanship
├---┤ Clanship by courtesy
├──→ Further unspecified clanship ties.

Diagram showing the relations of clanship between Zubiuŋ, Gbizug, Gbeog & Ba'ari in terms of overlapping fields of clanship of the component maximal lineages.

field of clanship. This means greater mutual dependence in both secular and ritual affairs, more frequent and regular co-operation, and a stronger solidarity than with linked lineages of other clans; it means the regular exercise of mutual privileges and the fulfilment of mutual obligations which are not so strongly binding on linked lineages of other clans, who therefore often omit to exercise them. The constituent maximal lineages of the same clan are united by ties of common interests and common values more powerful than those that bind any of these lineages to a linked lineage of a neighbouring clan. Thus the clan forms the region of greatest integration between a maximal lineage and any of its neighbouring maximal lineages, but it has no hard-and-fast social boundaries. Clanship ties cut across clans, and the basic rule of inter-clan linkage is that spatial proximity is translated into terms of putative genealogical connexion. It will be seen that these Talis clans have the same form as many composite Namoo clans. In principle, too, there is only a difference of degree between their structure and the more close-knit structure of the sub-clans of Mosuor biis. In both, the same kinds of common interests and common values form the basis of the unity and solidarity of the group, and these are expressed in the common ritual allegiance of its subdivisions.

The Mesh of Clanship among the Talis

The interlinkage of adjacent or neighbouring clans in accordance with the pattern we have described above runs in a complicated network through all the Talis clans. So complex is the overlapping of the fields of clanship of adjacent and neighbouring maximal lineages that the whole system might be compared to a piece of chain mail. It is worth while following up one or two of these series of linkages in order to get a clearer picture of the system.

We have described the linkage of Zubiuŋ-Yakɔra with Gbizug. At the level of clanship Gbizug, as we have seen, counts as one of the two major segments of Gbeog. Between Gbizug and the other major segment, Gbeog proper, runs a winding watercourse. The people of Gbizug and the people of Gbeog claim to be descended, respectively, from two brothers who were 'the sons' of the primordial tɛndaana, Genɔt. Both have clanship ties with the maximal lineage of Sakpar at Ba'ari, but not with the other sections of Ba'ari. There is also, however, an attached lineage at Gbeog who have an intercalary position between Gbeog and Ba'at-Lakum yiri (the Ba'ari lineage linked with Zubiuŋ-Kpaɣara-yaɣar) similar to the relationship of Zubiuŋ-Pulien biis and Sakpee, and explained by the same fiction. Members of this attached lineage may not marry women of the rest of Gbeog or of Gbizug or of Ba'at-Lakum yiri, but may marry into any lineages of other clans with which Gbeog and Gbizug and Ba'at-Lakum yiri have ties of clanship.

Corresponding to their close ties of clanship, which resemble those of the component maximal lineages of Zubiuŋ with one another, Gbizug and Gbeog have a common cult of the supreme tɔŋgban in their area, though its custody is directly vested in the former. Their relative autonomy, however, corresponding to their spatial division, is symbolized in the

88 THE STRUCTURAL RELATIONS OF THE TALIS

tɛndaanaship and in other religious cults. Each segment has its own tɛndaana, the Gbizug tɛndaana being the senior of the two, and in addition the Gbeogdɛm have the cult of the External Bɔyar, like Zubiuŋ and the Hill Talis, whereas the Gbizugdɛm do not participate in this cult. This cleavage comes into operation also in the political and jural relations of the two segments, so that in very many situations Gbeog emerges as an independent settlement.

Both segments have ties of clanship with Soog, the Talis clan sandwiched between Tongo and Wakii. But there is an additional bond between Gbeog and Soog, which is not shared by Gbizug, for one-half of Gbeog is associated with Soog in a common cult of an External Bɔyar, in the same way as the three sections of Zubiuŋ are associated in the cult of their External Bɔyar, Duunkpaləg. The other half of Gbeog has a separate External Bɔyar. Gbizug has ties of clanship also with Degal, the Tɛnzugu clan, in virtue of the alleged 'brotherhood' of the four primordial tɛndaanas. Yet Wakii and Ka'ar, the clans sprung from the other two primordial tɛndaanas, are merely the sunzɔp-by-courtesy of Gbizug, though both, and especially Wakii, have closer spatial, jural, and ritual relations with it than Degal has.

Soogdɛm have no ties of clanship with Zubiuŋ, but regard them as sunzɔp-by-courtesy. They are linked by a ritual relationship which comes into effect whenever a Zubiuŋ tɛndaana dies. There was for a long time an estrangement between the two clans, because some years ago a Zubiuŋ youth married the ex-wife of a Soog man. A ceremonial reconciliation under somewhat dramatic circumstances took place recently when ritual necessity compelled the elders of the offender's lineage to send a deputation to beg the pardon of the Soog elders. Apart from this intermittent and very limited ritual collaboration, the clanship-by-courtesy of Soog and Zubiuŋ is very weak. One of the standing jokes in Zubiuŋ concerned two of the lineage heads of Soog. These two old men are notoriously poor through bodily infirmity, and therefore make use of every opportunity of getting free food or drink. Thus, whenever there is a funeral at Zubiuŋ they appear as representatives of their clan to claim their share of beer and meat as sunzɔp-by-courtesy; but Zubiuŋdɛm have long ceased to go to Soog funerals.

From Ba'ari the mesh of clan linkages continues across the dialectal boundary with the Gɔrisi. Ba'at-Sakpar has clanship ties with Sanaab biis, a section of Bɔləga. 'They are our kinsmen', said the Ba'at-Sakpar tɛndaana-elect, 'even though they have become Gɔrisi.' Another Bɔləga section are similarly related to Ba'at-Lakum yiri. Ba'at-Guŋ, on the other hand, have ties of clanship with Tamboog on Tɛnzugu, and Ba'at-Dun biis have ties of clanship with Samiit on Tɛnzugu. Yayazuor and Gbee are sunzɔp-by-courtesy to all sections of Ba'ari.

The internal constitution of Ba'ari is interesting, in that the whole clan is grouped around Ba'at-Sakpar. Thus, Ba'at-Lakum yiri has the status of an attached lineage of Sakpar. Their founding ancestor was said to have been a sororal nephew of Sakpar, begotten by a Zubiuŋ man—hence also their ties with Zubiuŋ; and Ba'at-Guŋ is similarly an attached lineage of Lakum yiri. Being related to Sakpar by a remove, Guŋ is allowed to

THE STRUCTURAL RELATIONS OF THE TALIS 89

marry with them, though it is politically and ritually part of the clan of Ba'ari.

Apart from these variations the pattern of clanship at Ba'ari is the same as at Zubiuŋ, the pattern common to all the clans mentioned in the preceding paragraphs. Local relationships run parallel with clanship ties, so that spatially contiguous lineages are more closely linked than spatially distant lineages. The component maximal lineages of each clan have a well-defined autonomy in relation to one another, organized in each case around a ritual office (either the tɛndaanaship or some other office associated with the cult of the Earth or the cult of the External Bɔyar) which is exclusively vested in a particular lineage. Each maximal lineage has its distinctive field of clanship within which 'brotherhood' (sunzɔt) varies in degrees of closeness from that which prevails within the clan to that of sunzɔt-by-courtesy. The field of clanship of any one maximal lineage overlaps, but is not congruent with, that of any other maximal lineage of the same clan; and the unity and corporate identity of the clan are focused in the cult of the Bɔyar, the common shrine of all the ancestors, and the cult of the Earth. Lastly, every maximal lineage has an intercalary function corresponding to its local and clanship ties.

The further extensions of this mesh of clanship ties can be rapidly summarized. Soog is locally and structurally intercalary between the cluster of clans we have been discussing and Tɛnzugu. Internally constituted like Zubiuŋ, it has ties of clanship with Sakpee, Gundaat, and Kpata'ar, all three Tɛnzugu clans, and with Wopo'ohug near Gbambee. Gundaat and Tamboog are clansfolk as well as neighbours. Though they are more autonomous in relation to each other than two segments of the same clan, their reciprocal privileges and obligations are closer than those of linked lineages of different clans. They have similar ties to those of Gbizug and Gbeog, though their origins are said to be diverse. Both have ties of clanship with one segment of Sakpee but not with the other, and Gundaat also has ties of clanship with an attached lineage at Wakii and with Wɔyar.

Kpata'ar, contiguous with Gundaat but not related to it by ties of clanship, comprises three maximal lineages. It is the senior of these, Kpata'arna'ab yidɛm, who have ties of clanship with Soog; and they also have such ties with Degal and with one section of Sɛk, the Namoo group at the foot of the hills, as well as with their next-door neighbours Dakuor yidɛm of Bunkiuk. The second maximal lineage, Nakyeet yidɛm, is linked with Sakpee—but not with the lineages of other clans to which the other sections of Kpata'ar are linked. The third lineage of Kpata'ar is on the point of extinction, and its clanship ties need not be enumerated.

Bunkiuk, besides being linked with Kpata'ar through Dakuor yidɛm, includes two more maximal lineages, Gɔlibdaan yidɛm and Yiraan yidɛm, which have no ties of clanship with Kpata'ar. Gɔlibdaan yidɛm have clanship ties with one of the constituent lineages of Yinduuri but not with the rest of Yinduuri, and Yiraan yidɛm are the sunzɔp of Sipaat. The closest extra-clan sunzɔp of the latter are the people of Sii, from whose founding ancestor they also claim to be descended. But whereas Sii has clanship ties with Yinduuri, their neighbours on one side, and with a section of

Kpɔlɔg (Pwɔlɔg), Sipaat has no ties of clanship with either of these places. Yinduuri, a clan whose inner constitution is a miniature replica of the whole system of interlacing clanship ties which we have been describing, is contiguous with Zandoya but has no ties of clanship with it. Zandoya's clanship ties link it with Gorogo, which in turn is linked with a group of Gɔrisi, who live in the Bɔlɔga district.

This is but one series of concatenated clan linkages running from end to end of the Tongo district and even, like those of the Namoos, extending across to the Gɔrisi. Similar chains of clanship ties link the other Talis clans to one another and to this series; and the whole forms an elaborately reticulated system which stretches beyond the linguistic and cultural frontiers of Taleland. By these chains of clanship ties the Talis are linked on to peoples outside Taleland who live quite beyond the boundaries of their regular interests and concerns.

We have been discussing clanship in the narrow sense—that is, ties implying the prohibition of marriage, joint leviratic rites, the reciprocal privileges and duties of *sunzɔp*, and such things as the liability in former times to be raided for one another's debts. As a rule, every constituent maximal lineage of every clan has such ties with one or more territorially contiguous lineages of neighbouring clans. Most of them also have clanship ties with some lineages of clans not adjacent to them, but not very far away, reckoning the distance in terms of the number of unrelated clans intervening and not by geographical criteria. There is no fixed rule; but within this cluster of settlements it is always a safe prediction that the greater the distance separating two clans the less likely are they to be linked by clanship.

In addition, every clan recognizes one or more clans in its vicinity as *sunzɔp*-by-courtesy. Soog and Wakii; Gundaat, Kpata'ar, and Bunkiuk; Yinduur and Zandoya; Sii and Gorogo: these consider one another to be *sunzɔp*-by-courtesy, and they generally appear at one another's funerals in this capacity.

As with Zubiuŋ and the clans adjacent to it, so among the Hill Talis, the ties which make up the field of clanship of any maximal lineage are not all of equal strength. The critical norms have an absolute value. Clanship prohibits intermarriage, vests defined rights and obligations in each lineage, and implies a solidarity which is incompatible with hostile acts like war or abducting one another's wives, or raiding one another's cattle. If these norms are infringed, as inevitably happens now and then, they are not thereby invalidated. The infringement tends to provoke processes which cancel out its effects and either re-establish the invulnerability of the norms or bring about a new alinement of structural ties, which neutralizes the breach. At the same time spatial distribution has a selective influence on the extent and frequency of the intercourse between lineages linked by ties of clanship. Proximity encourages more frequent and regular co-operation in situations which mobilize ties of clanship. Other factors, too, influence the gradation of clanship ties, the most important of these being the fact that solidarity, co-operation, and mutual dependence are greater within the clan than between linked lineages of different clans. Besides having a specific field of clanship, each maximal

THE STRUCTURAL RELATIONS OF THE TALIS 91

lineage is also a region where different fields of clanship overlap. This is what gives it its intercalary functions (see Diagram on p. 86).

Quasi-Clanship: Joking Partnership

Beyond the lineage's field of clanship lies a zone of social relations with which it has no constituted ties. For example, Zubiuŋ has no constituted ties with Zandoya. When Pal of Zubiuŋ abducted the young wife of a Zandoya man, this was his justification for an act which would have been considered an outrage if she had been the wife of a Ba'ari man. Again, when Saɣabo of Kpata'ar clandestinely brought home the wife of a Gorogo man, the elders of his lineage were ready to shield him. A few months later another youth of the same lineage eloped with the wife of a man belonging to a linked lineage, and the same elders peremptorily sent her home to her former husband.

Somewhere between clanship and potential enmity come two other kinds of ties belonging to the same class of structural relations as clanship and generally accounted for as arising out of some form of kinship (*mabiirət*). Each clan among the Talis, and in some cases a particular maximal lineage, has one or more joking partnerships with other clans or lineages. Thus Ba'ari has a joking partnership with Gorogo, Zubiuŋ with Sakpee and Gundaat, Kpata'ar with Wakii, Degal with Samiit, and so forth. The natives describe these relationships in the following terms. They say, 'We tease one another (*ti kiehət ni taaba*)', or 'We abuse one another (*ti tura taaba*)'. If they are asked for an explanation they say, 'It is laughter (*la'at*)', 'it is brother-in-lawship (*dakiirət*)'. Talking of it always raises a grin.

The joking partnership has two conventional modes of expression. When, for example, a Ba'ari man meets a Gorogo man or woman on a path by chance they abuse each other with impunity, in such terms as 'you ugly thing (*bonlɔrəga*)', or 'you good for nothing (*boŋwari*)', or some similar objurgation. Spoken in anger, these are deadly insults. Between joking partners, who shout them out with mock seriousness, they arouse only a roar of laughter. As we have noted, the natives compare them with the joking relationship of affines of the same generation. A man will tease his wife's brother (*dakii*) or sister (*dakii-pɔk*) or his sister's husband (*dakii*) or a clansman's wife in this way, and a woman her brother's wife (*pɔyakii*) or her husband's sister (*pɔyakii*), to the amusement of both.[1]

The other gesture of privileged aggression which is a convention of the joking partnership I once observed at a Zubiuŋ funeral. A cow had been slaughtered in honour of the deceased, and the elders were distributing the meat. A huge crowd of people had gathered, as is usual, for the occasion, and the tumult was indescribable. The division of the meat was still in progress. This process is always accompanied by loud and what appears to be truculent argument. Suddenly a youth sprang forward from the middle of the crowd, snatched the leg of a sheep, and sprinted off at top speed. There was a moment's consternation, and then an uproar. Laughing and shouting taunts and mockery at the top of their voices, the crowd looked on as one of the most respected elders of Zubiuŋ dashed off

[1] But marriage is not prohibited between joking partners.

92 THE STRUCTURAL RELATIONS OF THE TALIS

in pursuit. The youth zigzagged through the crowd, flourishing his leg of mutton, and threw it to a companion as the old man reached and grappled with him. For a few minutes they wrestled on the refuse heap, the old man pretending fury with the most realistic mimicry, as he cried out, 'you thief, you scoundrel', and his opponent making a pretence of resisting vigorously. A horde of small boys pranced around them with joy, and the elders at the gateway shook with laughter. Then it was all over, and everybody's attention reverted to the serious business of dividing the meat. 'Those young fellows are Sakpeedem', an elder explained to me; 'we and Sakpee abuse each other, it is brother-in-lawship, and not fighting.' This incident was a striking instance of how a social definition steers a situation. Anyone but a Sakpee man acting thus would have been set upon and manhandled; even a Zubiuŋ man, if he were to commit such an unthinkable act, would have been severely mauled.

When the natives speak of this as brother-in-lawship, they make it clear that they are speaking figuratively. A clan's joking partners are usually clans that live just beyond the range of its effective ties of clanship. They are clans who actually are or might be the *sunzɔp* of its *sunzɔp* by clanship or by courtesy. Thus they lie on the border between two zones. On the one side lies the zone in which the clan has precisely defined social ties implying specific rights and obligations and resting on the assumption of amity and solidarity. Serious conflict with these clans is regarded as incompatible with the basic axioms of social relations, and when it occurs it always precipitates action designed to re-establish normal social relations. On the other side live people with whom no direct structural ties exist; they may be friendly if they wish, but they can be hostile with impunity. They are clans whose wives can be abducted or seduced, if one is bold enough, without infringing the loyalty of clanship or necessarily incurring instant reprisals.

Joking partners lie between these two sets of clans, and are likely to be connected with both by structural ties of one kind or another. Thus the joking partners of my clan are not our *sunzɔp* nor our possible but inaccessible enemies. They are the *sunzɔp* of our *sunzɔp*, in relation to whom both my clan and theirs have similar rights, obligations, and sentiments. This is a bond of friendliness between us. But they are also the *sunzɔp* of our possible enemies, who may side with them against us, and this is a source of latent opposition between us. The conventions of the joking relationship symbolize piquantly the interstitial status of joking partners between friends, who have rights, duties, and loyalties to one another, and potential enemies. Their privileged aggression reconciles the conflicting definitions of *sunzɔp*, whose right to a share of the meat symbolizes reciprocal bonds, and non-*sunzɔp* who have no right to it because of the absence of reciprocal obligations; of people who are near (*pɔrəga*)—a significant concept in Tale political thought indicating both spatial and social proximity—and those who are far (*zaa ha*); of people whose friendliness can be relied upon, and those who are incalculable.

This is obvious both in the custom of mock abuse and in the snatching of meat or other food at a funeral ceremony. The joking partners obtain a share of the meat almost as if they were *sunzɔp*—but by a burlesque of

THE STRUCTURAL RELATIONS OF THE TALIS 93

seizing it by violence, almost as if they were hostile intruders. *Sunzɔp* have *a priori* no need of force to assert their privileges; if they did resort to it the affront would be so grave as to rupture the ties of clanship with them. Unrelated strangers could only get one of the shares due to *sunzɔp* if they had the temerity to seize it—but they would be fortunate if they escaped with their lives, even in these days of curbed passions. The mock aggression of a joking partner is a caricature blending these contradictory ways of behaviour.

Joking partners are not obliged to tease one another. They do so spontaneously when the situation seems appropriate. People who are greatly unequal in years or status, or personally related by cognatic kinship, will not act in this way. The joking partnership merely fixes the group with whose members such behaviour is appropriate in appropriate circumstances; a casual encounter, for instance, where anybody but a joking partner or a close kinsman would be met with the customary greeting—'*ni i tooma*', lit. 'with your work'. It is also appropriate, as we have seen, in situations such as funeral ceremonies, where there is a very strict determination of attendance and behaviour by clearly defined social ties. But even there joking partners turn up largely by chance. They happen to be passing, or a few young men, hearing of the funeral and knowing that there will be dancing and girls, go for the lark of it. For distant *sunzɔp*, too, attendance at funeral ceremonies is very often a matter of chance, but it is also very often the result of a decision by responsible elders.

Such institutionalized joking partnerships do not appear to exist among the Namoos. This may be correlated with the less elaborate interlocking of constituted ties and cleavages among them than among the Talis. An analogous practice which throws light on the ideas implicit in standardized joking partnership was, however, in vogue among the several branches of Mosuor biis until recently. When there was a funeral at Yamɔlɔg a party of relatives-in-law (*deenam*) would sometimes pass through Tongo from Wakii or Tɛnzugu carrying the obligatory food contributions consisting of a basket of porridge and a whole sheep or goat cut up and cooked. Tongo youths would then, if they had a chance, intercept them and compel them to give up most of the food, leaving only a small portion to prove to the Yamɔlɔg people that their relatives-in-law had discharged their obligations. The Yamɔlɔg people would naturally be indignant; they would denounce the Tongo youths as thieves and rascals, and upbraid their relatives-in-law for yielding so timorously. Then they would wait for an opportunity to recoup themselves in kind. Next time a similar party of relatives-in-law bound for Tongo from Nabɔrug passed through Yamɔlɔg they would be waylaid and robbed in the same way. It was thought of as a practical joke, and accepted as such by the victims. The annoyance it caused soon blew over and did not leave a lasting grudge, for it was understood to be an exaggerated enforcement of the rights of *sunzɔp* to a prescribed share of such contributions if they happened to turn up at the funeral.

In the same way, twenty years ago, a Tongo man who chanced to be passing through Yamɔlɔg when the guinea corn was ripening or the

94 THE STRUCTURAL RELATIONS OF THE TALIS

ground-nuts ready for harvesting, might pluck a few twigs of guinea corn or pull up a bunch of ground-nuts to stay his hunger. He would shout out, 'Whose corn is this, yo-o-o? I am going to pluck some.' The owner, standing on his flat roof, would probably remonstrate and swear, but he would not raise a hue and cry, for this was not theft but an exaggerated assertion of clanship ties. Nowadays, since the political jealousies between the chiefs of Tongo and of Yamaləg have brought about a state of chronic hostility between the two places, this pleasant custom has fallen into disuse. It is impossible to tease people with whom one has open or suppressed enmity; it would certainly provoke a fight.

Such liberties, it is of interest to note, could never be taken with the people of Sie or Biuk, though they, too, are the clan *sunzɔp* of Tongo. For, as my informants explained, 'they are too far away, and therefore they would resent it'. On the other hand, while any Tongo man can pluck a handful of guinea corn or a bunch of ground-nuts from a clansman's field at Tongo if the two men are on good terms, no one would dare to intercept the food contribution of another Tongo section's relatives-in-law. A serious quarrel would inevitably result. 'We are too near each other, we are like the members of a single family', explained my informants. Every segment of Tongo is likely to be represented at the funeral ceremony at which these contributions from relatives-in-law are shared, to claim the share due to it. For any segment to anticipate this by violence would be a gratuitous insult implying that the other segments do not respect its rights. The people of Yamaləg and of Sie used to act in the same way towards each other before the political jealousies that to-day poison their relationship arose.

All Tallensi think alike on matters of this sort, which fall within the ambit of their common culture, whatever their particular structural affiliations may be. This Namoo custom and its recent obsolescence fit the pattern we have established for the more conventionalized joking partnerships of the Talis.

Yet another kind of joking which I have several times witnessed adds confirmation to our analysis, the more so because it is entirely informal. This occurs between the members of two maximal lineages which are bound to one another by inescapable ties of politico-ritual inter-dependence. They are usually maximal lineages which have complementary politico-ritual offices, such as a chiefship and the tendaanaship complementary to it. A large element of tension is necessarily involved in these relationships. Mutual loyalty and solidarity in situations involving common interests are counterbalanced by mutual suspicion in matters concerning the private interests and possessions of each lineage. Behind a strong sense of amity and interdependence lurks a jealous vigilance in regard to reciprocal rights and duties.

When, therefore, representatives of the two groups meet in a ceremonial or jural situation, the more aggressive among the elders often taunt one another playfully at moments when ceremonial formality is relaxed. Gbizug and Tongo men, for example, have a habit of doing this. The Chief of Tongo and the Gbizug tendaana, on the rare occasions when they meet in public, will interrupt a long and ceremonious discussion with a

THE STRUCTURAL RELATIONS OF THE TALIS   95

jesting altercation about their mythologically founded bonds of mutual coercion. Ta'aŋ, the Gbizug tɛndaana's brother, who often deputizes for him in public ceremonies, has a sharp tongue. When representatives of the tɛndaana and of the Chief of Tongo have to perform some ceremony together he always pretends to mock the Namoos. 'You are only guests here,' he jeers (referring to their immigrant origin), 'I (as representative of Gbizug) have given you land to sit on, but if you don't behave I'll drive you back to Mampurugu, where you came from.' The Tongo men laugh good-humouredly at this sally, and one of them might answer, 'Very true, but if we should decide to go back to Mampurugu and leave you to yourselves, you will just starve'—the reference being to the Chief of Tongo's ritual power over the rain. Elders of Kpata'ar and Gundaat, which have a similar politico-ritual relationship to that of Tongo and Gbizug, often tease one another in the same way when they meet to perform a ceremony together.

Tallensi say this is just fun, jesting (*koohǝg*); but we see again that this apparently spontaneous jesting acts as a means of reconciling and counteracting the tensions of a double-edged social relationship. Where two corporate groups are structurally divided from each other to the point of having potentially competitive interests likely to lead to conflict at one level of the social organization, but are at the same time bound to each other by strong ties of obligatory co-operation and goodwill in another aspect of their social relations, the undercurrent of hostility or mutual wariness is deflected by a jest. You jest with people who must be friendly to you in terms of one set of loyalties and may be hostile to you in terms of another, and with whom you are on an equal footing as far as mutual rights and duties go. In the social relations of individuals with one another, this configuration occurs between siblings-in-law; hence the notion that the joking relationship between corporate units is modelled on *dakiirǝt*, the relationship of siblings-in-law.

Privileged Moral Coercion

There is another peculiar tie belonging to the category of social relations which we have been discussing. So far as my information goes, it is also confined to the Talis and their congeners. Its moral aspect is of particular interest as a clue to the values that lie at the back of the basic principles of Talis social structure.

The natives have no name for this relationship. In virtue of it, pairs of clans or lineages usually on the margin of the field of clanship of each, but not joking partners, have the privilege of moral coercion over each other's members. The natives describe this as a taboo (*kihǝr*). No member of one group may refuse a request of any member of the other. 'They *dare not* refuse', one informant declared, with obvious solemnity, as if to emphasize that it was a question of deep moral values. 'If they don't give what we ask, they would die, their house (i.e. lineage) would fall to pieces (*ba yiri gbi'irme*).' In other words, if anyone violates this bond, not only he but his entire line of descent would perish—the most calamitous retribution conceivable to the natives and one which befalls only those who transgress the ultimate tenets of religion and ethics.

96 THE STRUCTURAL RELATIONS OF THE TALIS

Hence, people connected in this way are careful not to ask each other for things. In the hunt, if a member of one group kills an animal and any members of the other group happen to be on the spot, the slayer will not lay a hand on the kill until the latter have cut a portion for themselves.

Sometimes it happens that a great tragedy overwhelms a member of one group and he abandons himself to grief, refusing food, drink, and consolation. Then, as a last resort, his relatives send for the head of the lineage whose requests cannot be refused, to persuade the stricken man to face life again. This happened, for example, when Puyɛl of Wakii's child was accidentally burnt to death. He was prostrate with grief, and said that he wished to die. Thereupon his brothers sent for the Bɔyarna'ab of Gundaat, the clan to whose members Puyɛl's lineage must yield, and the Bɔyarna'ab persuaded him to accept food and water, a sign that he was ready to throw off his despair. 'It is a matter of our fathers and our ancestors', the Bɔyarna'ab declared when he told the story. 'He dare not refuse; I would call on the Earth, and my *bɔyar*, and our ancestors, to witness, and his house would be destroyed if he remained obstinate.' Elders of other Talis clans explained the inviolability of this bond in almost the same words. It rests upon religious sanctions, the cult of the Earth and the cult of the External *Bɔyar*, common to all the Talis.

The Rationalization of Clanship Ties

Tallensi have no explanation to offer for the joking partnership or the bond of privileged moral coercion between clans or lineages, though they regard them as being somehow connected with the network of clanship. 'It is a matter of our fathers and forefathers', is all that even the best informed elders have to say about these ties.

Clanship ties, however, always have the warrant of dogma or myth, as we have seen. It is worth while examining a few more instances.

Sometimes common agnatic ancestry is claimed, though no common ancestor can be cited by name or any point of convergence of the different genealogies suggested. This is the case with Yinduuri and Sii, for instance. Frequently the fiction of a cognatic link is used. Thus, in explanation of the clanship ties existing between Degal and Kpata'arna'ab yidɛm of Kpata'ar, it is said that the latter are the sororal nephews (*ahɔs*) of the former. The name of the Degal woman who is thus alleged to have been the progenitrix of the Kpata'ar lineage is unknown, and no Kpata'ar man would even speculate as to which of their ancestors might have been her husband. Similarly, Dakuor yidɛm of Bunkiuk are said to be the descendants of a sororal nephew of Kpata'arna'ab yidɛm with whom they have ties of clanship. The fictional character of this formula is revealed when we compare the neighbouring clan of Samiit. The people of Samiit say that their founding ancestor was a Wakii man (hence their ties of clanship with Wakii), who migrated to the top of the hills because he had by accident killed and eaten a python, which is a taboo at Wakii. After wandering about for some time, he found refuge with the people of Gundaat, one of whose daughters was later given to him as a wife. The people of Samiit are the posterity (*tu'u*) of this pair. Strictly speaking, therefore, the people of Samiit are the sororal nephews of Gundaat; and

THE STRUCTURAL RELATIONS OF THE TALIS 97

yet they have no ties of clanship with the latter. Questioned about this anomaly, Samiit elders brushed it aside coolly with the remark, 'That is a long time ago, so now we marry one another'. But this argument, which is also met with elsewhere, runs counter to the basic principle of Tale exogamy, that consanguinity, however remote, is always a bar to marriage, not to speak of its obvious contradiction of the explanation of the Degal-Kpata'ar and other similar clanship ties. The Samiit elders, characteristically, admit these logical contradictions, but remain indifferent to them. For the structural ties that constitute the field of clanship of a particular lineage are validated independently of those that constitute the field of clanship of any other lineage. Theory and myth are made to fit the facts of social structure. It is enough if the fictions and myths utilized to explain the different linkages of a particular maximal lineage are consistent with one another. The Samiit story, which is typical of many others, proves, incidentally, that the explanations alleged for present-day structural ties are often myths of origin. Even if a Taləŋ killed a tabooed animal by accident, it would be unthinkable for him to cook and eat it; and if by some mischance he did commit this sacrilege, he would not flee his settlement on that account.

Owing to the dominance of genealogical relationships and the ideology of kinship in Tale social organization, most of the formulas accounting for the clanship ties of maximal lineages are couched in the idiom of kinship. But in many cases this is not so. We have already had instances where clanship ties are attributed to local coalescence; but there are cases in which this rationalization cannot work.

Take, for instance, Gundaat and Tamboog. These two adjacent maximal lineages are considered to be on an equal footing with the other clans of Tɛnzugu. But they are united by clanship ties as intimate as those that unite the component lineages of a single clan. Thus, as we have already noted, when either clan celebrates mortuary or funeral ceremonies, the ritual duties which normally devolve on close *sunzɔp* are undertaken by the other. When the placation gift (*sɛndaan*) is sent for a bride from one of these units, the live cock which forms part of it is always presented to the head of the other. This reciprocal privilege is usually confined to the component lineages of a single clan; and it is the same with political and economic activities in which co-operation is usually restricted to the clan. But according to their nebulous myths of origin, these two clans have a totally diverse ancestry. To explain their clanship ties the elders of these two clans fall back on an *a posteriori* argument which is common in similar circumstances all over the country. They say, 'We sacrifice together at a single shrine, so how can we marry one another? (*ti kab kaabɔt bayɔr dekɔ'la, ti le na ntuo ndi taaba?*)'. The implication here is that clanship ties are a consequence of 'sacrificing together'. This is inaccurate as a description of fact, but the formula draws attention to the most important overt factor of organization in the social structure of the Tallensi. We have met it already in our study of the Namoos and some of the Talis clans; but its remarkable elaboration among the latter deserves further attention.

H

CHAPTER VII

CLANSHIP AND RITUAL COLLABORATION

The Significance of Sacrificing Together

SOCIAL ties and cleavages are most conspicuously affirmed in Tale ritual. Ritual collaboration and common ritual allegiances are indices of common interests and mechanisms of solidarity. The core of Tale ritual thought, doctrine, and performance is the sacrifice (*kaab*). In some situations a libation of water into which a handful of flour has been stirred (*zɔm kuom*, flour-water) is a sufficient sacrifice. In others, and more characteristically, domestic animals (fowls, guinea-fowls, goats, sheep, cattle, and dogs), with or without the addition of beer, are sacrificed. The selection of the animal depends on a multiplicity of factors, such as the relative importance of the shrine at which it is offered, the importance of the occasion, the status of the suppliant, or the group offering the sacrifice. No other situation evokes so vividly and so directly, both for the native and for the onlooker, the sense of the significance, for the Tallensi, of their continuity with their ancestors, and the strength and reality of the moral cohesion of such corporate units as lineages and clans.

To sacrifice together (*kab kaabɔra*) is the most binding form of ritual collaboration. According to the ethical and religious ideas of the Tallensi, it is totally incompatible with a state of hostility—that is, with an open breach of good relations. Personal feelings are of secondary importance in this connexion. One can sacrifice with a person whom one despises or dislikes, as long as these feelings do not lead to an infringement of the ties of mutual obligation. But one cannot sacrifice propitiously with someone who is an enemy. This, according to native theory, would cause the ancestors to become angry, for 'as you are towards each other so are the spirits of your ancestors towards one another'. Therefore, if avowed enemies sacrifice together, mystical retribution will follow. To sacrifice together means not only to acknowledge a common spiritual tutelage, but also to eat together of the sacrifice; in short, to unite in a sacrament. Thus it is both an expression and a pledge of mutual amity and dependence.

Ritual Relations in Namoo Clans

As our analysis of the clan structure of Mosuor biis has shown, the final barrier to the complete absorption of an accessory lineage into one of the sub-clans is its exclusion from sacrifices to the founding ancestor of the sub-clan. This is the disability that excludes accessory lineages from the right to hold the chiefship of the sub-clan. But accessory lineages participate in sacrifices to the shrine of the ancestor who is regarded as the founder of that segment of the sub-clan to which they are attached or assimilated. The shrine (*bɔɣar*) of the founding ancestor of the sub-clan is usually in the custody of one of its segments, whose head (*kpeem*)

CLANSHIP AND RITUAL COLLABORATION 99

has, by right of succession, the duty of sacrificing to it on behalf of the whole sub-clan. Whenever sacrifice is made, all the segments of the authentic lineage must be represented. Accessory lineages are not represented, but they regard the representatives of the authentic segments to which they are linked as representing them also.

Thus, Nɔŋsuur yidɛm, of Tongo, are assimilated to the authentic segment of Siiyɛŋ yiri, and are present at sacrifices made to the founding ancestor of Siiyɛŋ yiri. But no member of Nɔŋsuur yidɛm could ever succeed to the custody of Siiyɛŋ's *bɔyar*. Now when sacrifice is made to Mosuor's *bɔyar* on behalf of the whole sub-clan, representatives of Siiyɛŋ yiri must be present; and Nɔŋsuur yidɛm, who cannot be present, regard these representatives of Siiyɛŋ yiri as representing them as well. This view is justified, for when the portion of the sacrificial animal which falls to the share of Siiyɛŋ yiri is divided out, some will be given to Nɔŋsuur yidɛm also 'to cook and set out for their ancestor spirits (*kpiinam*).' As it is expressly forbidden for anyone not a member of the clan or the wife of a member to eat of this meat, this obviously signifies an acknowledgement of the indirect religious dependence of Nɔŋsuur yidɛm on the ancestors of the authentic lineage to which they are structurally linked. Though formally barred from the sacrament by the dogma of agnatic descent, accessory lineages are in practice indirectly admitted to it.

This arrangement is thoroughly in keeping with Tale ideas of the representation of corporate units. But where the centripetal forces of co-operation and solidarity within the local community are as great as at Tongo, it is an unstable compromise. In all secular affairs, and in other ceremonial and ritual events, the accessory lineages exercise all the duties and privileges that spring from solidarity and fellowship. They cannot be rigidly barred from the crowning ritual act that witnesses to the solidarity of the sub-clan, and most categorically pledges its constituent units to amity and co-operation. We have seen how this results in pressure to admit the accessory lineages to the cult of Mosuor's *bɔyar*, exerted indirectly by them but supported vigorously also by the most powerful agent of cohesion in the sub-clan, the chief. The unity of the sub-clan in practical affairs is evidently felt to be negatived by the ritual discrimination against some of its elements.

In other Namoo clans the correlation of ritual collaboration with the jural and material aspects of clanship is even closer. At Ŋkoog, for instance, the attached lineage, Alaa biis, participate in all sacrifices to the shrine of the clan's founding ancestor, but they are prohibited from holding the chiefship. Politically and locally Alaa biis form an integral part of Ŋkoog, even though they intermarry with the two segments to which they are not attached. But their strongest bond of unity with the authentic branches of the clan is their right to take part in the cult of the clan *bɔyar*. This has been made easier by the fact that the custody of this *bɔyar* is vested in Abɔkrɔ biis, the segment to whose 'sister's son' Alaa biis trace their origin. It can be interpreted as an extension of the right to participate in the cult of the founding ancestor of Abɔkrɔ biis. One sign of the close social affiliation of Alaa biis to Ŋkoog is that they do not participate in the sacrifices of the Wakii lineage with which they are linked by ties of

100   CLANSHIP AND RITUAL COLLABORATION

clanship. But on the day of the harvest festival at Wakii, they send an offering of a fowl and flour to be added to the sacrifices which will be made at the External *Bɔyar* of Wakii.

This pattern of ritual collaboration between the constituent segments of the clan is common in most of the other Namoo clans. Where a clan consists of one or more Namoo lineages united with one or more non-Namoo lineages, there is usually no common ritual cult, as, for example, at Zoo. The component lineages of such clans might more appropriately be considered as locally contiguous linked lineages.

Ritual collaboration in Namoo clans differs in substance though not in form from the ritual collaboration found in the clans of the Talis, as will be clearer shortly. The Namoos lack the elaborate cult of the External *Bɔyar* associated with the Great Festivals, and most of their clans are built up round a dominant maximal lineage. In Namoo clans the cult of the founding ancestor corresponds to the cult of the *dugni bɔyar* among the Talis—that is, the cult of the founding ancestor of a constituent maximal lineage of a composite clan. Thus, unlike the External *Bɔyar* of the Talis, a Namoo clan *bɔyar* is kept at the house of the segment head in whose custody it is, in the same way as the particular lineage *bɔyar* of one of the component lineages of a Talis clan. (The *bɔyar* itself consists of one or two small pots (*kpatarɔg*) inside a shallow platter-like vessel made by chipping off the bottom half of a large pottery basin (*sar*), and covered with another piece of pottery. Like all ritual shrines, it is usually indescribably grimy with the remains of many sacrifices.)

As a general rule, ties of ritual collaboration between corporate units in Taleland always imply the existence of other structural ties. Conversely, all significant ties which define the place of a corporate unit in the whole social system tend to be mirrored in some form of ritual collaboration. This principle is of special significance for the Talis and their congeners.

Ritual Collaboration among the Talis: The External Bɔyar and the Earth

A. *Zubiuŋ.* We have noted that the unity of a clan such as Zubiuŋ becomes explicit in the cult of their *Bɔyar*, Duunkpalɔg, the common shrine of all the ancestors of its constituent maximal lineages, and in the cult of the Earth. To sacrifice together here means to participate equally in the cults of the *Bɔyar* and of the Earth, and is an index of the closest ties of clanship. Among the people of Zubiuŋ the synthesis of ritual collaboration with the clan structure is relatively simple, and is analogous to what is found among their Namoo neighbours. The three constituent maximal lineages are jointly and equally responsible for the custody and cult of their focal ancestor shrine, the Duunkpalɔg *Bɔyar*. It is described as an External *Bɔyar* (*yɛŋha bɔyar*). It is 'outside' in the literal sense of being out-of-doors, in the open, and 'outside' also in the social sense of not being bound exclusively to any one of the three constituent lineages of the clan.

But each lineage, as we have previously noted, also has its *dugni bɔyar*, 'the *bɔyar* of the room'. (The term 'room', *dug*, implies that each maximal lineage has a segmentary relationship with the other maximal lineages similar to that of the co-ordinate segments of a single lineage.) The *dugni*

CLANSHIP AND RITUAL COLLABORATION 101

bɔyar, again, is both literally and socially the domestic replica of the External *Bɔyar*. It is kept at the homestead of the lineage head, and it symbolizes the particular ancestors of that lineage only. Only that particular lineage offers sacrifices through its head to its *dugni bɔyar*, that is, to its own ancestors; all three lineages meet at Duunkpaləg in ritual homage to all their ancestors. (The *dugni bɔyar* of a Zubiuŋ lineage, as among all the Talis, consists of two small pots embedded in a projecting bulge of the outside wall of the house, together with other sacred para-phernalia, and, as usual, smeared all over with the dried flour, blood, and feathers of many sacrifices.)

The two aspects of the *Bɔyar* cult mark the two poles of clan structure—on the one hand, the relative autonomy of the constituent lineages of the clan; on the other, the unity and the solidarity of the clan, synthesiz-ing these relative autonomies in a wider field of social organization, but according to the same principles of structure that operate to constitute these relatively autonomous units. Though less explicitly, the same pattern of ritual collaboration obtains at Zubiuŋ with respect to the cult of the Earth.

The lineages of other clans with which Zubiuŋ has ties of clanship never participate in sacrifices at Duunkpaləg or at any of the Zubiuŋ Earth shrines. A linked lineage has ritual ties only with the Zubiuŋ maximal lineage to which it is directly linked, but these ties are very elastic. Thus, in situations in which the corporate identity of one of the constituent maximal lineages of Zubiuŋ is emphasized—for example, in the ceremonies of inducting a new tɛndaana into his office, or in the funeral rites of a deceased tɛndaana—members of the linked lineages of that group are nominally obliged to participate in the exoteric phases of the ceremonies. This obligation, however, is not so rigorous as in the case of the other Zubiuŋ lineages.

B. *Ba'ari*. The pattern of ritual collaboration between the component units of Ba'ari is slightly different. There the focal shrine of the clan is the principal sacred grove (*tɔŋgban*) consecrated to the Earth, Ba'at Da'a. Important sacrifices there, particularly during the Great Festivals, require the presence of all the constituent lineages of Ba'ari, including the accessory lineages. This is not regarded as inconsistent with the fact that one of the attached lineages, Ba'at-Guŋ, is permitted to intermarry with two of the other lineages, though otherwise exercising the rights and obligations of close *sunzɔp*. Ba'ari lacks the cult of the External *Bɔyar*, and the lineage (*dugni*) *bɔyar* of each of its constituent lineages is associated with Ba'at Da'a, which doubles the functions of an External *Bɔyar* and a focal *tɔŋgban*. Ba'at Da'a has, in fact, two ritual aspects. In its esoteric aspect it is the ideological pivot around which the clan revolves. Only the clan takes part in the cult associated with this aspect; linked lineages of other clans have no share in it. It also has an exoteric aspect connected with certain phases of the cycle of the Great Festivals. Again, linked lineages take no part in the ritual that defines this aspect. But the people of Gbizug have a formal role in these rites, and so have Wakii and Yaɣazuor, who are *sunzɔp*-by-courtesy. These clans participate, not in virtue of ties of clanship with Ba'ari, but by reason of their ritual bonds. They have a

102 CLANSHIP AND RITUAL COLLABORATION

general ritual bond in the tɛndaanaship and the special ritual relationship with the Earth which this office imposes on a group that has the prerogative of it, and they have a specific ritual bond that comes into action during the Great Festivals.

At the level of these ritual relations, Ba'ari, Gbizug, Wakii, and Yaɣazuor are brethren (*mabiis*) to one another. Gbizug, it will be remembered, is also linked to Ba'ari by clanship ties; through it, therefore, the scheme of linkage by clanship ties is interlocked with the scheme of linkage through ritual ties; and the myth in which the social relations of Gbizug and Ba'at-Sakpar are symbolically pictured expresses this double-sided interdependence. As will be clearer presently, the organization of ritual ties between corporate units, like that of clanship ties, follows the field principle. Working at different levels of the social structure in the service of different interests, the two systems are interlocked but not congruent. They reinforce each other by counterbalancing each other; and both kinds of ties are translated into the basic idiom of Tale social relations, the idiom of genealogical connexion.

C. *Gbizug*. We shall see this more clearly if we consider the role of Gbizug in this configuration. As we have noted before, linked maximal lineages have the right to participate in exoteric ceremonies (such as funeral ceremonies) in which the corporate identity of the particular Ba'ari lineage with which they have clanship ties emerges; but clanship ties do not give them the right to take part in the religious cults in which the corporate unity and identity of the whole clan emerges. They have no bonds with the clan as a whole, but only with the relatively autonomous segments of the clan. Gbizug, however, is bound to a segment of the clan by clanship ties and to the whole clan by ritual ties, and the bridge between these two sets of ties is Ba'at-Sakpar. Gbizug has no loyalties to the rest of Ba'ari, other than Ba'at-Sakpar, on the level of clanship; in this respect Gbizug is a threat to the stability of Ba'at-Sakpar's field of clanship. The latter's loyalties to Gbizug might in certain circumstances clash with its loyalties to the rest of Ba'ari. Compromise and adjustment are made possible by the scheme of ritual ties. The partly independent fields of clanship of Gbizug and Ba'at-Sakpar are adjusted to one another at a different level of social organization. In the frame of ritual relations, Gbizug is, as it were, assimilated to the whole clan of Ba'ari, drawn into the field of clanship of Ba'at-Sakpar.

It follows that on this plane of ritual relations Gbeog and Zubiuŋ-Yakɔra are indirectly bound to the whole of Ba'ari, for Gbizug represents its whole field of clanship in its corporate ritual relationship with Ba'ari. At a further remove Zubiuŋ Yakɔra is the bridge between the whole of Zubiuŋ and the whole of Ba'ari through Gbizug; and this rule extends, by a series of removes, to all the Talis.

The Underlying Principles of Ritual Collaboration

We must try to see clearly the principles underlying this bewildering hierarchy of social ties between corporate units in Taleland. It is as difficult to state this principle simply and precisely as it was for the writer to elicit it from the confusing and, at first sight, inconsistent welter of

CLANSHIP AND RITUAL COLLABORATION 103

facts with which he was faced in the field. Maximal lineages are the smallest corporate units that emerge in political action. The social and political relations between maximal lineages are regulated by ties of clanship. These ties constitute fields of social relations in which larger corporate units, which we have called clans, emerge. These are the largest corporate units that act in political matters. At the level of social and political relations between clans—that is to say, where the fields of social relations, constituted by clanship ties, overlap one another—clanship ties no longer suffice as the organizing mechanism. Here we meet with the interaction of more complex units and regions of Tale social structure than the maximal lineage. The social interests in response to which these interactions occur are more complex and more diffuse than those that are served by clanship. Consequently, an organizing mechanism of a different order comes into play, the mechanism of ritual.

Ritual is the appropriate mechanism of social organization at this level because the interests involved are not of a practical or utilitarian kind but of a moral kind—in fact, the most general moral interests of the natives, the maintenance of their existing institutions and norms of social behaviour. We must emphasize that we are dealing here with levels of organization correlated with different grades of social interests, and not with hard-and-fast forms of social grouping. We are dealing with different expressions of the same underlying forces. The same categories of ritual values and forms of association serve as a differentiating and integrating mechanism both at the level of social relations between maximal lineages and at the level of interclan relations. And clanship forms the bridge between the two levels as well as the organizing factor at the lower level. Both factors operate at both levels but with inverse dominance. That this is so can be seen from the natives' habit of conceptually assimilating all their social ties to the pattern of genealogical relationship and evaluating them all by the touchstone of kinship. The basic pattern of organization is that which we have described in our analysis of the clan system.

The ritual configurations and connexions at the higher level are obviously modelled on clanship configurations and connexions. The reason for this is simply that the ritual relations we are here concerned with exist between corporate units, maximal lineages or clans, defined by the canon of agnatic descent and by their place in the whole system of clanship.

We can say then that a Talis clan has a field of ritual relations overlapping but not congruent with its field of clanship ties. The fields of ritual relations of adjacent clans are articulated with one another so as to form a connected system linking all Talis to one another. It is through this system that the major cleavage between the Talis and their congeners on the one hand, and the Namoos on the other, is transcended; and the cycle of the Great Festivals is the medium through which this ritual system is regularly, obligatorily, and conspicuously brought into action. Let us see how the system extends to the Hill Talis.

The Scheme of Ritual Collaboration among the Hill Talis

The ritual relations of clans and lineages among the Hill Talis, though based on the same principles as those of Ba'ari, have a much more complex

104 CLANSHIP AND RITUAL COLLABORATION

elaboration. Among them the cult of the External *Bɔyar*,[1] homologous though it is in function and doctrine with its Zubiuŋ counterpart, includes peculiar esoteric elements lacking in the latter. This cult is the pivot of their Harvest Festival, *Bɔyaraam*, which takes its name from the External *Bɔyar*, of which it is essentially a sacrament. The sacrament includes an initiation cult, by which the males are brought into the *Bɔyar* sodality and bound to its obligations and observances.

Each *Bɔyar* has a number of ritual functionaries who hold office by virtue of being the heads of the maximal lineages in which these ritual offices are vested. As a rule a particular maximal lineage has the exclusive ownership of one office, and the ritual offices connected with a particular *Bɔyar* are distributed among all or most of the corporate units (maximal lineages) that owe allegiance to that *Bɔyar*. They usually include maximal lineages of a single clan, maximal lineages of other clans linked to them by ties of clanship, and territorially adjacent maximal lineages not related to them by clanship.

The cult of the Earth (*Tɛŋ*), again, is localized at a number of sacred spots, the most exalted of which are the foci of ritual association and collaboration between groups of clans and maximal lineages *not* connected by clanship. As in the *Bɔyar* cult, the ritual roles are distributed among the heads of the corporate units owing allegiance to a particular Earth shrine. Each maximal lineage has, in addition, its private lineage *bɔyar*, the symbolic seat of its own ancestors, as well as the special shrine that symbolizes and is bound up with the ritual office vested in that lineage.

Though each ritual office of a particular *Bɔyar* or *Tɛŋ* congregation is vested in one maximal lineage, the other member-units of the congregation have an interest in that office. There are certain occasions when all the ritual functionaries must be present in order that the rites of worship may be performed. This is the case during the Great Festivals, and the concrete manifestation of this principle is the common sacrament partaken of in the rites at the *Bɔyar* and the *Tɛŋ*.

Again, there is an order of seniority among the ritual functionaries of a *Bɔyar* or *Tɛŋ*. The most senior is the chief custodian of that shrine. Members of his lineage have a private relationship with the shrine, in addition to their public duties in connexion with it. They may, through him, bring private sacrifices to it in misfortune, or out of gratitude. But this functionary is also the direct intermediary between the congregation and the shrine. The priestly duties of its cult fall mainly on him. He is obliged to preside at all rites in which the whole congregation takes part, and the lineages of the other functionaries are dependent on him for the proper performance of the rites. This does not give him political power over them, for he is only *primus inter pares*, but it enhances the prestige of his office and makes it the pivot of the whole constellation. Thus all the functionaries and their respective lineages have a particular interest in the senior, pivotal office.

Furthermore, the installation of a ritual functionary in his office is

[1] For the sake of clarity whenever reference is made to an external *Bɔyar*, a capital *B* will be used; when any other kind of *bɔyar* is referred to a lower-case *b* will be used.

CLANSHIP AND RITUAL COLLABORATION 105

always the privilege of another functionary of the same congregation, or of a neighbouring congregation. The effect of this is to maintain particularly close bonds of interdependence and mutual amity between pairs of clans or maximal lineages and thus to strengthen the force of ritual collaboration as a sanction of mutual loyalty and cohesion. If the *Bɔyar* or *Tɛŋ* congregation is coterminous with a clan (as at Zubiuŋ), the relationship tends to be mutual or circular—A installs B and B installs A, or A installs B and B installs C who in turn installs A. The arrangement is then plausibly subsumed under the relations of clanship. In a congregation of unrelated maximal lineages the relationship may be mutual between some pairs of lineages and circular between other sets of lineages, which will often include lineages belonging to mutually installing pairs. Thus, A installs B and B installs A; but A also installs C, C installs D, and D installs E.

It often happens, also, that the ritual functionary representing a maximal lineage belonging to one *Bɔyar* or *Tɛŋ* congregation is installed by a ritual functionary representing a maximal lineage of a neighbouring congregation. The two lineages may be connected by clanship ties and the arrangement explained by invoking these. Or they may be adjacent to each other; or they may belong to the same *Bɔyar* congregation but different *Tɛŋ* congregations (or vice versa), so that it is only with respect to one context that the parties can be said to belong to different ritual groupings.

In every case it comes to this: that maximal lineages bound to each other by one set of ritual ties, with respect to one focus of ritual cohesion, are divided from each other, and bound to maximal lineages of other congregations constituted with reference to the same category of ritual relations, by another set of ritual ties. Thus the division between adjacent *Bɔyar* congregations (or *Tɛŋ* congregations), mutually exclusive by reference to the particular *Bɔyar* or *Tɛŋ* at which each worships, is bridged by the ritual interdependence, in terms of another ritual category, of some of their respective member lineages. And the system extends chainwise throughout all the clans of the Hill Talis.

We have here a more elaborate reproduction of the pattern of ritual relations that was observed to hold between Ba'ari and its neighbours. Indeed, the schematic formulation attempted above gives only an inkling of the labyrinthine intricacies of these ritual relations among the Hill Talis. In this pattern the cult of the External *Bɔyar* and the cult of the Earth have a very significant relationship, as we have previously indicated. It can be seen more explicitly than at Zubiuŋ or Ba'ari that they form polar principles in the total system of public ritual values and relations.

This appears quite clearly in the doctrines and ritual practices of the Hill Talis. *Bɔyar* and *Tɛŋ* are always coupled together in ritual activities. Together they exercise a mystical rule over the life and health, the fertility and prosperity of man. The differences in the way in which they are concerned with these fundamentals of human existence are like a complementary division of labour. This is well shown in the annual cycle of the Great Festivals. Thus *Gɔlib*, the Sowing Festival just before the first rains, is centred on the Earth cult. It dramatizes man's dependence on the fertility of the soil and on the rain for his livelihood, and the dependence

106   CLANSHIP AND RITUAL COLLABORATION

of these, in turn, on the mystical power of the Earth. Its chief theme, through all the rites and ceremonies of the festival, is a plea for the beneficence of the Earth in the approaching farming season. Though the chief actors are the Hill Talis, it is a festival in which all the Tallensi take part, directly or through representative ritual functionaries, since they are all under the mystical jurisdiction of the Earth; and it seeks to mobilize the goodwill of the Earth for the prosperity and fertility of all the people of the country.

At the other end of the agricultural season, when the harvest has been gathered, comes the complementary Harvest Festival of *Bɔyaraam*, as it is called by the Hill Talis. As the name suggests, this festival is centred on the External *Bɔyar* and is dominated by the cult of the ancestors. It is celebrated independently by each *Bɔyar* congregation, not in common, as the *Gɔlib* is. The Namoos, and the other Talis, also have their Harvest Festivals at about the same time; and all have the same theme. They are dramatizations of man's gratitude for the crops that the soil, under man's labouring hand, has yielded, for the children that have been born, and for the welfare that has been granted to men by the Earth and the ancestors. Through all the rites and ceremonies runs the' reiterated prayer that the ancestors and the Earth may unite to grant long life to men so that they may enjoy these and further blessings of the same kind.

The natives sum up the relationship between *Bɔyar* and *Tɛŋ* in the following formula. The *Bɔyar*, they say, rests on the Earth and cannot act without it; but the Earth would be derelict without men, the children of the ancestors whose spiritual abode is the *Bɔyar*. The sacredness of the Earth is due to the fact that men live on its surface, tend it, and worship it.

Both the Earth cult and the *Bɔyar* cult have a parochial aspect and a universal aspect. There are the particular *Bɔyar* and Earth shrines, each exclusively worshipped by its own defined congregation and bearing its own name; and there are the universal cults of which these are the local embodiments. This is plain both in native comment and in the forms of rites and ceremonies. The natives say that all Talis *Bɔya* (including not only those of the Hill Talis but those of Zubiuŋ and other Talis of the Plain as well) are 'one and the same thing'.

So when a sacrifice is offered at a particular *Bɔyar*, the officiant in his invocation calls upon all the Talis *Bɔya*, enumerating them by name, to 'gather together and accept this sacrifice'. Similarly, while every *Bɔyar* has its own name—Bona'ab, Wannii, Samoo, and so forth—they also have the generic name of Tɔŋna'ab.[1] The *Bɔya* of all the Talis clans are

[1] Some of these names have obvious meanings, others have none, or have lost all semblance of meaningful forms. Bona'ab means 'Chief of Things', i.e. Great Benefactor; Samoo means 'the (uncultivated) bush at Soog', presumably because in the distant past the shrine was surrounded by uncultivated bush; Wannii can only be given a meaning by twisting the first syllable into a phonetically analogous meaningful form. Tɔŋna'ab breaks up into the two syllables *tɔŋ* (from which Tongo takes its name) which is cognate with *tɛŋ*, the Earth (cf. *tɔŋgban*, earth shrine, lit. surface of the Earth) and na'ab, chief. It means, therefore, Chief of the Earth, or in other words, Lord of the Country. And to the Hill Talis their *Bɔyar* cult *is* the most important religious phenomenon in the world.

CLANSHIP AND RITUAL COLLABORATION

'brethren' (*mabiis*) and, in fact, this brotherhood includes also the *Bɔya* of all the clans, Tallensi or non-Tallensi, that take part in the cycle of the Great Festivals.

The idea reflects the sense of belonging to a wider politico-ritual community than their own local cluster of clans that is at the back of every Talɔŋ's mind. This notion of the unity of their External *Bɔyar* cult is especially strong among the Hill Talis, though each congregation has its distinctive variants of some of the ritual conventions. Hence a man who has been initiated into the cult at the *Bɔyar* at which his own lineage worships can be present at sacrifices at the *Bɔyar* of any other congregation of Hill Talis, whereas a Zubiuŋ or a Tongo man would not be admitted to the ceremony. This corresponds to the close interlocking of clan with clan and lineage with lineage among the Hill Talis by spatial, clanship, and ritual ties.

It is the same with the cult of the Earth. All Earth shrines (*tɔŋgbana*) are 'brethren' (*mabiis*), the localized places of worship, for defined social groups, of the universal Earth (*Tɛŋ*). The pattern of doctrine and ritual practice of the Earth cult has a much greater uniformity over a wider area than that of the *Bɔyar* cult. In comparison with the practices of the Hill Talis, the *Bɔyar* cult among all the other non-Namoo clans of Tale-land appears to be whittled down to its barest essentials of rite and belief, and outside the Hill Talis, different *Bɔyar* congregations are strictly exclusive of one another. In the cult of the Earth identical beliefs and dogmas, norms of conduct, ritual conventions, and social settings hold throughout Taleland. Indeed this is true of the whole of the Northern Territories.[1] This reflects the fact that the economic relations of man to land are practically identical for all the peoples of this area; that the social relations of men, as these are determined by their occupation and exploitation of land, are all of the same pattern throughout this area; and that their mystical notions of the Earth are identical. Tallensi sum this up in the idea that 'the Earth is indivisible (*tɛŋ la pu bɔkəra*)'.

Bɔyar and *Tɛŋ* are the foci around which interclan and interlineage associations crystallize out and through which the two dominant religious conceptions of the Tallensi act as the mechanisms and the sanctions of loyalty, amity, co-operation, and respect for one another's corporate rights between genealogically independent units. And these two foci of ritual consolidation are complementary. In spatial relations every maximal lineage belongs to one set of adjacent lineages in the *Bɔyar* cult and to a different set of adjacent lineages in the Earth cult. It has, there-

[1] The cult of the Earth is a prominent feature of native religion throughout West Africa. The form it takes in the Northern Territories of the Gold Coast is common, in its main outlines, to all the peoples of the Sudanese Zone. Cf. references to it *passim* in the previously cited works of Delafosse, Tauxier, Labouret, and Monteil, *Les Bambarra du Segou et du Kaarta*. Rattray, op. cit., gives many data on the cult as found in the Northern Territories, but his interpretations of these data are open to question. He gives much information on its Ashanti form in his works on the Ashanti. The best information from Nigeria is given in C. K. Meek's *Law and Authority in a Nigerian Tribe*. A point of importance is that there is no convincing evidence of the Earth being personified as a 'Goddess' in the Northern Territories of the Gold Coast—certainly not among the Tallensi—as Rattray and Meek claim is the case for the Ashanti and the Ibo.

108   CLANSHIP AND RITUAL COLLABORATION

fore, two intersecting fields of politico-ritual relations so adjusted that its loyalties to the other component lineages of one field are counterbalanced by its loyalties to the component lineages of the other field. Both sets of politico-ritual loyalties are correlated with the same sort of social interests, symbolized in a single system of religious concepts and values. Their organization in two complementary configurations around polar symbols checks the dangers of disruptive conflicts that might spring from them. Thus the ties of clanship are regrouped around another axis of social integration. Every maximal lineage is a bridge between a *Bɔyar* congregation and a *Tɛŋ* congregation. In most cases, in fact, the component lineages of a particular *Tɛŋ* congregation all belong to, and in that context represent, different *Bɔyar* congregations, and vice versa. This is the fundamental mechanism of the remarkable politico-ritual equilibrium found among the Talis.

The Network of Ritual Ties between Talis Clans

This network of public ritual ties runs through all the Talis clans. Indeed, as we have mentioned before, in the context of the cycle of the Great Festivals, it embraces both Talis and Namoos in the Tongo district, the clans of the Sie district, and a number of adjacent clans beyond the borders of Taleland. Confining ourselves to the Talis only, we find among them an organization of ritual relations analogous in pattern to the network of clanship ties. Adjacent maximal lineages have fields of ritual relations that overlap each other. They are combined thus into a single system of interwoven chains of ritual ties which spread across all the Talis. The ritual field of each maximal lineage corresponds to the parochial aspects of the *Bɔyar* and the Earth cult, the all-embracing network to their universal aspect.

To illustrate this analysis let us take up again the chain of ritual ties that begins at Ba'ari and follow out its further extension from Gbizug to Tɛnzugu. Gbizug and Gbeog, it will be recollected, are segments of a single clan. The ritual focus of their clan unity is the supreme Earth shrine (*tɔŋgban*) at Gbizug. There the elders of the two segments are obliged to assemble for sacrifice at certain times, notably at certain phases of the Festival cycle and when the funeral ceremonies or the investiture rites of a Gbizug tɛndaana are performed. The Gbizug tɛndaana and the Gbeog tɛndaana install each other in office. But the supreme Earth shrine at Gbizug is in the sole custody of the Gbizug tɛndaana. The people of Gbeog have their own focal *tɔŋgban*, the custody of which is vested in the Gbeog tɛndaana, and the people of Gbizug have no ritual connexion with this *tɔŋgban*. The Gbeogdɛm, again, also practise the cult of the External *Bɔyar* in the manner of the Hill clans. Gbizugdɛm have nothing to do with this cult. In fact they speak of it with contempt and hold aloof from it as if it were a perversion, even though their own clansmen practise it. 'Our ancestors did not take part in that', they say.

In terms of the Earth cult Gbeog comes into the field of ritual relations of Gbizug. Though it is the closest and most important, it is not the sole component segment of that field. Other adjacent maximal lineages form a part of it. Next to their supreme *tɔŋgban* the most sacred lineage shrine

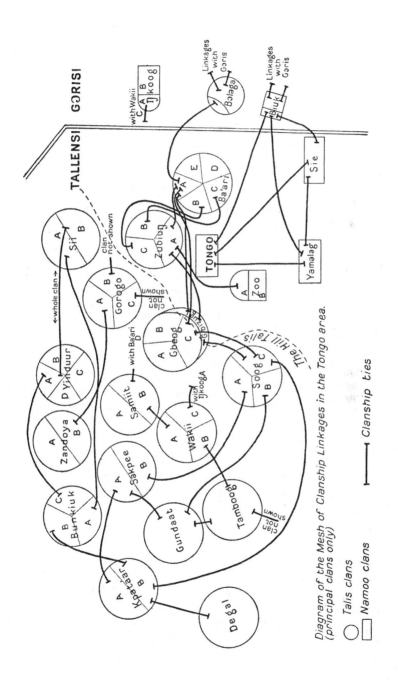

Diagram of the Mesh of Clanship Linkages in the Tongo area. (principal clans only)

of the people of Gbizug is the grave of their primordial ancestor, Tɛndaan Gɛnɔt. This grave, situated on the reputed house-site of Tɛndaan Gɛnɔt, is in the sole custody of Gbizug, and is associated with the tɛndaanaship, therefore with the Earth cult. But whenever a new Gbizug tɛndaana is installed, representatives of Gbeog, Ba'at-Sakpar, and Zubiuŋ-Yakɔra must be present at the rites performed at Gɛnɔt's grave. This is a matter of right and duty, subsumed under the rights and duties of their clanship ties and validated by the myth of the primordial tɛndaanas. But one segment of Wakii must also be represented at these rites, not in virtue of clanship ties but of the kinship (*mabiirɔt*) in the figurative sense that is held to prevail between all tɛndaana clans. It is effective in this case because of the proximity and the ritual collaboration in the Great Festivals of Wakii and Gbizug.

It is significant that the people of Soog, despite their clanship ties with Gbizug, do not come into the field of its ritual relations. On the surface this appears to be correlated with their spatial separation from Gbizug. It is only by their attendance at the exoteric ceremonies that accompany the installation or funeral of a Gbizug tɛndaana, and by the rights to special portions of meat and beer that they can exercise on these occasions, that the clanship ties between Soog and Gbizug impinge on the latter's field of ritual relations.

On the other hand, the clanship ties of Soog with Gbeog have a ritual embodiment in the cult of the External *Bɔyar*. All the segments of Gbeog practise this cult; but some of them owe allegiance to the *Bɔyar* of which the people of Soog are the senior custodians, and the others have a separate *Bɔyar* of their own. Soog and Gbeog do not have a common Earth shrine. In terms of the Earth cult Gbeog forms one united community and Soog another.

In this intricate tissue of ritual relations we see again, as at Ba'ari, the interweaving of clanship ties, neighbourhood ties, and ties of ritual interdependence *per se*, forming syntheses of politico-ritual relations at a higher level than those that are possible in terms of any one of these categories. This interweaving can be seen at any of the ceremonies in which a particular field of ritual relations is actualized. It is particularly clear among the Tɛnzugu clans, where we can see, more plainly than at Gbizug or Ba'ari, how it is produced by the counterbalancing of ritual ties against clanship and local cleavages, and of ritual ties of one sort against those of another sort.

Soog has a specific ritual tie with one major segment of Sakpee, the head of which installs the senior ritual functionary of the Soog External *Bɔyar*. This segment of Sakpee, Sakpee I, has its own *Bɔyar*. But it unites with the other major segment, Sakpee II, in the worship of a common Earth shrine, the custody of which is vested in Sakpee II; and Sakpee II owes allegiance to the External *Bɔyar* Bona'ab, the senior custodian of which is the head of Kpata'ar. Soog, though linked by clanship ties with Kpata'ar, has no direct ritual connexions with it. Their fields of ritual relations overlap at Sakpee, which forms the bridge between them at this level.

Kpata'ar provides a typical instance of the structure of the ritual fields

CLANSHIP AND RITUAL COLLABORATION 111

of any of the Hill Talis clans. Each of the two maximal lineages that constitute Kpata'ar, Kpata'arna'ab yiri and Nakyeet yiri, has its own private lineage *bɔyar*. Though bound by all the reciprocal duties and privileges that make them the closest clan *sunzɔp* of each other, the genealogical cleavage between them is somewhat more strongly emphasized than it is between the constituent maximal lineages of Zubiuŋ, for example. The head of Kpata'arna'ab yiri is the head of the clan, and *eo ipso* the senior ritual functionary and principal custodian of the Bona'ab *Bɔyar*. The head of Nakyeet yiri has a complementary role in relation to him in political, ritual, and jural affairs that concern the whole clan.

The politico-ritual office held by the head of Kpata'arna'ab yiri is symbolized in a shrine that is ancillary to the External *Bɔyar*. It is in the sole custody of Kpata'arna'ab yiri. But when sacrifice is offered at it on prescribed occasions Nakyeet yiri must also be represented; and in addition Dakuor yiri, the component maximal lineage of Bunkiuk with which Kpata'arna'ab yiri has ties of clanship, must be represented and share in the sacrament. Thus, both Nakyeet yiri and Dakuor yiri, though they themselves have no ties of clanship, take part in a common sacrifice with Kpata'arna'ab yiri because of their clanship ties with the latter. In this case the central region of the field of clanship of Kpata'arna'ab yiri becomes actualized in a sacrament that symbolizes the exclusive rights to a particular politico-ritual office held by that maximal lineage.

But what about the worship of the External *Bɔyar*, Bona'ab? As its senior custodians, the men of Kpata'arna'ab yiri can sacrifice there alone or accompanied by Nakyeet yiri, if they desire the intercession of the *Bɔyar* in matters that concern them only. When the Great Festivals come round, however, it is obligatory for the whole congregation of the *Bɔyar* to join together in the performance of the ceremonies. The other communicants, beside the two segments of Kpata'ar, are Gundaat, Samiit and two of its linked lineages, together counting as a single unit, and Sakpee II.

The cult of the *Bɔyar* Bona'ab is the central force uniting this group of maximal lineages. It is, we must emphasize, not a permanent bond of union that operates at all times and under all conditions, but a synthesis that emerges chiefly in the context of the Great Festivals. During the festivals their interdependence in the cult of the *Bɔyar* imposes mutual amity and solidarity on this group of maximal lineages. At other times this is not always an effective sanction of amity and goodwill. For these ties of ritual collaboration are not homogeneous. Underneath them run other ties which reinforce them in the context of the *Bɔyar* cult but might act against them outside of this context. There are first the ties of clanship linking Kpata'arna'ab yiri with Nakyeet yiri, Nakyeet yiri with Sakpee, Sakpee with Gundaat, in a chain, as it were. Then there are the ties of clanship-by-courtesy which link all these lineages with one another. Samiit and Sakpee have bonds of local contiguity because they 'sit together on the same land' under the ritual jurisdiction of the Sakpee tɛndaana. Gundaat and Samiit are *sunzɔp*-by-courtesy, bound by a covenant of mutual amity which they trace back to the alleged kinship ties of their mythological founding ancestors. Gundaat and Kpata'ar

112 CLANSHIP AND RITUAL COLLABORATION

have not only bonds of local contiguity, but an additional tie of ritual interdependence in that their heads install each other in their respective ritual offices. Similarly, Sakpee and Samiit have an added ritual tie in that their heads each have a special role in the ceremonial installation of the other. Finally, the head of Samiit exercises a special politico-ritual function in relation to the head of Kpata'ar. It is his task, in times of great social emergency, formally to adjure the head of Kpata'ar to initiate the ritual procedures necessary to avert disaster.

Thus, underneath the general collaboration of the communicants of Bona'ab with one another in the *Bɔyar* cult, and interweaving with it, spread these particular, divergent ties between different pairs of maximal lineages. In many situations these subordinate ties hold fast where the superordinate ties of ritual collaboration between all the communicants are not strong enough to override the cleavages between them. It is a striking thing, for instance, that whereas Nakyeet yiri and Sakpee have tended to side with the Gɔlibdaana of Bunkiuk in the struggle for power that has been going on between him and the head of Kpata'ar during the last few years, Gundaat has stood staunchly by the latter. The general bond of ritual collaboration in the *Bɔyar* cult has not ensured the support of the whole Bona'ab congregation for Kpata'arna'ab yidɛm in this struggle, and even the specific ties of clanship between them and Nakyeet yidɛm have not been proof against the lure of the Gɔlibdaana's fleshpots.

It is characteristic of Tale society that the structure of a community, whether it be a permanent community or a temporary community such as emerges in the cult of the External *Bɔyar*, is directly mirrored in every situation and every institution in which this structure becomes manifest. To take a very simple example: when the congregation of Bona'ab assembles there for a sacrifice, the representatives of the different maximal lineages sit in a fixed order. Kpata'arna'ab yidɛm sit in the place of greatest honour, since they are the senior custodians, and the other lineages are distributed as shown in the diagram opposite. It will be seen that this diagram gives a picture also of the structural relations between the different lineages, and incidentally of their local relations to one another. It shows in a nutshell how local, structural, and politico-ritual relations are interlocked with one another and converge to create and maintain interclan co-operation and solidarity. The diagram shows also how the ritual roles in any of the rites and ceremonies connected with the worship at the *Bɔyar* are distributed amongst the different maximal lineages.

Kpata'arna'ab yidɛm are the senior custodians also of the supreme Earth shrine of Tɛnzugu, Ɖoo; but in the cult of Ɖoo they have a completely different set of ritual collaborators from those associated with them in the cult of the External *Bɔyar*. They have a different field of ritual relations counterpoised to that of which the External *Bɔyar* is the focus. The units associated with Kpata'arna'ab yidɛm in the cult of Ɖoo are Degal (linked by clanship ties to them, but having its own External *Bɔyar*), Gɔlibdaan yidɛm of Bunkiuk (who have no clanship ties with Kpata'arna'ab yidɛm, and are the senior custodians of a different External

Bɔyar from theirs), and Tamboog (who also have no clanship ties with Kpata'ar, and have an independent External *Bɔyar*). These four units must be represented at all rites performed at Doo during the Great

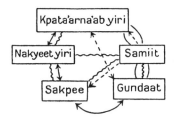

Diagram showing the seating arrangements at ceremonies in the sacred grove of the External Bɔyar **BONA'AB**, as reflecting the structural relations underlying ritual collaboration in the Bɔyar cult.

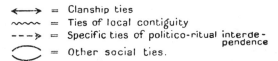

Festivals. Each one has also a private Earth shrine, with which the other three groups have no connexion, but their common allegiance to Doo binds them to one another in mutual ritual dependence. This should mean also, and by all accounts formerly did mean, a bond of mutual amity and cohesion; for there is nothing, according to Tale belief, which the Earth abhors so greatly as strife between those who worship it together at the same shrine.

To-day the cult of Doo furnishes an outstanding instance of the relativity of such ritual sanctions to the structural relations of the corporate units amongst which they are effective. During the Great Festivals, the four maximal lineages meet as of old to perform the prescribed rites at Doo. For this limited period and this objective they are obliged to set aside their antagonisms and collaborate amicably. At other times, however, they are divided by the struggle for power that has been going on between the Gɔlibdaana and the Kpata'arna'ab. Both Degal (in spite of their clanship ties with Kpata'ar) and the majority of the Tamboog people have been seduced by the wealth and power of the Gɔlibdaana.

The pull of loyalty to Kpata'ar sustained by the common cult of Doo has not, however, remained altogether ineffective. In order to make their religious relations with Kpata'ar consistent with their newly arisen political hostility to them, the supporters of the Gɔlibdaana have tried to oust Kpata'arna'ab yidɛm from their traditional status in relation to Doo. They would thus, if they succeeded, have put Kpata'ar in the position of a faction opposed to the rightful principals in the cult of Doo.

CLANSHIP AND RITUAL COLLABORATION

On the other hand, there are dissidents in the Gɔlibdaana's camp who rationalize their opposition to him and find a rallying motive for it in the traditional loyalty which they owe to Kpata'ar in virtue of their reciprocal ties of ritual collaboration.

For Kpata'arna'ab yidɛm, Degal, Bunkiuk, Gɔlibdaan yidɛm, and Tamboog, their common allegiance to Doo counteracts their divergent loyalties to their respective *Bɔyar* congregations. Doo, however, does more than merely bind these four units to one another. It is the focus of integration of the four *Bɔyar* communities they represent; and it is the point of confluence of the distinctive fields of clanship and of local ties of these four units. The ritual of the Gɔlib Festival when closely analysed shows that Doo is the palladium of all the Talis, the centre about which the equilibrium of all their corporate relations with one another swings.

Thus, to be specific, Tamboog is regarded as representing Wakii, and therefore, in virtue of the latter's ties with Gbizug, Zubiuŋ, and Ba'ari, these clans as well. Tamboog also represents Wɔyar and the other members of its *Bɔyar* congregation. Kpata'ar represents the other units constituting its *Bɔyar* congregation, and through them Soog and Gbeog. Degal represents the Talis on the east slope of the hills and the adjacent plain. Bunkiuk represents its *Bɔyar* congregation, which includes segments of Zandoya, Yinduuri, Sii, and Gorogo. And intersecting these groupings run the numerous ties of clanship, joking partnership, clanship-by-courtesy, privileged coercion, and local contiguity, that link up particular members of different groups.

We have considered only the two major ritual institutions through the medium of which the clans of the Talis are articulated into interdependent sets, and these again serially interlocked in a single system. There are also a number of other religious institutions ancillary to the cults of the *Bɔyar* and the *Tɛŋ* in which more localized forms of ritual collaboration unite maximal lineages and clans, not otherwise ritually related, on certain occasions. It would be tedious to deal with them at length. It is enough to say that their effect is to interweave more closely the numerous threads which form the amazing web of politico-ritual relations among the Talis. They make the system complete to its last detail.

The all-embracing range of this web of politico-ritual relations comes out most plainly in the Great Festivals. The cycle requires the ritual co-operation not only of all the Talis but of the Namoos as well. The distribution of ritual roles and responsibilities amongst the clans is such that every corporate unit has a specific role associated with a particular phase of the cycle and with particular ritual emblems. Thus the cycle of the Great Festivals unites all the Tallensi in the performance of one connected series of ritual acts, and this is a bond of profound importance for all their social relations with one another.

The Great Festivals are dramatizations on the plane of ritual symbolism of the most vital and universal values of the Tallensi. They express the idea that the common good of all the Tallensi is founded on the inescapable interdependence of their elaborately differentiated clans and lineages. This common good, the ritual of the Great Festivals might be interpreted

CLANSHIP AND RITUAL COLLABORATION 115

to declare, is not a matter of expediency or calculation but the essence of life for the individual and the community. It is a sacred necessity; and men must be in harmony amongst themselves and with the mystical powers that control their lives if they desire to gain the beneficence of these powers for this end. The ritual, the sacrifices, and the prayers to the ancestors and to the Earth, pleading for the fruitfulness of the land, of women, and of the flocks and herds, for health, prosperity, and peace, and offering thanks at the end of the agricultural year for these boons, eloquently express the Tale conception of the common good. In the rites of the Great Festivals the widest community that has social relevance for any Talaŋ emerges, not as a hard-and-fast political unit, but as a temporary synthesis of all the forces of social integration operative in Tale society. This is an expression of the fact that, though they have no centralized government, the Tallensi do form a single body politic, albeit one without defined territorial boundaries. This unit is built up on the widely ramifying structural ties which knit the independent corporate units together. But its ultimate basis is a body of moral and jural norms and values accepted as binding by all Tallensi, and defended from the disruptive action of conflicting sectional interests by the most solemn ritual sanctions of Tale religion. The function of ritual collaboration between clans and lineages is to maintain the un-challengeable validity of these norms and values; for upon their observance the attainment of the common good ultimately depends.[1]

Native Thought and the Realities of Social Structure

We have digressed to survey the scope and function of ritual collabora-tion among the Talis in order to see what truth there is in the maxim that 'those who sacrifice together do not intermarry'. As a generalization it is obviously inaccurate; but it is valid for particular instances of linkage by clanship ties, though only as an *a posteriori* inference.

Tale elders do not fall into this error of deduction through lack of intelligence or ignorance of their social organization. Among the Tallensi, as among most primitive peoples, what appears to us to be defective logic usually proves to be a product of the social organization as it is appre-hended by native thought. When an individual Talaŋ applies the maxim we have criticized to his own particular field of social relations—not to that of his lineage or clan—it is perfectly apposite. For an individual in his personal capacity can only sacrifice together with other individuals if they are his kinsfolk or clansfolk; and this implies automatically that he cannot marry their daughters or sisters.

In the social philosophy of the Tallensi, as will be shown in the next volume of this study, kinship is the model of all social ties between individuals and groups. The ties of clanship, ritual collaboration, or local contiguity are visualized as so many different extensions and transforma-tions of the fundamental patterns of kinship. For the individual this is accurate to a very large extent. There is a kinship element in all his social

[1] This aspect of Tale political organization and its wider sociological implica-tions are discussed in *African Political Systems*, cit. supra.

116　CLANSHIP AND RITUAL COLLABORATION

relations; for him they are all contained within a single frame of social reference, determined, at bottom, by his parentage. He cannot connect the rules and conditions that govern his own social behaviour with the general principles of Tale social structure. He has no means of ascertaining these, since the Tallensi do not make a systematic study of their own society. Every native knows only a limited sector of the social system, and the picture he has of it is built up out of his direct experience of the way in which it acts upon the day to day conduct of his life. Individuals who have the same or nearly the same field of social relations tend to have the same picture of their society; and individuals who have different fields of social relations tend to interpret their social behaviour and the structure of their society by the same concepts and along the same lines in so far as the same principles determine Tale social structure in every sector of the society. When we speak of Tale social philosophy or Tale thought, we do not mean that the natives have a systematic body of objective knowledge about their own society. We mean only the common denominators in the knowledge of their society that they have individually. Such knowledge, though partially inaccurate and transmitted only in face to face contact, is necessary for the existence of every society. For men employ their social notions in their relations with others and adapt their concepts to those of their fellows in carrying on collective life. Common notions emerge out of corporate and co-operative social action for common ends. In a society as homogeneous as that of the Tallensi this knowledge is widespread and tends to be uniform; hence the common denominators stand out.

When a native harks back to kinship in order to explain or interpret any social tie that directs his corporate or co-operative activities, he is putting forward a common point of view, but not an objectively accurate one. The outside student, seeing Tale social life on a wider scale than any native, can see differences in the significance of kinship for the individual, and of clanship for a corporate unit. Thus, matrilateral kinship has a different value for the individual from what it has in the sphere of clanship. In the former case, matrilateral kinship confers definite privileges and obligations on an individual in relation to other individuals or to defined groups, and it has the same value for everybody. In the latter case, it is one of several fictions used to rationalize ties of a particular kind between corporate units. For example, the sister's son (*ahaŋ*) of a Ba'ari man is not entitled by right of matrilateral kinship to participate in sacrifices at Ba'at Da'a; but Ba'at-Lakum yidɛm exercise this right in virtue of clanship ties accounted for by the fiction of descent from a sororal nephew. Similarly, it is evident to the sociologist that the exogamic barrier by which ties of clanship are distinguished from other social ties has a different structural value from the prohibition against marrying a maternal kinsman; for the former is a factor of solidarity between corporate units, and the latter the index of a particular tie between certain individuals. But the natives lump them together.

Thus it comes about that the Tallensi describe and discuss the social relations of corporate units in terms of kinship, using such concepts as *sunzɔ*, *mabii*, and *dɔyam*. The primary significance of these concepts will

CLANSHIP AND RITUAL COLLABORATION 117

be discussed in our next volume. It will be useful, however, to sum up the meanings attached to them in the context of the structural relations between corporate units.

The term *sunzɔ* (pl. *sunzɔp*) means literally sibling by the same father. It is applied by the members of a particular lineage or clan to another lineage or clan with which they have a defined structural relationship, involving reciprocal rights, duties, and interests, identical with or analogous to those that obtain between segments of a single lineage. The natives visualize this relationship, which they describe by the abstract noun *sunzɔt*, as modelled on the social relationship of brothers.

Mabii (pl. *mabiis*), literally mother's child, and the abstract noun *mabiirɔt*, are more loosely used and have a wider range of reference. In its primary sense *mabii* denotes a kinsman of the same generation, in particular a sibling, as distinguished from kinsmen of a preceding or succeeding generation. Its emphasis, however, is not on the reciprocal rights, duties, and interests of siblings, but on their equality of status and on the sentiments of brotherhood based on common descent. A man can speak appropriately of his brother as his *mabii*, but not of his son. Lineages of the same order of segmentation can be described as *mabiis*, but not a segment of a lineage in relation to the whole lineage. Related clans, or even clans that have some distinctive usage in common, can speak of one another as *mabiis*. In certain circumstances all the Tallensi may be described as *mabiis* by contrast with non-Tallensi. *Mabiirɔt* means 'to be akin to one another in some way'—by kinship in the narrow sense, in a kinship context; by local propinquity, political or ritual association, common custom, or merely common race, in other contexts. It is reminiscent of our own phrase 'kith and kin', which we apply to our actual kinsmen in one context, and to our 'cousins', the Australians or Canadians, in another. We have tried to convey this by translating *mabiirɔt* by 'kinship in the wide sense'.

Lastly, there is the concept *dɔyam*, derived from the verb *dɔy-*, to bear or beget a child. Its primary reference is to kinship by consanguinity; hence it is most appropriately used to refer to a structural tie based on a known or accepted genealogical connexion. It serves to distinguish such ties from apparently similar ties for which no genealogical connexion or at most a very general community of stock is postulated. Thus, a Tongo man will describe the people of Yamɔlɔg as 'our *dɔyam*', but not the people of Zoo; they are merely 'our *mabiis*'. *Dɔyam* has no reference to the relative status of the parties or to their precise jural relationship. Father and son, uncle and nephew, a person and his distant cognate, clansfolk, members of linked lineages, are all *dɔyam* to one another. The term refers to the tie of consanguinity itself.

All three terms are frequently used in a metaphorical way to express attitudes of amity, solidarity, or goodwill, such as are taken for granted amongst kinsfolk, even where the parties concerned have no social ties based on genealogical connexion. To give an instance, Soog and Zubiuŋ were estranged from each other for a long time. At length they were compelled for ritual reasons to meet and become reconciled. Pledging their clans to everlasting amity and goodwill in the future, the two spokes-

118 CLANSHIP AND RITUAL COLLABORATION

men declared fervently '*ti a dɔyam*—we are consanguineous kin'. Let no one betray this kinship in the future; and if a man of either clan does so, let the ancestors and the Earth visit punishment on him. *Dɔyam* was used here to express in the most emphatic way both the state that it was desirable to maintain between the two clans and the special cordiality they felt for one another on this signal occasion of a ceremonial reconciliation after a long breach in their good relations. Similarly, when Tallensi wished to express particular cordiality towards, and confidence in, me they used to say, with great self-satisfaction, '*Nyɛn pana ɛŋ ti dɔyam*—you have now become our kinsman'.

The concept *dɔyam* is the link between the individual's notion of ritual collaboration as a function of kinship and the common idea that ritual collaboration between corporate units is a sign of a corresponding genealogical connexion. For consanguineous kinship[1] is the fundamental condition that permits individuals to join together in a common ritual activity, and the individual's scheme of ritual values is linked to his social frame of reference through the medium of his kinship ties. It is in his relations with his consanguineous kinsfolk that a person has the most direct experience of that amity and solidarity which are assumed to be intrinsic to all ties of ritual collaboration.

The Network of Structural Ties among the Gɔrisi and in the Sie District

The intricate network of structural ties and cleavages that links the Talis clans and lineages among themselves stretches across into the country of the Gɔrisi. There, at Bɔlɔga, at Zuarungu, and elsewhere, we find similar aggregations of local clans and lineages, differentiated from one another and interlinked in a similar pattern to that which we discovered among the Talis; but from the superficial inquiries I was able to make, it seemed that the organization is much less elaborate among the Gɔrisi than among the Talis. These clusters of Gɔre clans and lineages adjacent to the Tallensi are hooked on to the Tale cluster by intercalary lineages such as the Biuk Namoos and Sanaab biis at Bɔlɔga. Thus, Sanaab biis are connected with Ba'ari (cf. p. 88) both by spatial proximity and by ties of clanship, but they lie outside the social horizon of an average member of any of the Hill Talis clans.

The same pattern of interlinked structural ties is found also among the non-Namoo clans and lineages of the Sie district, but again it is not so elaborate and complete a system as that of the Talis. In this district we find the same type of composite clan bearing a local name, considering itself a unit, expressing its corporate identity and solidarity in its relationship to *bɔyar* and *tɛŋ*, and composed of relatively autonomous maximal lineages each with its own lineage head holding a particular ritual office. Again we find contiguous maximal lineages linked with one another by ties of clanship and of clanship-by-courtesy.

But in this area the chains of linkage are more variable than among the Talis. Political and territorial ties often unite neighbouring groups which

---

[1] As opposed to affinal kinship (*deen*) which is the prototypical social relationship that excludes sacrificing together.

CLANSHIP AND RITUAL COLLABORATION 119

among the Talis would be linked by clanship as well. There is therefore greater variation in the degree of overlapping between the fields of clanship of contiguous lineages than among the Talis.

Some clans in this area are closed units forming by themselves a miniature replica of the whole system. Thus, Duusi proper consists of three maximal lineages, bound together by ties of clanship, but none having clanship ties with any other lineages or clans. These three lineages are said to be 'consanguineous kin with one another (dɔyam ni taaba)'. But there is no myth to account for their coalescence, nor is it rationalized by genealogical fictions. They are structurally differentiated in a similar way to the maximal lineages of Zoo. Thus, one lineage has the exclusive right to the chiefship, another to the tɛndaanaship, and the third to the ritual office of Yiraan, which holds the balance between chiefship and tɛndaanaship. The ritual observances of the three maximal lineages differ from one another and they have no common ancestral bɔyar. One focus of integration for the whole of Duusi is the supreme tɔŋgban, Ziug, whose custody is vested in the lineage that holds the tɛndaanaship, but whose cult requires the co-operation of the other lineages as well. The other focus of integration is the chiefship, which demands both political co-operation and ritual collaboration among all three maximal lineages.

The loose articulation of this set of clans as compared with the Talis is reflected in their lack of a common appellation. One reason for this, no doubt, is that the line of cleavage between Namoos and non-Namoos in terms of structural relations, ritual observances, and politico-ritual roles and offices, is not so clear cut as in the Tongo district. At Sie, where it is most precise, the Namoos are identified as *naditib*, those who hold (lit. eat) the chiefship, in contraposition to the *tɛndaanditib*, those who hold the office of tɛndaana, namely the people of Sawalɔg and Tɛndaaŋ; and this cleavage runs parallel to their clanship relations and ritual observances. (Throughout the area, as among the Gɔrisi and Namnam, a settlement or part of a settlement occupied by *tɛndaanditib* is usually referred to as Tɛndaaŋ, and *tɛndaanditib* lineages are often described as Tɛndaaŋdɛm.) But in several other clans *naditib* and *tɛndaanditib* are constituent maximal lineages of the same clan. This is similar to the distribution of ritual offices amongst the maximal lineages of a Talis clan; but in this case the *naditib* lineages are usually Namoos, whereas the *tɛndaanditib* lineages fall into line with non-Namoo clans like Sawalɔg and Sie-Tɛndaaŋ in their ritual observances and social alliances. Among these clans, therefore, the ties of clanship often cut across the cleavage between Namoos and non-Namoos; the social and political alinements of clans or maximal lineages in accordance with their ritual observances cut across their alinements by clanship ties. The general effect is to link Namoos and non-Namoos more closely together than in the Tongo district, but in a looser system than is found among the Hill Talis.[1]

The *tɛndaanditib* clans and maximal lineages of the Sie district declare

---

[1] *Naditib* is compounded of *na'am*, chiefship and *di* to eat—here in its metaphorical meaning of 'to have the prerogative of an office'—and the plural suffix *-b* (< *ba*), people; *tɛndaanditib* comes in the same way from *tɛndaan*, *di*, and *-b*.

CLANSHIP AND RITUAL COLLABORATION

themselves to be akin to the Talis, and are so regarded by the latter, though only in the very broadest sense. There is, of course, no clear boundary between the two aggregates of clans, either territorially or structurally. The *tɛndaanditib* maximal lineage of Gbee and the people of Yaɣazuor have ties of clanship, but Gbee is considered to belong more closely to the Sie district than to the Tongo district, whereas Yaɣazuordɛm are definitely Talis united by ritual bonds and clanship-by-courtesy to Ba'ari. Indeed Yaɣazuordɛm were always regarded as potential enemies by the clans of the Sie district. In two famous wars still recollected by the old men, almost all the clans of the Sie district, both *naditib* and *tɛndaanditib*, including even the *naditib* maximal lineage of Gbee, were ranged against Yaɣazuor and Ba'ari. Thus, Gbee forms one interstitial group between the Tongo district and the Sie district. Similarly, Sɔk, near Yamaləg, forms another interstitial group, considered by each aggregate to be more closely allied to the other.

CHAPTER VIII

TOTEMISM AMONG THE TALIS AND OTHER NON-NAMOOS

The Unity of all the Talis

IT is commonly said, everywhere in Taleland, that the Talis are 'all one' (*bonyɛni*). The Talis themselves, in spite of their elaborate differentiation by clanship ties, always picture themselves as a cohesive group. As might be expected, the implications of this idea vary considerably as between the Talis adjacent to Tongo and the Hill folk. For any of the latter, with the exception of Yinduur and Sii, it meant in the old days, among other things, mutual assistance in war against the Namoos. Yinduur and Sii, however, never fought against Tongo, and sometimes took the side of Tongo on account of their ties with it through the chiefship held by the clan head of Sii. Yet nobody would be more indignant than a Sii man if it were seriously suggested that this indicated closer bonds between his clan and the Tongo Namoos than between his clan and the other Talis; for in a fight between the Talis and any settlement other than Tongo, Sii and Yinduuri would rally unhesitatingly to the side of their 'kin', the Talis. The people of Zubiuŋ, again, invariably took the side of Tongo in war, whereas the people of Ba'ari generally ranged themselves with the Hill clans. Gbizug, bound by equally strong politico-ritual ties to the other Talis and to Tongo, was ritually prohibited from taking part in war between them at all. In keeping with its function of maintaining the political balance between the Namoos and the Talis, it was the traditional peace-maker. But Gbeog fought with its Talis kin and might even attack Zubiuŋ. Thus by the crucial test of warfare the Talis do not form a single, permanently cohesive group. But at the same time, clans that stood outside the Hill Talis cluster, or opposed them in warfare, never infringed their specific ties of clanship by doing this. Zubiuŋ, for instance, would fight against the Hill Talis in a general war, but not against Ba'ari, with which it has clanship ties. For the same reason Sii, coming to the aid of Tongo, would attack Gorogo or Gbeog but not a Tɛnzugu clan.

These divergent loyalties in war are indices of divergent social and political ties springing from the internal structural differentiation and local relationships of the Talis. They are an aspect of the interlocking of Talis and non-Talis in the social system. They do not invalidate the claim of the Talis to be a cohesive group. Their unity is based on the network of structural ties binding them to one another. It is symbolized, in native thought, by a number of ritual observances that are closely correlated with their social ties and cleavages; and its most significant expression is the cycle of the Great Festivals.

Funeral Customs as Criteria of Social Alinement among Talis Clans

For a Namoo, the social definition of the Talis is primarily 'those who

122 TOTEMISM AMONG THE TALIS AND OTHER NON-NAMOOS

gird their dead with a sheepskin loin cover (*ba suona pɛhug*) and taboo (*kih*) the tortoise (*pakur*) and the water-tortoise (*mieŋ*)'. The people of Zubiuŋ, as we have seen, also fix upon their mortuary and funeral rites and their totemic avoidances as the two main indices of their affinity with the Talis. They add to this their special ritual relationship with the Earth, symbolized by the office of the tɛndaana.

Most of the Talis, it is true, gird the dead (that is, males who have begotten children before they die and are therefore considered to be socially mature) with a sheepskin; but there are a few exceptions. The people of Ka'ar use an oribi (*waləg*) skin, and the people of Gorogo, as well as some of the Teeləg lineages, use only a piece of string.

The sheepskin has the same ritual value for the Talis as the goatskin has for the Namoos. Identical beliefs and attitudes lie behind these differences of usage, which are clearly a function of the social cleavage between Namoos and Talis. Members of either group often have great knowledge of the mythology, the ritual practices, and the distinctive beliefs and customs of the other group. They pick up this knowledge when they go on visits to their maternal kin in the other group, and the underlying identity of beliefs and values makes this easy. Yet it would be inconceivable for the people of either group deliberately to take over the usages of the other group. The assimilations of custom that have taken place have been unconscious.

Talis explain deviations from the common ritual, such as those of the people of Ka'ar or of Gorogo, by the cliché, 'Our ancestors desired it so'. Thus the Gorogo people claim that their founding ancestor originally came from the Wooləga country. They still have ceremonial ties with the people of Chana, which they say was their ancestor's place of origin. They connect their custom of putting a string on a corpse with this myth, for both myth and custom distinguish them from the other Hill Talis. It is significant that the Teeləg lineages which have the same custom have no clanship ties with Gorogo, nor is any explanation offered by either group of the common ritual usage.

The Tallensi see the binding force of any observance held by the lineage or clan as deriving from an ancestor whose edict it is said to have been. The concept *kih*, it must be remembered, is applied not only to ritual prohibitions but also to ritual injunctions. The sheepskin loin cover for the dead is also a *kihər*. The moral imperative of a ritual prohibition or injunction—a *kihər*—is connected with the dependence of the lineage on its ancestors' goodwill for its survival and welfare. And there is another point. The most sacred duty owed by son to parent or parent to child is the performance of his or her funeral ceremonies. It is unthinkable, and it has never been known, for a native to fail in this duty, though nobody can compel him to do it. This is the case in spite of the fact that funeral rites are also the concern of the whole lineage and clan. In funeral ceremonies the structure of the lineage and clan emerges into action as perhaps in no other Tale institution. And it emerges in such a way as to show up clearly how the moral responsibility of the individual to his forbears is a function of his rights and duties as a lineage member and is a factor in the cohesion of the lineage.

TOTEMISM AMONG THE TALIS AND OTHER NON-NAMOOS 123

Funeral rites have a twofold symbolic value for the Tallensi. They symbolize the corporate unity and identity of the lineage and clan and its ties with other clans; but they also symbolize the group's dependence on and moral responsibility to their ancestors, collectively and individually. This is shown very well in the custom of each clan's using a particular kind of loin cover for the dead and in the associated custom of swearing an oath by the father's loin cover. They show that ritual symbols of social differentiation and association among the Tallensi are not mere emblems of intergroup differences. They are emotionally charged symbols of the fact that the corporate unity and identity of the group is created by the moral bonds of its members among themselves and of each member with the ancestors of the group. We shall return to this presently.

In spite of their deviant mortuary customs, the people of Gorogo, Ka'ar, and Teelɔg consider themselves to be, and are considered to be, as much a part of the Talis aggregate as any other Talis clans. Conversely it is known among the Talis that some clans of Gɔrisi and Namnam, as well as many of the *tɛndaanditib* lineages of the Sie district, dress their dead in a sheepskin loin cover. The Talis do not on this account acknowledge any of these groups as Talis or as being kin to them. Again, some clans in the Sie district gird their dead with an oribi skin. But they deny having any ties with Ka'ar. Indeed, their elders are quite unaware that they have this custom in common with Ka'ar, and are not in the least interested in hearing of it. This is a significant difference between the Namoos, all of whom have the same mortuary observances, and the Talis and their congeners. This difference extends to other manifest ritual usages that serve to differentiate corporate units from one another.

Certain other funeral rites are also stressed as rigorously distinctive of the Talis and as common to all of them. All Talis, it is said, conclude a funeral by the rite of *ŋma ma'ala*. Members of the deceased's maximal lineage, and the heads of the other lineages of the clan, contribute a large number of fowls, which are slaughtered as a sacrifice to mark the final departure of the dead person from the social sphere of the living and his aggregation to the ancestors. In reality, almost every clan has its own modifications in the details of the rite. In some clans it is performed for all males who have begotten children, in others for lineage heads only, in others for both men and women; and the people of Kpata'ar omit the rite altogether. The rite is found also among many of the *tɛndaanditib* lineages of the Sie district, with diverse local variations.

Similar local variations from clan to clan appear in the other parts of the funeral ceremonies where the usages of the Talis contrast with those of the Namoos, and many, if not most, of these distinct customs are found among the *tɛndaanditib* of the Sie district.

These variations in ritual observances, and their correlation with structural ties and cleavages, are constantly brought to an observer's attention. They form a common topic of discussion and comment at funeral ceremonies. One is often reminded of them by the behaviour of women at these ceremonies. A woman's husband's clan very often has different ritual practices from those of her father's clan. Now, married

124 TOTEMISM AMONG THE TALIS AND OTHER NON-NAMOOS

daughters always come to funerals in their paternal family. They have special ritual duties, some specific to that clan, some more general. They are apt, then, to follow the procedures to which they have become accustomed in their husband's home and have, therefore, to be closely supervised.

In all these mortuary and funeral rites there is a tendency for the plainsmen to have one type of variant, while the Hill clans favour another. There is less variation in the details of rites among the clans of either group than between the two groups, and the clans at the foot of the Hills show variants of ritual usage intermediate between those of the plains Talis and of the Hill clans. Thus, one of the most solemn and sacred of the rites which transform the brute fact of death into the mystical fact of spiritual status is the rite of *kpe kpiintaŋ*. It is usually regarded as distinctive of the Namoos, but it occurs also in the funeral ceremonies of tɛndaanas and elders at Zubiuŋ, Ba'ari, Gbizug, and Wakii (the Talis clans contiguous with the Namoos) as well as among some of the non-Namoo clans of the Sie area. The Hill Talis attribute this to contamination by the customs of the Namoos. There are one or two rites which the plains Talis have and the Hill Talis lack altogether. There is, therefore, a broad distinction corresponding to the division between the clans that celebrate *Da'a* and those that celebrate *Bɔyaraam* as their Harvest Festival. But the two clusters overlap, as they do structurally, and the Talis overlap with the *tɛndaanditib* of the Sie area by the criterion of funeral customs as they do by those of locality and structure.

The funeral customs of the Talis, it is clear, are directly correlated with the structure of the society. The broad patterns of doctrine and ritual practice are the same for all Tallensi, and are an indication of their uniform culture and of a social structure which embraces all the Tallensi in a single system. More specific patterns of doctrine and practice are followed exclusively by the Talis and their congeners elsewhere in Taleland. They are an index of the structural differentiation of these clans from the Namoos. Some of these patterns are common to all or most of the Talis clans, and correspond therefore to the network of clanship and other structural ties linking them all to one another. Other specific patterns of funeral customs mark off lesser regions within the whole cluster of Talis clans. And finally, variations in detail correspond to the genealogical differentiation of clan from clan and lineage from lineage, and to the fact that each unit has a specific field of social relations not wholly congruent with that of any other unit of a like sort. The natives understand this. As we have noted before, they see variant ritual beliefs and practices of all kinds, and especially variant mortuary and funeral customs, as ways in which the corporate identity and the continuity of lineage and clan are expressed. They consider such variations within the limits of common patterns as belonging to the very fabric of their social organization.

Totemic Avoidances and Clanship Ties

The connexion between ritual observances and the social structure can be even more plainly seen in the totemic avoidances of the Talis and the

TOTEMISM AMONG THE TALIS AND OTHER NON-NAMOOS 125

other non-Namoos. It is recognized by all Tallensi that these taboos are on a par with the fowl taboo of the Namoos, though they have, in many respects, a more complex meaning. Among both groups of clans, no doubt because totemic taboos are so clear-cut and categorical, it is considered unthinkable for an adult in full command of his faculties to violate (*galəm*) a totemic taboo deliberately. The sanctions for an accidental breach are the same in both groups, but this is an extremely rare occurrence. It is enough to see the spontaneous repugnance of small children to unaccustomed or forbidden food to understand why they keep totemic taboos so conscientiously. A man never allows a prohibited animal into his house; and women married to men who may eat animals forbidden to themselves take scrupulous care to avoid a possible lapse. His totemic taboos appear to the individual as a simple, unequivocal moral precept.

Talis state their totemic avoidances in the form: 'We do not eat (*ti pu ɔbət*) or we taboo (*kih*) such and such an animal', meaning a particular species of animal. They explain that these avoidances are obligatory on a person through the fact of his being born a member of a certain maximal lineage; they are obligatory on both men and women from birth to death. Hence the wives of Talis have to refrain from eating animals prohibited to their husbands, though not to their own maximal lineages, when they have infants at the breast, or, in some clans, throughout their child-bearing period. For, as the natives explain, 'Food changes into milk', and the infant would be committing a sin indirectly. This problem does not arise amongst the Namoos, since all Tale women avoid eating the domestic fowl from the beginning of pubescence onwards. It is one of several food taboos observed by women with the utmost strictness, not for ritual reasons but purely as a matter of feminine propriety.

As with the Namoos, Talis totems and the totems of their congeners in the Sie area, are mythically validated, as we shall see presently. But like Namoos, Talis never express awe or reverence for a clan or lineage totem animal. It is an ordinary, commonplace creature devoid of anything in the nature of a halo of sacredness. They do not, for example, call a totem a sacred object (*bayər*). The emphasis is on the avoidance, the act of conduct as such. There is a notion of moral obligation in keeping the avoidance, but it is directed, as we shall see, to the ancestors and not to the totem animal in its own right.

Talis are not forbidden to kill an animal which is their totemic avoidance, though they would not wantonly do so. They may, and often do, catch these animals alive and sell them to people who are permitted to eat them; for many of these totem animals are considered to be great delicacies.

In one respect, however, the totemic avoidances of the Talis and their congeners differ from the fowl taboo of the Namoos. The former swear an oath by their totems, whereas the Namoos never invoke the fowl in this way. Like the Namoos, Talis can swear by the loin cover they put on their dead. The formula is the same as for the Namoos, with the substitution of the name of the animal whose skin is used: 'By my father and his sheep (or oribi) and his three cowrie shells.' This is a solemn oath, uttered in response to a serious accusation, in proof of one's innocence,

126 TOTEMISM AMONG THE TALIS AND OTHER NON-NAMOOS

I was told. I have never heard it used by anybody, and this itself shows how seriously it is taken.

The oath by the totem is not quite so serious a matter, though it could not be uttered with impunity. The formula is: '*Pakur ni nnuoni*—the tortoise and inside my mouth', if the totemic animal is the tortoise, or, in free translation: 'By the tortoise which I may not eat.' This oath might be used in trivial circumstances. Thus, if a man were wrongly accused of adultery he might swear by his father. But if he were accused of having appropriated something belonging to a friend or relative without permission, though admittedly without intending to steal it, he would swear to his innocence with an oath by his totem. It is the sort of oath, too, informants said, that one might use to assert one's truthfulness in an argument. A person who swears falsely by his totem would decline in health and begin to waste away (*burəm*), but he could probably be saved by atoning sacrifices. A person who swears one of the greater oaths, including the oath by one's father, falsely, will probably die. That is how the natives distinguish the degrees of sacredness they attach to these oaths. Again, I have never heard a totemic oath used, but I have discussed the matter with many people, both young and old, and their views are unanimous. Tallensi are reluctant to swear an oath except in an issue of real importance, and then they resort to the most solemn oath that is appropriate in the situation.

There is nothing secret about these totemic avoidances. Knowledge of them is public and widespread, though not always accurate where the totems of other clans than one's own are concerned. People become acquainted with the totemic avoidances of other clans through their ties of extra-clan kinship, and women spread the knowledge of the totemic avoidances of their paternal clans among the clans into which they marry. An amusing instance of the way in which this knowledge spreads occurred with one of my own boys. He was a Namoo, and one day bought a live water-tortoise from a Tɛnzugu youth. This is a great delicacy, but, as he told me afterwards, the cooking of it cost him almost more trouble than it was worth. For he had to cook it himself, out of doors in a borrowed pot, because his wife, a Tɛnzugu woman, was prohibited from eating this animal and refused to let him contaminate her kitchen or her cooking utensils with it.

It is never necessary for Tallensi to ask one another what their totemic avoidances are. When a person is required, for ritual reasons, to observe the taboos of another clan, the people of that clan who come to perform the rites that impose these taboos on him tell him about them. But one can ask a person, 'What do you (i.e. such and such a clan or lineage) taboo? (*ya kiha lani*)', or, 'What do you swear by? (*ya pɔta lani*)', in order to ascertain a group's totemic avoidances.

The animals most widely avoided among the Talis are the tortoise (*pakur*) and the water tortoise (*mieŋ*). Zubiuŋ, Gbizug, and most of the Hill clans taboo both these animals. But there are several exceptions. None of the clans on the Degal side of the Hills keep these avoidances, nor do the people of Tamboog, and only the senior maximal lineage of the three constituent lineages of Soog has them. The people of Degal,

TOTEMISM AMONG THE TALIS AND OTHER NON-NAMOOS 127

for example, avoid the squirrel (*sinsɛrɔg*); the Tamboog people do not eat the dog (*baa*), the leopard (*yeogbaa*), the monkey (*ŋmaaŋ*), and the hare (*suoŋ*).

The majority of the clans which observe the two characteristic avoidances of the Talis have additional discriminatory totems. Zubiuŋ has the cat (*sakoo*); at Wakii it is the snake (*waaf*), and this includes all species of snake, even the innocent little green *bɛnɔrɔg* which children of other clans kill and eat. A whole group of clans, including all that part of the network of linked lineages that connects Bunkiuk, Yinduur, Sii, and Gorogo, taboo the snake and the crocodile (*baŋ*) in addition to the land and water tortoises. Among these clans a snake that injures a domestic animal or a person is killed without hesitation, and if it is of an edible species, such as the python (*wayakpɛm*), it will be given to a friend or kinsman of a neighbouring clan which does not taboo snakes. This rule applies to all species of dangerous animals that serve as totems to a clan. If they injure mankind, or man's property, they are transgressing (*galɔm*) and deserve to be killed. This does not mean, however, that the Tallensi conceive of a special tie of friendship or kinship between a clan and its totem animals. But we shall come back to this point later.

Ba'ari and Yaɣazuor, with the exception of one accessory lineage, do not fall into the same circle of totemic avoidances. Their taboos vary from one maximal lineage to another. Thus, Ba'at-Sakpar taboos the dog and the hare; but Lakum yiri has no totemic avoidances.

When a clan or lineage has several totemic avoidances they are all considered to be of equal importance. In some situations the totems common to several clans are stressed, in others the natives draw attention to those which differentiate units among a number that have some common totems. There is no precise correlation between the ties of clanship and the distribution of totemic avoidances. Tamboog and Gundaat, closely allied as they are by ties of clanship, have different totemic avoidances. The constituent maximal lineages of clans like Soog and Ba'ari have no common totems, nor have the linked lineages of Zubiuŋ and Ba'ari, or Soog and Sakpee. Conversely, common totemic avoidances do not by themselves indicate the existence of clanship ties. Ba'at-Sakpar has no clanship ties with Tamboog, though both taboo the dog and the hare, and the avoidance of the Degal people is found also among some clans of the Sie area which have no ties of clanship with Degal. It follows from this that (as among the Namoos) common totemic prohibitions are not a bar to marriage; lineage and clan exogamy operate in terms of clanship ties only.

On the other hand, clanship ties are in some instances associated with totemic avoidances. Dun biis of Ba'ari are said to observe the same avoidances as the Hill Talis, because they have clanship ties with Samiit. Alaa biis of Ŋkoog have the totemic taboos of Wakii, as well as those of Ŋkoog proper (a Namoo clan), because of their clanship ties with Wakii. Both these are attached lineages, whose descent is attributed to a son of a clan sister who had been married to a Samiit and a Wakii man respectively and had subsequently been divorced and sent back home with her children. The two lineages thus preserve the avoidances of what would

128 TOTEMISM AMONG THE TALIS AND OTHER NON-NAMOOS

have been their founding ancestors' paternal clans. In other cases the correlation is not so clear, since the attached lineages concerned are intercalary between clans that have the same avoidances. But it is not a general rule that attached lineages preserve the avoidances of the clan of the alleged father of their founding ancestor, as can be seen from the case of Ba'at-Lakum yidɛm, who do not keep the Zubiuŋ taboos.

Thus Talis sometimes cite common totemic and other ritual observances as a sign of clanship ties, and at other times deny any necessary connexion between ritual observances and clanship ties. When they want to emphasize the close interdependence, or the sense of community of a particular group of clans, by contrast with other Talis or non-Talis clans, they tend to pick on common ritual observances in proof of this. But on the other hand, they are equally ready to quote peculiar totemic taboos as signs of the genealogical or social singularity of a clan or lineage. The apparent inconsistency does not worry them. For, as we have seen, Tallensi cannot visualize precisely the structure of their society in its entirety, and there is good evidence for both views in the ritual observances of the Talis. There is a tendency for some clans that are closely interconnected to have some totems in common, and for others to have different totems.

The totemic avoidances found among the clans of the Sie district in general follow the pattern found at Ba'ari; but in this area there is no close-knit nuclear aggregate of clans like the Hill Talis. The relative autonomy of the maximal lineage stands out more markedly, and there is consequently a greater diversity of totemic avoidances.

Totemic Myths

We have previously remarked that Namoos show little interest in the mythology of their totemic taboos. This attitude is characteristic of all Tallensi. Talis elders, whose authority and wisdom in ritual matters were widely respected, and who willingly gave me information of the most secret kind, were content to dismiss the question of the origin of their totemic taboos with some trite remark such as, 'We grew up to find it thus'. But here and there one comes across a myth accounting for the origin of a totemic taboo, especially in the Sie area. They are all expansions of the text 'The animal conferred a benefit on our ancestor (*u daa maal ti yaab la*)'. Though they all have the same moral, they vary greatly in substance.

Thus, according to one version, the avoidance of the tortoise and water-tortoise among the Hill Talis began in this way: 'Our (anonymous) ancestor' was suffering severely from thirst once and could find no water. He saw a tortoise crawling along and followed it. The animal reached a heap of dry leaves, which it scratched aside revealing a spring. Thereupon 'our ancestor' vowed that never again would he or his descendants eat the tortoise; and as the water-tortoise is merely another species of the same family, this taboo naturally extends to it as well.

According to another version, which is worth quoting as an example of the variations in these myths, 'our ancestor' was on a journey and was

TOTEMISM AMONG THE TALIS AND OTHER NON-NAMOOS 129

held up by an impassable river. He noticed a water-tortoise descending the bank, and followed it. Thus he was led to a ford, which enabled him to cross. Thereupon he vowed that he and his descendants would refrain from eating this animal and its brother species, the tortoise.

Similar myths are current among other clans that taboo aquatic animals. Thus one of the segments of Sie have the special avoidance of the crocodile in addition to the usual fowl avoidance of the Namoos. The head of this segment told me the following myth in explanation. There was a communal fish drive, during which their ancestor, Layεn, disappeared. He was given up for lost, and next day a party was dispatched to search for the body. But when they reached the river, they found him sitting on the bank with a crocodile at his feet. He told them that the crocodile had saved his life (*fa u ɲovor bah*) by holding him down and covering him up. Hence he vowed that he and his descendants would never again eat crocodile.

In the same way the elders of Gban narrate that 'their ancestor' was suffering with a swollen hand. He asked friends to lance it, but they thought this was unnecessary. Then one day, as he sat resting his hand on his head because of the pain, a large grasshopper of a species with sharply serrated legs (*saŋkaan*) landed on it. The ancestor scared it away. As it leaped off, it kicked out and ripped the skin of the festering hand with its saw-edged legs. This let out the accumulated pus and cured the hand. Thereupon the ancestor vowed, in the phrase that usually concludes these myths, 'May he grow old with his grandson, but no descendant of his should ever again eat the *saŋkaan* (*ɔn kɔragɔn ni u yaaŋa, ka ɔn bii ku le di saŋkaan*)'.

Other myths of this kind relate how the anonymous ancestor was saved from an enemy about to slay him by the opportune appearance of the totemic animal. Thus, according to one of the elders of Sawalɔg: 'Bows were in conflict (*tap ndaa ŋme*)', ('Perhaps', he added, as an afterthought, 'there was a fight with Mamprusi who came to raid for slaves') 'and our ancestor fled, seeking refuge in an animal's burrow. The enemy was about to break open the burrow when a squirrel (*sinsεrɔg*) darted past. They turned to pursue it, and left our ancestor. Thereupon, he vowed never to eat the squirrel again, neither he nor his descendants.'

As this sample of totemic myths shows, the pattern is the same as that of the Namoo myth accounting for the fowl avoidance. They are more unstable in content, however. The two versions of the tortoise myth were obtained from two equally authoritative elders of the same clan. There is, indeed, always an element of speculation, or of *ad hoc* construction, in these myths. Listening to them one often has the feeling that they are being elaborated by logical deduction. The starting-point is the premiss that the totemic avoidance was due to a vow made by 'our ancestor' in gratitude for an extraordinary service that saved his life. The process of reasoning is to deduce an action on the part of the animal consistent with its known peculiarities of appearance and of behaviour. Informants are never able to tell one where and when they first heard these myths. They say vaguely: 'We heard them from our fathers.' This method of reasoning, however, is congenial to the Tallensi. It forms the

K

130 TOTEMISM AMONG THE TALIS AND OTHER NON-NAMOOS

basis, for instance, of their technique of divination, which depends on rapid and spontaneous inference from stereotyped signs and symbols.

These myths provide yet another illustration of the indifference of the Tallensi to the origins of their customs. The emphasis in their culture is on conduct, not on creed; on performance rather than on doctrine. At the same time, these myths express, as we have previously noted, the basic postulate of Tale philosophy—that the ancestors are the *fons et origo* of their whole social order—and they show also how the natives visualize their totemic taboos as symbols of the moral and ritual bonds imposed by agnatic descent.

The Totemic Avoidances of the Talis as a Reflex of the Social Structure

We can now resume our analysis of the relationship of Talis ritual observances to the social structure. We have considered certain funeral rites and totemic avoidances as the chief indices of structural differentiation. We have seen that they are not, as the natives sometimes imply, hard-and-fast criteria. They mark off the Talis cluster from the Namoos in a broad way, but reflect the overlapping between them which our study of the clanship system has brought out. And among the Talis themselves, though there is a considerable congruence between genealogical grouping as determined by the canon of agnatic descent and distinctive ritual observances, it is not a one-to-one relationship.

The funeral customs and totemic taboos we have reviewed have one feature in common which helps to explain why the natives think of them as indices of social differentiation. They are tied to the agnatic line, passed on from father to child just like membership of the lineage. They owe their binding force to the fact that they were, according to native belief, instituted by the ancestors of the lineage or clan. Hence arises a significant common element, the oath associated with the observance. Breach of the ritual observance or using the oath falsely is blasphemy against the ancestors.

We pick up this thread again in another sphere of the ritual system of the Talis. It is a common opinion in Taleland that the taboos against eating the tortoise and water-tortoise are specially characteristic of the Hill Talis. And the reason always given for this is that these taboos are connected with the Talis cult of the External *Bɔyar*. Among the Hill Talis, if a child transgresses the taboo (*galɔm kihɔr*) by eating of the forbidden animal, its father 'pays' (*yɔ*) a fowl to the External *Bɔyar* of which his clan is an adherent. The fowl is sacrificed at the *Bɔyar*, with apologies for the transgression and pleas for the child's future well-being. A fine is thus paid to annul the trespass, and the smallness of the fine is evidence that the trespass is not considered serious.

As a rule, the group of clans and maximal lineages forming the congregation of a particular External *Bɔyar* all have the same avoidances. Thus, all the units that owe ritual allegiance to Bona'ab, the External *Bɔyar* of Kpata'ar and its associated lineages, taboo the tortoise and the water-tortoise. Hence, individuals who are the spiritual wards of Bona'ab may not eat these animals, and, if they belong to other clans or other

TOTEMISM AMONG THE TALIS AND OTHER NON-NAMOOS 131

tribes with different taboos, they must observe these in addition to the taboos of their own clan. One segment of Samiit, which also belongs to this congregation, is prohibited in addition from eating the snake, so a supplicant coming to the *Bɔyar* sponsored by Samiit must refrain also from eating the snake. Wannii, another well-known External *Bɔyar* in the Hills, includes in its congregation only clans and lineages which taboo the snake and crocodile as well as the tortoise and water-tortoise. Hence, children of strangers who are the spiritual wards of this *Bɔyar* must avoid all four animals. Clans and lineages that have atypical totems also have independent External *Bɔya*.

Among the Hill Talis, then (and this applies also to the people of Zubiuŋ and Gbeog), common totems generally indicate membership of the same External *Bɔyar* congregation. This means that the clans and lineages concerned are subject to common ritual sanctions in terms of the ancestor cult, embodied in common cult objects and ceremonies. It implies obligatory bonds of amity and interdependence on the politico-ritual plane, prohibiting recourse to arms, for example, as a means of redressing wrongs between member lineages of the same congregation, or acts of hostility such as the abduction of a fellow member's wife, though he may not be a kinsman. It implies formal duties of member lineage to member lineage in funeral ceremonies; and it creates a feeling of belonging together, of spontaneous goodwill towards one another, among the member lineages, which even the bitter political dissensions of to-day have not altogether destroyed. Belonging to the same religious community in itself connotes social ties analogous to those of clanship.

The *Bɔyar* cult resembles other forms of ritual observance tied to the notion of descent in that there is an oath associated with it. It emphasizes the key idea of the cult, the dominance of the collective ancestors, as we shall see shortly. For that matter, this idea is the main theme of all the rites and doctrines of the cult—the initiation of youths by 'handing them over to their ancestors' as the Talis put it; the Harvest and Sowing Festivals; and no less in such minor things as entrusting a recalcitrant wife, the source of future descendants, to the *Bɔyar* or the coercion of an adulterous wife by means of it.

But before we deal with these points, an aspect of the *Bɔyar* cult to which we have previously referred must be further discussed. An External *Bɔyar* can become the spirit-guardian (*sɛyɔr*) of an individual. An ancestor spirit who becomes a person's spirit-guardian is defined in native religious doctrine as 'He who has my life in his keeping so that I exist (*ɔn m-mar n-ŋovor ka mbɛ*)', and the ward (*sɛyɔraan*) must keep the totemic avoidances of the *Bɔyar* community. This applies particularly to non-Talis (Mamprusi, Dagomba, Bulisi, and others) who come as pilgrims to the *Bɔyar* to supplicate for children. The special bonds of ritual dependence thus created include both the parents and the children born, as the natives believe, in answer to their prayers. The Hill Talis themselves keep the avoidances whether or not they are personally the wards of the *Bɔyar*; for, as they put it, they are all *ipso facto* under its spiritual guardianship.

If a stranger pilgrim has a child in answer to his prayers, his first duty

132 TOTEMISM AMONG THE TALIS AND OTHER NON-NAMOOS

is to pay over the gifts and sacrifices he has promised the *Bɔyar* in return. Later, when the child is old enough to travel, it is brought to the *Bɔyar* to be ritually dedicated to it and named, and thus brought into communion with it. Wards of the *Bɔyar* have prescribed names according to their order of birth. First-borns are always Tɔŋ or Bɔyare; later children have names compounded of these two names and suffixes indicative of sex or birth order—Tɔndoog or Tɔnpɔk or Tanzoo, and so forth. A girl ward must remain chaste until she marries; and when she is given in marriage she has to be released from this bond by means of gifts and sacrifices to the *Bɔyar* before she goes to her husband.

The ritual dominion of the Hill Talis' External *Bɔya* extends, also, to whole clans and lineages of non-Tale tribes as we shall see later. Here it is enough to mention that every External *Bɔyar* of the Hill Talis has a traditional network of client lineages and clans among the adjacent non-Tale tribes, the Mamprusi, Dagomba, Bulisi, Woolisi, and even Mossi; and nowadays also in Ashanti and the Colony. Every year, at the time of the Harvest Festivals, these client lineages send messengers with gifts and sacrifices to the *Bɔyar* to which they adhere, to give thanks for the benefits of the past year and to pray for good crops, good health, peace, and offspring during the coming year. Client lineages also observe the totemic and other ritual rules of the *Bɔyar*. From time to time reciprocal visits are paid to the client lineages by representatives of the Hill Talis lineages that sponsor them before the *Bɔyar*. These visitors, coming as emissaries of the *Bɔyar*, are received with the hospitality due to honoured kinsmen and travel long distances in hostile country under the safe conduct of their client associates without danger. It is chiefly from its client lineages that pilgrims come to a particular *Bɔyar*.

The personal totemic avoidances of wards of a Talis *Bɔyar* are instances of a more general rule. It often happens that a child's spirit-guardian is a matrilateral ancestor or ancestress, its father's maternal grandfather, for instance. Then the ward (*sɛyəraan*) is obliged to observe the totemic avoidances which were held by his spirit-guardian during the latter's lifetime. He must do so, according to native doctrine, because he will have to offer sacrifices throughout his lifetime to his spirit-guardian; and as a sacrifice is an act of communion, both between the living, and between the living and the dead, he would be unable either to offer or to partake of sacrifices to his spirit-guardian if he did not keep the latter's taboos. Thus he would nullify the bond of mystical tutelage and lay himself open to inevitable disasters. He would also gravely damage his relations with the agnatic descendants of his spirit-guardian, upon whom falls the duty of maintaining the cult of the latter's spirit and whom he will sometimes have to join in sacrifice. There are many people among the Namoos who observe Talis taboos for this reason, and many Talis who avoid both the totems of their own clan and those of other clans as well. The fowl taboo of the Namoos is an exception to this rule, for the obvious reason that it is restricted to first-born children. Even if a man had to avoid the fowl in his lifetime, it ceases to be relevant after his death, and is no longer remembered by his descendants. But the rule does apply to the ancillary totems of those Namoo clans and lineages that have any, such as the

TOTEMISM AMONG THE TALIS AND OTHER NON-NAMOOS 133

leopard taboo of Ŋkoog; for these taboos are of the same class as those of the Talis.

An individual's avoidance of his matrilateral spirit-guardian's totems is, of course, an avoidance of the totems of the latter's lineage. They are the people who have the custody of the shrine at which sacrifices must be offered to the *sɛyɔr* spirit; their mediation is essential for a correct relationship between ward and spirit-guardian. It is with them, the living members of the spirit-guardian's lineage, that the ward shares the communion of sacrifice, and this is the fundamental condition for preserving the mystical goodwill of the *sɛyɔr*. On the same principle, a person given as ward to a Talis *Bɔyar* would be precluded from sacrificing to the *sɛyɔr*, that is from sharing in the communion of sacrifice with the members of the *Bɔyar* congregation through whom alone ritual access can be gained to the *Bɔyar*, if he does not observe their totemic avoidances. This is the symbol of the unique religious and moral bond between them. There are other ways, too, in which a matrilateral ancestor can be endowed with direct and permanent ritual efficacy for a man. Such a spirit may become (*naam*) his divining spirit (*bakologo*) or his Destiny (*yin*). Then he will have to call upon this ancestor's agnatic descendants to come and consecrate a shrine to the spirit at his house. He will have to sacrifice to this spirit and share the communion of sacrifice with the spirit's agnatic descendants. Therefore, he, too, must respect the totems of this matrilateral ancestor's lineage.

We see, therefore, that an individual can have private totemic observances not shared by other members of his lineage or clan. Like clan totems, however, they become obligatory on him in virtue of a particular tie of descent. Superficially, they can be understood as emblems of this tie and of the living kinship ties that flow from it. But there is more to it than this, as we see from the totemic bond between stranger wards of an External *Bɔyar* and the *Bɔyar* congregation.

The stranger ward and his parents are not kinsmen of the lineage that sponsors them. But they do acquire a relationship of what might be called quasi-kinship with their sponsors and a ritual bond with the *Bɔyar* which carries social duties and religious obligations equivalent to those of adherents by descent of the *Bɔyar*. These relationships are based on the fact that stranger pilgrims establish a line of descent through the mystical aid of the *Bɔyar*. It is, as the natives put it, 'because it is on his (the *Bɔyar's*) account that we have begotten children'.

Similarly, the association of totemic and other ritual observances with lineage and clanship groupings is seen to have a wider significance when the client lineages of Hill Talis *Bɔya* are brought into the picture. The ties between client lineages and the true member lineages of the *Bɔyar* to which they owe ritual allegiance may be called quasi-clanship, to sum up the native interpretation of the relationship in one word.

Totemic Taboos and the Patrilineal Principle

We have endeavoured to keep the information adduced in the preceding pages down to the minimum necessary for our argument. It is enough, however, to justify the conclusion that the ritual observances we have

134 TOTEMISM AMONG THE TALIS AND OTHER NON-NAMOOS

been discussing have a deeper meaning to the natives than merely as convenient indices of social differentiation. It is on account of their deeper meaning that they serve also, in certain contexts, to identify corporate units. The very casualness with which Tallensi speak of their totemic taboos; the unquestioning way in which they take their funeral customs for granted; and at the other extreme, the connexion of these ritual observances with the supreme religious institution of the Hill Talis, whose influence pervades their whole social life, all show that we are dealing with something that goes down to the axiomatic ideas and values that underpin the social structure.

These ritual institutions, with their common pattern of injunction, oath, and determination by descent or quasi-descent, form part of an interlocked system of religious values that springs directly out of the social structure. Their common focus is the notion of dependence on the ancestors determined by the fact of descent. But it is not descent in its physiological sense that they refer to. They symbolize the fact that descent, to the Tallensi, axiomatically creates bonds of moral and ritual interdependence and obligation. It is because, as we have previously seen, Tallensi tend to read into all ritual relations, whatever their derivation, corresponding genealogical relationships; because the relations of mutual amity and co-operation, even though only in a limited sphere of conduct, imposed by ritual ties are of the same type as those imposed by ties of kinship; because all the rights and duties determined by descent are kept in force by the sanction of the ancestor spirits, that the values appropriate to the sphere of kinship and descent merge with those expressed in religious cult and doctrine. There is a syncretism in the Tale system of ideas and values that images their syncretic social structure. Lineage system and ancestor cult interfuse and at the same time mirror each other.

Our analysis can be carried farther if we consider what lineage membership means. It is created by the bare physiological fact of patrilineal descent. But the physiological links between the individual and his ancestors and between all the living members of the lineage have no social significance except as the kernel of the social relations and bonds that come out in economic affairs such as the ownership and use of land; in the exercise of moral and jural rights and duties, as in marriage or parenthood; in ritual belief and practice, as in the ancestor cult. This is the stuff of individual and collective life for the native wherever—and this applies to almost everything he does—the fact of descent is relevant. Membership of his lineage, or his clan, or of a religious community means, to the individual, a particular collection of people taken severally in some situations, collectively in others, with whom he has certain kinds of known and regular social relations reflecting their common interests, and based on the continuity and integrity of the group; and he submits to a number of restraints on word and deed in order to maintain his relations with them. A man experiences this in a multitude of particular actions and events, day after day.

As a member of a particular lineage a man has definite rights and duties and enters into a stream of social relations from which all who do not

TOTEMISM AMONG THE TALIS AND OTHER NON-NAMOOS 135

belong to that agnatic line are excluded. It is a fact that marks him off from a great many people who come into his range of contact. It determines, for example, whom he may or may not marry, what social roles he may or may not exercise, who will support him in his troubles, where he will make his farms, and especially which named ancestors ritually accessible at certain definite, material shrines govern his life. Of course lineage membership, as we know, isolates only the central area of a person's field of social relations, as this is determined by his birth. Lineage membership, clan membership, and membership of the wider community of the Hill Talis, or of a *Bɔyar* congregation, are all primarily determined by the fact of birth; and the social relations by which one zone is distinguished from the next in the total field all belong to the same category.

All the members of the lineage are equally members of it, irrespective of age, sex, or status. The social bonds that define the limits of the lineage and mark its social identity for its members are equally binding on all its members. They all share the sentiments engendered by membership of the lineage. They all feel themselves to be embraced within its corporate unity. These are matters of everyday practical experience. But behind them lies the deep sense of the continuity of the agnatic line. This takes the form, in the individual, of a great pride in his ancestry and a strong feeling of identification with the other members of the lineage and with the lineage as a unit in their common dependence on their ancestors.

At their simplest, the totemic and funeral taboos of the Talis are symbolic expressions of the irrevocable and supremely important fact of lineage membership. But if that were all, they might not have taken a ritual form. Among the Talis we can see more plainly than among the Namoos why these symbols of the social identity conferred on individuals and groups by agnatic descent take the form of ritual observances.

Agnatic descent, as we have pointed out, automatically puts one under moral bonds to certain other people. There is no choice about membership of one's lineage. And there can be no questioning or choosing in the matter of the basic norms of lineage relations. One has rights and duties towards one's co-members of the lineage, amity for them, interest in them, common concerns with them, simply and solely because they are of the same agnatic line. Lineage norms are absolutely binding, and the sanction for this is the common ritual dependence of all the members on their ancestors. This is crystallized in the cult of the lineage *bɔyar*, the thing in which the spiritual jurisdiction of the ancestors over all the lineage members is made tangible and accessible to human thought and action. The lineage as a social entity is founded on moral and ritual imperatives. This is how the natives feel it: we need not here concern ourselves with possible scientific explanations of this fact. What matters is that this sense of the moral and ritual imperatives behind lineage relations, explicitly brought out as it is in the cult of the ancestors, is also diffused through all the relations of lineage members. The function of totemic taboos is to crystallize in a clear-cut, concrete, external object of no intrinsic significance this diffused sense of the moral and ritual imperatives behind lineage bonds. The taboos are simple and definite

136 TOTEMISM AMONG THE TALIS AND OTHER NON-NAMOOS

imperatives symbolizing those other more fundamental imperatives. The very fact that they are trivial in themselves and can be easily remembered and kept without hardship by young and old make them the more effective as social symbols.[1] The natives, of course, cannot formulate such an explanation of their totemic taboos. It can only be inferred from their attitudes and actions just as we infer from our economic actions and attitudes that coins and notes are the symbols of goods and services.

Totemic taboos, it must be remembered, are not the only ritual observances through the medium of which the Talis mark the fact of lineage membership. Lineage membership has many facets, as we have seen, and sometimes one facet is uppermost in thought or action, sometimes another. Two of these facets have principally concerned us here. A person's membership of the lineage emerges in its corporate activities as a unit of social structure; common interests and concerns prevail and the individual counts only as a component of the group. It is as a corporate unit that the lineage has its ritual focus in the lineage bɔyar. Though each member stands under the governance of the bɔyar, he cannot approach it except through the lineage head and in association with representatives of every branch of the lineage. On the other hand, every member of the lineage carries his lineage membership about with him, as it were, even on his private occasions; it is an abiding attribute of his social personality. We see this most plainly in the case of a woman member who is debarred by her sex from sharing completely in the corporate unity of the lineage. Yet she retains her membership of it all her life as a birthright.

It is this aspect of his lineage membership that is symbolically projected in the totemic taboos for the individual himself. They are to him a sign of his lineage membership and all that it means, a constant reminder of his moral bonds with his fellow members and his ancestors. Through them he expresses his pride in his ancestry and the deep value he attaches to the body of custom bequeathed to him and his fellows by his ancestors.

We can see, now, how the totemic equivalence of distinctive funeral customs comes about. Everything symbolized by totemic avoidances comes ultimately from the fact of birth, as a gift from one's father. On his death he goes to join the ancestors. The rites that transform him into an ancestor spirit express recognition of his role as transmitter of the unique agnatic line, and of the ritual sanctions he represents for the correct conduct of his son as a member of the lineage.

But membership of the lineage by birth makes one also a member of the clan. And this entails obligatory social relations with members of

[1] The connotation given to the word *symbol* in this argument will strike the reader as a cross between Freudian usage and Durkheimian usage. We mean by it (a) a complex of a material object, together with the ideas, beliefs, attitudes, and conventional actions associated with it, which (b) has no self-evident utilitarian or logical significance to the observer or even to the natives but (c) can be understood as explained in the text above. The point of importance for us is that the symbol carries a strong emotional charge and has the value of a direct moral imperative. If this were lacking we should have preferred to call Tale totems emblems or distinguishing devices.

other lineages. Though the norms of clanship and the social bonds that define the clan are an extension of those that hold within the lineage, they mark out a wider field of social relations for the individual. It is through his clanship ties that the individual gets bound up with the social order as a whole; through them he becomes a member of the wider community of the Hill Talis, which in turn forms part of the yet wider and looser community, the Tallensi in general. Through clan membership one belongs to a community, defined not by specific rights and duties based on the spiritual jurisdiction of one's own ancestors, but principally by common values and common ritual interests. Within the lineage the social personality of the individual is an important factor of his behaviour and of the behaviour of others towards him. Sex, age, and status are significant. In relations between lineages the social personality of the individual fades into the background. It is submerged in the corporate unity of the lineage.

Totems, Clanship, and External Bɔyar

The social bonds of clanship, like those of the lineage, derive their validity from the ancestors. But it is now not a question of a particular known line of ancestry, but of the ancestors in general; and among the Hill Talis these are associated with the External *Bɔyar*.

The External *Bɔyar* is an elaboration of the lineage *bɔyar*, parallel to the elaboration of the lineage structure into the structure of the clan and the network of clanship. It is the seat of all the ancestors of the clans and lineages that make up its congregation. As we have previously learnt, each External *Bɔyar* is the pivot of a group of structurally connected clans and lineages, and at the same time the local embodiment of a single cult embracing all the Hill Talis. Thus the cult of the External *Bɔyar* maintains ritually sanctioned social bonds between a particular group of maximal lineages, and at the same time symbolizes the fundamental common values of all the Hill Talis. It is the quintessence of the social identity of the Hill Talis. Hence, they say that when a boy has been initiated into this cult, 'he at length knows (what it means to be) a Talɔŋ (*u pana baŋ Talɔŋ*)'. The esoteric significance of the fact of being a Talɔŋ has been revealed to the boy. Before that he was a 'woman', a 'child'; now 'he has become an elder'. These terms are used metaphorically to indicate the boy's transformation from a person who was merely a member of the lineage by birth into a full social member of the clan and the wider community.

The *Bɔyar* is the apex of the whole ancestor cult of the Talis. It symbolizes the idea of the ancestors in general, the concept of ancestry, one might say, in contrast to the notion of a particular named line of ancestors. Thus, the Hill Talis speak of the External *Bɔyar*, and often invoke it in ritual, as *Yaab*, Ancestor, that is, the generic, prototypical, anonymous ancestor. The External *Bɔyar* symbolizes the ritual value of the Ancestors to all the Talis. It implies the subjection of all the Talis to a common spiritual jurisdiction, deriving from the Ancestors. It symbolizes the continuity of the whole social order conceived as brought into being by the Ancestors, and kept in being under their spiritual

138 TOTEMISM AMONG THE TALIS AND OTHER NON-NAMOOS

aegis. Initiation into the *Bɔyar* cult binds the individual by the most solemn covenant known to the natives to uphold the social order bequeathed to the living by the Ancestors; and this is a bond that transcends the lineage. It requires the interests of the lineage to be subordinated to those of the wider community in particular circumstances.

That this is so can be seen from the fact that the most solemn oath of the Hill Talis is the oath by the External *Bɔyar*—'(By) my Ancestor Tɔŋna'ab and his late-millet flour water (*Nyaab Tɔŋna'ab ni u za zɔm kuom*)'. It is strictly forbidden to use late-millet flour in sacrifices at the External *Bɔyar*. The climax of the initiation ceremony is the administration of this oath to the novices at the *Bɔyar*, pledging them, in the name of a thing sternly excluded from its rites, to observe the tenets of the cult and keep the secret of its rites. This oath, in contrast to the oath by the totem animal, is a matter of the utmost gravity. 'If we swear thus', an elder of one of the Hill clans explained to me in tones of obvious awe, 'we all who are Talaŋ, you know we are speaking the truth. If you swear thus and lie you will die.' It is an oath which would be resorted to only in an extremely serious matter; and its gravity for the Hill Talis is known all over Taleland.

The sanction of the oath is the covenant entered into by a man when he is initiated. The *Bɔyar* destroys a perjurer. 'Will you not be going into the *Bɔyar* to sacrifice, and eat of the (sacrificial) flour and (sacrificial) fowl? This is what kills you (if you swear falsely)', a ritual functionary of the cult declared. It is not even a question of literal participation in the ritual of worship at the *Bɔyar*. A man who has offended it cannot offer sacrifice to his own dead father at his own home; for his father had, in his lifetime, taken part in the sacraments of the cult, and was joined to all the ancestors, whose common shrine is the *Bɔyar*, on his death. By the same reasoning even uninitiated members of clans that belong to a *Bɔyar* congregation can validly use the oath, though they would be unlikely to do so. For they are also 'the children of the *Bɔyar*'; their life, too, is 'in the keeping' of the ancestors who abide there. They will become initiated members of the cult if they are men, and they are members of the lineages incorporated into the cult if they are women.

When Hill Talis are asked how their totemic taboos are connected with the cult of the External *Bɔyar*, they say 'they belong together (*ba tɔŋa taaba*)'. The phrase implies that the two things are different but intrinsically related. In fact, the Hill Talis think of all their ritual institutions as being somehow connected with the *Bɔyar* cult. For behind all of them stands the sanction of the ancestor spirits. Totemic taboos hold independently of the *Bɔyar* cult. Breach of them, or a false oath by the totem animals, does not provoke the wrath of the *Bɔyar*. Fines are paid to the *Bɔyar* for a breach of totemic taboos because it is the supreme manifestation of the ancestors. If a person transgresses an obligation that falls on him by virtue of his descent, it is obviously necessary to appease the ancestors. On the same principle, the Hill Talis hale an adulterous wife to the External *Bɔyar* in order to force her to confess; for her sin endangers the life of her husband and children and thus jeopardizes their line of descent. This is a matter of concern to the ancestors, not only

TOTEMISM AMONG THE TALIS AND OTHER NON-NAMOOS 139

to the husband's own ancestors, but to all the ancestors, for the whole social order is based on the continuity of the patrilineal line.

One reason why the totemic taboos of the Hill Talis 'belong together' with the cult of the External Bɔyar is because all Tale ritual institutions tie up with the ancestor cult; for Tale ritual ideas and values are, as we have several times emphasized, a reflex of the social structure and this rests on a genealogical basis. But the connexion can be seen in more precise terms. Membership of the lineage, which means adherence to the norms of lineage relations symbolized in the totemic taboos, is a prerequisite for membership of the clan and for admission to the Bɔyar cult. Just as the constitution of the Bɔyar congregation embraces and rests upon the lineage and clan, so the ritual values and observances of the Bɔyar cult draw the ritual symbols of lineage identity and continuity into their orbit. The External Bɔyar is a transposition of the lineage bɔyar to a higher level of social integration; allegiance to the External Bɔyar is an extension, on this higher level, of the bond with the lineage bɔyar. In terms of ritual observances, admission to the covenant of the External Bɔyar presupposes observance of certain totemic taboos. And this mutual implication is strengthened by the fact that every male of a Talis lineage is bound to become a member of the Bɔyar cult. Lineage, clan, and Bɔyar congregation represent three interconnected levels of social relations and the ritual observances that correspond to them. The simplest level of this field system implies the existence of the most complex which in turn presupposes the existence of the simplest.

It is a point of significance that women, though bound by the totemic taboos as members of the lineage, are not admitted to the cult of the External Bɔyar. This is not only because the cult of the ancestors is the exclusive province of men. Women marry out of the lineage; they do not pass on to their children physical or social membership of it; they do not perpetuate the lineage. It is the men who maintain and perpetuate the corporate unity and continuity of the lineage; and it is on these that both the clan structure and the Bɔyar cult rest. It is the men who both keep the lineage going as a social entity symbolized in its totemic taboos, and maintain the social order of which the External Bɔyar is the pivot.

In sum, then, the totem stands for the relative autonomy of the maximal lineage, the External Bɔyar for the interdependence of lineages in a single religious community; and the two ritual principles fuse owing to the fact that this ideological community is constituted by the knitting together of maximal lineages in local clusters. At the geographical centre of the ideological community, the summit of the Tong Hills, the fusion is most complete. The avoidance of the tortoise and the water-tortoise is shared by all the clans of the centre, and is felt by all the Talis to symbolize particularly membership of the ideological community as well as the narrower allegiance to the lineage. But some clans and lineages at the centre have additional or exceptional totems; and the farther we move from the centre towards Gbizug and Ba'ari out of the region of the External Bɔyar cult as practised by the Hill Talis, the more conspicuous do these extra avoidances become. Maximal lineages and clans which have

140 TOTEMISM AMONG THE TALIS AND OTHER NON-NAMOOS

extra or exceptional avoidances usually consider them to be more distinctive of themselves, though not more important, than the general taboos. In other words, these avoidances emphasize the relative autonomy of the maximal lineage in opposition to the coherence of the ideological community; and this is the more conspicuous the farther away from the centre a clan is located.

It is significant, however, that clans with additional or exceptional totems are not considered to be the less Talis for that reason. The people of Degal, for instance, who belong to the central cluster of Hill Talis, claim to be 'Talǝŋ' *par excellence* in virtue of their supposed descent from the primordial, earth-begotten tendaana of the Hills. It is a question of degree, the primacy of lineage membership being relatively stressed in the totemic avoidances of the deviant clans, the interdependence of corporate units in the greater aggregate being relatively stressed by most other Talis. From the point of view of the Hill Talis, there are, as we have learnt, two levels of interdependence amongst the Talis. There is the interdependence of the Hill clans *inter se*, focused in the External Bɔɣar cult, which extends as far as Zubiuŋ; and there is the interdependence of all the Talis—and in fact of Talis and Namoos—in the wider politico-ritual synthesis which emerges most conspicuously in the cycle of the Great Festivals. The clans associated in the narrower synthesis all tend to have the tortoise and the water-tortoise taboos; the clans associated only in the wider synthesis tend to have taboos stressing their genealogical autonomy; Zubiuŋ and Gbizug, which form the transition region, as it were, between the narrow association and the wide association, observe the tortoise and water-tortoise taboos, but do not consider them to be as distinctive of themselves as their special avoidances.

But this, we must not forget, is not the whole story. Totemic taboos, funeral rites, and Bɔɣar ritual are symbols. What they symbolize is the body of moral and ritual norms correlated to each of the three zones of social relations we have been considering—the norms which are the organizing values of lineage, clan, and ritual community. As these rest, in the final count, on the mystical supremacy of the ancestor spirits, we can say summarily that these ritual observances symbolize the ancestors in the various aspects under which they govern social and individual life among the Talis.

The Significance of Animals as Totems

The totemic avoidances of the Tallensi all refer to animals, and it may well be asked if they have any common characteristics or outstanding peculiarities from the native point of view. Totemic avoidances of the type we have recorded are found throughout Voltaic culture; in fact, they are a notable feature of social organization among all the negroid peoples of the western Sudan. Not only is their pattern the same throughout this region, but the animal species most commonly prohibited are the same, and the myths accounting for the taboos have the same form.[1] To

---

[1] Cf. for example, the reference to the *Tne* among the Bambara, in Monteil, Charles, op. cit. 134–5.

TOTEMISM AMONG THE TALIS AND OTHER NON-NAMOOS 141

speak only of the Voltaic area, the animal species referred to above occur among the totemic avoidances of people as remote from the Tallensi, both spatially and linguistically, as the Isala and the Lobi,[1] as well as among all the other 'tribes' of the area.

Confining ourselves to Taleland and to the settlements of Gɔrisi fringing this area, we find that the totemic avoidances include birds like the canary (*wurɔg*), the turtle-dove (*daŋman*), the domestic fowl (*noo*), and several other species; reptiles, like the snake, the tortoise, the water-tortoise, and the crocodile; fish, like the *tunɔg*; insects, like the large grass-hopper (*saŋkaan*); rodents, like the squirrel (*sinsɛrɔg*) and the hare (*suoŋ*); ruminants, like the goat (*buu*) and the sheep (*pɛhug*); carnivores, such as the cat (*sakoo*), the dog (*baa*), and the leopard (*yeogbaa*); and a variety of other animals, such as the monkey (*ŋmaaŋ*) and the bush-pig (*dee*).[2]

It is impossible to find any common trait amongst this variety of creatures. Some play an important part in the economic life and the food-supply of the natives, but the majority are negligible in this respect. Many are prized as delicacies by those who are permitted to eat them; and, on the other hand, some are despised as food. No adult would willingly eat grasshoppers, canaries, or small edible snakes, though little children, who eat almost any small animals they can lay their hands on, quite often do so. Several of these animal species are regarded as always potentially dangerous in the magical as well as the physical sense. Such are the crocodile, snakes, the leopard, and other wild carnivores. But many, on the contrary, are entirely innocent both in the magical and the physical sense. Some have a place in the meagre folk-lore of the Tallensi, including such diverse creatures as the monkey, the turtle-dove, and the cat. Cats, for instance, are considered to be pre-eminently the domestic companions of women, but with a streak of the wild animal in them. Women treat them with a mixture of solicitude, appropriate to a valued pet, and of pseudo-ritual respect that meets with good-humoured ridicule from the men. Incidentally, clans that have the cat as a totem show no particular respect towards household cats, nor are household dogs treated differently by people who may and people who may not eat the dog.

The totemic animals of the Tallensi thus comprise neither a zoological nor a utilitarian nor a magical class. All that can be said of them is that

---

[1] For the Isala and other 'tribes' of the Voltaic area, see Rattray, op. cit. His report on the Isala is in vol. ii, pp. 465 ff. For the Lobi, see ib., vol. ii, pp. 425 ff., and Labouret, op. cit., pp. 227 ff. Rattray does not distinguish clearly between the different kinds of ritual prohibitions and injunctions coupled with patrilineal descent, some of which are not totemic in the sense we have given to this term. But his observations and those of Labouret confirm the conclusion that there is no precise correlation between these avoidances and clanship ties. Labouret's account of the attitudes and values associated with totemic avoidances among the Lobi shows them to resemble closely those of the Tallensi.

[2] Rattray's list for this area, op. cit., vol. i, p. 236, includes also several big-game animals, such as the roan (*koo*), hartebeest (*sɛbɔg*), bush-cow (*yeognaaf*), and elephant (*wɔbɔg*), as well as the lion (*gbiaɣmɔr*), the hyena (*gbiŋgbɛr*), and the hippo (*ɛmɔr*). But here, as elsewhere in the book, Rattray appears to have lumped together ritual observances that are similar in form though not in function, and he does not state clearly what clans or settlements hold particular taboos.

142 TOTEMISM AMONG THE TALIS AND OTHER NON-NAMOOS

they are generally fairly common domestic or wild creatures. We have shown that the totemic avoidances of the Tallensi have a symbolic value in relation to their social organization. They are not, however, explicable simply as a function of the social structure. We cannot dismiss the choice of animal symbolism for this function as an accident of history or as mere coincidence. To understand it we should have to probe more deeply into the religious beliefs not only of the Tallensi but of all the peoples of this culture area. Animal and food taboos play a very important part in the ritual symbolism of Voltaic culture and indeed of West African cultures in general. We have repeatedly emphasized the intrinsic relation of the religious system of the Tallensi to their social structure. In a social system such as theirs, ritual ideas and values and the morphology of the society are interrelated as mind and body in the higher primates. But these two aspects of Tale society are not merely the obverse and reverse of the same coin. Though Tale religion springs directly out of the social structure, it is fed by streams whose sources lie beneath and beyond the social structure. We cannot pursue this theme here in detail, for it leads to problems of Tale psychology, and indeed of human psychology, that lie outside the scope of this study. We can only give an indication of the line such an enquiry would take. To do this we must consider some other forms of animal symbolism that appear in Tale religious beliefs.

Taboos of the Earth

Animals of all kinds can be endowed with ritual significance for individuals or groups among the Tallensi. They become sacred objects (baɣa, sing. baɣǝr) forming part of shrines (baɣa, sing. baɣǝr) dedicated to named ancestor spirits, on which sacrifices are offered. A baɣǝr animal is an individual animal or a species found in a particular place. Totem animals are not baɣa, since they are whole species respected everywhere and not associated with particular shrines.

Certain 'taboos of the Earth' (tɛŋǝn kiha) form a class of animal taboos standing between baɣa in the narrow sense and totems. Some Earth taboos are universal. Thus, throughout the Voltaic region it is a taboo to appropriate any unclaimed object of iron found lying on the ground. Other Earth taboos are specific to localities coming under the ritual jurisdiction of particular clans or lineages. All over Taleland large reptiles such as the crocodile (baŋ), the python (waɣakpɛm), the tree- and water-lizards (uuk and wuu) are taboos of the Earth. They may not be killed within the precincts of any important Earth shrine. In the bush, where men have no social bonds with the land, and therefore no ritual bonds with the Earth at specific places, they are not sacred. Binding on everybody, these taboos hold with extra force for members of lineages that have tendaanas (see also pp. 187–8 below).

Tallensi say these animals are 'the people of the Earth (tɛŋǝn nirǝba)' as men are people of such and such a settlement. They symbolize the mystical power of the Earth as it acts on human life, sometimes beneficently, sometimes punitively. This is what the natives mean when they say 'The Earth is a living thing (tɛŋ la a bonvor)'.

TOTEMISM AMONG THE TALIS AND OTHER NON-NAMOOS 143

This mystical power is focused for a particular social group in the Earth shrines of their own settlement—that is why the Earth animals are not sacred in the bush. And the ritual efficacy of the Earth at a particular place depends on its connexion with a particular social group holding the office of tɛndaana for that place. The animals therefore symbolize the moral relations of men, as these are determined by their social ties with particular tracts of the earth. They symbolize the function of locality in Tale social organization.

One logical element in this symbolism is obvious. The mystical 'livingness' of the Earth is symbolized in the living creatures it harbours. But this is not all, for otherwise other earth-dwelling creatures might have been selected as well.

The special relationship of the sacred Earth animals with the clan holding the tɛndaanaship for the area is focused in one species, as a rule. Thus the python is specially sacred at Gbizug, the crocodile at Zubiuŋ. To kill one of these animals at home is almost as bad as murder. For they are more than Earth taboos; they are 'ancestors' (*yaab*, pl. *yaanam*) to the group concerned. If found dead in the settlement, they are given a token funeral. The sacred crocodiles living in the Zubiuŋ water-hole are treated with an almost human familiarity. 'They are our ancestors, they would not injure us', the people say. In some clans carnivores like the leopard or the lion have this function, but are not considered Earth taboos. The natives say that their ancestors who have held politico-ritual office 'rise up again (*ihigərəme*)' after death as these animals. Tallensi deny that this is a belief in reincarnation or in the transmigration of souls. These taboos have attributes of totems, of Earth taboos, and of personal ancestor symbols; and the common thread is the notion of the ancestors as a living mystical force, symbolized in living creatures. The animals symbolize the immortality of the ancestors, that is, their efficacy and power in the life of their descendants. The ancestors are where their descendants are. One reason why the lineage is tied to its locality is because the ancestors are tied to it. They are spiritually present in the social life of their descendants in the same way as the sacred animals are present in sacred pools or in the locality with which the group is identified.

Functional Differentiation and its Symbolism

An important inference emerges from our argument. Lineage and locality are interwoven and interdependent factors of Tale social structure. But they are functionally discrete factors. We have previously seen how their interdependence is reflected in Tale religious ideology. We see now that their functional discreteness within the pattern of interdependence is also expressed in ritual symbols. The formally similar and associated but functionally distinct symbols we have discussed bring this out.

Tale society is highly homogeneous and integrated. But this is a resultant of the balanced interplay of a number of functionally discrete factors and of the inter-articulation of many clearly defined social units. Tale religion gives ritual expression and sanction to these principles.

144 TOTEMISM AMONG THE TALIS AND OTHER NON-NAMOOS

Every functionally differentiated aspect of the social life carries specific norms of conduct. It implies specific social obligations, jural rights, and, very often, economic relationships. It usually has a morphological correlate, as offices are vested in particular lineages, localities are associated with lineages, and social roles are transmitted by descent or determined by kinship. Hence every functionally differentiated aspect of social life tends to be subject to specific ritual sanctions within the general frame of the ancestor cult and to be identified by particular ritual symbols. In terms of the individual's place in the social system, this means that Tale religious ideology recognizes the fact that a man's social personality is compounded of many roles corresponding to the different functional aspects of social life in which he takes part. But this multiplicity of social roles does not obliterate the individual. Though he is a microcosm of his society he is always, also, uniquely himself. At times this is the prime determinant of his behaviour, at others a particular social role or membership of a corporate group is decisive. Totemic and other ritual symbols are the ideological landmarks that keep the individual on his course.

We see this very well in the case of a chief or other politico-ritual functionary. The man himself with his personal qualities, his career, his good or ill fortune is one thing. He also belongs to his lineage, and is subject to the code of lineage rights and duties. His title to his office rests on this. Then he is also a chief, with the special ritual and secular privileges and responsibilities of his office. Each facet of his social personality corresponds to a different functional aspect of social life—the aspect of private relationships, of lineage membership, of politico-ritual office representing common or corporate interests. Each aspect has its ritual imprimatur, made explicit largely in the form of symbolic actions or taboos, especially animal taboos. Chiefs, for instance, may not eat the bush-pig (*dee*) and the dog (*baa*); the natives say that is because they are scavengers and therefore unclean in both the physical and the mystical sense.

The use of ritual symbolism in this context is not fortuitous. It reflects the supremacy of the ancestors as the sanction of the social order. Men cannot visualize their ancestors, but they experience their intervention in human affairs; and this gives a clue to the importance of animal symbolism in Tale religion.

As a member of a corporate group, a man comes under the spiritual jurisdiction of the common ancestors of the group, focused in the lineage *bɔyar*. This relationship is symbolized, *inter alia*, by his totemic taboos. As a unique individual his immediate ancestors have most relevance for him. The pattern of his life is broadly the same as that of his contemporaries. But particular events such as an illness, or the birth of a child, have a personal significance in his own biography. The Tallensi sum this up in the notion of Personal Destiny (*Yin*). Certain ancestors of his become a man's *Yin*. They are revealed to him gradually in the course of years. The process begins with some stroke of good or, more usually, ill fortune that singles him out. He builds a shrine to his *Yin* ancestors in which are incorporated material symbols of the occasions on which they were revealed to him. And animals play a big part in these

TOTEMISM AMONG THE TALIS AND OTHER NON-NAMOOS 145

symbols. It may be a domestic animal peculiarly associated with the man because he reared it. But far more significance is attached to a bush animal killed in the hunt, or an aquatic animal caught in a fish drive. Encountering such an animal is a matter of luck. Overcoming it demands skill and has an element of danger; and this singles out the successful hunter or fisherman from his fellows. It is a sign of the intervention of his *Yin* ancestors in his life and the animal is an obvious choice as a symbol for them. It should be stressed that the question of economic value does not come in at all. Bush and aquatic animals have very little economic value. It is as symbols of personal achievement and luck that they have meaning.

But what is the common psychological theme in these different categories of animal symbolism? The relations between men and their ancestors among the Tallensi are a never-ceasing struggle. Men try to coerce and placate their ancestors by means of sacrifices. But the ancestors are unpredictable. It is their power to injure and their sudden attacks on routine well-being that make men aware of them rather than their beneficent guardianship. It is by aggressive intervention in human affairs that they safeguard the social order. Do what they will, men can never control the ancestors. Like the animals of the bush and the river, they are restless, elusive, ubiquitous, unpredictable, aggressive. The relations of men with animals in the world of common-sense experience are an apt symbolism of the relations of men with their ancestors in the sphere of mystical causation.

It is an interesting point that the commonest and most widely respected totem or quasi-totem animals are what Tallensi call 'teeth-bearers' (*nyindɛm*)—reptiles and carnivores, whose weapons are their teeth and who live and defend themselves by attacking other animals or even men. The symbolical link with the potential aggressiveness of the ancestors is patent.[1] This is, no doubt, the chief reason why other species of earth-dwelling animals are not selected as Earth taboos.

To sum up, animals are peculiarly apt symbols for the livingness—the immortality—of the ancestors as this emerges in the various functionally differentiated aspects of the social life. They symbolize, in particular, the potential aggressiveness of the ancestors as the supreme sanction of Tale cultural values. They serve to crystallize in simple, concrete, unequivocal imperatives and images the notion of the binding force of the moral code which is not clearly apparent in the diffused and particularized imperatives that make up the day-to-day experience of it. Different animal symbols stand for different aspects of the moral code, but they all form a connected series corresponding to the unitary basis of that code and the all-embracing sanctions of the ancestor cult. The principles of right and wrong, of duty and justice, of what is permissible and what is prohibited in social life fall into a consistent scheme among the Tallensi. And as the existence of the society depends on the maintenance of this code, its ultimate sanctions are necessarily of mystical form.

[1] Teeth are a common symbol of aggression among many peoples. The association is familiar to psychologists. We have it ourselves—witness our expression 'to show one's teeth'.

L

146 TOTEMISM AMONG THE TALIS AND OTHER NON-NAMOOS

This digression on the significance of animal symbolism has been necessary in order to put Tale totemism and related ritual ideas into the perspective of the social structure as a whole. We have, however, only touched the fringe of a vast subject in Tale social life. Even the material used here would lend itself to deeper analysis. A psychoanalytic interpretation (which I am not competent to undertake) would shed interesting light on the structure of the moral conscience among the Tallensi.

CHAPTER IX

THE PLACE OF WOMEN IN THE CLAN ORGANIZATION

The Concept of a Clanswoman

WE have occasionally referred to the role of women in the clan organization of the Tallensi, but this subject deserves further consideration. In a certain sense women illustrate the principle of the corporate unity and identity of lineage and clan more strikingly than men. On marriage women leave their paternal settlements to reside with their husbands. They never, however, lose their status as members of their own patrilineal lineage and clan. It is true that they have not the same jural rights and duties as their clan brothers and cannot exercise a responsible role in lineage or clan ritual; for, as we shall see in the second part of this study,[1] a woman is a minor in jural and ritual matters. Nevertheless, women are subject to the critical norms of clanship in the same way as men. They are bound by the same rules of exogamy as the men, and by the same ritual observances that distinguish maximal lineage from maximal lineage or clan from clan. They also have certain privileges as members of their patrilineal descent group. We deal with these points in outline here. The details will come more appropriately in our next volume.

The term *pɔyayabɔlɔg* sums up the status of a woman as a member of her patrilineal maximal lineage and clan. It can best be translated as 'woman of the clan'; and it refers to a woman of the clan or maximal lineage whether she is residing at her father's house or living with her husband. *Pɔyayabɔlɔg* denotes the general status of clanswoman irrespective of what segment of the clan she may belong to. At all funeral ceremonies, for instance, certain duties and tasks both of a ritual and non-ritual kind fall on *pɔyayabɔlis*. Some of these tasks, such as the gathering of firewood, are usually performed by young unmarried *pɔyayabɔlis*. The girls who volunteer for these tasks are treated as a single group, irrespective of what segment of the clan they belong to. Other tasks and ritual duties that have to be carried out by clanswomen fall upon older women, usually married women who return home specially for the funeral. Any woman of the clan who is qualified by her knowledge and seniority can perform these duties. If a married woman living with her husband is asked where she comes from, she always replies: 'I am a *pɔyayabɔlɔg* of such-and-such a clan.'

It is a maxim that all *pɔyayabɔlis* are equal to one another in relation to their natal clan. 'No one owns a *pɔyayabɔlɔg*, we all own her (*sɔ pu sɔ pɔyayabɔlɔg, ti waabi nsɔ ka*)', is the native formula. The implication is that the clan as a whole is the primary unit claiming the allegiance of a

---

[1] Forthcoming shortly under the title of *The Web of Kinship among the Tallensi*.

148 THE PLACE OF WOMEN IN THE CLAN ORGANIZATION

pɔɣayabəlɔg, particularly of one who is living at her husband's house. To be sure, her kinship ties with her own family and with the segment of the maximal lineage to which her father belongs are not severed; indeed, a woman's relations with her paternal clan are largely regulated and mediated by these ties. The concept of *pɔɣayabəlɔg* implicitly stresses the fact that it is a woman's fate to be married out of the clan and to be cut off from its routine corporate activity; and it contains the idea that a woman thus separated from her parental home is felt to belong primarily to the widest corporate unit that stands in contraposition to her husband's, where his relations with her are concerned.

Thus outside the range of the lineage segment in which generation differences are recognized, a *pɔɣayabəlɔg* is referred to as 'our sister (*ti tau*)' by any of her clansmen, and she speaks of them as *ntap*, 'my brothers'. A man visiting the settlement of another clan makes himself at home in the rooms of any *pɔɣayabəlɔg* of his clan. When the cow-peas are ripening, a *pɔɣayabəlɔg* visiting her clan settlement—her 'father's house' (*ba yiri*), as it is described by extension of the concept of the father's house or lineage in the narrowest sense—may pluck cow-pea leaves (*bɛŋɔt*) for herself anywhere in the settlement. A Yamələg or Sie *pɔɣayabəlɔg* can do this at Tongo, for instance, if she is merely passing through on her way elsewhere. No one would resent it; but if the wife of a member of a segment of the clan other than his own were to pluck a man's cow-pea leaves without his express permission, it would lead to a quarrel. Similarly, it is customary for women to come and collect a basket of grain from the men of their parental family after the harvest. A *pɔɣayabəlɔg*, however, is permitted to ask any of her clansmen for a gift of this kind. Thus it sometimes happens that a Yamələg or Sie woman married to a man at Yinduuri comes to a clansman at Tongo after the harvest for a gift of grain, or a Tongo woman married to a man at Datɔk or Duusi calls on a clansman at Sie for such a gift. As these examples indicate, a *pɔɣayabəlɔg* of a linked maximal lineage counts as a *pɔɣayabəlɔg* of the clan.

When a woman's funeral is celebrated by her husband's people the last act is 'to send her home (*kulh*)' to her father's house. For this ceremony a large party of men and women in their gayest clothes, led by the nearest agnates of the dead woman and escorted by drummers and musicians, sets out for her husband's settlement to 'receive her funeral (*die koor*)'. When such a party is being assembled, messages are sent to the heads of all the constituent lineages of the clan, and representatives are generally sent from all the lineages to accompany the party. It is partly a matter of duty, and partly an act of courtesy and a voluntary demonstration of clan solidarity. Sometimes young people of linked lineages join the party, knowing that it will be lavishly entertained by the affinal clan and that there will be dancing and girls to flirt with. Fetching the funeral of a *pɔɣayabəlɔg* is an affair of the whole clan.

The *pɔɣayabəlɔg* has a formal status in the lineage and clan, and this status is recognized as an intrinsic element in the structure of the lineage and clan. The fiction behind this is the idea often explicitly stated by the natives that but for an accident of birth she might have been a man

THE PLACE OF WOMEN IN THE CLAN ORGANIZATION   149

and her sons might have been able to exercise all the rights and duties of clanship. There is, in fact, a submerged feeling of rivalry in the relations between the men of the clan and the *pɔyayabɔlis*, deprived by an accident of birth of effective jural and ritual membership of the clan. This is shown, for example, in a curious taboo affecting the oldest living *pɔyayabɔlɔg* of a maximal lineage. She may never spend a night in the homestead of the head of the maximal lineage, even if he is her own brother. If she did, either or both of them would die. For the lineage ancestors abide in this homestead, and they object to her presence there simultaneously with that of their proper male custodian. The natives, of course, simply state this taboo as a fact, but to anyone familiar with Tale culture the interpretation is obvious. The senior *pɔyayabɔlɔg* might, in her own person, have been the head of the lineage but for the accident of birth. Her presence in the homestead which she might have occupied as a man is a hidden challenge and reproach both to the male head of the lineage and to the ancestors. It would be tantamount to a symbolic rejection of the fundamental principles of the lineage organization. For these reasons she cannot stay with the man who most conspicuously represents the extrusion of women from the full heritage of patrilineal descent.

Institutionalized Recognition of a Clanswoman's Status

There are many institutions in which the status of the *pɔyayabɔlɔg* as an intrinsic element in the lineage organization is recognized. For example, a new-born child is confined to its father's house for some months. When it is big enough to be allowed out of doors it must be ritually taken out for the first time by a *pɔyayabɔlɔg* of the clan. Usually she is a near agnate of the father, but any clanswoman may be asked to carry out the rite. The child's father consults a diviner to find out who will be a suitable *pɔyayabɔlɔg*; for the rite is implicitly a blessing of the ancestors, and it is they who are believed to appoint a woman of the clan to carry their blessing to the child. It can be surmised that a *pɔyayabɔlɔg* is chosen for this rite because she is by birth identified with the child's father and its lineage, and by sex identified with the child's mother and the function of motherhood. Taking the child out of the house is in part a question of maternal care, therefore a woman's task; it is also a step that involves the child's physical and spiritual well-being. Outside the walls of the homestead lie greater dangers, both material and mystical, than inside the homestead, and this is the concern of the child's patrilineal ancestors.

The role of *pɔyayabɔlis* in relation to the lineage *bɔyar* is significant in this connexion. A woman cannot become the custodian of an ancestor shrine, except nominally if she is the sole survivor of a lineage. In that case she cannot sacrifice to the shrine directly, but must call in a collateral male agnate to deputize for the man who might have been the custodian of the shrine. This is the most important distinction between the status of male members and that of female members of the lineage, and it is a consequence of the fact that women do not help to maintain the continuity of the lineage. Nevertheless, *pɔyayabɔlis* have the right to take part

150 THE PLACE OF WOMEN IN THE CLAN ORGANIZATION

in sacrifices to their lineage ancestors. When an important sacrifice is due to be made to a lineage *bɔyar*, the married *pɔyayabɔlis* of the lineage who live near enough to be able to attend, and especially the senior *pɔyayabɔlɔg*, must be informed. Those who can, will attend the rite, and a prescribed portion (*tɔrɔg*) of the animal sacrificed is the due of the *pɔya-yabɔlis*. This portion, consisting of the 'waist' (*sie*), i.e. part of the vertebral column and some of the ribs, together with prescribed bits of various internal organs and the intestines, is divided among the *pɔya-yabɔlis*, both married and unmarried, who are present. The allocation of a prescribed portion of a sacrificial animal to any group or individual is the most significant indication, in Tale culture, that that group or indivi-dual has a recognized formal status in the social structure.

An outstanding event in the life of a lineage is the inheritance (*vaagɔr*), that is, the formal assumption of the custody, of a lineage *bɔyar* by a new lineage head. Being old men generally, lineage heads seldom survive succession to this status for many years. Thus, the inheritance of a lineage *bɔyar* is an event of fairly frequent recurrence at periods varying from five to ten years. It is an occasion on which the integration of the lineage is at its maximum. Every member, male and female, who can do so makes an effort to attend. Those who are heads of families contribute fowls and flour to be added to the sacrifices on their behalf. All cognates by descent through women of the lineage who live near enough are invited, and those who are heads of families also bring contributions for the sacrifice. In short, the occasion is a sacrament in which all the descendants of the lineage ancestors, through both men and women, participate, and it is regarded as a particularly auspicious sacrament.

One of the first rites in the inheritance of a lineage *bɔyar* is the transfer of the shrine from the homestead of its late custodian to that of his succes-sor. This rite is carried out by one male member of the lineage, almost invariably a member of the segment whose head has become head of the lineage, and one *pɔyayabɔlɔg* of the lineage, both selected by divination. Later, when many fowls brought by those present are sacrificed to the *bɔyar* to mark its transfer to a new lineage head, this pair are the first of the lineage members to present their offerings. Thus is symbolized the equality of status of men and women members of the lineage before the *bɔyar*, and the rights of women members and their descendants to the spiritual protection of the lineage ancestors.

As we have seen in our consideration of attached lineages, and as we shall learn more fully when we examine the relations of maternal uncle and sororal nephew,[1] there are circumstances in which descent through a woman is partially assimilated to the true agnatic line. To give only one example here, a sororal nephew (*ahɔŋ*) of any degree whatsoever, that is, any member of another clan who has a cognatic link with the clan in question through an ancestress however remote, is formally equated with the sons of the clan in the matter of leviratic rights. An *ahɔŋ* has the right to seek the hand of a widow of his maternal uncle's clan (*ahɔb yiri*) on the same terms as a true member of that clan. He is, so to speak, exercising the right, corollary to the obligation of clan exogamy, that

[1] In *The Web of Kinship among the Tallensi.*

THE PLACE OF WOMEN IN THE CLAN ORGANIZATION 151

might have been his mother's if she were a man. In practice sororal nephews are rarely allowed to assert this right, and then only if their cognatic link with their maternal uncle's clan is not more than about four generations back.

Though the *pɔyayabəlis* of a lineage or clan never act together as a single group, since marriage disperses them among other clans, they are often thought of as forming a united body, the feminine counterpart of the men of the clan. This is seen most conspicuously in funeral ceremonies; and we can easily understand why, if we remember that funeral ceremonies are the concern of the whole clan. We have made a passing reference to the role of *pɔyayabəlis* in funeral ceremonies, but it deserves some amplification. For it is in funeral ceremonies that one constantly hears 'the *pɔyayabəlis*' spoken of as if they were a regular, organized group, sees them called upon to undertake tasks in a purely representative capacity, and observes the allocation of prescribed portions of food to them as of right.

Naturally, this is most noticeable at the funeral of an important member of the lineage or the wife of a lineage elder. Large quantities of beer and food have to be prepared for distribution at various times during the ceremony, and this is the work of the women. All the women assisting in the work at the 'house of the funeral' (*koor yiri*) are divided into two groups, in a way which shows clearly the division of the women in whom a lineage or clan has jural and moral interests, into those who belong to the clan by birth and those who are married into it. The *pɔyayabəlis* form one group. They have separate cooking quarters, and special tasks. The other group consists of the *dubɛnib*, 'those who stay in the room'. They are the clanswomen of the wives of the bereaved house, who are themselves wives of other members of the clan or of nearby linked lineages or allied clans. They may include the *pɔyayabəlis* of several clans, except, of course, those of the clan celebrating the funeral. They, too, have their own cooking quarters and special duties and privileges. They are called *dubɛnib* (from *dug*, room, and *bɛ*, to stay or be) because they are identified with the *dugdɛm*, the 'mistresses of the rooms', that is, the wives of the bereaved clan who are their clan sisters. Their principal task is to remain indoors with their clan sisters in order to attend to their needs, to console them, and to help them in the duties that would fall upon wives in this situation. Clan sisterhood sometimes has a very wide connotation in these circumstances. There are many Wakii women married to Tongo men. If one of them requires the help of her clan sisters as *dubɛnib*, those of them who live nearest to her or are most closely related to her will be the first to come, and her distant clan sisters will probably not come at all. On the other hand, there are very few women of Hill Talis clans married to men at Duusi. So if one of them needs the help of *dubɛnib* she will call on all the women of Hill Talis clans at Duusi and in neighbouring settlements. In such a case the solidarity of clanship merges with that of locality and of common values. This principle is carried so far that if a Gɔre woman married to a Tɛnzugu man requires the help of *dubɛnib*, she calls upon all the other Gɔre wives, of whom there are very few, of Tɛnzugu and of immediately adjacent clans, whatever part of Gɔreland

152 THE PLACE OF WOMEN IN THE CLAN ORGANIZATION

they may come from. For these women feel themselves to be as closely akin to one another as members of the same clan, by contraposition with the Tallensi whom they have married.

The *pɔyayabɔlis* act together as a single group under the leadership of the oldest among them at funeral ceremonies. The young girls perform such tasks as bringing in the great bundles of firewood required for cooking the beer. The older *pɔyayabɔlis,* expert in the preparation of beer, undertake that task themselves. The younger women do the more strenuous jobs connected with cooking, such as grinding flour and preparing the other ingredients of a meal. The older women cook the porridge and meat relishes required for such rites as the setting out of consecrated food for the dead. All food required for ritual use is prepared by the *pɔyayabɔlis*, since all the ritual is the preserve of the clan. As members of the clan they can be associated with the ritual activities of the clan, and as women they can carry out tasks which are appropriate to their sex in accordance with the usual division of labour. The *dubɛnib* do not prepare the food required for ritual purposes, but only the food used to give hospitality to clansmen, kinsmen, and other visitors.

The *pɔyayabɔlis* have also to be directly represented by one of them, most appropriately by one of the older women, in many of the rites. A *pɔyayabɔlɔg* has to assist in such rites as the offering of the initial sacrifices to the spirit of the departed and to the ancestors he or she is about to join. A *pɔyayabɔlɔg* and a man of the clan see to the ritual feeding of the orphans, which takes place at different stages of the ceremonies. The various mourning strings (*miis*) which the orphans and widows have to wear during the funeral ceremonies are tied on, and at the end removed, by an elderly *pɔyayabɔlɔg*. The setting out of consecrated food for the dead is always done by one male and one female member of the clan. And then, when the final divination takes place, a man and a woman of the lineage together carry out the simple rite of restoring the dead person's body dirt (*dayat*), the symbol of his individual self, to the house where his life was spent, and whither he now returns as a spirit to whom sacrifice must be offered.

Lastly, a married *pɔyayabɔlɔg* is a link between her paternal clan and her husband's clan, both in herself and in the line of descent which springs from her. This is evident nowadays from the role of the *pɔyasama* —a clansman of the bridegroom and a matrilateral kinsman of the bride's lineage—as an intermediary in marriage negotiations. It was shown in former days in peace-making ceremonies. If two clans, or groups of clans, had been at war, peace was concluded by a ritual reconciliation. In this the opponents were usually represented by a *pɔyayabɔlɔg* of each side who was married to a member of the other side, who was therefore bound by jural and moral ties to both sides and had strong emotional attachments to both, and thus symbolized the underlying interdependence of the opponents.

Lineage and clan consist of both their male and their female members. Though the women do not contribute to the continuity and perpetuation of the lineage, they are a source of strength to it. This is most obvious in the fact that the bride-price paid for them adds to the resources by

THE PLACE OF WOMEN IN THE CLAN ORGANIZATION 153

means of which the lineage acquires wives. But what is more important, the women carry the descent of the clan into other clans, and thus build up that network of interclan kinship ties which breaks down the rigid exclusiveness of the lineage and clan, interweaves clan with clan, and is one of the factors that restrain strife between clans and prevent Tale society from splitting into anarchic fragments. Since the tie of descent is indestructible, women members of the lineage and clan have definite rights and duties in all those practical and ritual institutions which bring out most precisely the solidarity and corporate identity of the lineage through the passage of time and the mutability of generations.

CHAPTER X

THE SOCIAL STRUCTURE OF A SETTLEMENT

Introduction

A TALE settlement is a miniature of the whole society, and reveals all the basic principles of the social structure. No two settlements are identical in topography, shape, size, or social composition; but all have the same social form, based on the same principles. Yet it is no easy task to describe a settlement as the natives see it. It cannot be isolated from neighbouring units of the same kind by inspection; for though it is locally fixed it is not territorially circumscribed. Its structure is unintelligible without reference to the lineage system, but ecological exigencies and political and ritual ties and cleavages play an important part in it as well.

The anatomy of a settlement appears in fullest relief during the dry season. Then the homesteads stand out starkly against the dun background of bare earth or the glare of rocks and boulders piled up in red-grey masses in the hilly areas. The foot-paths winding between the homesteads scar the land as if etched into it by generations of feet. Every shade tree in front of a homestead is an inviting landmark. Sacred groves, looking temptingly cool when the sun is high, are unmistakable. The water-holes, pits, and ditches, flooded beyond recognition in the latter part of the rainy season, can easily be distinguished. The boundaries of farm-plots, overgrown with crops and weeds during the rains, are now clearly visible. The landscape is a map of the social relations of the people. This is the season, too, when life goes on largely in the open. There is leisure for gossip and conversation; for paying visits, strolling in the market, going a-courting, making long journeys, dancing in the moonlight; for hunting and fishing drives; there is time also, and the necessary supplies, for the performance of funeral ceremonies and other ritual activities. It is in such events that the structure of Tale society is most vividly actualized.

Types of Settlement and Distribution of Population

Two main types of settlements are found: those of ancient habitation (*tɛŋkɔrɔg*, old country), covering all the centre of the country, especially on and around the Tong Hills, and including the majority of the Tallensi; and those of recent foundation (*tɛŋpaalɔg*, new country), towards the periphery of this area. Though the basic plan is the same, the principles on which a settlement is built operate with different emphasis in each type.

Neither territorial extent nor density of aggregation affects the basic plan of a settlement. The range of variation is very great. Moreover, processes of expansion and contraction continuously alter the extent of a settlement. Thus, Yamɔlɔg and Tongo are ancient settlements of the same general structure, though the latter is four or five times the size of

THE SOCIAL STRUCTURE OF A SETTLEMENT 155

the former; and Biuŋ, with 25 homesteads and less than 400 inhabitants, is a peripheral settlement of the same type as Datɔk, which has over 600 homesteads and between 5,000 and 6,000 inhabitants. The whole of Biuŋ can be seen from one of the hummocks on which it stands, but it takes an hour's ride on horseback to get round the whole of Datɔk.

The density and distribution of habitation varies somewhat from one part of the country to another. The broad undulating plain on the north side of the Tong Hills permits of dense settlement, whereas the plain stretching south and south-east of the hills carries a relatively sparse population.[1]

Differences of altitude and of drainage probably explain this. During the rains a large part of the southern plain becomes too waterlogged for cultivation or for human habitation. Many of the Hill Talis went to live there when they were dispersed in 1911.[2] Though they have always cultivated bush farms there, wherever the lie of the land is suitable, they look back on their exile as a doubly miserable interlude on account of the uncomfortable and unhealthy conditions in which they had perforce to live. Accustomed to their well-drained hills, they hated the interminable swamp, as it seemed to them, into which the plain is transformed during the rains; and hardened though they are, they found the mosquitoes and other noxious insects that swarm there during this season an intolerable plague.

From the top of the Tong Hills, looking northwards, one has a view of what seems to be an endless plain, dotted meagrely with trees, and studded closely, as far as the eye can reach, with homesteads. They are identical in appearance, squat, circular, drab-grey or red, like the soil itself, mostly thatch-roofed, and seem to be scattered indiscriminately, some close together, others farther apart. There is nothing to indicate where one settlement ends and the next begins. Homesteads here, in the old settlements, are often no more than 20 yards apart.

The density of population is greater in the old than in the new settlements, and greater in the vicinity of the Tong Hills than in settlements nearer to the periphery. I cannot state how great the difference is, as I had neither the time nor the training for a comprehensive demographic survey. Sociological observation suggests that the amount of arable land available is an important factor, though not the only one, determining density of population in the older areas of settlement. This is as one would expect of a sedentary population of subsistence farmers. In the new settlements there is ample land, and men have large home farms immediately adjoining their homesteads, which are therefore often as

---

[1] I have no exact figures. From the statistics given in the census of 1931 (*Appendices containing Comparative Returns and General Statistics of the 1931 Census, Gold Coast*, Government Printer, 1932) it appears that the large area lying between Pwɔlɔg (Kpɔlɔg), the centre of the Tong Hills, and a straight line from there to the Red and White Volta—that is, this southern plain—had about 5,000 inhabitants in 1931, only one-seventh of the total population of Taleland. This included many people who were then in exile and now live on and around the Tong Hills.

[2] By order of the British Administration, after the punitive expedition against them. Cf. p. 12 above.

156   THE SOCIAL STRUCTURE OF A SETTLEMENT

much as a quarter of a mile apart. The greater congestion of the older settlements is correlated with greater fragmentation of holdings, due to the greater length of time they have been continuously occupied.

The population of Taleland, as of the remainder of the trans-Volta plateau, appears to have been increasing steadily in the recent past. In the older settlements it is clearly excessive in relation to the available land and the level of technical skill of the natives. This is the opinion both of Government officials and of the natives themselves. The natives always say that shortage of cultivable land was the main incentive for the migration of young men to the peripheral 'bush' zone in the past; and the men who have come to settle permanently in the peripheral settlements during the last two or three decades always ascribe their move from their natal settlements to the same cause. Labour migration during the past ten or fifteen years has been much influenced by pressure of population on the land in the most congested areas.

These economic adaptations of the natives and their general standard of living, as well as the territorial distribution of such clans as Mosuor biis in Taleland, compel the inference that the population has been increasing for some time. But adequate statistics for measuring the present rate of increase in the population, or for establishing its trend in the past, are lacking.[1]

There are no clear-cut geographical features regulating the distribution of homesteads in most settlements. The location of water-supplies has no bearing on it, since Tale agriculture relies wholly on rainfall, and domestic requirements are a secondary consideration, and offer no difficulties in the wet season. Towards the end of the dry season the domestic consumption of water is cut to the minimum necessary for cooking and drinking. When water is scarce, the average Taloŋ is content to go unwashed for weeks at a stretch. By the end of the dry season most surface supplies have vanished, and water is usually obtained from shallow pits, artificially deepened and enlarged from time to time by those who use them. These pits are regular water-holes (buləg), utilized solely for that purpose throughout the year. A large settlement has several, situated in the dry beds of what are strong streams (koləg), or in the depressions (bo'og) which become swamps and pools during the rains. A water-hole generally serves the needs of the homesteads within a radius of about a quarter to half a mile. But at times of acute shortage the women and girls may have to go a mile or more to fill their water-pots.

Variations in elevation influence the scatter of homesteads to some extent. Inured though they are to the discomforts of their climate, the Tallensi prefer to build on high ground if possible. Thus, in the older settlements, homesteads tend to cluster closer together where there is a rise in the ground, and to be few and far between where there is a de-

---

[1] Reliable reproduction rates, either for the Northern Territories as a whole or for Taleland in particular, cannot be calculated from the data given in the abstract of the census of 1931, and there are no other official statistics, published or unpublished, which could be used for this purpose. My own exiguous demographic data suggest that the population of the older Tale settlements is increasing, though not steeply.

THE SOCIAL STRUCTURE OF A SETTLEMENT 157

pression liable to flooding in the rainy season. The people of the Tong Hills consider themselves to be particularly fortunate in this respect. Their homesteads stretch densely across the slopes of the hills, and amid the great boulders and rocky piles of the summit. Singing the praises of their tiny fastness, they contrast it with the plain, where one is always ankle-deep in mud and slush during the rains and scorched by the sun in the dry season. On the hills, they say, a sheltered nook can always be found among the rocks, shady when the sun is most cruel, dry in the severest storm, where the children can play or the grown-ups sit and talk.

The Stability and Continuity of a Settlement

Stability and continuity are essential characteristics of a settlement. They are implied in the native concept of a *tɛŋ* (settlement) as both a definite locality and a fixed community. The ancient settlements have attained a very high degree of stability and continuity. The peripheral settlements are rapidly ceasing to be mere economic apanages to the older centres of habitation, and are taking on the form of permanent and stable units. Being still in process of organization, their structure is fluid compared with that of the ancient settlements, and the dynamic factors of Tale social structure sometimes appear more conspicuously in them than in the latter.

But the older settlements are by no means static. The bounds, the layout, and the internal constitution of a settlement alter continuously, if very slowly. Even in a single year one can see how processes of expansion and contraction, of segmentation and incorporation, are at work all the time. Whenever land changes hands by inheritance, or an office passes by succession, or a man achieves economic independence, a minor reshuffle in the collocation of homesteads takes place. The cumulative effects of these processes of slow but progressive readjustment are clearly exhibited in the contemporary structure of a settlement. They are documented in its constitution and layout, in the location of ancestral graves, the ownership of farm plots, and in ceremonial and political relations. Fixity of location and of the structural plan ensure the stability and continuity of a Tale settlement.

Topographical Distinctions and the Natives' Knowledge of Natural History

Precise local orientation is essential in the economic activities and social relations of the Tallensi. Place-names are often derived from prominent topographical or geographical features. Thus, Tɛnzugu means the head (*zug*) or highest part of the country (*tɛŋ*), Yaɣazuor means 'perched on a hill', and many other place-names are popularly believed to be corruptions of topographical or spatial metaphors. Within a settlement topographical variations are distinguished by terms like *tɛŋr*, the lower part (the locative of *tɛŋ*, here in the sense of 'ground'), and *saazugu*, the higher part (lit. head-high, or high up). Conspicuous patches of low-lying land, hillocks, rock piles, ditches, water-holes, streams, &c., are named, and are very often sacred spots. The name may indicate peculiar qualities of the soil, prominent trees, or other landmarks formerly or still

158 THE SOCIAL STRUCTURE OF A SETTLEMENT

found at that spot. Thus, Sielug is an uninhabited part of Zubiuŋ, where clay (*siela*) is abundant near the surface, making it unsuitable for cultivation and therefore a favourite pasture. Naɣabɛraabo'og ('cattle-poison-grass valley'), the tract of low-lying land renowned as the traditional battle-field of Tongo and Ba'ari, appears to be named after a kind of grass believed to be noxious to cattle. Other such names have a legendary flavour, but the Tallensi, with their characteristic realism, have no myths or legends to account for them. Locality names of this kind are Kumpeɣalɔɣat ('Death carries quivers') and Kurbɔk ('Stooping ditch'). Sacred groves (*tɔŋgbana*) often serve as landmarks to identify a locality; e.g. Dooni (at Doo), means the precincts of that *tɔŋgban*, vaguely defined, as are all such localities, by position and not by definite boundaries.

We shall see later how the social structure of a settlement is anchored to a locality. The physical environment is built into the whole edifice of native life. Tale economic pursuits demand an intimate knowledge—unscientific but remarkably efficient at the level of their social organization and technical development—of natural history and topography. Tale leechcraft, on its empirical side, depends on this knowledge; and every prominent and many an inconspicuous feature of the landscape has its meaning and place in native social relations. A great boulder may be the children's playground, or the women's pounding-floor, or a shrine. A hoary baobab tree is not only an amenity and a source of useful products, but also a lineage shrine. A furrow, an outcrop of laterite, or a fringe of grass, may mark the boundary of a farm plot. A shrub, hardly noticeable on the bank of a dry watercourse, is a medicine. In consequence, the natural environment forms a very important aspect of the native's social space. In his own settlement, and especially in his section of the settlement, he knows every rock and tree and almost every tuft of grass, the qualities of the soil, and the ownership of farm plots.

In addition to his own settlement a man usually knows pretty thoroughly the natural environment of neighbouring settlements with which his clan has close social bonds and, more superficially, that of his mother's natal settlement and of settlements in which close extra-clan kin live. The great majority of men, even the younger men who have been abroad for lengthy periods, are all well versed in the geography, the vegetation, and the fauna of the tracts of bush and river-bank on the borders of Taleland, the economic exploitation of which is indispensable for the subsistence of the natives. Every dry season many men and boys have to go out to the nearest bush to cut grass for thatching, rafters for roofing, shafts for their implements, *baɣana* (*Bauhinia*, spp.) bark for the rope used in house-building, canes for their bows and reeds for their arrows, tree-stumps for their shrines, and many medicinal roots and leaves. They go hunting in near and distant tracts of bush, so that most adult men are familiar with every hunting bush within a day's march of their settlement; and they go fishing in the pools left in the river-beds during the dry season. Women are as expert as men in these matters. They take part in the big fishing drives, comb the fields for edible herbs, seek out deposits of clay for pottery and gravel for beating floors, explore the neighbouring bush for firewood, for reeds to make sleeping mats, for fruits and edible leaves.

THE SOCIAL STRUCTURE OF A SETTLEMENT 159

In marked contrast is the average person's ignorance of settlements, even near at hand, with which his clan has no close social bonds or with which he has no personal links of kinship or friendship. Tallensi acquire their knowledge of geography and natural history gradually in childhood, by direct experience. It is already well established by the age of 9 or 10, and grows *pari passu* with the expansion of the child's social space. The basis of this is the child's natal settlement, where, except for occasional visits to kinsfolk elsewhere, it spends its entire childhood. But even adults had little liberty of movement in the past, since they could hardly go unmolested in settlements unrelated to theirs by clanship or political ties or where they had no kinsfolk. Most of the older people have never been outside Taleland, and many of them have never, or only rarely, visited some of the settlements within an hour's walk of their own.

A Talǝŋ inevitably has a profound emotional attachment to his native settlement. It is striking how many Tale emigrants return home eventually after years of absence, casting aside the flesh-pots of Ashanti or the rich fields of Mampurugu. '*Kpala m-mah*—Here it is pleasant', they say, in spite of the penury of existence; for here are your kith and kin, here is the scene of your childhood joys and sorrows, and above all, the abode of your forefathers. The Talǝŋ's empirical knowledge of his habitat is the precipitate in his thought and experience of the economic and structural facts that determine the local fixity of his native settlement. His affective attachment to it finds an institutionalized expression and support in the ancestor cult.

Settlement Boundaries

The hub of Taleland is Tongo (see map on p. 15). This ancient settlement, geographically central and politically nodal in the network of interclan relations, provides a very good model of the structure of a typical Tale settlement.

As we know, the Tongo branch of Mosuor biis live in such close spatial and social propinquity with Zubiuŋ, Gbizug, and Zoo that these clans are often spoken of collectively as 'the people of Tongo (Tɔŋdɛm)'. For precision, Tongo proper is referred to as Tɔŋ-Nayiri—the Chief's House of Tongo—all over Taleland. Throughout the Mole-Dagbane-speaking region clans which hold a chiefship are thus identified by reference to it. Those which have tɛndaanas are sometimes called Tɛndaaŋ, on the same principle. Thus outsiders distinguish between Sie-Nayiri and Sie-Tɛndaaŋ.

Tɔŋ-Nayiri, Tongo proper, forms an irregular block of homesteads, somewhat less than three square miles in area and is one of the largest settlements in Taleland. It comprised, in 1934, 192 homesteads and a total population of about 2,400.[1] This does not include Tongo people

---

[1] Calculations, based on my own census samples and on figures kindly supplied to me by the A.D.C. Zuarungu, show that in Taleland the average number of people of both sexes and all ages occupying a homestead is 12 to 14. Owing to the variation in the constitution of homesteads this figure must be accepted with reserve; but it is sufficient for a rough estimate of population in a country where accurate statistics do not exist.

160 THE SOCIAL STRUCTURE OF A SETTLEMENT

living at Zoo and Gbambee, though they are an integral part of the community.

Like all Tale settlements Tongo has no fixed territorial boundaries. (See map at end of book.) Its frontiers with the circumjacent settlements take the form of a social circumference, kept in being by local, genealogical, and politico-ritual ties and cleavages. This is the line of ecological and social balance between Tongo and its neighbours, more or less stable now, but still undergoing minor readjustments as this balance changes with alterations in the internal equilibrium of any of these units. It is most stable and firm where the genealogical, political, and ideological cleavages between Tongo and its neighbours are clear-cut and dominant; it is more pervious where Tongo's structural ties with an adjacent clan have greater strength than the cleavages between them. Thus, there is a distinct though sometimes narrow territorial separation between the outermost homesteads of Tongo and those of Wakii, Soog, Gbeog, and Ba'ari. At one point on the west side of Tongo only a stretch of cultivation separates Tongo homesteads from Wakii homesteads a stone's throw away. Tongo homesteads actually lie on the Wakii side of the watercourse which might have formed a natural boundary between them. On the south this watercourse and a straggling outcrop of rocks and boulders hedge in Tongo and mark it off from Wakii. A prominent landmark here is Samoo, a mass of huge rocks overgrown with trees and scrub. It is a sacred spot, the External *Bɔyar* of Soog and Gbeog. North of Samoo lies Tongo, the nearest Tongo homestead being about 50 yards away; south of it are Wakii and Soog. It would be most unlikely for a Tongo man to build his homestead on the south side of Samoo, or for a Soog or Wakii man to live north of it. For Samoo symbolizes all that the Namoos consider alien, hostile, and to some extent repugnant, in the cultural differences and structural cleavages between themselves and the Hill Talis. In olden days the immediate vicinity of Samoo was the no-man's-land where the two groups used to meet in battle.

Soog, Wakii, Gbeog, and Ba'ari, all Talis clans that were among the traditional enemies of Tongo in war, are all demarcated from the latter. On the border between Tongo and each of these clans is a stretch of land, cultivated or uncultivated, but free of homesteads, which is still thought of as the traditional battle-ground of the two groups. It is significant that these battle-grounds are all associated with Earth or *Bɔyar* shrines under the ritual jurisdiction of the Talis clans.

By contrast it is impossible to draw a clear line between the homesteads of Tongo and those of Zubiuŋ or Zoo. They merge completely. This corresponds to the close ties which have always existed between these three units and have enabled them to fuse easily into a single political community under the authority of the Chief of Tongo, since his acquisition of judicial and executive power under British rule.

In the old days Zubiuŋ and Zoo always fought on the side of Tongo against the Hill Talis. Both clans have direct politico-ritual roles in connexion with the Tongo chiefship, and come into its immediate field of influence, whereas the Hill Talis and Ba'ari come into its secondary field of influence. The three clans act as *sunzɔp*-by-courtesy (cf. ch. V) to

PLATE VII

(a) The Unity of all the Talis: The chief tɛndaanas of all the Talis settlements assemble to perform the rite of 'blowing the whistles' to inaugurate the Gɔlib Festival.

(b) A sacred crocodile at Zubiuŋ crawling out of the water-hole to take a live frog offered to him by a youth of the clan. Note the latter's fearlessness.

PLATE VIII

(a) The solidarity of clan sisters. During the funeral of the family head clan sisters of the widows, who have married into the same or adjacent clans, come to sit with them and console them.

(b) One of the senior clan-sisters (*pɔyayabəlis*) of the deceased supervises the cooking of the beer for his funeral rites.

THE SOCIAL STRUCTURE OF A SETTLEMENT   161

one another in funerals and similar ceremonial events. These ceremonial reciprocities do not prevail between Tongo or Zoo and any of the Hill Talis clans adjacent to them.

Nevertheless, a palpable social boundary still prevails between Tongo and Zubiuŋ, but one far less determinate than that between Tongo and its other Talis neighbours. No Zubiuŋ homesteads are so situated as to be surrounded on all sides by Tongo homesteads, and vice versa; there is no indiscriminate mingling of the homesteads of the two clans. Looked at from within, both Zubiuŋ and Tongo are self-contained spatial units within their respective social circumferences. This is correlated with their contrasting totemic observances, clan cults, and politico-ritual offices; their mutual exclusiveness by the canon of agnatic descent and the liberty to intermarry that goes with this; and their consequent divergent jural interests as distinct corporate units; the people of Tongo are Namoos, the Zubiuŋdɛm Talis. The observer is constantly apprised of this in the attitudes and opinions of individuals, in economic activities, and in jural and ritual events, the very activities and events which reveal the close bonds of the two groups. Tongo people never scrupled to raid their weaker Zubiuŋ neighbours for cattle owed to them, as many old men relate from personal experience. On the other hand, responsible elders and chiefs of Tongo, in those days, disapproved strongly of resort to violent self-help against Zubiuŋ by their people, though they could not always prevent it—an attitude they would never adopt in regard to the other Talis. To-day Tongo and Zubiuŋ people regard one another with a certain amount of suspicion and good-natured superiority, tempered with a tolerance which the former never show towards the other Talis.

A similar, but more elastic, social boundary exists between Tongo and Zoo. There are no Zoo people living inside Tongo, but no less than 11 of the 39 homesteads situated on the land under the ritual jurisdiction of Zoo-Yiraaŋ, within the social circumference of Zoo, are the homes of permanent immigrants from Tongo. The bond of common stock (buurət) between these two locally allied and politically associated Namoo clans blurs the cleavages between them. Tongo people find it the more congenial to live amongst Zoo people in considerable numbers because they have the same ritual observances, mortuary and funeral customs, and politico-ritual offices and values. It is mainly cultural differences of this kind that deter them from settling amongst the people of Zubiuŋ.

The one-sided filtration of Tongo people into Zoo, and the absence of the reverse process, are due mainly to the density of habitation—which is so great as to preclude immigration—and the obvious excess of population at Tongo. Zoo people who wish to emigrate, temporarily or permanently, move farther afield, to Gbambee or Biuŋ. In any case, the flow of migration from Tongo to Zoo has apparently reached saturation, for it has now practically stopped. But this movement, though at bottom an ecological readjustment, has been canalized by the social structure; and while it brings out the affinities of Tongo with Zoo, it also emphasizes their separateness. Because they are structurally independent of each other, Tongo people only migrate to Zoo if they have matrilateral kin there who will grant them land to build on and farm. By contrast,

M

162   THE SOCIAL STRUCTURE OF A SETTLEMENT

people from Tongo and Zoo settle at Gbambee, which is only an overflow settlement, irrespective of kinship or lineage relationships, usually on land formerly utilized by their forefathers as bush farms.

Elastic as it is, the social boundary between Tongo and Zoo has not disappeared. This is shown in the effort made by the people of Zoo, during the past two generations, to resist being swallowed up politically by Tongo. To preserve the autonomous status of the chiefship of Biuŋ, which is vested in the Zoo Namoos, the chiefs of Biuŋ now reside there permanently instead of at Zoo, as in former times. It is evident, also, from the recognition by leading men of both groups, that they are now more closely united than in the days of their fathers. They describe this as part of the general trend towards wider political consolidation, both within clans and between neighbouring communities, 'since the white man tamed us (*nasaara m-maa ti*)'. They commonly quote a trivial but telling sign of this. Nowadays one often finds a group of Zoo boys pasturing their cattle side by side with a group of young cattle herds from Tongo, and playing amicably with them. 'When I was a boy', a Zoo elder said, 'this never happened. The Tongo children were strangers to us, and our fathers used to warn us not to go near them, for we always used to fight and that would cause bad blood.'

Between Tongo and Gbeog dwells the numerically small (they number under fifty males) but socially powerful maximal lineage of Gbizug. A social boundary, intermediate in character between that which separates Tongo from Zubiuŋ and that which demarcates it from the Hill Talis, runs between it and Gbizug. They are more distinctly separated, territorially, than Tongo and Zubiuŋ, yet so closely contiguous that constant friendly intercourse and mutual assistance is a regular feature of the relations of members of the two units with one another. At the same time, the cleavage in terms of descent, ritual observances, and jural interests goes deeper than with Zubiuŋ. Gbizug is closely allied to the Hill Talis and Ba'ari by ties of clanship, politico-ritual collaboration, and common ritual values. It is also bound to Tongo by inescapable ties of politico-ritual interdependence and mutual constraint. This accentuates the social boundary between them. The politico-ritual function of Gbizug is to hold the balance between Tongo and the Hill Talis. It stands aloof in their disputes, taking neither side, for it belongs equally to both and wholly to neither. Thus, important ceremonial events at Gbizug are attended both by representatives of Tongo and by representatives of the adjacent Hill Talis clans and Ba'ari, though the former take a more distant, passive, and extraneous part in them than the latter.

We have mentioned Gbambee, a settlement of about 25 to 30 homesteads straggling over a row of stony hillocks alongside a great stretch of low-lying bush, most of it uncultivable, which lies just beyond Zoo. This is regarded as merely an outpost of Tongo and Zoo, where the younger men, who are most handicapped by the scarcity of land at home, can find an economic outlet. Hence a man may live there for many years, grow old and die there, but he is generally brought back to Tongo or Zoo for burial among his ancestors. There are many indications, however, that Gbambee will soon become stabilized as a permanent settlement.

THE SOCIAL STRUCTURE OF A SETTLEMENT   163

A small number of Tongo people have gone yet farther afield in search of
a livelihood: to Biuŋ and other peripheral settlements, to Mampurugu,
and, increasingly in recent years, to the tempting Eldorado of Ashanti
and the Colony. Thus, not all the members of the Tongo branch of
Mosuor biis and its accessory lineages live at Tongo at any given time;
but within its confines live only members of the sub-clan and their
families; and for all members of the sub-clan, wherever they may be
living, Tongo is their home, the centre of gravity of their social existence.

We have said before that no two Tale settlements are exactly alike.
Allowing for specific differences, however, the local and social circum-
scription of Tongo may be taken as typical. The general rule is that
boundaries exist in terms of social cleavages co-ordinated with residential
distribution, and not of geographical or topographical features; and this
rule applies both to the spatial relations of contiguous settlements and to
those of parts of a settlement with one another. Community and locality
cannot be dissociated. The maxim, 'A tɛŋ is not a tɛŋ if there are no
people in it', always cited to explain the strong sense of ethical obligation
felt by the natives to accept a suitable immigrant in any community, if
land is available, sums this up. The boundary disputes that have become
common between chiefs and headmen in recent years turn on the contradiction between the conception of a defined territorial boundary
fostered by British rule, and the type of social boundary inherent in the
native social structure.

A revealing case occurred among the Hill Talis. The elaborate interlocking of the Hill Talis clans with one another through clanship ties,
ritual collaboration, local cohesion, and political loyalties, and the diffused
solidarity to which this gives rise, impel them to common or mutually
supporting action in crises. Yet even among them, social boundaries
divide clan from clan and maximal lineage from maximal lineage both
spatially and structurally, and come into operation in certain situations.
But these social boundaries are far less firm than those between Tongo
and its neighbours. Groups of contiguous clans cohere to nearly the same
extent as a genealogically organic community like Tongo. Tɛnzugu, in
particular, and Yinduuri-Zandoya, form two such close-knit sub-
communities within the wider community of all the Hill Talis.

Since 1936 a boundary dispute has embittered the relations of the
Gɔlibdaana and the Yinduurna'aba, who are recognized by the Administration as headman of Tɛnzugu and headman of Yinduur-Zandoya
respectively. It is an insoluble dispute, bound to remain a chronic source
of friction as long as these two headmen exercise the territorially
defined powers entrusted to them by the Administration.

The dispute concerns a segment of Zandoya living on the slope of the
Hills between Yinduuri and Tɛnzugu. It was at length, after many
evasions on the Gɔlibdaana's part, brought before the Chief of Tongo for
arbitration. But this ended, inevitably, in a deadlock. The Gɔlibdaana,
crafty and overweening, as only a man of his extravagant wealth and un-
yielding temper could be, when he knew himself to be in the wrong,
took his stand on a criterion often used by Administrative officers in such
disputes. The group in question, he claimed, was living on land that

164 THE SOCIAL STRUCTURE OF A SETTLEMENT

comes under the ritual jurisdiction of the Degal tɛndaana, the ritual 'owner' of the land of Bunkiuk, the Gɔlibdaana's clan. As the head of Bunkiuk and headman of Tɛnzugu, which includes Degal, he held political authority over all the territory under the ritual jurisdiction of the latter. Hence this strip of territory, as far as the watercourse, belonged to him. The people dwelling there were no concern of his; let them go elsewhere if they wished.

The Yinduurna'aba, a simple and inarticulate old man, who has never mastered the wiles of modern headmanship, protested vehemently. The Gɔlibdaana's arguments were untenable. The ritual jurisdiction of tɛndaanas had nothing to do with the matter. In any case the Zandoya tɛndaana would contest the Degal tɛndaana's claim. Everybody knows that tɛndaanas acknowledge no boundaries. The group in question was a segment of Zandoya. How could they belong to any other political unit than the latter? To talk of their abandoning the land on which their ancestors had dwelt was preposterous. Indeed, the whole situation was something quite unheard of; it could never have occurred before the coming of the white man, when everyone had his acknowledged place in the society. The truth was that the Gɔlibdaana was deliberately trying to entice his people away from him.

There the matter rested. The case was widely discussed and public opinion, except for the Gɔlibdaana's supporters, sided unanimously with the Yinduurna'aba. Five other cases of the same kind came to my notice; and in all of them the verdict of native custom is unequivocal; social affiliation and not alleged territorial boundaries define the extent of a community. Even the new settlements, though they sprawl more widely than the old settlements and are usually surrounded by considerable tracts of uninhabited land, have no defined geographical boundaries. They can and do go on expanding.

The Concept of the Tɛŋ

A Tale settlement can only be identified as a unit by reference to the lineage relationships, politico-ritual ties and cleavages, and jural rights and duties, prevailing within it and between it and its neighbours. That is why we have avoided the word 'village', which conjures up the image of a neatly isolated, compact territorial unit. *Tɛŋ* (pl. *tɛs*) is the native concept denoting a settlement; but no English translation can convey its exact sense. In some ways it is reminiscent of the deme of ancient Greece, a coalescence of local association, lineage organization, common religious cult, and political solidarity. None of these factors serves to demarcate a *tɛŋ* absolutely from adjacent *tɛs*; all of them link together neighbouring *tɛs* or parts of *tɛs* as closely in respect of that one category of social relations as they unite segments of the same *tɛŋ*. A settlement is only a relatively autonomous community. One might perhaps define it as the region of maximum overlap of all the categories of social relations found among the Tallensi.

Native linguistic usage reflects this, for *tɛŋ* has a width of reference varying with the situation. A man beginning a discourse on marriage with '*ti tɛŋɔ, nyɛn di pɔya . . .*—In this our land, if you marry a wife . . .'

THE SOCIAL STRUCTURE OF A SETTLEMENT 165

is thinking of the country at large as a unit with respect to marriage customs. Hill Talis often describe Tongo, Zubiuŋ, and Zoo as one *tɛŋ*. They are thinking of the close bonds uniting these places in opposition to themselves. But Tongo, Zubiuŋ, and Zoo are always distinct *tɛs* to one another. Tɛnzugu is described as a single *tɛŋ* when the coherence and close interdependence of the group of clans inhabiting it are emphasized; but when their genealogical cleavages loom foremost they are designated as separate *tɛs*. In the struggle for political dominance now going on between the head of Kpata'ar and the head of Bunkiuk, the partisans of both bitterly denounce one another for 'breaking up the unity of the *tɛŋ*', but insist, at the same time, that each clan holds its *tɛŋ* in its own right and does not come under the jurisdiction of any other, according to native custom.

Underlying these variations in usage is the generic conception of *tɛŋ* as a locality defined in relation to a corporate unit of social structure, a lineage, clan, or interconnected group of clans; and the variation in the width of reference of the concept reflects the variation in the range of corporate solidarity that is effective in different situations. In war the Tɛnzugu clans all hold together; in the matter of marriage one of them might quite easily come into conflict with another. The confluence of local, lineage, and politico-ritual relations, as we have previously noted, is the keel of Tale social organization.

Tɛŋ, like all the key concepts of Tale social organization, has a ritual significance as well. It denotes the Earth in its mystical aspect, either in the generic sense or in the specific sense of a particular sacred spot and its precincts. What is a *tɛŋ* in the sphere of secular relations may be, but often is not, a *tɛŋ* in the system of religious beliefs. There are two aspects to locality as a correlate of social structure: the secular aspect and the sacred. They merge in the social organization and the social philosophy of the Tallensi, and consequently also in linguistic usage. Sometimes one aspect is the focus of a social activity, sometimes the other, sometimes both together. If a man repeats the conventional formula, '*Tɛŋ la pu sayat ziem la ni*—The Earth does not permit bloodshed', his exclusive reference to the mystical aspect of the Earth is obvious; if he says of another settlement or region, '*Ba tɛŋ la mar ki pam*—Their land has plenty of grain', he is thinking solely of the material and secular denotation of the word; if he says of Ba'ari, '*Bam tɛŋ kuob la pu dara*—In their settlement farms are not sold', his implication to anyone familiar with native beliefs is that it is a taboo of the Earth (in its mystical character) at Ba'ari to sell parcels of the earth (in its material character).

Postponing for the moment the further elucidation of these ideas, we may note their most commonplace expression in Tale custom. A settlement name is *ipso facto* the name of the clan or group of maximal lineages whose home it is. A custom arising out of the rule of clan exogamy is that of addressing a wife by an appellation indicating her clan of birth. Most often it is the clan place-name, e.g. Zubieŋa, Wakiiŋa. It may be the name of a well-known *tɔŋgban* in her natal settlement, e.g. Ba'ari women are called Saniiga, after the sacred grove of that name in Ba'ari. It may be a name indicating differences of custom and belief that distinguish her

166   THE SOCIAL STRUCTURE OF A SETTLEMENT

clan from her husband's, e.g. Namooga, the appellation used by Talis for their Tongo wives. Lastly, it may be a name taken from some politico-ritual office vested in her clan or maximal lineage, e.g. Bɔyaraan, for Sii women, Tɛndaan-bii for Gbizug women. This shows how, without explicit formulation, the notions of locality, lineage, sacred attributes of the Earth, distinctive customs, and politico-ritual office—the major themes of Tale social and political organization—are linked together in a single ideological configuration.

The Section—Yizug

With the exception of the settlements of a few small clans not divided into maximal lineages of independent descent, all clan settlements are further divided into sections. The principles that regulate the structure of the settlement as a whole also determine the structure of its sections and of segments of these sections. This rests on the fact that the different orders of segmentation in the maximal lineage are serially homologous. An old-established settlement is the home of a clan or sub-clan. It is built up on the lineage system. All groupings and alinements that emerge in corporate affairs tend to follow lineage ties and cleavages. Thus, a section is a local subdivision of the *tɛŋ* occupied by a defined segment of the clan or maximal lineage. *Yizug* (pl. *yizugɔt*), the native term here translated by 'section', means literally 'Superior House',[1] and shows that the genealogical criterion predominates in the native definition of a section. Occasionally people speak of a *yizug* or part of a *yizug* as a *faaŋ* (quarter, pl. *fɔna*), using a term more common among the Mamprusi, when they are thinking of it primarily as a residential unit.

In the new settlements, however, the *yizug* is predominantly a local subdivision. This is due to their genealogical heterogeneity and political immaturity. At Datɔk, for example, one finds Gɔrisi, Tallensi, and Namnam from many different clans, drawn thither by the need for land, and connected with one another not by lineage but by ties of extra-clan kinship and affinity. Moreover, before British rule brought security and gave the titular chief of Datɔk real authority over it, its population was small and largely temporary, and constituted a group of loosely associated neighbours, not a political community. In these circumstances the sub-division of the settlement on strictly local lines is inevitable, the more so as the present-day administrative organization is based on territorial groupings.

Primarily, a *yizug* is a localized lineage segment of a clan settlement. But, characteristically, the Tallensi often extend its reference to denote a whole clan, considered as a member of an interlocking group of adjacent clans that have a greater degree of political solidarity and social cohesion *inter se* than any of them have with other clans. Tɛnzugu, as we have seen, is the outstanding instance of such a community. Tɛnzugu elders often describe the six clans dwelling there as 'our six *yizugɔt*' when they recapitulate stories of fights with Tongo in the days of long ago. It is a phrase constantly heard in the invocations to the ancestor spirits

[1] *Yir*, 'house', or, in this context, 'lineage', and *zug*, 'head', or by extension, 'superior, supreme'.

THE SOCIAL STRUCTURE OF A SETTLEMENT   167

and the Earth when representatives of the various clans gather to perform
one of the great annual ceremonies, as their ritual obligations compel
them to, even though they are nowadays divided into two hostile camps.
For these are the occasions when the essential unity of Tɛnzugu—a unity
in relation to which the six clans rank merely as *yizugət*—can rightly be
insisted upon, when frank reproaches verging on warnings of spiritual
retribution can be directed against the destroyers of this unity.

Yet in other situations the component maximal lineages of a particular
Tɛnzugu clan are referred to as its *yizugət*. Thus, in connexion with their
distinct ritual offices in the cult of the External *Bɔyar* or their divergent
clanship linkages, the three maximal lineages of Bunkiuk are always
described as *yizugət*. For, like the clan in relation to its neighbour clans,
the maximal lineage forms a distinct genealogical and residential unity
within the clan settlement. Looked at from within, each maximal lineage
is a relatively autonomous integral unit, the majority of whose members
live close together inside its social boundaries, which are defined in
relation to the other lineages of the clan in the same way as those of the
clan settlement are defined in relation to neighbouring clans. The
difference is one of degree only, the social boundaries of a lineage within
a clan being more fluid than those of a clan. The stability of a settlement
rests on the equilibrium of its sections with one another, and this depends
upon their being precisely differentiated from one another.

The Sections of Tongo

Tongo proper (Tɔŋ-Nayiri) has four *yizugət*—Puhug, Guŋ, Seug, and
Kuorəg. Two roads, laid down some years ago by the Administration,
which intersect almost at right angles where the Resthouse stands (see
map at end of book), by chance afford a convenient set of co-ordinates for
describing its layout. Puhug occupies most of the south-western quadrant and a corner of the south-eastern quadrant, most of which is Kuorəg.
Seug is an irregular block in the north-eastern quadrant. Guŋ is divided:
part of it, Guŋ proper, lies across the watercourse to the west of Puhug;
but the majority of its members live in the north-western quadrant, in a
broad wedge between Zubiuŋ and Gbizug known as Dekpieŋ. A few Guŋ
homesteads also lie on the border between Seug and Zoo. Nevertheless,
scattered as it is, Guŋ constitutes a single *yizug* in all corporate affairs
except those connected with modern administrative demands. In the
latter the local criterion prevails, Dekpieŋ having its own headman and the
Guŋ homesteads at Seug coming under the supervision of the Seug
headman. Members of all four sections live at Zoo and at Gbambee, but
they always act with their respective sections in matters of common
concern.

The names of these sections are typical of section and settlement names
all over the country. Puhug gets its name from an ancient *puhug* or *pusəga*
(*Tamarindus Indica*) tree, which is said to have stood at the edge of the
sacred dancing-ground in the centre of the section from time immemorial.
It died long ago, but old men still remember seeing its stump. Guŋ is
called after the silk-cotton tree (*Ceiba Pentendra*; Talni, *guŋ*) so common
in the country. Trees of all kinds, and especially those as tall as the

168   THE SOCIAL STRUCTURE OF A SETTLEMENT

silk-cotton, are prominent landmarks in a country of monotonous plains; hence settlements and sections often bear the names of species of trees found there.

Kuorəg was thus named, according to popular etymology, because the Soog Yikpɛmdaana, who holds the ritual jurisdiction over the land on which the homesteads of Kuorəg stand, ritually allocated or 'cut' (*kuo*) the sites for all these homesteads when Tongo men first settled there. In the same way popular etymology explains the name Dekpieŋ ('it is hard') as derived from the hardness (*kpeoŋ*) of the soil in that part of the settlement as compared with that of Puhug or Seug. Seug literally means 'the rainy season', but no one in Tongo was ever able to suggest how this section acquired its name; and this is characteristic of very many settlement and section names in Taleland.

To the people of Tongo their present residential constellation is the visible deposit, as it were, of the continuous expansion of the sub-clan through many generations within the limits of its geographical environment and social boundaries. They read the spatial disposition of the four sections as a record of their structural evolution, as a map of the contemporary constitution, and as proof of the chronological retrospect of the sub-clan. Mosuor came to settle at Puhug, where his grave still marks the site of his homestead. As his posterity increased in numbers, they began to move outwards in the same way as young men migrate to Zoo, Gbambee, and farther, nowadays, and for the same reason, shortage of farm-land. Thus Guŋ, Kuorəg, and Seug were occupied. Later, the descendants of those who founded Guŋ became too numerous for the land available there, and, prevented from expanding into Wakii by the social barriers between Tongo and that clan, filtered gradually into the area that is now Dekpieŋ. Arguing from what may be observed nowadays, they say that this was largely a process of occupying hitherto vacant land at a time when the population was very small. But it was partly, also, a process of dispossessing and pushing out to their present location the people of Zubiuŋ and of Gbizug, who claim to have lived at Puhug originally. In proof of this they cite their myths of origin, the fact that the dancing-ground in Puhug is sacred because it is the site of Tɛndaan Gɛnət's homestead, and the ritual jurisdiction exercised over part of the land of Puhug by Gbizug and over the remainder by Zubiuŋ. Indeed, there are Zubiuŋ graves on land now occupied by Dekpieŋ men which are said to date back only three to five generations. This proves that the people of Zubiuŋ were still yielding ground to the Tɔndɛm, as they themselves admit, when elders alive to-day were 'already born'.

There is nothing derogatory in such a retreat. On the contrary, Gbizug and Zubiuŋ elders boast of it as additional evidence of the dependence of the people of Tongo on their ritual benevolence and bounty. It is a cardinal rule of Tale ethics that a request for land to build on and farm— especially if it comes from a kinsman, friend, or neighbour—may not be refused if it can be granted without hardship. There was formerly, and there still is to a small extent, land to spare at Gbizug and at Zubiuŋ. Tongo people have innumerable ties of kinship and neighbourhood with Gbizug and Zubiuŋ, which are the more effective on account of the ties

THE SOCIAL STRUCTURE OF A SETTLEMENT 169

of politico-ritual unity and solidarity existing between the three clans. To give up land to them is, therefore, an act of virtue that creates yet closer mutual bonds.

The four sections of Tongo are not marked off from one another by territorial boundaries. But each is more or less concentrated in one locality, forming a more or less exclusive local unit, looked at from within. Members of one section are not found living right in the middle of another section. In theory they are at liberty to do so. In practice they would find it impossible, owing partly to the absence of unowned land at Tongò, but mainly to the pull of lineage loyalties. For the territorial segmentation of Tongo is a function of its precise and definitive lineage segmentation; a section is the local framework of a lineage segment. By the lineage criterion the sections are relatively autonomous units within the limits set by their common descent, but they are held together in a remarkably stable social equilibrium by their common interests. This has a counter-part in their territorial relations, which show them to have reached a stable ecological equilibrium *inter se*. The area occupied by each section is now finally fixed in location and more or less fixed in extent. Where any of them has expanded in the last three or four generations it has been chiefly at the expense of Zubiuŋ and Gbizug, not of another Tongo section. Thus, as in the case of composite clans, a social boundary exists between one section of Tongo and another. There is more intimate and regular daily intercourse, more mutual aid, closer and more binding moral, jural, and ceremonial bonds, between the members of a section, both children and adults, and between their wives, than between them and members, or wives of members, of another section. There are latent hostilities and hence a greater probability of dissension between sections than within sections. Thus they have a competitive orientation towards one another where some common interests, like the chiefship, are concerned.

Territorial Distribution and the Tɛŋ in its Mystical Aspect

As with many other Tale settlements, there is no relation between the territorial distribution of the people of Tongo and the distribution of ritual jurisdiction over the land on which they live. This was the point emphasized by the Yinduurna'ab in the case previously quoted. Tongò stretches over the ritual domains of several tɛndaanas. Guŋ proper lies on the outskirts of the Gbeog tɛndaana's tɛŋ; most of Puhug is on the Gbizug tɛndaana's ritual territory; Kuorɔg is on land under the ritual jurisdiction of the Soog Yikpɛmdaan; Seug partly on Zoo tɛŋ and partly on Zubiuŋ tɛŋ, Dekpieŋ mostly on Zubiuŋ tɛŋ.

The bearing of this on the internal structure of Tongo is only indirect. The section or part of a section dwelling on a particular tɛndaana's tɛŋ and thus coming within the scope of his ritual powers has closer ties of neighbourliness and of affinal and cognatic kinship with that tɛndaana's clan than other sections have. Differences in the local taboos of the Earth (*tɛŋɔn kiha*) observed by the people of Tongo symbolize these ties. For example, a red pot must be left on a new grave at Kuorɔg, because this is a taboo of Soog tɛŋ. Elsewhere in Tongo this is not done. Soog elders and youths always take part in the festive phases of a Kuorɔg funeral, in a

170   THE SOCIAL STRUCTURE OF A SETTLEMENT

representative capacity; they attend funerals elsewhere in Tongo only in a personal capacity as kin or affines of the bereaved family. Similarly, when the Gbizug tɛndaana invited the men of Tongo to a collective hoeing—an invitation to which his politico-ritual relations with Tongo gave the weight of a command—it was to Puhug mainly that he directed the invitation, and the elders of Puhug saw to it that their sons turned out in full force. For, as they explained: 'We stand in awe of the Gbizug tɛndaana, he sacrifices (to the Earth) on our behalf.' From Dekpieŋ, the neighbours of Gbizug, came only three young men, and the other sections merely sent messengers to convey their good wishes for a fruitful day's work. Such ties, however, are only effective as long as amicable relationships prevail between Tongo as a whole and the particular tɛndaana's clan.

This brings us back to our starting-point: the social boundaries of Tongo. It is evident that they are largely a function of the social and political relations which each section has with its immediate neighbours, and which differ slightly from section to section.

CHAPTER XI

LAND, LOCALITY, AND THE EARTH

Definition of the Bonds between People and the Land

As we have already seen, there is in Tale social organization an intrinsic connexion between every defined social group or part of a social group and a specific locality. Now there are, as yet, no communities in Taleland consisting of aggregations of individuals or families of completely heterogeneous cultural or genealogical origin, whose sole common interest in the locality they occupy is utilitarian, and whose sole bond with one another is their common subjection to a single political authority. As we shall see, even in the new peripheral settlements, which are now, under the pressure of land shortage, being permanently occupied by mixed populations, the decisive bonds of association are ties of consanguineous and affinal kinship. It could hardly be otherwise in a society so homogeneous and also lacking centralized government.

The connexion between community and locality has the three aspects found in all Tale social institutions. It is utilitarian—for men build their homes on the land and get their livelihood from it; it is also morphological, particular units of the social structure being tied to defined localities so that the social unit and its locality form a single entity; and it has a moral and ritual coefficient. Men have moral and ritual relations with one another and with the land in virtue of their occupancy or utilization of particular portions of its surface. We have touched on this in our preliminary remarks on the Tale concept of *tɛŋ*. We return, here, to the further elucidation of this concept.

The bonds between a community and a locality, or between an individual or a lineage and land, are summed up in the idea of 'ownership' (*soləm*). This concept, which occurs in various contexts, has certain general implications. Where it is a matter of property such as land, or where persons or localities associated with social groups are concerned, to 'own' (*so*) them means to have responsibilities towards and for them, rights over and on behalf of them, privileges and duties in relation to other individuals or corporate groups in virtue of being the 'master' (*daana* or *-raana*) of the land, locality, or person in question. In every case, there is no such thing as purely utilitarian ownership. Utilitarian ownership exists within a framework of the relations of a defined social group to the land, the person, the locality; and this framework, in turn, is held together by a scheme of moral and ritual values and sanctions.

Thus, in the case of land, exercising or acquiring 'ownership' for productive purposes is regulated by clanship and kinship ties and limited by the moral and ritual values of the ancestor cult and the Earth cult. In some circumstances clanship or kinship may be the more important determinant, in others ritual considerations may be the vital factor. The three aspects of 'ownership' may be vested in the same individual or group, or in different individuals or groups. But they are always there.

172   LAND, LOCALITY, AND THE EARTH

The natives cannot imagine any tract of land or territory being totally unconnected with a human group. Most tracts of uninhabited bush are 'owned' by chiefs, who have ritual jurisdiction over hunting rights. But some tracts of untilled and uninhabited land (e.g. between Biuŋ and the river) appear to have no 'owners', either secular or ritual. The natives say the 'owners' have died out. The land did at one time have a connexion, perhaps only a ritual connexion, with a human group, and this connexion remains mystically effective still. Such areas of *wasak*, as the natives call them, are economically a free good. Anyone can come and build or cultivate there. But a man who does so will try to find some person or some clan to offer sacrifice to the Earth on his behalf, as the residuary legatee of the defunct 'owners', through local or clanship ties with them. If he fails to find anyone, he will consult a diviner to find out for himself where the sacred spots are in this stretch of *wasak* and make the sacrifices himself, thus creating a moral bond with it. Nowhere is the Earth inert; and its mystical powers are a reflex of its relations with human groups.

The three functionally differentiated aspects of man's relations to territory in Taleland are interconnected in Tale thought and custom in a rather complex way, and local differences blur the general principles. The simplest approach will be from the starting-point of land used for agricultural purposes. This is by far the most important economic use of land, but not the only one. There are few products of nature on the earth's surface that the natives do not make some economic use of, or rely on for other practical purposes. It is easy to see, therefore, why the natural environment is built into the social organization and invested with values and meaning in the social philosophy and ritual beliefs of the Tallensi. Our analysis would lead to the same conclusions if we started from uncultivated bush (*moog*), for instance, the source of essential products such as firewood, wild fruits, shea nuts, thatching grass, reeds for mat-making, rafters, medicine roots, and so forth, as well as of game and wild fowl.

Farm-land and Subsistence

Land means many things to the Tale farmer. He distinguishes, firstly, between the soil (*tam*) and the arable, or tilled land (*kuob*). He recognizes and takes into account different kinds and qualities of soil. This is something independent of the tillage of the land; and, conversely, cultivation (*kuo*, from *kɔ*, to hoe) turns any kind of soil (*tam*) into arable (*kuob*). Tilled land, again, is classified, without reference to soil qualities, by its location and by the kind of crops grown on it. Thus, every farmer has one or more home farms (*saman*) in the settlement and one or more bush farms (*poog*) in an area free of human habitations. In addition, a particular farm is merely a parcel of land, a bit carved out of a *tɛŋ*. In this context a *tɛŋ* is a stretch of territory in its useful, material aspect. One can speak of such and such a *tɛŋ* as being very fertile, or as having a sandy soil (*tambiihug*).

Farming is the basis of the Talaŋ's livelihood. A failure of crops, nowadays, spells widespread privation. Thirty years ago it would have brought famine. Tallensi often talk of this, especially when unpropitious

LAND, LOCALITY, AND THE EARTH

weather causes anxiety about the crops; for famine is the greatest social calamity they can imagine and is a very real menace. I have heard people speak of the last great famine that swept the country, some forty years ago, with a poignancy that made one realize how deeply dread of famine is stamped into the native's outlook on life. 'It is our black man's thing this (*ti gbansablǝg yɛl n-a-de*)', they say, 'from the days of our fathers and forefathers'—or, as we might put it, it is a law of nature for the black man. 'The white man has saved us. If there is hunger now we can buy grain from Mampurugu or Kusaa.' Sombrely they describe how in times of famine people ate grass and weeds fit only for animals, and died on the footpaths. Men deserted wife and child to seek sustenance among distant relatives who had a little food. They took their own children to sell into slavery among the Mamprusi for food. The social order broke down completely.

Sufficient crops of the staple cereals mean survival, good crops mean joy to the Tallensi. They show it in the Harvest Festival that marks the end of the farming year. If the harvest is poor, they say, people attend the dances perfunctorily and dance without enthusiasm. But in a good year, as I saw in 1936, no one can be held back from the dances. Young mothers steal out to them with their babes in their arms, sedate elders fling themselves into the rout with the zest and energy of striplings. There is a general feeling of elation. 'Our bodies are full of strength (*ti nɛŋ kpɛŋya*)', is how the natives describe it.

A successful farming year not only provides for the satisfaction of the fundamental physical needs of existence; it gives security to the social order. There is ample evidence of this in the busy and cheerful atmosphere of the market-places, and, more significantly, in the space of ceremonial activities that follows on a satisfactory harvest; for all Tale ceremonial activities express and fortify relationships of amity and interdependence. For the individual the physical well-being of himself and his dependants—sufficiency of food, good health, and the increase of offspring—is a sign that all is well with the social order. The ritual symbols in which the forces that shape Tale social organization and keep it on a steady course are objectified and made emotionally tangible go back to this fact of native experience. The stereotyped formula with which a prayer offered at any shrine is usually concluded epitomizes this: 'Grant that fields be farmed (fruitfully), that live-stock breed, that offspring be born, that (undisturbed) sleep be slept (*Kye ka kuo kɔ, ka guul guul, ka dɔyam dɔya, ka guom gbis*).'

Productive Efficiency and the Bounds set by Nature

Now what does the achievement of sufficiency of food and general physical well-being depend upon? It is quite clear, from the way the natives carry on their agricultural activities and the way they think and talk about them that, other things being equal, they consider skill and industry to be the main factors of efficiency. But variations in efficiency between a *pukpaa*, a slothful farmer, and a proper *kpa'at*, an industrious hoe-man, mean only a difference in their respective standards of consumption. One has rather less food and other goods than the other.

174 LAND, LOCALITY, AND THE EARTH

Whether there is food or famine, a bare sufficiency or a surplus for the majority of people, depends on other things than human efficiency. It depends enormously on the weather. Drought (*waar*) in the early months of the rainy season brings hunger; an erratic distribution of rainfall causes a poor harvest; an unusually violent tornado (*sanziug*), crushing and uprooting the young millet, produces a shortage. Locusts (*tinta'aba*) descending suddenly, inexplicably, on the half-grown crops and devouring them, ruin the most efficient farmer's work. These are public calamities beyond human control, and they are an ever-present danger. During my first tour in Taleland a long gap in the normal sequence of the early rains threw everybody into a state of foreboding. Men went about restlessly, waiting anxiously for a sign of rain. During my second tour locusts destroyed the crops in one part of the country. The grief and chagrin of those whose crops had suffered showed that they felt they had suffered an irreparable loss.

Another possible natural disaster which would destroy physical well-being and rend the social fabric is an epidemic of small-pox (*zinzaaŋ*) or of measles (*kasoo*).[1] Cases of *kasoo* occur every year and the mortality is high. I have heard of more than one family in which several children died of it in a week or two. Naturally the natives, who have no remedy for it, regard it with terror. The last small-pox epidemic (before 1937) occurred about a generation ago. The natives know that the white man's precautions will check any future epidemic, but they still dread the danger. For small-pox, when it comes, devastates social life. People stop visiting their kinsfolk and neighbours; stricken families are isolated by a wall of thorn bushes; those who die of small-pox are not even given proper burial but are interred in the midden heap or thrown into the uncultivated bush. At such times small-pox must be referred to by a euphemism. It is 'the chief' (*na'ab*), and a death due to it is 'the chief has bestowed a boon (*na'ab maalya*)'.

These are the ever-possible public calamities which defeat human effort and skill. Private dangers also threaten the individual farmer. A snake might bite him as he stoops to hoe; blight might destroy his millet but leave his neighbour's farms unaffected; sickness might lay him low or deprive him of the help of wife or son.

It must not be thought that the Tale farmer goes about in a permanent state of fear of these external dangers to his welfare and security. When things are going well he does not give a thought to them. Living, as they do, at a subsistence level that gives them no regular surplus over what they require to satisfy their normal wants, the Tallensi take no long-term precautions, either individually or collectively, against the dangers of starvation or pestilence. They have neither the technical means nor the social institutions for such measures. But these threats do materialize often enough for them to serve as the realities towards which Tale acts of ritual self-protection, both individual and collective, are directed. Tallensi do not believe that these ritual acts will prevent natural disasters

---

[1] From the natives' description of the symptoms, I think the sickness they call *kasoo* is probably measles, but I am not certain and I have not been able to obtain medical corroboration.

LAND, LOCALITY, AND THE EARTH 175

or personal mishaps. They do not attempt to control nature by means of ritual, though the content of their prayers might persuade the superficial observer that this is their object. Their ritual is concerned with the effects of natural phenomena and physiological happenings on the fate of the individual and the coherence of the community. Ritual is the means of fortifying the individual and the society against these effects. Tallensi believe that the fate of individuals and of communities depends on their relationships with mystical powers. Natural phenomena are the medium, as it were, by means of which these powers intervene in human affairs. If men offend them, they will intervene disastrously; if men please them, they will intervene beneficently. And men offend or please the mystical powers by the manner in which they behave to one another and by the way in which they observe the moral norms of the society and the ritual duties that symbolize these norms. Ritual—that is, sacrifice and prayer— is a means of keeping up a good relationship with the mystical powers. These, as we know, are principally the ancestors and the Earth.

Striving after Security: the Ritual Background

We have tried to state briefly how the Tallensi connect their ritual conceptions with their striving after personal prosperity and social security. This can be put in another way. The individual farmer, working his own land with the aid of his dependants for their common subsistence, looks to his and their immediate ancestors for spiritual protection. He and his dependants are personally responsible for the success of their efforts in the working of their fields. They are also personally responsible for the goodwill of their immediate ancestors. The sacrifices and prayers they offer to their ancestors at sowing and harvest express these private concerns. They enable them to enjoy the fruits of their labour with a clear conscience and to overcome the demoralizing effect of accidents, which they regard as private misfortunes.

On the other hand, public calamities are associated with the mystical powers of the Earth, which are a symbolical projection of the common concerns of mankind. By prayers and sacrifices the ritual officers who represent the community in relation to the Earth and the Earth in relation to the community, the tendaanas, preserve the benevolence of the Earth towards mankind. Even though ritual measures often and obviously fail to prevent a public calamity, they serve to reintegrate the community after the calamity has passed. The idea of the Earth's being concerned with the common good corresponds to the fact that the cultivations of individuals are but parcels of land cut from the limitless earth.

Just as the earth's surface is limitless, so the mystical power of the Earth is universal.[1] All men everywhere acknowledge this in the ritual observances by which they show their respect for the Earth. The most important of these observances are the rules concerning 'things found on

---

[1] The word *tɛŋ* belongs to the *ka—si* Noun Class and takes the third person singular pronoun *ka*. This is the pronoun always used to refer to the earth in its material aspect. But in its mystical aspect the Earth is commonly referred to by the third person singular pronoun *u* which is primarily used for persons. To conform with this rule, we write 'earth' in the first sense with a lower-case initial letter, and 'Earth' with a capital letter for the latter.

176   LAND, LOCALITY, AND THE EARTH

the earth (*tɛŋənpiima*)'. As we have previously noted, any article or stray animal, the owner of which is unknown, is a *tɛŋənpiimər*. It must be handed to a tɛndaana. The rule applies to stray fowls, goats, sheep, and especially to objects of iron; and it is most scrupulously observed. A hoe or an axe, for instance, can safely be left lying about on a farm. Tallensi speak with awe of the sacrilege of appropriating a 'thing found on the Earth'. They say that swift retribution invariably overtakes a sinner, and they quote the example of those who occasionally break the taboo, by accident or purposely. It is particularly heinous to take anything found near an Earth shrine, where the mystical power of the Earth is directly localized. Even children are fearful of picking up bits of rubbish near *tɔŋgbana*. Breaches of Earth taboos serve, in the long run, to increase the respect in which they are held. The native is constantly reminded, by these taboos, that the useful, material earth is only the façade of the universal mystical Earth. They remind him that the security and satisfaction he derives from the utilization of the earth's resources are conditional upon his moral behaviour.

We have examined the relation of the concept of the Earth in its mystical aspect to the great public calamities that threaten the physical basis of the existence of the natives. But this concept has a positive side, too. When men do not offend it, the Earth permits crops to flourish, women to bear children, and men's enterprises to succeed. Locusts, Tallensi say, when they rationalize the powers they attribute to the Earth, come up out of the earth; tornadoes sweep across its surface; but, also, crops grow on the earth; homesteads stand on it; men walk on it; out of it they dig the roots they use to cure their illnesses and make magical defences for themselves; in it they bury their dead. All these services of the material earth have their reflex in the ritual values attached to the mystical Earth.

All Tallensi stand in awe of the Earth. We have learnt that they speak of it as 'a living thing', meaning by this that it intervenes mystically in human affairs in the same way as the ancestor spirits do. When they talk of the Earth they mention its remorseless punishment of sacrilege, and the things it prohibits, not its blessings. Yet it is the symbol to them of the forces that promote the common welfare of all mankind without discrimination. Thus a wandering stranger is a 'thing found on the earth'; but he is given to a chief and not to a tɛndaana. Chiefs are ritually qualified to sell a human being into slavery; a tɛndaana would commit a sacrilege against the Earth if he did so. As the priest of the Earth it is his duty to protect human beings, keep the peace among them, and be watchful against the dangers that threaten them. The dog lives in such close association with man that it has quasi-human qualities, and therefore stray dogs must also be surrendered to chiefs. And this holds for stray cattle, too, which are also closely identified with man owing to their great economic value and their special importance as sacrificial animals.

Everywhere, too, the Earth forbids the shedding of blood in strife, and, in the neighbourhood of important Earth shrines, the raising of the alarm signal (a long-drawn-out, high-pitched cry *ya-a-a-a-hi*) as a call to arms, and therefore to bloodshed. Men who transgress have to pay heavy

PLATE IX

(a) A large boulder in the middle of a settlement forms a natural mortar where young girls go to stamp guinea corn.

(b) Women at a waterhole in the early rainy season. This waterhole serves homesteads within a radius of over a quarter of a mile.

PLATE X

(a) The Gbizug tɛndaana dressed for a specially important ritual occasion. Notice his black string cap, one of the distinctive emblems of his office.

(b) Kparəg bush near Biuŋ. The chief of Biuŋ's son about to fire the bush on the morning of the annual communal hunt. Though uncultivated, Kparəg is under the ritual jurisdiction of the chief (who is also tɛndaana) of Biuŋ.

LAND, LOCALITY, AND THE EARTH

sacrifices of expiation or else 'their house—i.e. line of descent—is destroyed (*ba yiri ŋmaarǝme*)' in retribution. This is the strongest sanction against homicide among the Tallensi. Whether it is intended or accidental, whether the victim is a clansman or a stranger, and has been slain at home or abroad, homicide is a sin against the Earth and must be expiated. But it is so grave a sin that it can, in fact, never be wholly atoned for. 'You cannot finish paying' the Tallensi say. It is a sin that pursues the wrongdoer's agnatic descendants for generations.

The Tallensi have no juridical machinery for taking penal action against a murderer and do not exact compensation. Between clans homicide may lead to vengeance and war; within the clan it does not. In the latter case it is like a cow that has trampled on its calf and killed it, the natives say. In either case the matter is left to the arbitrament of Earth. Tallensi who have shed human blood take no pride in it. A man who can be persuaded to confide the story of how he killed another speaks of his deed as if it were forced on him by circumstances. Though homicide seems to have been an infrequent occurrence in the past, it was by no means rare; but every instance I have heard of was presented as a reprehensible action, even if it was due to provocation or done in self-help. Informants always draw the moral prescribed by Tale ethical values. So-and-so killed a man and died childless; So-and-so left only one young son; deaths pile up in such-and-such a family because their father had shot a man. In the long run, again, the reaction to sacrilege is greater respect for the moral norm and its ritual sanction.

Bloodshed and strife are symptoms and causes of deep rifts in or between human communities. The taboos against them show us the Earth as a sanction of solidarity within and between communities; and this is of particular interest in relation to the structure of the settlement. The bond between community and locality has moral implications for the natives that transcend the crude facts of spatial distribution and economic organization in which they are rooted. It is worth while tracing out these implications somewhat further from the starting-point of the individual farmer again.

The Social Framework of Production: Land Tenure

The farming unit among the Tallensi is the group of male agnates of a single household who usually form a nuclear lineage. Most of the plots it farms are owned by the farming unit, but some may be borrowed for a shorter or longer period and some held by gift. In the case of borrowed or gift land the farmer—distinguished as the 'owner of the farm' (*kuoraana*) —pays no rent to the owner—distinguished as 'the owner of the soil' (*tamraana*)—or tribute to a political authority. An annual gift of grain, when crops are good, is the only return he makes to the owner of the land, and this is a voluntary gesture of gratitude, not a jural obligation. Borrowed land always reverts to the owner. Theoretically gift land can also be resumed at will by the owner. In practice it often becomes the property of the recipient's lineage in the third or fourth generation after the gift, if it has been farmed continuously by that lineage. This is either because donor and recipient are usually kin, related in such a way that

178 LAND, LOCALITY, AND THE EARTH

the latter can claim a contingent right to the land and cannot be dispossessed without offence to their common ancestor or ancestress; or because the land was virgin at the time of the gift and the donor 'cut' (*kie*) it for the recipient in virtue of being the tɛndaana of the area. Thus all farm-land is either owned or in process of becoming owned.

The ownership (*solɔm*) of farm-land is a precise jural concept among the Tallensi. Briefly, it is vested in a lineage and forms the most important part of the lineage patrimony (*faar*). When, in course of time, this lineage splits up, some of the *faar* land will be apportioned among the resulting segments, each of which will retain perpetual and exclusive ownership of its portion. The rest of the *faar* land remains the common property of the whole lineage. Though the bulk of farm-land is owned by nuclear lineages, there is land owned by lineages of larger span than the average nuclear lineage.

To say that land is owned by a lineage is equivalent to saying that it is generally acquired by right of inheritance. All males of the lineage have the right to inherit lineage land, but at any given time control over it is vested in the head of the lineage, by right of seniority. He inherits (*vaa*) what amounts to full usufructuary rights within the limits of the co-existing rights of the other members of the lineage. The utilization of the land is at his discretion; he disposes of the crops; and in some settlements he is nominally free to pledge or to sell the land. But he is subject to restraints which observation shows to be very effective. He is bound to provide fairly for the wants of those who share the labour of farming with him. Tallensi formulate this obligation in terms of reciprocity within the productive unit, which they regard as a matter of natural justice and moral duty. They emphasize, however, that there is also a strong practical sanction behind the rule. A man who deals meanly or unscrupulously with his younger brothers, sons, or brother's sons will find that they leave him at the first opportunity; and the strength of this sanction has increased now that young men, and even girls, can easily slip away to work abroad. In accordance with this obligation a lineage head always consults his dependants about the disposal of land, crops, or other patrimonial property.

There is also a religious sanction, the converse of the obligation to one's dependants, and the ritual projection of the common interest of the lineage in its patrimonial land. Inherited farm-land is a sacred trust of the ancestors. Their labour won it for human use, hallowed it, and preserved it for their descendants. It belongs to them. To pledge it is a slur on them; to sell it a sacrilege. 'It will kill deaths (*de kura kum*)'— the offended ancestors will cause deaths in the family of the seller—the natives say. And the strength of this sanction is such that only dire necessity will make a man sell ancestral land in the settlements where this is allowed. It is, in fact, an uncommon thing for farm-land to be sold, both for technological reasons, and on account of the ritual sanction against sale. In places like Tongo, land sales do occur, however, but appear to have been more frequent in the past than at present. Three out of every four nuclear lineages at Tongo possess farm plots that they claim have been purchased during the past two or three generations.

LAND, LOCALITY, AND THE EARTH   179

In the past hunger or a pressing bride-price debt often left a man with no other resource than to sell his land; and a man in a tight corner, the natives say, does not care about ritual sanctions. Nowadays there are other ways in which a man can struggle through (*waləg*) such difficulties.

Where land is concerned Tallensi always connect the fear of mystical punishment by the ancestors with the obligations towards one's dependants and coheirs. The religious sanction and the practical sanction are thought of as aspects of the total economic and kinship configuration. The head of the nuclear lineage is not only bound to but wants to preserve his patrimonial land for his successors, because it is the foundation of the lineage's subsistence. And his brothers and sons do not rely solely on ritual and moral sanctions. They will use every legitimate means to prevent him from selling or pledging land that is due to come to them on his death.

Despite these sanctions the pledging of farm-land is not uncommon; and judging by what happens in such cases, it is probable that much land now regarded as having been bought came into the possession of its present owners by having been pledged, in the first instance, and not redeemed. But the attitude of the natives in such cases is well illustrated by the behaviour of a man I knew very well. He was an extravagant man and had accumulated debts to the tune of about thirty shillings in the past few years. But he was also, like most Tallensi, touchy about his reputation. So when his creditors began to press him, and his failure to pay began to arouse gossip, he borrowed money on the security of his ancestral land. For months afterwards, whenever I met him, he could talk of nothing else but his pledged land. His remorse and apprehension were obvious, for he knew that only a windfall would ever enable him to redeem the land. It was like a Damocles sword over his head. 'If I do not repay the loan my forefathers won't allow it. They will kill deaths in my family', he told me anxiously.

Borrowing land for a season or a period of years is very common. I have never heard of a case in which the lender has been cheated of his right of resumption. Here, again, the sanction of the ancestor cult is the significant factor. When land is borrowed for a long time, the decisive act in the transaction is a sacrifice to the lineage ancestors of the lender's lineage. This is performed in the presence of the other members of the lineage who have an interest in the land, and of the borrower, who must provide the animals and libations for the rite. Though the loan is made at the discretion of the head of the lineage owning the land, his co-members must consent and the lineage ancestors must be informed. The ancestors who 'own' the land are exhorted to prosper the borrower. Without this covenant, expressing the consent of all concerned, the transaction is void. The borrower would not venture to farm the land, even if this were possible. He believes that the owners' outraged ancestors will bring disaster on him, if he did so.

It is important to note that, with rare exceptions, such land transactions always take place between kinsmen or clansmen. All forms of land ownership and utilization exist only within the genealogical frame of the

180 LAND, LOCALITY, AND THE EARTH

social structure. The economic utilization of land is regulated by the process of segmentation in the lineage and by the system of co-operation in the household. It turns upon the acceptance, by the members of the household, of the norms governing their relationships and the enforcement of these norms, in accordance with the principle of reciprocity, by direct action. Behind these norms stands the ancestor cult, the supreme sanction of solidarity in the pursuit of common interests by the lineage. Granted favourable external conditions, the efficiency of production, among the Tallensi, with the technical means at their disposal, depends on the organization of the household and lineage.

Broadly speaking, then, every unit of farm-land corresponds to a unit of social structure. More specifically, the elementary utilitarian unit of territory corresponds to the elementary unit of the social structure, and the relationship between them, summed up in the concept of ownership, is a permanent one. The history of a nuclear lineage is *eo ipso* the history of its farm-land. Every change in the structure of the lineage implies a corresponding change in the distribution of the usufructuary rights in its farm-land. While the lineage exists it never forfeits ownership of its farm-land, whether its members cultivate it or not. The strength of the tie felt to hold between a lineage and its ancestral farm-land (*banam kuo*) is shown in the rule that purchased land is redeemable at any time by repayment of the purchase price (or more probably, as we have suggested, of the original loan) by the vendor lineage.[1]

The keystone of the institutional framework of Tale agriculture is security of land tenure. But what, we may ask, guarantees to the lineage security of ownership of its farm-land, in the absence of judicial institutions and instruments? The answer is contained in the Tale concept of the *teŋ* as a community. The landowning unit is a segment of a maximal lineage and its property rights are an aspect of its corporate relationship to the maximal lineage and clan. Within a settlement the stretch of land parcelled out into farm plots corresponds to the clan occupying that locality as it segmented into a hierarchy of lineage units. All segments of the clan of the same order are equal to one another. They have an equal weight in the structure of the clan, equal power in its affairs. They have, in consequence, equal property rights (though not necessarily equal amounts of property), equal opportunity for holding and farming land (though not necessarily equal achievement), and equal social duties to one another. Hence each segment respects the land rights of all other segments, just as it respects their rights in relation to their wives and children. This is an aspect of the solidarity of the clan, one of the indices of the common interest of all members of the clan in one another's welfare. It is a feature of the equilibrium of interlineage and intra-clan relationships. The relative structural autonomy of the nuclear lineage, which is a basic factor in the equilibrium of the maximal lineage and clan, presupposes corresponding economic autonomy. Just as members of the same

[1] In practice, the rule does not hold beyond three generations, by which time all witnesses to the transaction, and their sons (whom they would have told of it) are dead, but attempts are often made to assert the right of redemption after three generations.

LAND, LOCALITY, AND THE EARTH 181

clan must not kill one another or abduct one another's wives, so they must not trespass on one another's land. For this would wreck the mutual loyalties of segment to segment and make impossible the maintenance of the reciprocity of rights and duties on which their corporate life depends. There is, in other words, a generally accepted body of jural and moral norms, binding on all members of the clan and cementing its solidarity, and supported by the powerful sanctions of the ancestor cult and the Earth cult. The security of land tenure is guaranteed by this.

Tallensi say that it is unthinkable for any man to take another's farmland. It is his ancestral land. You would not borrow a patch for a groundnut plot without his permission: how could you think of seizing any of it for yourself? The idea is either fantastic or simply ludicrous to them. And in fact, disputes over farm boundaries or trespassing on another's land are almost unknown. The most remarkable proof of this occurred in 1936, when the Hill Talis returned to their ancestral homes after twenty-five years of exile. Several hundred men took possession again of their ancestors' farm plots without a single boundary dispute. If there was doubt about a particular plot the elders were consulted and settled the matter, not by the exercise of authority but by reason of their knowledge of where every member of the clan had farmed in the old days. Boys of thirteen or fourteen know in detail the ownership and boundaries of every farm plot in the settlement, or at any rate in their section, if it is a large settlement.

It should be noted that there is no communal production for communal use of foodstuffs or any other commodities among the Tallensi, and there is, accordingly, no concept of the communal ownership of the farm-lands of the community. A nuclear lineage has indefeasible rights of ownership over its land. No one has an over-right over it, either real or fictitious. This rule applies between clans as well as within the clan. Trespassing on the farm-lands of members of clans other than one's own is unheard of. For, as we have learnt, adjacent clans are interconnected by structural ties. Every clan is a member of a wider community of interdependent clans, emerging at the level of politico-ritual relations and including, at its widest extent, all the Tallensi. This is the *tɛŋ* at its widest extent, symbolically recognized in the Great Festivals and in the chain of interdependent politico-ritual offices held by the heads of all the different maximal lineages and clans. It is the counterpart, in the social structure, of the notion of the Earth in its mystical aspect as a universal power acting on the lives of all men.

Security of land ownership, which means security for every man of the opportunity to supply the basic needs of himself and his dependants, is, therefore, conditional upon the integration of the community; in the first place, of the clan, but also of the wider community of interdependent groups of clans. Its ultimate basis is the politico-ritual organization of the Tallensi.

The Integration of the Community: Chiefship and Tɛndaanaship

The politico-ritual integration of a Tale clan is focused in the politico-ritual office or offices vested in it or in its component maximal lineages.

LAND, LOCALITY, AND THE EARTH

These offices are either chiefship (*na'am*) (or its equivalent, the senior office connected with an External *Bɔyar*) or tɛndaanaship.[1] Chiefship is primarily associated with the Namoos, though not exclusively so, tɛndaanaship with the clans and maximal lineages claiming to be the autochthonous inhabitants of the country, though, again, not exclusively so. Both chiefship and tɛndaanaship are, to the natives, unitary institutions made up of offices distributed among a number of clans and lineages. The range of these institutions is not even limited to Taleland. All chiefs are 'brothers' since they derive their office from a common source, the Paramount Chief of Mampurugu; all tɛndaanas, similarly, are 'brothers' since their office has the same function and ritual value everywhere in relation to the Earth. The chain of ritual collaboration is one expression of this notion.

Among the Tale chiefs (*na'ab*, pl. *nadɛm*) the Chief of Tongo (*Tɔŋraana*) ranks highest. He has no political, administrative, or judicial authority over any other chiefs, or any other clan than his own, but his office incarnates the quintessence of *na'am*. He represents all the chiefs of the country in the ritual attributes of chiefship. Tɛndaanas, in keeping with the elaborate segmentation of the clans in which this office is vested, are more equal in status. But in every cluster of closely interdependent contiguous clans there is one tɛndaana who ranks higher than his confreres. The Gbizug tɛndaana ranks above the tɛndaanas of Zubiuŋ, Gbeog, and Wakii, and the Ɗoo tɛndaana above the other Tɛnzugu tɛndaanas.

As we have seen, the Earth cult and the External *Bɔyar* cult function as polar opposites in the structural dynamics of the Hill Talis' clan system.[2] In terms of politico-ritual office it is chiefship and tɛndaanaship that have this polar relationship. Within a particular clan and between interdependent contiguous clans the complementary politico-ritual roles of chief (or his equivalent) and tɛndaana form the axis about which the body of moral, jural, and ritual values that binds the community into a unity revolves. Such a community may be a clan (as, for example, Ɗkoog) or a cluster of interdependent clans (as, for instance, Tongo and its immediate neighbours); and at the times of the Great Festival, the community that emerges includes all the Tallensi and some non-Tallensi.

Chiefs and tɛndaanas had no political power, as we understand it, before the coming of the white man. They had no administrative, or executive, and only rudimentary judicial powers. They were the leaders and not the rulers, the fathers and not the princes of their clans. Where the social ends served by the native political system are concerned, this pat-

[1] We are concerned here with the role of these politico-ritual offices in the native social system as it was before the establishment of British rule and as it still functions vigorously in situations that fall outside the orbit of the British Administration's sanctions and demands. It is convenient, however, to follow the usage of the Administration in calling the functionary who holds the office of *na'am* a chief rather than overload our analysis with an excess of native titles. But there is no comparison between Tale 'chiefs' and the rulers of great African nations like the Ashanti or Bemba, or even the chiefs of southern Bantu tribes. Cf. *African Political Systems* previously cited. My article in that book deals more fully with the subject of this section.

[2] Cf. Chap. VII.

LAND, LOCALITY, AND THE EARTH 183

tern still prevails. Their function is 'to prosper the community (*maal tɛŋ*)'. Overtly and most conspicuously this is a ritual function. By their conscientious observance of the ritual rules of conduct that symbolize their respective offices, their responsibilities for the community to the mystical powers, and their mutual relationships, as well as by taking the lead in ritual acts calculated to preserve or restore the goodwill of these mystical powers, they maintain the well-being of the community. Actually, these ritual attributes symbolize the fact that chief or tɛndaana is the hub of clan unity and solidarity, the representative of the common interests and of the common values that enable men to visualize and to hold fast to this common interest.

The polar conjunction of chiefship and tɛndaanaship is expressed in the obligatory ritual collaboration, with complementary roles, of chiefs and tɛndaanas. It mirrors the fusion of the two principles that shape the total social field which ultimately determines the prosperity of the individual. One is the principle that the fate of the individual and of the community is determined by the practical and utilitarian concerns and needs that bind man to the earth and put him at the mercy of natural phenomena. The other is the principle that the attainment of prosperity and security, both for the individual and the community, depends upon the integration of the community. The two principles fuse in the notion that the prosperity of the land (*tɛŋ*)—that is, of the community dwelling on its territory—depends on the united strength of the chiefship and the tɛndaanaship, in the last resort. When drought or an epidemic threatens, chiefs and tɛndaanas meet together to decide on ritual measures to be undertaken to avert it. When war temporarily cuts through the tissue of structural ties that holds the clans of Taleland together, the social equilibrium is finally restored by the ritual collaboration, according to ancient custom, of chief and tɛndaana. The death of a chief or tɛndaana leaves 'the land empty (*tɛŋvoog*)', as if its sentinel has departed, until his successor is installed. The death of a chief, Tallensi say, portends want— at best a scarcity of food in his own clan, at the worst a famine throughout the whole country. 'The land dies (*tɛŋ la kpiirəme*)', the people starve, and social life breaks up. This always happens when a Chief of Tongo dies. It is the one disaster, Tallensi declare, which even the white man's rule cannot avert. The death of an important tɛndaana is also ominous, but not likely to be so disastrous, since there is usually at least one other tɛndaana in the same clan and there are a great many tɛndaanas in the country.

The principles underlying the structure of a society are never embodied in a perfectly unambiguous way in its social institutions. Social life, even in the most stable and unprogressive of societies, demands continual reshufflings, readjustments, and revaluations of social relationships. Though the distant past has no record among the Tallensi, their society exists in time like every human society. Events leave a deposit in its structure, though they themselves vanish into the limbo of oblivion. Thus, in some clans the two principles we have been examining are very clearly brought out in the precise separation by office, ritual observances, and genealogical limitation of the functions of chiefship and tɛndaanaship.

184 LAND, LOCALITY, AND THE EARTH

Elsewhere their differentiation and relationship are obscured by the fusion of the two roles in a single office or by the subdivision and distribution of the two roles among a group of offices.

Broadly speaking, however, chiefship symbolizes the plexus of social relationships, based on lineage and kinship, which unites a defined group of people into a community; and tɛndaanaship symbolizes the bonds of men, as members of a community, with land, locality, and the material earth. Chiefship and tɛndaanaship are ritual offices because the principles of social structure they stand for are so fundamental that they appear to the natives as axiomatic. Projected on to the ritual plane, they are transformed into unchallengeable values and so become beacons that guide men's behaviour. Both chiefship and tɛndaanaship are vested in maximal lineages and therefore have the ritual sanction of the ancestor cult; both are associated with the organization of the Tallensi into local communities and the utilization of natural resources, and therefore have the sanction of the Earth cult. But in their complementary conjunction the emphasis in the chiefship is on its transmission from the ancestors, while the emphasis in the tɛndaanaship is on its specific ritual bonds with the mystical Earth.

This is brought out by one curious point of difference between the burial customs of Namoos and those of most non-Namoo clans. Namoos bury their dead at the entrance to the homestead, so that the ancestral graves of every segment of a lineage are separate. Men know the graves of their particular forebears and the graves of remoter ancestors who are significant for the structure of the lineage. The tombs of chiefs, in particular, are known and cared for by their agnatic descendants. Namoos also sacrifice to a particular ancestor on his grave. Clans which have tɛndaanas usually bury their dead in cemeteries within the settlement. They do not sacrifice to their ancestors on their graves and within two generations forget which is the grave of a particular individual. In other respects their ancestor cult is exactly the same as that of the Namoos. In clans that have the chiefship (naditib), the natives explain, the most important thing is for every man to be able to show exactly how he is connected by descent with previous holders of the chiefship; whereas in tɛndaanditib clans this is unimportant as all the members of the clan have the same ritual bonds with the Earth.

The Tɛndaana's Tɛŋ

Everywhere in Taleland men utilize the earth's resources in the same way and owe respect to the mystical powers of the Earth. But the natural resources of the Earth are of direct importance for them at particular places—where they farm, build their homesteads, hunt, fish, or collect bush products. It is at these places that the mystical power of the Earth impinges directly on their lives. Men's utilitarian interests in the earth's surface are sectional, not global; and so also are their social interests in it since they are divided into maximal lineages and clans which are precisely localized. Thus the earth's surface is divided into sections relatively to the social organization of the Tallensi. Each section has its own Earth shrines for the worship of the Earth at that place, and they are in the

LAND, LOCALITY, AND THE EARTH 185

ritual custody of a particular clan or maximal lineage. Such a territorial section is the *tɛŋ* of a particular tɛndaana. He is the master (*daana*) of that locality (*tɛŋ*), exercising ritual jurisdiction over it on behalf of the maximal lineage or clan which has the ritual ownership of it, in virtue of being the head of that unit. He is the mediator between the Earth and the people whose interests lie in that fraction of its physical surface. When the concept *tɛŋ* is coupled with a tɛndaana it has a double meaning. It denotes both a stretch of territory and a place of contact with the mystical Earth. It may be used to designate a single Earth shrine (*tɔŋgban*) and its precincts, a total area of anything from about 20 square yards to an acre or two; and it can be applied to the whole of a tɛndaana's *tɛŋ*, which includes a number of *tɔŋgbana*.

Tɛndaanas' *tɛs* vary greatly in extent. As I have no exact measurements, I can only indicate roughly the range of differences. Small *tɛs* are the rule in the older and more densely settled part of the country. The area of a clan settlement on Tɛnzugu, for instance, perhaps a square mile altogether, may be divided amongst three or four tɛndaanas. On the other hand, at the peripheries tɛndaanas have ritual jurisdiction over large tracts of land, many square miles in extent. This is largely due to the absence of permanent settlement in these parts until recently, and the still relatively scanty population living there.

Tallensi do not think of a tɛndaana's *tɛŋ* in terms of its size but in terms of its position relatively to the *tɛs* of neighbouring tɛndaanas. Tɛndaanas themselves claim that their *tɛs* have definite boundaries, but when asked to show them they become very uneasy and quote the maxim 'The boundaries of a *tɛŋ* must not be pointed out (*Tɛŋən tentɔris pu pa'ana*)'. When my bona fides was, at length, accepted by the Tallensi I was able to persuade several tɛndaanas to have the boundaries of their *tɛs* shown to me. My guides were always ill at ease, and apparently felt that what they were doing verged on sacrilege. Chiefs and elders of clans that do not have tɛndaanas usually declare that it is impossible for tɛndaanas to have boundaries (cf. p. 164); for are not neighbouring tɛndaanas always 'kin' (*mabiis*)—by clanship or by ritual ties? Do they not often sacrifice together at one another's Earth shrines (*tɔŋgbana*) or go by stealth, at night, to sacrifice at a neighbouring tɛndaana's Earth shrines? Tɛndaanas do not deny this. In every group of contiguous maximal lineages, each presided over by a tɛndaana (as for instance Gbeog, Gbizug, and Zubiuŋ), the senior tɛndaana (in this instance the Gbizug tɛndaana) always claims to be the real 'owner' of the aggregate of *tɛs* held by the group of tɛndaanas. He talks of this aggregate of *tɛs* as if it were one *tɛŋ* apportioned amongst his junior 'brothers' and himself for the greater convenience of performing the priestly duties of the tɛndaanaship. They divide their common spiritual jurisdiction rather than a distinct stretch of territory; and in principle this rule embraces the whole of Taleland. For the powers of the Earth are indivisible, the Earth is a unity. When the Gbizug tɛndaana sacrifices to his supreme *tɔŋgban*—or, as he often phrases it, his *tɛŋ*—Kpɔŋkparəg, he invokes all the important *tɔŋgbana* of Taleland, up to the limit of the field of politico-ritual relations in which Gbizug participates, from Duusi in the north-east to Biuŋ in the south.

186   LAND, LOCALITY, AND THE EARTH

Like the tɛndaanas all the tɔŋgbana of Taleland, and even beyond Tale-land, are described as 'kin' (mabiis) to one another. In principle, tɛŋ, the Earth, cannot be divided up; it is the tɛndaanaship which is distributed.

This explains the diversity and lack of precision one finds in the boundaries of tɛndaanas' tɛs. Like settlement boundaries they are deter-mined by social rather than physical facts, though here and there con-spicuous topographical features may be fixed upon as landmarks from which to take a bearing. Doo tɛŋ, the area immediately surrounding and including the supreme tɔŋgban Doo of Tɛnzugu, is an example of a tɛndaana's tɛŋ that can easily be distinguished. Homesteads on Doo tɛŋ may not have roofs of thatch (mopin) but must have flat roofs (bɛa, vb.) of mud. This is a quasi-totemic taboo of this tɛŋ (cf. p. 142). Standing on the wall of granite boulders that overlooks this part of Tɛnzugu one can see where the mud roofs end and the thatched roofs begin. I was very reluctantly told about, and later shown, what purported to be the fixed physical boundaries of Doo tɛŋ by men of Kpata'ar, the clan which has ritual jurisdiction over it. A ditch, a line of large boulders, a prominent tree, a path, such were the landmarks by which they went. But the striking thing about this boundary was that, almost all the way, it followed the social boundaries between Kpata'ar and Gundaat on the one side, and between Bunkiuk and Samiit on the other. In the closely settled parts of the country, wherever tɛndaanditib clans are in occupation of the areas under their ritual jurisdiction, there is a noticeable tendency for the alleged physical boundaries of tɛs to coincide with social boundaries between clans or maximal lineages.

Settlements like Tongo, where people believed to be of immigrant descent occupy land under the ritual jurisdiction of other clans, are instructive. Tongo, like many other Tale settlements, stretches over the ritual territories of several tɛndaanas (cf. p. 169). The alleged boundaries between the tɛs of the Gbizug, Soog, and Zubiuŋ tɛndaanas run through Tongo. As the people of Tongo put it, these clans at various times allotted portions of their own land for Tongo people to build and farm on. Physical landmarks are pointed out as indicating these boundaries. But if they are examined it will be seen that they tend to coincide with the social boundaries between sections (yizugɔt) or between segments of sections (dugɔt). (See map at end of book.) Wherever part of a tɛndaana's boundary runs between homesteads of men of the same segment (dug), the homesteads (rarely more than one or two) on the wrong side of the boundary have not been sited there for more than a generation. The continual slow shifting about of homestead sites in a settlement through the course of generations is paralleled by a shifting of the boundaries between farm plots; for they pass through alternate phases of being divided up, wholly or in part, among the segments of a nuclear lineage that has reached a phase of fission, and of being reconstituted, wholly or in part, at a later stage of lineage integration. These internal adjustments often result in a spilling over of one section of a clan into what was till then regarded as the area of a neighbouring unit of like sort.

We lack historical documents; but we can infer from the contemporary dynamics of Tale social life that the boundaries of tɛndaanas' tɛs shift

LAND, LOCALITY, AND THE EARTH

gradually with the passage of generations in adjustment to changing social boundaries.

It is significant how frequently in settlements like Tongo tɛndaanas' boundaries are adjusted to cognatic ties between a particular tɛndaana's clan and a segment of the immigrant clan. In Tongo all Dekpieŋ, barring two or three homesteads, is on Zubiuŋ land; there is not one segment of Dekpieŋ that has no cognatic or affinal ties with Zubiuŋ. The few men who live on Gbizug land are all matrilateral kin of Gbizug. All Kuorəg is on Soog land; and the Kuorəg tradition is that one of their ancestors was a Soog *ahəŋ* (sister's son) who was granted land to settle on by his *ahəb* (maternal uncle), the Soog tɛndaana. Similarly, Lɛbhtiis yidɛm of Puhug call themselves the classificatory sister's sons of Gbizug, and most of them live on Gbizug land. This is a further indication that the ill-defined boundaries of tɛndaanas' *tɛs* are shaped by social relationships.

Not all Namoos live on land under the ritual jurisdiction of other clans. The Chief of Biuŋ, though a Namoo, is also the tɛndaana of Biuŋ. The people of Ŋkoog live on land under their own tɛndaana, a member of their own clan. They have both a chief and a tɛndaana.[1] In these cases the natives maintain that the original settlers of their clan found no one living there. Being Namoos they brought the chiefship with them, or, as at Biuŋ, held the chiefly rights over the bush out of which Biuŋ has been carved. But the Earth cannot go unworshipped where men dwell; so they undertook the tɛndaanaship themselves.

A tɛndaana's *tɛŋ* is the area in which he exercises priestly duties and responsibilities and the rights and privileges that correspond to them. It is primarily on behalf of the people dwelling or farming there that he constantly consults diviners to find out what sacrifices he must offer in order that the Earth may bless the strivings of men. Lost and unclaimed property or objects found anywhere on his *tɛŋ* must be delivered to him, to be used by him or sacrificed to the Earth. If anybody wishes to build a house on a virgin site, even on farm-land belonging to his own lineage, the blessing of the Earth is essential if the house is to prosper. Therefore the tɛndaana of that *tɛŋ* must come and 'clear the house-site (*kuo yir*)' ritually for the family, receiving, in return, only certain prescribed portions of the meat of the animals sacrificed. If a new grave has to be dug, the tɛndaana, or someone deputizing for him, has to mark it out ritually (*kyieb*) and supervise the digging. This is not only because the dead are laid to rest inside the earth, but also because interring the dead is an act of crucial social and personal importance, charged with ritual meanings of great intensity. It is one of the points at which man's life and the mystical powers of the Earth come into contact in a way that is fraught with the deepest affective and social meaning for the individual and wide consequences for the organization of the society. Thereafter,

---

[1] But, characteristically, the tɛndaanaship is vested in one segment only of the clan, and that segment is prohibited from holding the chiefship. Moreover, their right to the tɛndaanaship and their exclusion from the chiefship are both validated by their lineage status. They form an attached lineage claiming matrilateral descent from a lineage of Wakii that has the tɛndaanaship. The chiefship is confined to the authentic lineages of Ŋkoog. Thus the polar relation of chiefship and tɛndaanaship asserts itself within the clan.

188   LAND, LOCALITY, AND THE EARTH

one who was human (*vor*) becomes a spirit (*kpiim*). For this service, too, the tɛndaana receives only prescribed portions of the sacrificial animals. If a man wants to break virgin land for cultivation, he requires the consent of the tɛndaana in whose *tɛŋ* the land lies. Unless the tɛndaana comes to cut the boundaries (*kie*) of the farm, its cultivation will bring nothing but disaster on the farmer. The tɛndaana's reward is, again, only a portion of the sacrifices and occasional gifts of grain in subsequent years. Lastly, there are the circumstances in which a tɛndaana must be called upon to make peace between man and the Earth. The weightiest of these is in the case of blood shed in strife, whether the victim dies or not. Atonement sacrifices must be offered by both parties through the tɛndaana of the *tɛŋ* where the blood was shed, and, in clans that have the tɛndaanaship, through their own tɛndaanas as well. There are also less heinous sacrileges and even venial sins—such as wearing cloth garments near certain *tɔŋg-bana*—for which small atonement sacrifices must be offered through the tɛndaana; and there are some minor accidents which must be ritually cancelled out by a sacrifice to the Earth. If a house burns down, for example, it is thought of as a quasi-mystical disaster, like a failure of one's crops, and the fire must be ritually 'quenched' by the tɛndaana, after it has been physically put out.

For all these ritual services, which tɛndaanas regard both as duties that can be neglected only at peril of life and as rights indicating their status and ritual jurisdiction, no payment is given other than portions of the sacrifices. To people with the standard of living of the Tallensi the value of such perquisites is by no means negligible. It is a common saying that all tɛndaanas are gluttons and that they are never short of meat. Cynics say that the office of tɛndaana is coveted for the meat it brings in. We must remember, however, that when we speak of a tɛndaana here it would be more appropriate to speak of a tɛndaana and his lineage or clan. For a tɛndaana can and frequently does send one or more of his clansmen to deputize for him and sometimes even delegates some of his duties to cognates not of his clan; and the rewards of his services must be shared with them and with his close agnates.

Certain taboos of the Earth are obligatory on all tɛndaanas. Thus it is a taboo for cloth garments to be worn in the vicinity of any of the important *tɔŋgbana* like Ðoo or of the homesteads of all except a few tɛndaanas. My clothing was a constant embarrassment to tɛndaanas even after they had resigned themselves to my European shortcomings. As tɛndaanas can never lay aside their priestly bonds with the Earth, they may never wear cloth. Instead, they wear dressed skins of domestic or wild ungulates. A tɛndaana dressed in his finest skins on a solemn occasion has an appearance of hieratic dignity that is most impressive.

There are also, as we have learnt (cf. p. 142), local *tɛŋ* taboos obligatory on everybody who lives on that *tɛŋ*, and serving to mark it off from other *tɛs*. Among the commonest are the prohibition against using red ochre (*tandaɣanze'e*) for plastering the homestead or grass for roofing it, and the taboos against killing certain reptiles. In the observance of these taboos, as in their compliance with all the obligations and observances connected with the Earth, Tallensi are extremely conscientious. In consequence,

LAND, LOCALITY, AND THE EARTH 189

his ritual powers and duties give a tɛndaana very great prestige and considerable moral authority over people living on his *tɛŋ* whether or not they belong to his clan. At Tongo, for instance, the Gbizug tɛndaana is spoken of and treated with a respect little short of reverence, both in the formal interclan politico-ritual relations and in commonplace relations of everyday life. 'He owns the land (*ɔn nso tɛŋ la*)', Tongo people say gravely, 'we are strangers here. We only grow our millet here to feed ourselves. If we offend the tɛndaana he can drive us away from here.' The last part of this statement is not literally true. A tɛndaana cannot drive people off their ancestral dwelling and farm-land; to say the least it would be ethically evil. It is not legal but ritual action that the statement implies. I have seen a tɛndaana's curse throw a person into a state of anxiety that persisted for days, until a reconciliation was effected. But this was anxiety concerning the mystical consequences of the tɛndaana's curse, without any assumption as to its jural implications. The term 'owner' applied to a chief or tɛndaana, as we have stated earlier, is simply a means of subsuming in one concept the configuration of rights and duties, privileges and obligations which defines the relations of a community with its politico-ritual heads in reference to its local framework and to the common values symbolized in ritual doctrine and practice. The material earth and the mystical Earth meet in the functions of tɛndaanas.

Many Tallensi are able to formulate the distinction between the earth in its physical, utilitarian aspect and the Earth in its ritual manifestations. But in general the distinction is inherent in the economic and politico-ritual institutions of the natives rather than expressed in explicit doctrine or language. Whenever or wherever the concept *tɛŋ* comes up it tends to be ambiguous. It suggests both aspects of the earth, though the major emphasis may be on one or the other. It is as if neither aspect of the earth can appear without the other following like its shadow.

This holds particularly with the *tɛndaanditib* clans. Their ritual bonds with their *tɛs* form a halo around their utilitarian relations with the earth. In most of these clans, therefore, it is a taboo of the Earth to sell parcels of land. To sell farm-land (*kuo*) is like selling pieces of the mystical *tɛŋ* to which they are bound by the strongest ties of interest, emotion, and values. Namoo clans which do not have tɛndaanas do not feel this strong and direct tie with their *tɛŋ* in its mystical aspect. The utilitarian, material aspect of the earth falls apart from its mystical counterpart more easily for them. Hence it is mostly in such communities that farm-land is sold. But even Namoos say that the earth as such, the *tɛŋ*, cannot be sold. In practice the sale of farm-land is a sale of usufructuary rights and is confined to clansmen or kinsmen as we know. It is, always, a transaction between men who are bound to one another by the fundamental common and mutual interests of Tale collective life. Men cannot buy land in a Tale settlement in which they have no kin. In this, as in other aspects of their relationship towards locality, the Namoos put the major emphasis on the coherence of the community as this is focused in the chiefship. And fundamentally the coherence of the community is as indivisible as the continuity of territory. The Chief of Tongo, for example, exercises an ever-present influence on the prosperity and welfare of the members of his own sub-clan. This is the central field of integrated social relations pivoting on this chiefship. But his ritual status also affects the prosperity and welfare of Zubiuŋ and Zoo directly and that of the Hill Talis indirectly. In fact, in the last resort, it affects all the clans of Taleland that have a place in the cycle of the Great Festivals. 'The community (tɛŋ) cannot be subdivided (bɔk)', the Chief of Tongo once told me in explanation of the ritual significance of his office. Famine, pestilence, war cannot be dammed and confined to one place. And so if the Chief of Tongo dies the whole country suffers, though his own clan will perhaps suffer most and the remoter zones of his politico-ritual influence least.

The bonds between man and land, community and locality that are so fundamental in the structure of Tale society cannot be understood apart from this context of ritual values and moral norms. Difficult as they are to grasp and pin down in exact language, they are as ever present to the native's mind as his sentiment of attachment to his native soil. They cause men who have been away from home for many years to give up splendid farms in Mampurugu or good jobs in Kumasi to return to take up their patrimonial land.

CHAPTER XII

THE LINEAGE IN THE LOCAL COMMUNITY

General Features

A CENTRAL factor in the continuity and stability of a Tale settlement is the economic organization; but the persistent morphological framework, the factor that gives its peculiar stamp to the form of a Tale community, is its lineage skeleton. The critical feature is the congruence of local aggregation and continuity with lineage aggregation and continuity.

To observe the operation of the lineage principle in the structure of a Tale settlement, we must isolate for consideration its male population. '*Bumpɔk pu meet yiri*—a woman does not build a house', say the natives, in words reminiscent of the Roman formula, *mulier finis familiae est*. That is to say, a lineage is not perpetuated by its women members, but only by its male members. We have previously studied the Tale lineage system in its macroscopic structure, from the outside, as it were. We proceed, now, to study it from within.

We shall keep Tongo as our model. Tongo is the *tɛŋ* of the senior of the four branches of the clan of Mosuor biis, each of which has the form of a maximal lineage though it is in reality only a major segment of a maximal lineage. In addition, there are at Tongo several accessory lineages linked to the authentic line of Mosuor biis by some genealogical fiction or other. If allowance is made for the special linkage of these accessory lineages to the authentic line of Mosuor biis, we can place all the men of Tongo on a single, patrilineal, chart. All their lines of ascent converge in Mosuor. They all belong to the same set of lineages, graded in segments of increasing span and rising order of segmentation and contained within the lineage limits fixed by their unilineal ancestry.

Births and deaths among its members continually change the composition of the sub-clan. Deaths of male members often cause further segmentation in the lineages of smallest span. They do not affect the lineage equilibrium of the sub-clan as a whole, for this is a function of the relations between the segments of highest order. The structural relations of all segments of an order higher than the minimal segments are finally fixed. If we take any one of these supra-minimal segments by itself, its place in the whole system can be altered only by the extinction of a co-ordinate segment of a lineage of greater span of which it forms a part. Hence the point of time chosen for an analysis of the system is immaterial.

Analysis of a Lineage from Within

Since all the men of Tongo can be included in a single genealogical tree, it is immaterial whom we choose as the starting-point for our analysis. Yidaan-Yin-Kurug is as convenient a person for this as anybody else. Lean and angular, like most Tale men, with the greying hair of a man past middle age, he occupies homestead No. 6 in Puhug, near the rough track that used to be a Government-made road. He is a man of some substance as wealth goes in Tongo, a section headman[1] (*Kambɔnaaba*) and one of the lesser elders (*Kpɛmtayɔlis*). But one would have to know the Tallensi very well to detect his status if one saw him in his usual garb of a loin-cloth stiff and greasy with body dirt, and an equally soiled body-cloth. Kurug is an average man of his age in Taleland, an industrious farmer by native standards, a law-abiding citizen, a loyal member of his section and of the settlement. (Cf. following genealogical chart and map at end of book.)

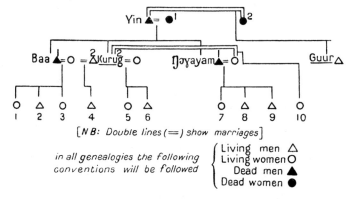

The unit of interest to us here includes: Kurug, the head (*kpeem*), his younger brother (*pit*) Guur, more strictly described as his *sunzɔ* (half-brother), his own children (*biis*), Nos. 4, 5, 6, and 10; his deceased older full-brother (*bier-soog*) Baa's children, Nos. 1, 2, 3; his deceased younger full-brother (*pit-soog*) Dɔyayam's children, Nos. 7, 8, 9. He describes these children of his dead brothers as his children (*biis*), and they speak of him as their father (*ba*). Except for two of the girls, who are married and therefore away from home, all the other children live under Kurug's roof and authority. His *pit*, Guur, is away too, in Mampurugu, where he went to live a few years ago.

This lineage is typical of what we may call the effective minimal lineage, that is, the lineage of the smallest span which emerges as a corporate unit in economic, jural, and ritual activities and is differentiated from other units of a like sort. It is not, it should be noted, an amorphous, internally undifferentiated unit; differences of generation, age, and maternal origin regulate the relations between its members. What is more important, the

---

[1] These headmen are an innovation due to the British Administration. They are appointed by chiefs and other heads of clans or locally associated groups of clans to assist them in carrying out the tasks demanded by the Administration. Before 1933 a headman's position gave him many opportunities of enriching himself by extortion.

THE LINEAGE IN THE LOCAL COMMUNITY

germs of a further segmentation by agnatic lines is present in this unit. Baa's children and Dɔyayam's children, being minors, still form part of Kurug's joint family; they are economically, jurally, and ritually dependent on him. But they have different fathers from Kurug's children. The effective minimal lineage, which is functionally the corporate unit of lowest order, may, and here does, comprise several morphologically lower minimal lineages.[1]

By the canon of agnatic descent Baa's children form one segment of the effective minimal lineage, Kurug and his children another, Dɔyayam's children a third, and Guur a fourth. As, however, they have no functional autonomy at this phase of their development, they may be regarded as minimal lineages submerged in the effective minimal lineage identified by reference to their immediate common progenitor, Yin. Eventually each of these submerged segments will become segregated as a relatively autonomous effective minimal lineage.

About 80 yards from Kurug (homestead No. 11), live Lɛbhtiis and Zupibig (II), whom he describes as his *pirib* (sing. *pit*), younger brothers, with their families. They have the following genealogical relationship to each other and to Kurug:

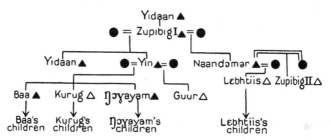

Lɛbhtiis is the head of an effective minimal lineage (Naandɔmər yidɛm) of exactly the same span and order as that (Yin yidɛm) of which Kurug is head. They are segments of the inclusive lineage of greater span and next higher order, Zupibig yidɛm, named after their common grandfather (*yaab*), or, more usually, Yidaan yidɛm, after their common great-grandfather (*yaab*). Kurug, the oldest of the four brothers (*sunzɔp*), is the head of this lineage, which we shall call a nuclear lineage.

Next door to Lɛbhtiis (homestead No. 10) live Deemzeet, whom Kurug and his brothers refer to as *ti ba* (our father), and his deceased brother's two sons (*biis*), Tɔbəg and Dɔbil, whom Kurug describes as *mpirib* (my younger brothers), and Lɛbhtiis as *mbiernam* (my older brothers).

---

[1] The introduction of so many indicator terms for the different grades of lineage segments requires an apology, but experience has shown that some such artificial device is necessary if the Tale lineage system is to be made clear to the English reader. The distinction here drawn between the *effective minimal lineage* (or segment) as the functional unit of lowest order, and the *minimal lineage* (or segment) as the morphological unit of lowest order, is important. An effective minimal lineage is usually the framework of a domestic family and includes women members.

Deemzeet's house (*yir*) has the following genealogical relationship to Zupibig yidɛm:

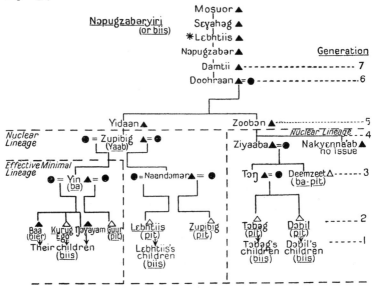

Taken by itself, Deemzeet's house has the same internal structure as Kurug's or Lɛbhtiis's; but Tɔbəg and Dɔbil are men of mature years with grown children. Though still formally under the jural, economic, and ritual authority of Deemzeet, they have considerable autonomy in ritual, jural, and economic affairs that concern their own segment (Tɔŋ biis) of the nuclear lineage. If Deemzeet, a timid old bachelor, had any children, the relative independence of Tɔŋ biis would be more obvious. The nuclear lineage of which Deemzeet is head has reached a more advanced phase of internal differentiation than that of which Kurug is head. This is due, partly, to its being an older lineage, which existed in its present form when Kurug and Guur were still minors under the tutelage of their own father, Yin, and Lɛbhtiis and Zupibig (II) were minors dependent on their father, Naandɔmər. But Deemzeet's house is not the older lineage in the sense that its members are older than the members of the lineages with which we are contrasting it; it is older in that it represents an earlier phase of the segmentation of the inclusive lineage of which Kurug's house, Lɛbhtiis's house, and Deemzeet's house to-day form the constituent and co-ordinate segments. Its head is a generation superior to Kurug and Lɛbhtiis in terms of their common descent. Thus it is the senior of the two segments. The span of a lineage being a function of its internal genealogical constitution, a three-generation lineage has a wider span than a two-generation lineage. But the order of a lineage is determined by its segmentary relationship to other lineages which are complementary to it—brother (*sunzɔ*) segments—in a greater, inclusive

THE LINEAGE IN THE LOCAL COMMUNITY

lineage. Lineages are differentiated in terms of their genealogical distance from one another within their common agnatic descent.

The whole lineage we have been analysing is often designated Doohraan yidɛm (or biis), by reference to its ancestor, Doohraan; but it is more frequently described as Nɔpugzabər yidɛm (or biis), going back to Doohraan's putative grandfather. This lineage is the skeleton of what may be called an expanded family, each of its component effective minimal segments being the foundation, similarly, of a domestic family.[1]

Nɔpugzabər yidɛm constitute a major segment of a wider lineage. Homesteads 5, 7, 8, and 9, the closest neighbours of the homesteads of Nɔpugzabər yidɛm, are occupied by the various branches of a lineage of the same order as Nɔpugzabər yiri. Its genealogical structure is briefly as follows:

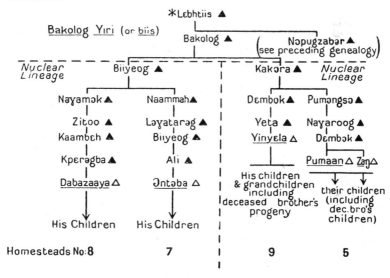

[1] Tale domestic organization is analysed in our next volume. Here it is sufficient to say that the modal family unit is the polygynous, agnatic joint family occupying its own homestead. This is the prototypical *yir*, house (pl. *yɛa*). Its typical substratum is an effective minimal lineage of two, or less commonly, three generations. Thus it may consist of two or more brothers (half or full brothers or cousins); or a man and some or all of his sons, and, occasionally, grandsons, together with the wives and young children of all the males. The joint family always constitutes a single jural unit; most often, but not always, it is also a single economic unit. The pivot of this *yir* is its male head (*yirdaana*, owner of the house). He represents the continuity of the patrilineal line in the structure of the family. He is the (patricentral) focus of cooperation and of jural and ritual unity in the family. This is symbolized by the position of the granary in the centre of the homestead and by the reservation of the space in front of the gateway (*zanɔr*) for the affairs of the men. Complementarily, each woman has her own separate quarters in the homestead where her children live under her care, and where she is mistress in domestic affairs. This is her *dug* (lit. room, pl. *dugət*); and this is the prototype of the lineage *dug*. Thus the children of the family—that is, the lineage growing out

196   THE LINEAGE IN THE LOCAL COMMUNITY

We have set down only the agnatic affiliation of the heads of the effective minimal segments of the lineage, for the relations of these segments with one another are determined by these ties, not by their respective internal constitutions. The head of this lineage (Bakolog yiri) was Yinyɛla; he died in 1937—a hoary ancient and one of the oldest men in Tongo, at least 75 years of age. He called Ɔntɔba *yaaŋ* (grandson), and Dabazaaya *yaaŋkalee* (great-grandson), and Pumaan, a man in the late forties or early fifties, *bii* (child).

Mutatis mutandis, Bakolog yir has the same internal organization and residential distribution as Nɔpugzabɔr yir, though it is more differentiated.

Nɔpugzabɔr yidɛm and Bakolog yidɛm are two co-ordinate segments (*dugɔt*) of the wider lineage (*yir*) Lɛbhtiis[1] yidɛm. From Deemzeet to Lɛbhtiis inclusively seven generations are reckoned. From Yinyɛla to Lɛbhtiis only six generations are reckoned. This is not fortuitous, for Yinyɛla claims to belong to the generation of Deemzeet's father.

Lɛbhtiis yidɛm include three more *dugɔt*, segments co-ordinate with Nɔpugzabɔr yidɛm and Bakolog yidɛm. These are:—

(a) Nɔdɛyɔr yir, the only surviving branch of which comprises but a single segment of narrow span consisting of three full brothers and their children who live in homestead No. 12.

(b) Pɔyasɔŋ yir, whose members occupy homesteads 17, 22, 28, 29, and 33.

(c) Gbɛn yir, in homesteads 18, 19, 20, 23, 24.

As with Nɔpugzabɔr yidɛm, a count of seven generations, inclusive, separates the heads of these three lineages from their ancestor, Lɛbhtiis. All these segments preserve the names of what appear to be redundant ancestors, like Damtii in the genealogical chart of Nɔpugzabɔr yidɛm. For, in conformity with their structural relations as co-ordinate segments of a single lineage, their particular genealogies must be congruent (see Ch. III). Bakolog yidɛm, with one ascendant generation less in their pedigree, fit into the set on the assumption—which they uphold vigorously—that their head belongs to the generation of the *fathers* of the other segment heads.

We need not analyse the internal organization of these last-mentioned segments of Lɛbhtiis yir. With variations of detail they duplicate the plan of Nɔpugzabɔr yir. The segments are homologous with one another; their sub-segments are constructed on the same plan; and so, on a bigger scale, is the greater lineage which embraces all of them. Bakolog yidɛm within Lɛbhtiis yidɛm, like Zoobɔn yidɛm within Nɔpugzabɔr yidɛm, is relatively senior to its brother-segments, and Nɔdɛyɔr biis, though a segment of a very narrow span compared with the other segments of Lɛbhtiis yir, is nevertheless co-ordinate with them.

of it—are genealogically and socially united by reference to the patricentral *yir* and the patrilineal line, and similarly divided into distinct segments by reference to their respective matricentral *dugɔt*. This is the pattern on which lineage segmentation is based. Again, what is a joint family in one generation generally splits, as the children grow up, into two or more joint families in the next generation. They then constitute what we have called an expanded family.

[1] The founding ancestor, Lɛbhtiis, of this lineage should not be confused with his living descendant of the same name, previously mentioned. In the genealogies given in this chapter Lɛbhtiis the ancestor is distinguished by an asterisk.

Diagrammatically, the agnatic filiation of the branches of Lɛbhtiis yir (or biis) can be represented as follows:

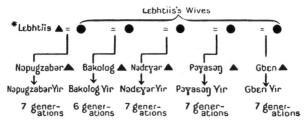

These five segments form a set of co-ordinate segments, all except Bakolog yidɛm reckoning seven generations inclusively between their present lineage heads and their common ancestor, Lɛbhtiis. Their corporate unity and common interests are symbolized by the ancestor shrine dedicated to the 'fathers' (*banam*) of the lineage, culminating in Lɛbhtiis. This is the *bɔyar* of Lɛbhtiis, the *banam bɔyar* (shrine of the forefathers) held by the head (*kpeem*) of the whole lineage, who may be a member of any of the five *dugɔt*. In 1934 the head of Lɛbhtiis yidɛm, Naandɔmɔr, who was also head of his own segment of Nɔpugzabɔr yiri died, and as his final funeral rites were not immediately performed, the *banam bɔyar* remained in the custody of his son, who carried out the duties of head of the whole lineage in his late father's name. Naandɔmɔr's prospective successor as *kpeem* of Lɛbhtiis yir was Yinyɛla, the *kpeem* of Bakolog yir.

Each segment also has its particular *dugni bɔyar* (shrine of the 'room'). This, as will be explained presently, is known as its 'mothers'' *bɔyar* (*manam bɔyar*)—the shrine of its eponymous founding ancestor among the sons of Lɛbhtiis, and his mother—the symbol of its differentiation, by reference to maternal origin, from its brother (*sunzɔ*) segments of the same descent, and of its specific corporate unity and identity in contraposition to those other segments.

Each segment tends to form a coherent residential cluster, situated on land which has been owned by its members for several generations, and in close proximity to the graves of their ancestors. The lineage as a whole tends to form a local aggregate, though a somewhat looser one than any of its segments. But not all the members of the lineage reside in Puhug, or at Tongo, at a given time. There are its married *pɔyayabɔlis* (women members) and absent male members. In Nɔpugzabɔr yiri two young men were away in 1934, one farming in Mampurugu, another working somewhere in the colony; three of the younger 'sons' of Bakolog yir were away at Kumasi, where they had been for several years. One subsegment of Pɔyasɔŋ yidem has been established at Yamɔlɔg for a generation or so; and several members of the other two segments were away in Mampurugu and Ashanti.

Numerically Nɔdeyɔr yir is exceptionally small, for it has only eleven male members. The other segments have between twenty and thirty male members each, counting infants as well. Numbers, we must again emphasize, do not in any way affect the status of a lineage or the rights

198   THE LINEAGE IN THE LOCAL COMMUNITY

and duties vested in it. Nɔdeyɔr yidem suffer no jural or ritual disabilities because they are so much inferior in numbers to their brother segments.

The Principle of Segmentation in the Lineage

There are two factors of great importance in the dynamics of the lineage system: the principle of segmentation in the lineage and the connexion between lineage aggregation and locality.

A striking characteristic of the Tale lineage is the rigorous precision with which its members fall into a set of hierarchically articulated segments, of homologous form but all exactly differentiated both genealogically and functionally (cf. Ch. III). This segmentary differentiation of the lineage follows the pattern of the family even to nomenclature. For the lineage grows out of, and through the medium of, the family, and throughout its existence a lineage develops uniformly, so that it preserves the form in which it was originally moulded.

To put it more accurately, a lineage grows by continuous internal differentiation in successive generations. It grows by the continuous multiplication of its parts, not by the mere accretion of new members. And this takes place by the splitting up of its cells, the minimal segments, into new minimal segments in successive generations. This process follows the lines of cleavage laid down in the joint family.

The polygynous joint family forms an integral unit with respect to its male element, the group of agnates upon which it is based and which gives it stability and continuity. This unity of the joint family is summed up in the concept of the patricentral 'house' (*yir*). But it is a unity superimposed upon a strict cellular differentiation into matricentral 'rooms' (*dugət*), each centred upon a wife.

The group of male agnates in the joint family constitutes an effective minimal lineage at a given time. Each male is a potential agnatic line; a pair of brothers are two potential segments of a lineage. In terms of their common patrilineal descent this group of males forms a single corporate unit. This is the essential *yir*. But this unity contains within itself two sets of cleavages: firstly, a stratification by generations, and secondly, a differentiation by descent. The generation principle acts in this way (cf.

Hypothetical Genealogy, I

Three generations of agnates in the joint family

Head & founder

Sons

Grandsons

Two patri-segments.

the hypothetical genealogy, I): Two brothers who are distinct as individuals are identified with reference to their common father; in all social activities in which they take part as the *sons* of their father they are, as it were, merged. During their father's lifetime they have, in fact, no independent jural status, but are, to speak figuratively again, submerged in his jural personality. Their sons, if the joint family survives as a unit for another generation, will be divided into two patrilateral groups with reference to their respective fathers, but fused into a single jural and economic as well as genealogical unit with reference to their grandfather. In this way the stratification of the effective minimal lineage into generations automatically splits it into patri-segments.[1]

Simultaneously, however, the centrifugal influence of the *dug* is at work. Brothers by the same father may have different mothers. Among the Tallensi this carries with it an emphatic affective discrimination. Half-brothers (*sunzɔ*, pl. *sunzɔp*) are divided by a wedge of sentiment which arises not only out of their independent emotional ties with their particular mothers, but also out of the structural, economic, and moral relations of the *dugət* within the *yir*. It reflects the social autonomy of the *dug* in relation to other *dugət* of the *yir* and the polarity of *dug* and *yir*. Conversely, full (*soog*) brothers have the most intimate bond in the whole gamut of Tale social relations, a bond implying an identity of interests, an emotional cohesion, and mutual loyalty so great as to override any kind of personal or social variance.[2] Thus, within the joint family, maternal origin (*ma dɔyam*, lit. 'mother's bearing') may divide the sons of one man in sentiment and by an additional index of descent. The patrilateral unit is segmented into incipient matrilateral segments.

What happens in the next generation can best be seen from the following hypothetical genealogy:

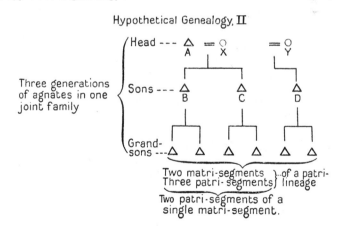

[1] This terminology is borrowed from Daryll Forde, *Marriage and the Family among the Yakö*, L. S. E. Monographs on Anthropology, No. 5.

[2] Cf. my paper 'The Significance of Descent in Tale Social Structure', *Africa*, xiv, 7, 1944, for a discussion of the concept of *soog*.

THE LINEAGE IN THE LOCAL COMMUNITY

We assume a joint family containing three generations of male agnates—the head, his three sons, and his six grandsons, and we neglect the maternal origins of the latter. The six grandsons are divided into three equal patri-segments with reference to their respective fathers, and form a single corporate lineage with reference to their common grandfather. But they are genealogically split into two segments with reference to their respective *grandmothers*; and one of these matrilaterally defined segments (matri-segments) can be split into two patri-segments, of a lower order. Patrilateral origin and matrilateral origin work in polar opposition to each other. An agnatic group united by their patrilateral origin can be subdivided in accordance with their matrilateral origin; and vice versa, an agnatic group united by reference to their matrilateral origin can be subdivided by closer patrilateral origin.

Note that this is not a question of matriliny versus patriliny. Matrilateral origin works as a factor of cleavage only within a patrilineal group, in contradistinction to strict patriliny. Either focus may be the critical one in a given situation; but the other is not thereby obliterated; it merely becomes latent. The pattern operative here is that of the joint family. Patri-segment and matri-segment are related as *yir* and *dug* in the joint family, matri-segment and matri-segment as *dug* and *dug*. They are, indeed, nothing other than the parallel, in the structure of the unending lineage, of the balance of forces that characterizes the joint family. Members of one matri-segment are the offspring of one *dug*, members of one patri-segment may be the offspring of several *dugət*. The natives use the terms *yir* and *dug* to define the relations of lineage segments to one another. *Dug*, then, always bears the implication of a cohesive integral segment within the fissile *yir*. It stands for solidarity as opposed to the latent divisions in the *yir*, obviously reflecting its primary sense of the irreducible, uncleavable matricentral cell within the potentially divided *yir*.

Segmentation by matrilateral lines in the nuclear lineage plays a very important part in the development of both the joint family and the lineage. Economic, jural, and affective relations in the joint family are influenced by matrilateral (*dug*) affiliation; and when in course of time a joint family splits up, fission takes place in the first instance between matri-segments. Members of the same *dug* hold together longer than members of different *dugət*. Thus, two full brothers (*soog*, pl. *saarət*) continue to live in the same homestead, to farm together, to be jurally and ritually one, long after two half-brothers (*sunzɔp*) have found it necessary to separate. Often the split, which inevitably comes between separate lines in the nuclear lineage, is retarded in the case of *soog* brothers, and does not take place until their death. Children of *soog* brothers even after fission have closer ties than children of half-brothers.

These principles of segmentation are not merely a method of genealogical classification of individuals, but an indispensable regulator of corporate activities, operating at every level of lineage organization. This requires the preservation of the names of all relevant ancestors and ancestresses, but genealogical classification has no meaning except as a shorthand for the many and complex relations of individuals and groups.

The living members of a lineage are continually experiencing, in their

THE LINEAGE IN THE LOCAL COMMUNITY 201

daily life, the antithesis between patrilateral and matrilateral ties in the joint family. There is also the principle of the continuity and identity of the lineage. Members of the same lineage are identified with one another and with their lineal ascendants. Tallensi think of a lineage as a continuous, even eternal, group, a unit persisting through time as well as existing at a given time. A particular lineage to-day is the same lineage that it was at its inception two, three, or x generations ago. Segments of a clan or maximal lineage have the same structural position relatively to one another as they had in the beginning, only on a different scale; and in the beginning segmentarily related lineages sprang from brothers. As these founding ancestors were related, so are their contemporary agnatic descendants related. Hence co-ordinate segments of a lineage are described as *sunzɔp* ('brothers by the same father'), and the bonds of brotherhood (*sunzɔt*) are the nucleus and prototype of the bonds between co-ordinate segments. Two co-ordinate segments whose founding ancestors were full (*soog*) brothers have closer ties than similar co-ordinate segments descended from a pair of half-brothers. The lineage is always growing, but can never break the unchanging frame laid down at its beginning. It is almost as if a single person has undergone a quantitative metamorphosis with the passage of generations.

Lineage ties cannot lapse or be renounced. A maximal lineage once established can never split into two or more independent (i.e. mutually exogamous) maximal lineages, as in some other areas of Africa, and territorial dispersion does not break the lineage tie, even after many generations. In fact, the whole stream of Tale social life emphasizes and reinforces the sense of lineage continuity, and of the identification of members of a lineage with one another, with their predecessors, and with their prospective successors. This is the basis of the corporate unity and solidarity of the lineage, and of the lineal transmission of rights and duties, ritual observances, office, property, and debts; and for this reason any member of a lineage can represent any other member, living or dead, or the whole lineage, in relation to other lineages of a like sort. This, too, underlies the usage by which members of a lineage can refer to their founding ancestor either as their 'father' (*ba*) or as their 'ancestor' (*yaab*), a term which denotes any patrilineal ancestor beyond and including the grandfather. It explains the conception of the lineage progenitrix—the founding ancestor's mother—as the 'mother' (*ma*) of the lineage. It must be added that even when a lineage is envisaged as a *dug* deriving from its progenitrix, it takes its name from her son, as its agnatic founding ancestor as a branch of a more inclusive lineage.

The rules of lineage segmentation can be summed up as follows: Whenever a lineage is envisaged as an inclusive corporate unit embracing two or more subordinate segments, it is identified by reference to its founding *ancestor*, as the starting-point of its descent. It is thought of as a *yir*, house, 'the children of one father (*ba yɛni biis*)', on the model of the patricentral joint family (*yir* in the primary sense) in which the offspring form a single genealogical and social unit with reference to their common father. Its focal ancestor shrine is designated the '*bɔɣar* of the fathers (*banam bɔɣar*)', a notion that stresses the dominance of the father-figure

202   THE LINEAGE IN THE LOCAL COMMUNITY

in the unity of the patrilineal descent group and in the coherence of the family. But when a lineage is visualized as a set of segments, these are differentiated by reference to their respective *progenitrices*, just as in the joint family the offspring can be subdivided in accordance with their maternal origins. The focal ancestor shrine of each segment is then called 'the *bɔyar* of the mothers (of the segment) (*manam bɔyar*)'. It is identical in form with the 'fathers' *bɔyar*' but complementary to it in function. Its name stresses the predominance of matrilateral origin in the differentiation of the segments of a lineage, by contrast with the patricentral lineage as a whole. Tallensi speak of a 'mothers' *bɔyar*' as being the shrine of the segment's founding ancestor and his mother, by contrast with the 'fathers' *bɔyar*', which they say is the shrine of the founding ancestor of the lineage only. But they recognize that a 'mothers' *bɔyar*' will in the course of time become a 'fathers' *bɔyar*' when the segment undergoes internal differentiation into sub-segments, and may function as a 'fathers' *bɔyar*' if the segment is already so differentiated. When a segment of a lineage is thus distinguished from co-ordinate segments of the same lineage, it is also implicitly contrasted with the whole lineage. It is thought of as a matri-segment, though named after its founding ancestor, and is described as a 'room', *dug*—'the children of one mother (*ma yeni biis*)'—of the 'house', *yir*, on the model of the joint family in which the matricentral *dug* is a segment of the patricentral *yir*.

Maternal origin (*ma dɔyam*) thus has significance only within the frame of patrilineal descent, as the polar opposite of paternal origin (*ba dɔyam*). Taken by itself, every lineage, no matter what its span or order may be, has only one founding ancestor and one progenitrix, this man's mother. The progenitrix of a lineage becomes significant only when it is considered in conjunction with other lineages of the same descent. Both morphologically and functionally every lineage represents an equilibrium based on the polarity of maternal filiation and patrilineal descent which runs through the whole genealogical structure of Tale society.

Obviously any segment of a lineage which comprises two or more sub-segments can function as a *dug* in one context or situation and as a *yir* in another. Its focal ancestor shrine thus functions as a *manam bɔyar* in one context and as a *banam bɔyar* in another. In principle a maximal lineage of wide span must always act as a *yir*—and hence its focal ancestor shrine is always a *banam bɔyar*; but by a stretch of the term it may be referred to as a *dug* when someone wishes to lay special stress on its genealogical unity and corporate solidarity in contrast to other similar units. The murder of a fellow member of the same maximal lineage is, for instance, always dealt with as 'an affair of the room (*dugni yɛl*)', which stringently excludes reprisals.

A few maximal lineages have so narrow a span, due, no doubt, to the extinction of collateral lines, that they function as medial or inner lineages (wide *dugɔt*), a distinction that will be clearer presently. Thus the maximal lineage of Gundaat is not subdivided into ritually and jurally differentiated major segments. Its head, the Gundaat-Bɔyarna'ab, explained this in a manner which shows how clearly many Tale elders grasp the mechanics of their own social structure. 'We have not yet achieved

THE LINEAGE IN THE LOCAL COMMUNITY 203

sunzɔt (division into brother (patri-) segments)', he said, 'but we shall eventually do so. Our line of descent has not yet gone far enough, for we are all the children of one woman (i.e. the descendants of a common progenitrix not very far back). A woman's offspring do not split up, it is a man's offspring that split (*Bumpɔk dɔyam pu bɔkɔra, buraa dɔyam m-bɔkɔt*).' In fact, Gundaatdɛm form a lineage of rather narrow span considering the number of ascendant generations which they reckon to their founding ancestor.

Incidentally the Bɔyarna'ab's statement brings out vividly the native conception of a lineage as a perpetual entity, 'going on (*kyɛŋ sa*)' for ever, unitary and identical beneath the surface of its changing personnel, the 'children of one woman (or one man)' as long as it lasts.

According to this scheme, in the set of lineages we have been analysing, Nɔpugzabɔr yidɛm, the agnatic descendants of Nɔpugzabɔr, constitute one of the five *dugɔt* of the *yir*, Lɛbhtiis yidɛm, which in turn is a *dug* of the section (*yizug*) of Puhug, and this in its turn is a *dug* of the sub-clan of Tongo. Nɔpugzabɔr yir, again, may in certain situations be regarded as consisting of two *dugɔt*, Yidaan biis and Zoobɔn biis; and as Tɔbɔg and Dɔbil are *soog* brothers, their agnatic descendants will form a single matricentral segment, with greater cohesion than Yidaan biis.

Though *dug* and *yir* are relative concepts—relative both to each other and to the particular situation in which a given order of lineage segmentation is critical—there is a sense in which *dug* has a more precise connotation. As usual in Tale social organization no rigorous criterion can be found for this. It can be defined only in dynamic terms. Tallensi tend to think of the field of lineage relations as made up of three broad zones: the zone of clanship,[1] as when a man says, 'I am a Tongo man'; within this zone, the zone of section (*yizug*) relations, as when a Tongo man says, 'I am a Puhug man'; and within this zone, the zone of *dug* relations, which lies between the limits of the major segment of the *yizug* to which the individual belongs, on the one hand, and a level of segmentation of about the order of Doohraan yidɛm—that is, with a common ancestor placed about five generations back, on the other. Thus, if a man says of another member of his clan, 'We are *dugdɛm* (members of the same *dug*)', one can infer that he is thinking of a lineage segment of an order between that of Doohraan yidɛm and that of Lɛbhtiis yidem of Tɔŋ-Puhug, though the exact genealogical extension of the lineage intended will vary from clan to clan.

This notion of the *dug*, to which we have given a purely morphological formulation, is a reflex of the configuration of social interests that regulate the corporate functions of the lineage. The zone of clanship is correlated with interclan and intersettlement political and ritual relations, and with the maximum extension of the rule of exogamy. The zone of *yizug* relations is correlated with intra-clan political and ritual relations, with the aliquot distribution between segments of the clan of rights to politico-ritual offices, and with the complementary rights and duties of the major segments of the clan, upon which the maintenance of its structural equilibrium depends. The zone of *dug* relations corresponds to a field

[1] Cf. Chapter IV.

204 THE LINEAGE IN THE LOCAL COMMUNITY

of closer common interests. It is related to the *yizug* as the *yizug* is to the clan. At the limit it marks off the widest lineage within which there is a strong feeling of moral solidarity, a tendency for corporate unity to prevail in all circumstances, and a strong sense of undivided common interests. Beyond this range, in the zone of section relations and in that of clanship, corporate unity and solidarity tend to be a function of politico-ritual interdependence and of a balance between the competitive interests and the obligatory bonds of reciprocity of the major segments of the clan.

At Tongo the widest range of the *dug* in this definitive sense is a lineage segment of the order of Lɛbhtiis yidɛm. This is constantly shown in economic life, as when a man invites his neighbours to a collective hoeing party or to help him build a new house. Then all the members of his widest *dug* feel bound to turn out, but not members of other *dugat* of the same section. Members of other sections will not be asked to come at all, and if one or two turn out it will be because they have personal ties of matrilateral kinship with the man issuing the invitation. It appears similarly in all other concerns of the individual which require corporate support. It is shown in the incidence of marriage prohibitions. Tallensi may not, according to strict rule, marry cognatic kin of any degree whatsoever. A man may not marry a daughter of his maternal uncle's lineage (*ahab yiri*). But the restriction is limited to his mother's widest paternal *dug*. Thus a man whose mother belongs to Lɛbhtiis yidɛm of Tɔŋ-Puhug would not be allowed to marry another daughter of this *dug*, but he can— and innumerable cases show that this often happens—marry a daughter of another *dug* of Puhug.

Dissension occurs between segments of such a *dug* now and then, but this arouses severe reprobation. Members of the *dug* feel it as a direct threat to their well-being, in a way that they do not feel conflict between such *dugat* to be; they feel it as verging on the sinful, challenging the wrath of the ancestor spirits, whereas conflict between such *dugat* or between sections, though morally reprehensible, is not mystically dangerous. Within this *dug* sexual relations between a member and the wife of one of his agnates are branded as incest, and produce a serious if not irreparable rupture in the unit; and sexual relations between classificatory brother and sister meet with strong censure. Beyond this range sexual relations between a man and the wife of a clansman are merely adulterous, a violation of clan solidarity, not a sin; and intercourse with a clan sister is not censured. These distinctions go back to one fundamental principle. The wide *dug* marks the widest range within which differences of generation and birth order are recognized for jural and ritual purposes; beyond that range these differences are not recognized. The lower limit of the *dug* corresponds to a segment of about the order of Doohraan yidɛm. This narrow *dug* frequently forms the core of an expanded family; it determines the widest field within which domestic relations prevail. Its members have differentiated person-to-person relations, based on the recognition of generation differences and proxy-parenthood, as well as corporate lineage relations. Their moral bonds are correspondingly stronger than in the wide *dug*, though of the same kind. Within this unit sexual intercourse with a sister arouses very strong reprobation, and

THE LINEAGE IN THE LOCAL COMMUNITY

sexual relations with a brother's or father's wife is a grave sin. What is more important, the solidarity of this *dug* very often rests on a common economic interest in patrimonial land, to which every male member of the lineage is a potential heir. This common interest in land gives the cohesion of the narrow *dug* a foundation upon which its moral solidarity, reinforced by the close bonds of sentiment its members have with one another, rests so firmly as to make it almost infrangible. The narrow *dug* is the widest lineage unit that always stands together like one man, right or wrong. Dissensions between its members are regarded as personal quarrels even when they follow the lines of genealogical cleavage within it. However acrimonious they may be, they are not permitted to divide the unit into mutually hostile segments.

Neither the wide nor the narrow limits of the *dug* can be fixed by a count of ascendant generations. The narrow *dug* may place its founding ancestor from four to six generations up the tree of ascent, the wide *dug* from five to seven generations back, reckoning from its present living head inclusively. It varies from clan to clan, the dimensions of the *dug* being always relative to the span and the degree of internal segmentation of the maximal lineage of which it forms a segment. As we have seen, there are maximal lineages like Gundaat which are so little segmented that they still function as wide *dugət*. Furthermore, a unit that is counted as a *dug* to-day may in a generation or two segment into two or more *dugət*. And it must be remembered also that in composite clans the section (*yizug*) is genealogically a maximal lineage, so that the *dug* constitutes a major segment of a maximal lineage.[1]

Thus the *dug* is a flexible unit and more difficult to visualize than the maximal and minimal lineages. It cannot, like them, be isolated by a morphological criterion; we identify the *dug* only when it emerges in social action.

It will simplify our analysis and save some confusion if we give a name to the *dug* in the context of the lineage structure. This is justifiable as well as expedient, for in a particular clan the *dug* has a determinate lineage span and segmentary order at any given time. We shall therefore use the terms 'medial lineage or segment' for what we have called the wide *dug*, and 'inner lineage or segment' for the *dug* in its narrow limits. We thus have a hierarchy of lineage segments: the effective minimal lineage or segment, the nuclear lineage or segment, the inner lineage or segment, the medial lineage or segment, the section or major segment, the maximal lineage.

[1] In many maximal lineages we find an intermediate grade of *dug* which is less closely integrated than the narrow *dug*, but more so than the wide *dug*. In diachronic terms it readily falls into place as a phase in the process of internal differentiation by which the narrow *dug* develops into a wide *dug*. In the set of lineages we have been considering the segment of Bakolog yidɛm of Lɛbhtiis yidɛm behaves like a *dug* of this sort. It has a somewhat wider span than Doohraan yidɛm, but a powerful contributory cause has been the personality of the *dug* head, Yinyɛla, whose actions have led the heads of the effective minimal lineages to reject his headship on several occasions and to stress the relative autonomy of their sub-segments in consequence.

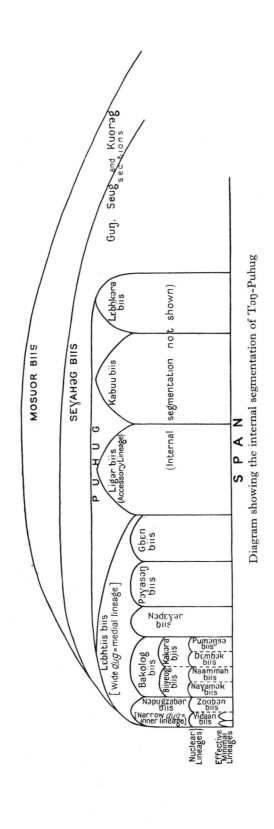

Diagram showing the internal segmentation of Tɔŋ-Puhug

Lineage Grouping and Local Grouping

We come now to the question of the connexion between lineage grouping and locality. A lineage like Nɔpugzabɔr yíri, though its span is comparatively small, exhibits all the important principles of lineage structure and will suffice as a crucial example.

In all the old-established settlements we find a very close correlation between lineage proximity and residential proximity among the members of the clan who live there. Close agnates tend to live near one another, so that residential proximity is almost a measure of lineage proximity. A segment of small span tends to be a close residential cluster, and segments of larger span, up to the major segments of a maximal lineage, tend to form residential blocks.

We can see this most readily if we look again at the residential dispersion of a group of agnatically related joint families, bearing in mind that the men of a joint family form a lineage. For as the homestead is the material integument of the living structure of the joint family, so is the localization of the lineage, growing out of the spatial arrangement of the homestead, the spatial counterpart of the lineage structure.

As will be remembered (see p. 199), the elementary case is that of two full (soog) brothers, who often continue to occupy a single homestead long after they have set up separate families. Each will have more or less self-contained quarters, but the homestead will have only one gateway (zanɔr), one cattle-yard (sapak), and one room for the family head (zɔŋ), signifying that it is a single homestead. Half-brothers (sunzɔp) may share a homestead in this way, but they usually separate more distinctly when they have growing families. Each will have his own gateway, &c., and party walls divide his section of the homestead completely from those of his brothers, making it what may be called a semi-detached homestead. Such a set of semi-detached homesteads may house a man and his mature first-born son, or a man and his deceased brother's sons. Sometimes two or more ortho-cousins (brothers, in native terminology) live thus side by side.

More usually, however, men whose nearest common ancestor is a grandfather occupy completely separate dwellings, often very near to one another. Men whose nearest common ancestor is a great-grandfather never have permanent homes adjoining one another in this semi-detached way. These conditions of residence signalize successive stages of segmentation as the effective minimal lineage expands and splits into new effective minimal lineages. But what residential arrangements will prevail in a particular lineage segment depends, also, upon other circumstances, the most important of which are the economic and religious relations, and the character and disposition of the individuals concerned. Residential collocation is not a simple function of lineage relationship. There is a tertium quid linking them: the combined effect of land tenure, on which the whole economy of the household rests, and of the ancestor cult. For example, when a joint family splits, the man who leaves the ancestral home usually builds a homestead for himself on land belonging to the

208 THE LINEAGE IN THE LOCAL COMMUNITY

nuclear lineage; but this land may be some distance from the ancestral home, owing to the scattering of holdings.

Looking at it from the native point of view, we should say, not that individuals tend to live near one another because they are agnatic kin, but that all lineages down to the effective minimal lineage tend to be tied to localities; and the more closely lineages are related, the greater is the spatial propinquity of their dwelling areas. The distribution of households is not rigidly parallel to the lineage structure at a given time. Mere spatial proximity cannot be directly translated into terms of lineage proximity. There is a diachronic element as well. Kurug's homestead (No. 6), for example, is nearer to Pumaan's (No. 5) in yards and feet than to Lɛbhtiis's; but Kurug is closer to Lɛbhtiis than to Pumaan in lineage. This is due chiefly to changes in the internal structure of their respective nuclear lineages in the last twenty or thirty years. The spatial relations of homesteads to one another reflect lineage relations in their diachronic aspect.

The Concept of the Lineage Home

Lineages tend to be tied to specific localities even if many of their members are permanently or temporarily away from the lineage home. Some representatives of the lineage will generally continue to reside near the ancient home where the spirits of the ancestors still dwell. The *daboog*, the site of the original home of the lineage, the first dwelling-place of its founding ancestor, is a hallowed spot. It is identified by reference to ancestral land and to the graves of the ancestors. These are the fixed things. Homesteads are not eternal. Their collocation reflects the structure of the lineage at a given time; but it changes as the composition and segmentation of the lineage alters. Whenever an alteration of this sort occurs, there is a corresponding reshuffle in the housing arrangements. New homesteads are erected, old homesteads replanned and rebuilt or abandoned. A lineage being an organic unit has, in native eyes, but one home (*yir*), though the material embodiment of this home is distributed at any given time. The *daboog* of the lineage of Nɔpugzabər yidɛm, the original homestead site of their ancestor Nɔpugzabər, is on what was in 1934 the home farm of the head of the lineage, Deemzeet, a stone's throw from his gateway. The graves of Nɔpugzabər and his sons, and a tree which sprouted on Nɔpugzabər's grave and is believed, therefore, to enshrine his spirit, mark the spot where his gateway (*zanɔr*) stood.

From this arises the concept of the lineage *zanɔr*. All the homesteads of its members together make up the lineage home (*yir*), and this home has its single gateway (*zanɔr*), the lineage *zanɔr*. The notion is preeminently symbolical, but its material embodiment is the homestead of the lineage head, and therefore, specifically, the gateway of his homestead. It applies to all levels of lineage organization, up to the maximal lineage. In a maximal lineage the site of the founding ancestor's homestead is generally a sacred spot, often marked by the erection on or near it of a miniature room to represent the ancestral *zɔŋ*. This room is one of the shrines connected with the lineage *bɔyar*, and its custody is vested in a

THE LINEAGE IN THE LOCAL COMMUNITY 209

segment of the lineage whose head always takes the title of *Yikpɛmdaan*[1] and has the duty of sacrificing to the collective ancestors of the lineage on behalf of all its members. Among clans that have tɛndaanas the senior tɛndaana often has to build his homestead on the site of the founding ancestor's homestead; and when a tɛndaana dies his successor takes possession of the ancestral homestead and his children move out. But many other arrangements exist all serving the same end of keeping alive the idea of the lineage home.

In the lineage we are discussing the three homesteads of the members stand on ancestral land quite close to the graves of the lineage ancestors, Doohraan, Damtii, and Nɔpugzabər. When Deemzeet formally became the head of the lineage his homestead housed the lineage *bɔyar* and other shrines of its common ancestors, and his gateway became the lineage *zanɔr*. The ancestral graves of this lineage are actually on land owned by its members. This is not always the case. Changes in the ownership of land as the population shifts frequently result in the land surrounding the ancestral graves of a lineage-segment passing into the hands of members of another segment of the same lineage, sometimes even into the hands of members of a neighbouring clan. The spot continues, nevertheless, to be regarded as the *daboog* of the lineage whose ancestral graves lie there. The conception of the lineage home is split. For jural and social purposes it is the *de facto* home of the lineage, the place where its head actually resides. The site of the ancestral home, marked by the graves of the ancestors, comes to be regarded primarily as the religious focus of the lineage.

The Influence of Lineage Localization in the Social Life

This fact, that in the older settlements the core of a lineage is a locally organized unit, and that its location is associated with its ancestor spirits on the one hand and its patrimonial land on the other, moulds the entire life of its members. The corporate unity and identity of a lineage is a real and tangible thing when its male members can see one another every day, and when most of them, certainly most of their leading men, can gather together easily and in a very short time to consider and take action in affairs of common interest. Classificatory kinship is no mere formality where an individual's childhood companions are his or her own siblings and ortho-cousins of various degrees; where a man's daily intercourse is carried on chiefly with close agnatic kinsmen, and almost entirely with men of the same patrilineal descent, in his section or settlement; where a man can readily, and indeed is compelled to, by the fact of physical accessibility in a culture lacking rapid and indirect means of communication, have immediate and almost exclusive recourse to his patrilineal kin for help in economic activities, support in maintaining his rights or performing his duties, advice and guidance in the conduct of his life, or solace in misfortune. Ceremonial co-operation is not an empty formula

---

[1] Tallensi are poor etymologists and various equally plausible etymologies are suggested for this title. The most probable is that it is compounded of *yir*, house; *kpiim*, spirits of the dead, and *daana*, custodian or master. This can be translated 'Custodian of the House of the Spirits of the Lineage Ancestors'.

P

210   THE LINEAGE IN THE LOCAL COMMUNITY

where it always and necessarily brings together men of the same descent group, bound together not only by ties of blood but also by ties of residence, common interests, and common experience. The local concentration of the lineage in such close association with the graves of its ancestors and the land hallowed by their life and labour gives to the cult of the ancestors a binding power and directive force in the social life of the natives which is hardly equalled elsewhere in Africa. The likemindedness, common values, mutual loyalties, sense of unity and continuity, so prominent in a lineage of small span and distinctive only to a lesser degree of lineages of greater span, can be translated directly into terms of contact, co-operation, and experience. So also the conflicts and rivalries that inevitably spring up in a human community, and occur as often in a Tale settlement as anywhere else in the world, have an additional significance, since they necessarily involve men who are kin to one another and belong to the same corporate unit. The principle of lineage representation and the concept of the equivalence of members of the same lineage have the maximum efficacy in these conditions.

The effect of the congruence between lineage ties and local ties is of no less importance for a woman than for a man. In childhood her closest playmates are the children of her father's inner lineage, that is, the children of her father's nearest neighbours, and their principal playground is the immediate vicinity of their parents' homesteads. Among her classificatory patrilineal relatives she knows best and depends most on the members of her father's inner lineage. Members of her father's medial lineage are next in order of importance for her, and more distant clansmen and clanswomen least important, though far from irrelevant. When she marries into another community she does not cease to belong to her natal clan. She maintains close ties with it, the most intimate being with the members of her father's inner lineage; and she thinks of these ties as ties with a corporate social unit, not with particular individuals only. Both to herself, her husband and his clansmen, and to her children, her 'father's house' (*ba yir*) is, in the broadest sense, her natal clan pictured as a local community, in a narrower sense, her father's medial lineage, thought of as a localized subdivision of her natal clan, in the narrowest sense her father's inner lineage thought of in the same way.

In her husband's home, too, the correlation of lineage proximity with local proximity enters continuously into the routine of her life. Her relations with the members of her husband's clan are graded in accordance with their lineage proximity to him. The men of her husband's clan with whom she has closest contact are her husband's nearest agnates and the nearest neighbours of her conjugal family. With him they form the segment of his clan which has the greatest jural interest in her and her children. If her husband dies, it is one of these men who is most likely to inherit her. The wives of all her husband's clansmen are nominally her co-wives or daughters-in-law; but in fact it is only the wives of his close agnates, women who are her nearest neighbours, whom she regards as effective classificatory co-wives and daughters-in-law. She and they will help one another in such tasks as floor beating or ceremonial cooking, and at critical times like a confinement or a death. She has bonds of

THE LINEAGE IN THE LOCAL COMMUNITY 211

comradeship with all women married into her husband's clan, owing to their common status as wives of the clan, but this bond is stronger with the wives of her husband's close agnates than with the wives of his distant agnates. It is most effective within the group of families built up round her husband's inner lineage, and becomes purely nominal outside the range of the group of families whose male members form a medial lineage.

Neighbourhood ties are *ipso facto* lineage ties, and therefore economic, religious, jural, and moral ties. The closer a man's neighbourhood ties with another, the more closely are they likely to be related by lineage and the greater are likely to be their common and mutual interests. A man's central field of social relationships is integral with his central field of spatial relationships. His range of physical communication with others is a function of his range of social relations, and is graded, both as to intensity and frequency of communication, in accordance with the gradation of his genealogical relationships. For, as we have previously noted, most men's lives are almost wholly tied to their natal settlements.

This close correlation between genealogical relationships and local relationships operates in the wide sphere of clanship as well as in the narrow sphere of individual conduct, in the corporate relationships of lineages and clans, no less than in the emotional bonds of individuals. We have seen how it emerges in the organization of the lineage, and its enormous importance in a person's relations with his patrilateral kin. It is equally significant in the establishment of affinal ties and in the efficacy of the ties of matrilateral kinship.

In this respect the Tallensi exhibit a feature of primitive society that has often been stressed: their overwhelming dependence on face-to-face communication and association in the organization of their collective life. Among the Tallensi it can be clearly seen that this is conditioned by their mode of economic life, their lack of the art of writing, and the absence of mechanical equipment and sources of power for transport, communications, and other technological purposes. But the student of Tale society cannot avoid the conclusion that social factors, in particular the complex of interrelated elements revealed in the narrow range of political and economic relations, the lack of a centralized political system and the dominance of genealogical connexions in all social relations, are the most important factors in the situation.

The Section

We can return now to our account of the lineage framework of Tongo.

Adjacent to Lɛbhtiis yidɛm, between them and Gbizug, lies the cluster of homesteads of the assimilated lineage of Ligər yidɛm (see above, p. 57), homesteads Nos. 1, 2, 3, 4, on our map. Lɛbhtiis yidɛm are the authentic lineage with which Ligər yidɛm are most closely linked, but they count as segments of equal order in the larger unit of the section (*yizug*). Another cluster of homesteads (Nos. 13, 14, 15, 16) belong to Kuŋkɔŋto'o yidɛm, the attached lineage reputed to be derived from a divorced sister's son (*tau bii*) of Lɛbhtiis yidɛm. Both these accessory lineages have a number of male members living away from Tongo.

The structure of Puhug (see diagram, p. 212), the section (*yizug*) of which it forms a segment, is the structure of Lɛbhtiis yidɛm writ large. Discounting the accessory lineages, Puhug comprises three major segments. It has two more lineages of the same order of segmentation as Lɛbhtiis yidɛm: Kabuu yidɛm and Lɛbhkɔra yidɛm. One segment of the former occupies the south-west or topmost (*zugni*) corner of Puhug (homesteads Nos. 25, 26, 27), abutting on the mass of great boulders that lies between Puhug and the watercourse that separates it from Wakii. The other segment occupies the group of homesteads at Kumpɛyalɔyat. A minor branch, including the head of this segment, migrated to Yamɔlɔg some twenty years ago, and other members of it are settled at Gbambee, Woo, and in the outlying parts of Taleland, while some are abroad. Lɛbhkɔra yidɛm, together with their attached lineage, Zɔŋ yidɛm, live in the group of homesteads—Nos. 30, 31, 32, 34—adjacent to Kuorɔg. These three major segments of Puhug (reckoned as *dugɔt*, medial lineages, in this context) are agnatically related as follows:

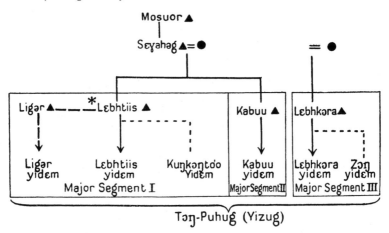

———— Authentic segments
— — Assimilated Lineages
· · · · · · Attached Lineages

Lɛbhtiis yidɛm and Kabuu yidɛm are *soog* (full brother) segments, it will be noted, and though they are not considered to form a single *dug* within Puhug, they have somewhat closer ties than either has with their *sunzɔ* segment of Lɛbhkɔra biis, while Ligɔr yidɛm have closer ties with Lɛbhtiis yidɛm than with the others, on account of their special connexion with the former. In the economic, ritual, and jural concerns of the section all the segments have the same status and the same degree of relative autonomy. But Lɛbhtiis yidɛm are recognized as the senior branch, and so rank above the others. The head (*kpeem*) of Lɛbhtiis yir is *ipso facto* the *kpeem* of Puhug.

The lineage structure of the other three *yizugɔt* of Tongo follows the same

THE LINEAGE IN THE LOCAL COMMUNITY 213

plan; and the architecture of the sub-clan as a whole is that of the *yizug* on a larger scale. A skeleton genealogy (see p. 214) will suffice to show this.

Guŋ, Seug, and Kuorəg are constituted according to the same general plan as Puhug. But each section has features peculiar to itself, specializations of the general principles of *yizug* structure due to the particular genealogical constitution of each, and to the demographic and structural relations with one another of the four sections. This is characteristic of Tale social organization. Like the maximal lineages of a composite clan, co-ordinate segments of a maximal lineage are homologous with one another in structure, but frequently different in genealogical composition.

Viewed in terms of its own diachronic and local constitution, each is unique, its present form the precipitate of its own peculiar history. Thus Guŋ, as we have seen, is not a single local aggregate like Puhug. But the principle that lineage proximity and residential proximity go together prevails. Leaving aside those who have settled permanently or temporarily in outlying places, the Guŋdɛm at Guŋ proper are almost all Kəbər yidɛm. The centre of settlement of Siiyɛŋ biis is Dekpieŋ. Bəɣayiedət yidɛm are most scattered; but each of its segments tends to be a small local aggregate, and wherever in outlying places a cluster of homesteads belonging to Guŋ men is formed—at Zoo, at Gbambee, and at Woo—these men are almost invariably members of a single minor segment of the lineage.

The three segments of Guŋ (excluding Nəŋsuur yidɛm, the assimilated lineage) are considered to be more closely united than the segments of Puhug because they have a single common progenitrix. They speak of themselves as 'members of one *dug* (*dug yɛni dɛm*)' in contraposition to the other sections of Tongo. Seug is the most homogeneous section of Tongo, both residentially and genealogically, for it consists of only one segment, of the same order as the component segments of the other *yizugət*. The members of Seug, too, speak of themselves as members of one *dug* in contraposition to the other three sections. Kuorəg is the most heterogeneous, genealogically, of the four sections. Its members are also more widely dispersed, most of them having moved to Gbambee in the past thirty or forty years.

Puhug and Kuorəg both show clearly how local association is a factor of section organization in a maximal lineage in the same way as it is a factor of clanship in composite clans. Genealogically, Lɛbhkərə yidɛm of Puhug are a lineage of the same order of segmentation as Seugdɛm; yet they do not, like the latter, constitute a separate *yizug*. Close local association with Puhug makes them a part of that section. Similarly, Yikpɛmdaan yir of Kuorəg on genealogical reckoning alone should rank as a section. Its founding ancestor is said to have been a kinsman (*mabii*), possibly a 'brother' but certainly not a son, of Mosuor, who accompanied him on his flight from Mampurugu. The head of this lineage, who has the hereditary title of Yikpɛmdaan, has a position of special dignity at Tongo. He is in one sense the senior elder (*kpeem*) among all the elders of the sub-clan. Yikpɛmdaan's high status is due to his hereditary ownership of a special shrine (*bəɣar*), Zoonkpaləg, which is both his lineage *bəɣar* (*banam bəɣar*) and a clan *bəɣar*, analogous to the External *Bəɣar* of the Talis, for the whole of Tongo. It is the shrine

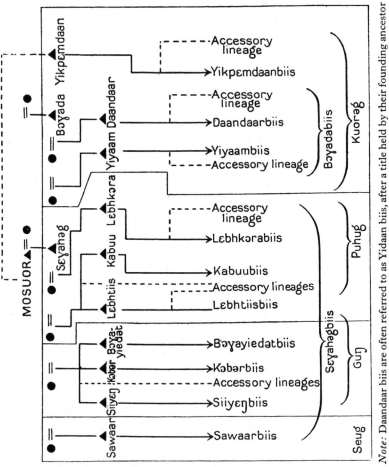

Note: Daandaar biis are often referred to as Yidaan biis, after a title held by their founding ancestor

THE LINEAGE IN THE LOCAL COMMUNITY 215

of all the ancestors of the whole maximal lineage, and it symbolizes the 'gateway' (*zanɔr*) of the whole maximal lineage (cf. p. 208). The natives maintain that the original Yikpɛmdaan accompanied his kinsman Mɔsuor to Tongo as the custodian of this *bɔyar*, in virtue of which he is the *zanɔr kpeem*—the elder in charge of the lineage gateway—of the maximal lineage. Hence it is a common saying at Tongo that 'Yikpɛmdaan is not a Kuorɔg man, but he belongs to the whole of this our Chief's House (*Yikpɛmdaan ka Kuorɔg nit, u a ti Nayirɔ waabi nit*)'. Nevertheless, Yikpɛmdaan yidɛm are always reckoned as part of Kuorɔg in the affairs of that section. Yikpɛmdaan himself acts as the senior elder of the section in jural and ritual affairs that concern it as a whole, superseding the *kpeem* of Bɔyada biis in virtue of his exalted status.

Segmentation and Equilibrium in the Sub-clan

By genealogical reckoning Tongo consists of two major segments: Sɛyahɔg biis (Puhug, Guŋ, and Seug), and Bɔyada biis (Kuorɔg), each with its accessory lineages. In some circumstances the unity of Sɛyahɔg biis in contraposition to Bɔyada biis is recognized. This is the reason why Zɔŋ yidɛm, the attached segment of Lɛbhkɔra biis of Puhug, are permitted to marry Kuorɔgdɛm but not any members of Seyahɔg biis, who are felt to be the widest lineage of which Zɔŋ yidɛm form a segment. But there is a distinct tendency towards the obliteration of the sense of contraposition between Kuorɛg and the rest of Tongo as the sentiment of unity, reflected in the conduct of accessory lineages at the great sacrifice to Mosuor in 1936, becomes stronger (see pp. 53–4). I have heard members of Zɔŋ yidɛm say that it is not becoming (*de pu nara*) for them to marry into Kuorɔg, even though it is no breach of the rule of exogamy to do so. In another decade or so they may well insist that it is not merely unbecoming but forbidden (*kih*), and it would then be a grave discourtesy for anyone at Tongo to remind them publicly of their indirect connexion with Mosuor biis by disputing this.

At funeral ceremonies this primary segmentation of Tongo often emerges. Thus, when the funeral of Yɔrug Yin of Kuorɔg was celebrated, contingents of elders from all the other sections of Tongo, and from Zoo— coming as *sunzɔp*-by-courtesy—as well as Soog (the clan adjacent to Kuorɔg and the 'owners of the land' on which Kuorɔg is situated) came in force to the second divination ceremony; for Yɔrug Yin had been the head of Bɔyada biis and headman of Kuorɔg. But his son was a poor man and had to temper with economy the munificence that pride dictates on such occasions. So when the beer was brought for the guests, Zoodɛm and Soogdɛm were each given a medium-sized pot, and then one large pot was given to *Nayidɛm*, the 'people of the Chief's House', that is, the other three sections of Tongo reckoned as a unit in contraposition to Kuorɔg. Had more beer been brewed, or had the *sunzɔp*-by-courtesy and the neighbouring clan not been present, each section would have received its own pot of beer. Similarly, at the funeral of Saɣawuob of Puhug's mother, representatives of Zoo came to claim the forequarter (*bɔak*) of the cow slaughtered in her honour, which they were entitled to as *sunzɔp*-by-courtesy. This left only two *nundaas* (major portions, or

216   THE LINEAGE IN THE LOCAL COMMUNITY

quarters) for the other three sections of Tongo, since one of the hind quarters (*gbɛr*) remains with the 'owner of the funeral', the man who is celebrating it. Thus the genealogical cleavage between Kuorəg and the rest of Tongo asserted itself. Kuorəg was treated as the *sunzɔp* of the rest of Tongo and received a forequarter, the remaining hind quarter going to the other three sections. There are stories of intra-clan quarrels in the old days in which Puhug, Guŋ, and Seug banded themselves together against Kuorəg.

Nevertheless, in the corporate affairs of Tongo as a whole Kuorəg emerges as a segment of the same order as the other three sections. It is one of the four co-ordinate sections (*yizugət*). A significant index of this is the fact that in all four sections nine generations of ascendants are reckoned inclusively between the present section heads (*yizug kpeem*) and Mosuor. No Tongo man, however profoundly versed in the traditions and customs of his clan, is aware of this, however. Tallensi never have occasion to work out the genealogical relations of all the minimal segments of a maximal lineage with one another.

A man's genealogical knowledge is built up gradually and piecemeal in the give and take of social life, by participation in jural, ritual, and ceremonial activities. But a man of wide experience knows the lineage ancestry of the component segments of his own *dug* as far as its founding ancestor; he will know who were the putative brothers of this man, the founding ancestors of the other major segments of his section, and their sons, the founding ancestors of large sub-segments like Nɔpugzabɔr yidɛm, in his section; and he will know the founding ancestors of the other *yizugət* of the clan, and possibly their sons; but he will not know the whole descent of other major segments of other sections.

The nine-generation ladder of ascent found at Tongo is an index of the structural differentiation and internal equilibrium of the clan. As we have already observed, the maximal lineage (and Tongo functions as a maximal lineage, though strictly speaking it is not one) is unalterably fixed. Its major segments cannot be altered in relation to one another by further segmentation of its minimal segments. Its internal equilibrium is a function of the relations between its major segments; and the same principle applies to each major segment. This is symbolized in the tree of ascent of the people of Tongo. The structure of the maximal lineage does not permit of the recognition of more than one generation between Mosuor and his nine putative grandsons. Following the simplest possible pattern of symmetrical lineage segmentation, all Mosuor's progeny are first divided into two major (matri-)segments in accordance with the stereotyped scheme of differentiation by reference to their progenitrices; and each of these is again segmented on the same principle. Kuorəg counts as a section of the same order as Puhug, Guŋ, and Seug in the corporate affairs of the whole sub-clan, because this is necessary for the equilibrium of the sub-clan. The internal differentiation of Sɛyahəg biis has reached an advanced stage. The relative autonomy of the three sections that constitute it is now so great that they can only act together as equal partners. Each of these three sections has a corporate unity and common interests that sometimes bring it into conflict with the other two

THE LINEAGE IN THE LOCAL COMMUNITY 217

or with Kuorəg. They have no greater common interests uniting them in opposition to Kuorəg. Whenever they unite for action they do so in the service of the common interests of the whole sub-clan, and this necessarily includes Kuorəg. This involves a distribution of roles and responsibilities equally amongst all four sections (Puhug, Guŋ, Seug, and Kuorəg), which places them all on a footing of equality.

Demographic factors have perhaps contributed to this development, though its determining principles lie in the structure of the maximal lineage. I estimate the total population of Kuorəg (men, women, and children), including members of the section and their families who live at Gbambee and Biuŋ, at about 400. Numerically it is considerably less than half the size of Guŋ, less than three-quarters as large as Puhug, and barely bigger than Seug. Kuorəg occupies a correspondingly smaller area than any of the other sections.

These demographic conditions have, it may be conjectured, enhanced the effect of the forces operating to maintain a balance between the segments of the maximal lineage. Looking at Tongo as unit, we may compare it with an arch which stands firm as long as the thrust and counter-thrust of its component forces are balanced. But it is a living arch, the elements of which are in a continuous process of mutual adjustment controlled by the need to maintain the equilibrium of the whole. The same principle can be seen at work in the maximal lineage and in every segment of a maximal lineage down to the smallest, and that is why Kuorəg has been forced into the position of a segment co-ordinate with the other three sections of Tongo, even though it is genealogically super-ordinate to them. This is a necessary condition of its continuing to be a part of Tongo.

The analogy of the arch is particularly pertinent to the structural equilibrium of Tongo. For whenever the four sections co-operate in a ceremonial or jural situation involving the clan as a unit, Puhug and Kuorəg are grouped together in contraposition to Guŋ and Seug, also grouped together. It is shown in small things as well as big things. When, for instance, the beast offered at an important sacrifice or ceremonially slaughtered at a funeral is to be flayed, the elders of each section, as befits their equality of status in the maximal lineage, select two of their younger co-members to do the flaying. Then Puhug and Kuorəg take the left flank, Guŋ and Seug the right; the titbits (*siit-numət*), which are the perquisite of the skinners, are divided equally between the two sides. Similarly at the initial divination for the Harvest Festival, Puhug and Kuorəg take one calabash of flour-water (*zɔm kuɔm*), Guŋ and Seug the other. Whenever the elders of all the sections gather in the chief's *zɔŋ*, that is how they sit—Puhug and Kuorəg on one side, Guŋ and Seug on the other.

The corporate activities and common interests in which the unity and solidarity of a maximal lineage are manifested vary according to the range of segments they mobilize and the degree to which participation in them is obligatory. Funerals and marriages are typical of situations in which there is a variable field of corporate action. Rights and duties associated with them are graded in accordance with lineage distance. The age, sex, station in life, character, and reputation of the deceased all influence the reactions of people to a death and the range of participation in the funeral ceremonies. Every death is the corporate concern of the deceased's medial lineage—his *dug* of the *yizug*. It is less stringently the corporate concern of the whole *yizug*. Funerals of old and important men evoke the participation of the whole clan or sub-clan, but it is clan solidarity and corporate obligation on the level of the section that draw *sunzɔ* sections to the ceremonies. Only the death of a chief, a tɛndaana, or other politico-ritual functionary, is the obligatory concern of every segment of the clan or maximal lineage. Funerals of women and young people or children impose no obligations on *sunzɔ* sections of the

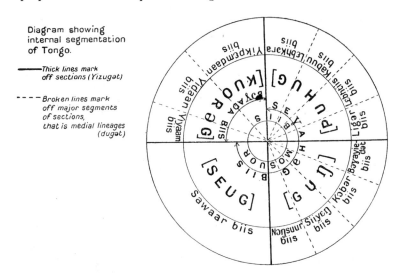

Diagram showing internal segmentation of Tongo.

——— Thick lines mark off sections (Yizugat)

- - - - Broken lines mark off major segments of sections, that is medial lineages (dugat)

deceased's (or her husband's) section. Whether or not their representatives come to condole with the bereaved household or to take part in the burial and funeral ceremonies rests entirely with the individual members of these sections and depends on individual ties of neighbourhood, kinship, or friendship with the deceased's family and *dug*. A funeral, even that of a politico-ritual officer, is primarily the direct concern of every member of the deceased's segment of the clan or maximal lineage. It concerns *sunzɔ* segments only at the level of corporate relations, because every event that affects the existence and constitution of one part of the clan or maximal lineage impinges on its common interests.

We may contrast with this a corporate activity in a wider sense, such as the sacrifice to Mosuor at Tongo, to which we have several times referred, the Harvest Festival, or the communal hoeing of the chief's bush farm, which has become an established custom under British rule. The pivot of these activities is always the chief, who stands for the whole sub-clan and its common interests and values, and whose office transcends the cleavages inherent in its lineage segmentation. In these activities the

THE LINEAGE IN THE LOCAL COMMUNITY 219

four major segments of the clan have an equal role. All have the same obligations and the same rights, vested in them as corporate units defined in relation to the whole clan; and all the segments must participate in equal degree. A similar corporate activity in a clan like Zubiuŋ is a sacrifice to the External *Bɔyar*, Duunkpalɔg.

The four sections of Tongo are equal and co-ordinate in political and jural matters. In religious matters of common interest Puhug is senior (*kpeem*) to the other sections. This is because Mosuor's grave and *bɔyar* and Sɛyahɔg's grave and *bɔyar* are the exclusive charge of Puhug, whose section head (*yizug kpeem*) always has custody of these shrines and officiates in sacrifices to them.

The Local Embodiment of the Ritual Focus of the Sub-clan

Puhug was the original home (*daboog*) of Mosuor. There he dwelt beside Tɛndaan Gɛnɔt, the site of whose *daboog* is now the sacred dancing-ground of the *Giŋgaaŋ* Festival, hence called Giŋgaaŋ Puhug. This is the hub of Tongo as an enduring and stable local unit. Whatever vicissitudes the clan may suffer, whether it expands or contracts, however widely its members may be dispersed, Giŋgaaŋ Puhug remains for ever fixed and inviolable, the heart of the clan and the visible and consecrated sign of its existence and persistence. At the edge of Giŋgaaŋ Puhug is the grave of Tɛndaan Gɛnɔt, and nearby are the graves of the first ancestors of Mosuor biis—Mosuor, Sɛyahɔg, and Bɔyada—marking the sites where their homesteads stood. Thus the ritual and ideological focus of Tongo's corporate unity as a descent group (and the same rule applies to all Tale clans) is directly bound up with its physical counterpart, the local focus of Tongo's unity and identity. In clans that have tɛndaanas, it is usually the principal Earth shrine (*tɔŋgban*) that is the consecrated local focus of the clan.

Mosuor's grave, marked by an irregular flat heap of large stones, lies under an enormous old baobab tree which the people of Tongo say *is* Mosuor (see map of Tongo). On the side of the trunk facing the grave are signs of the sacrifices offered there—dirty streaks of dried blood and flour-water, and patches of fowl and guinea-fowl feathers stuck to the trunk with blood. It is a prominent landmark in Puhug, and a favourite shade tree for the people of the nearby homesteads. There the old men come and rest on hot afternoons, infants are put out to sit, well protected from the sun, while their mothers get on with the household work, and older children come to play or to swing in the branches. It is characteristic of the Tallensi that the people of Tongo treat their most sacred shrines in this realistic and matter-of-fact way in the context of everyday life. The tree is sacred, it is a *Bayar*, but it is also just a tree, whose ritual significance is not relevant except on a ritual occasion. Then it is treated with appropriate reverence. And this is true, also, of ancestral graves, which are often treated very casually and sometimes allowed to fall into such neglect that none but the elders of the lineage descended from him know exactly where a particular ancestor's grave is. Mosuor's grave, however, being of such outstanding ritual importance for the whole of Tongo, is more carefully kept and is always treated with respect.

220 THE LINEAGE IN THE LOCAL COMMUNITY

The graves of Sɛyahɔg and Bɔyada lie within a couple of minutes' walk of each other and of Mosuor's baobab in Puhug. Though Bɔyada's grave is in the middle of the home farm of a Puhug man, its custody is vested in Kuorɔg, whose head comes to sacrifice there periodically. Similarly Siiyɛŋ, Kɔbɔr, and Bɔyayiedɔt, the ancestors of Guŋ and Dekpieŋ, lie buried at Guŋ proper, at the *daboog* of this *yizug*, though the majority of their descendants live at Dekpieŋ.

For the people of Tongo—and this also applies to all Tallensi except the Hill Talis—the disposition of graves maps out the gradual increase or diminution in numbers of the clan or any segment of the clan through the generations, and its gradual territorial expansion or retraction. Thus Tɛndaan Gɛnɔt's house site and grave in the centre of Puhug are accepted as proof that the Gbizugdɛm lived there at the time of Mosuor's arrival and were gradually pushed out to their present location by the spreading of Mosuor's progeny. The founding ancestor of Zubiuŋ Yakɔradɛm, Gɛnɔt's putative brother, is also believed to have lived at Puhug at that remote period, and they, too, are said to have been dispossessed by Mosuor biis. Similarly the location of Bɔyada's grave is proof to the natives that the growing numbers of Puhugdɛm caused his descendants to withdraw gradually into what is now Kuorɔg.

Structure of the Clan Settlement among non-Namoos

Among Talis as well as Namoos in the older part of Taleland, the clan settlement is built up round the lineage in this way. In composite clans the tendency is always for each constituent maximal lineage to form a locally distinct though not strictly demarcated aggregate, and for the segments of these *yizugɔt* to follow the same rule more markedly. The correlation of residence with lineage, ancestral lands, and the graves of the ancestors holds. At Zubiuŋ, at Ba'ari, and among the non-Namoo clans living in the vicinity of Yamɔlɔg and Sie—the group of clans which the Hill Talis regard as having been culturally influenced by the Namoos —a person is buried among his own (or her husband's) immediate forebears near the homestead. The Hill Talis bury their dead in small cemeteries, each section (*yizug*) or main segment (*dug*) of a section usually having its own. Among all the Talis and the non-Namoos of the Sie district a sacred grove (*tɔŋgban*) or an External *Bɔyar* takes the place of the sacred dancing-ground at Tongo as the local and spiritual focus of the settlement. The homestead of the *yizug* head, housing the most important shrines of its ancestors, whatever his ritual office may be, is often fixed, so that when a man succeeds to the office he takes possession also of the homestead that goes with it; thus the idea of the home of the maximal lineage has an everlasting and consecrated embodiment in the actual homestead occupied by its head.

Among the clans which have tɛndaanas the local anchorage of the clan and of its constituent maximal lineages is, in some respects, even stronger than among the Namoos. It is more conspicuously wrought into their institutions and more obviously sacrosanct, since the office of tɛndaana presupposes very special ritual bonds, the strongest bonds known to the Tallensi, of a maximal lineage with locality.

THE LINEAGE IN THE LOCAL COMMUNITY

Structure of Peripheral Settlements

In the newer settlements there are no lineages of large span. Where segments of maximal lineages, whose homes are in the old settlements, have been settled for more than a generation, those of their members remaining in the peripheral settlements do not always live in close proximity to one another. People shift readily to take up new land, and spread widely so as to have a large area for cultivation immediately around the homestead, as we have learnt. But the tendency for a lineage to become locally stabilized on the land of its ancestors, near their graves and original home, operates strongly too, and has been strengthened in recent years.

Many men at Woo, Biuŋ, and Datɔk now live on land originally broken for cultivation by their fathers, grandfathers, and even great-grandfathers. A powerful incentive to remain there is the fact that they now hold this land by right of inheritance. An irresistible sanction binding them to these new settlements is the fact that their fathers and grandfathers lie buried there. Born and bred in these settlements, they look upon them as their homes, while maintaining strong ties with their original clan settlements, which they regard as the clan homes.

The effect is to establish new, permanent, local nuclei for minor branches of lineages anchored in the old settlement. Around these nuclei we sometimes find a small cluster of homesteads, the heads of which are all members of a lineage segment of two, three, or at the most four generations. But this is far from common. As we have mentioned before, these settlements have been, and are being, occupied by people of very diverse genealogical origin from all parts of Taleland and neighbouring areas. This is particularly marked in the case of Datɔk. Biuŋ and Woo have been settled chiefly by people from Tongo and the places immediately adjacent to or socially connected with Tongo. In addition to the bonds of local cohesion the inhabitants of these places have also the ties of political and ritual interdependence which they bring with them from their original clan settlements. At Datɔk no such bonds are carried over into the new community. A Gban man may have as his nearest neighbours a man from Ba'ari, a man from Bɔlɔga, a man from Yamɔlɔg, and a man from Bongo. The basis of political unity is locality rather than lineage. The sections of Datɔk, for example, are local units, wards, or quarters, not genealogical-cum-local units.

But it is characteristic of Tale social organization that the bonds of local association never stand alone and are never sufficient in themselves to generate bonds of solidarity. Mere contiguity requires some degree of mutual accommodation. It does not, in a society without a constituted legal system or territorially organized political units, create mutual legal obligations, or provide a basis for corporate relations between individuals. Hence it must be reinforced by, and indeed founded on, more fundamental ties which are morally and jurally binding in their own right. In the older settlements lineage ties have this function; in new settlements kinship ties take their place.

The following excerpt from a census of a part of Datɔk illustrates this.

It will be seen that both affinal and cognatic kinship ties regulate the collocation of homesteads.

Section: Zalənwuuri. (A local subdivision of Datɔk, named after the stream forming one of its boundaries.)

Homestead 1. This belongs to Latammi, a man of about 55, whose father, a Gar man, came to build his house and to farm here about fifty years ago. He died and was buried at his new home. Latammi, his eldest son, then inherited the homestead and the surrounding farm-land, and remained living there.

Homestead 2. About 200 yards away, is owned by Latammi's father's younger brother's (*pit soog*) son. This young man formerly shared Latammi's homestead but recently moved out to set up in his own.

Homestead 3. About 250 yards away from 1. Latammi's father's half-brother (*sunzɔ*) built this homestead, having come to settle here shortly after Latammi's father. This man died recently and the homestead and surrounding farm-land now belong to his son.

The following genealogy shows how the heads of these three homesteads are related:

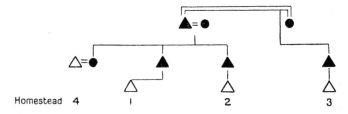

Together they constitute a lineage of small span, a segment of a greater lineage whose home is at Gar. Their residential collocation is exactly the same as it would be if they were living at Gar or in any of the older settlements.

Homestead 4. About 200 yards from 1. This is the homestead of a Ba'ari man who migrated to Datɔk about three years ago. He is a brother-in-law (sister's husband) (*dakii*) of Latammi's late father (see genealogy above), and was, on this account, given land on which to build and settle by the latter's half-brother's son of Homestead 3.

Homestead 5. About a quarter of a mile from 1. This belongs to Naambɔn, whose father, a man from Bɔləga, came to build and settle here some forty years ago. This man had first migrated from Bɔləga to Kosabɔləg, on the outskirts of Duusi. While he was living there Teroog (now an old man), a member of the same maximal lineage as Latammi's father, who lives in another section of Datɔk, married one of the Bɔləga man's daughters. The land he held at Duusi proved to be unsatisfactory, so Naambɔn's father decided to move to Datɔk. Through the good offices of his son-in-law, Teroog, he was introduced to Latammi's father, who (as a son-in-law (*deem*) in the classificatory sense) gave him land to settle on near the fringe of the huge area he had marked out as a farm for himself.

THE LINEAGE IN THE LOCAL COMMUNITY   223

This small sample is typical of the relationships that unite neighbours at Datɔk. The settlement is divided up into such clusters of homesteads, numbering anything from four or five homesteads to about a dozen, which have grown up around the homestead of a man who migrated to settle there forty or fifty years ago when Datɔk was still uninhabited bush.

Gradually the original settlers were joined by younger members of their lineages and kinsmen, migrating for economic or psychological reasons but drawn to this particular place by their kinship ties. Often several such clusters of homesteads close to one another, the owners of which are linked among themselves by ties of lineage or kinship, are grouped round men who are themselves linked by lineage or kinship. They are the original settlers, or more usually the sons or grandsons of the original settlers, who built their homesteads far apart from one another so as to have ample land for cultivation close at hand, and then 'cut' (ŋma) parcels of this land for the immigrants who filtered in subsequently.

In these conditions a great deal of intermarriage takes place between neighbours and within the local community, since many different clans are represented in the community. Tallensi are more inclined to marry people who live nearby than to take spouses from a distance; and at Datɔk marriage between the children of men who happen to be neighbours because of their kinship with a third man, but are themselves not related, is very common.[1] This weaves the mesh of kinship ties yet more finely, binding neighbour to neighbour still more closely and firmly.

It is evident that the corporate life of a community like Datɔk—and this applies only in a lesser degree to other peripheral settlements of mixed origins—must differ in many ways from that of the older settlements. Two clans, Gar and Gban, are numerically and politically dominant at Datɔk, just as Zoo is at Biuŋ, and the Hill Talis are at Mɔɣaduur, and the people of these numerically superior clans or lineages can co-operate and unite for action in the same way as the segments of the clan do in the old settlements. People who have very few or no clansmen or lineage brothers in the settlement are in a different position. In Tale jural and ceremonial relations all matters of importance are dealt with corporately by lineages. Thus, if a Ba'ari man living at Datɔk suffers a bereavement, takes a wife, marries off a daughter, gets involved in a dispute, or has to make an important sacrifice, he has to call upon the elders of his lineage and clan at Ba'ari to support him in the action required. His extra-clan kinsmen at Datɔk cannot give him corporate assistance, though they would be individually helpful. Similarly he takes part in the economic, jural, and ceremonial events in which his Datɔk neighbours and kinsmen are involved only as an individual actuated by ties of personal kinship and concern for the welfare of particular people. In other words, these outlying settlements are still politically inchoate. They are still mainly social and political apanages of the older settlements from which they have been colonized; very many of their members are still tied into the structure of their natal clan-settlements, and are still

[1] I state this in a general way, as I did not take a sufficiently large sample of marriages at Datɔk to give a numerical indication of the extent of marriage within the settlement.

224 THE LINEAGE IN THE LOCAL COMMUNITY

loyal to the interests of these clan settlements. But the political structure of the newer settlements is rapidly crystallizing out, on the basis of a territorial unity reinforced by inter-individual kinship ties. This process has been greatly accelerated under the influence of British rule, with its stress on the territorial definition of political units and the support it gives to chiefs and headmen in the exercise of administrative and judicial functions.

Seniority and Authority in the Lineage

In the course of our morphological analysis of the lineage system from within, we have made many references to the corporate activities in which this system emerges. As in our study of clanship, it has been convenient to speak as if the lineage structure exists and persists apart from the activities in which it emerges. But this is only an analytical device which we shall consider more fully presently. The implied distinction between the structure of the lineage and its functions does, however, bring out the important fact that the lineage structure is more than any of its functions. It is the integral of what is common to all Tale institutions in which the patrilineal line operates as an organizing principle. It is the general factor of consistency, coherence, and continuity in the social structure.

The concept of social structure essentially implies ordered extension *in time* as well as ordered articulation *at a given time*. This is often overlooked in the study of primitive society. Among the Tallensi the lineage system enables us to see the operation of the time factor in social structure in a very concrete way.[1] We see how the lineage structure at a given time incapsulates[2] all that is structurally relevant of its past phases and at the same time continually thrusts its growing-points forward. The dynamic equilibrium of a lineage is an equilibrium in time.

The key position, whenever a lineage emerges in function—and this applies to lineages of any span and all orders of segmentation—is that of the lineage head (*kpeem*). He is, to revert to an analogy previously used, the keystone of the arch. He does not stand above the lineage; he is part of it. *Kpeem* literally means 'senior': a *kpeem* is a senior, an elder. The head of the lineage is the most senior male of the group. The head of a lineage and his age or generation equals in the lineage are collectively designated 'the elders (*kpɛm*)'. They are for the most part the heads of the component segments of the lineage.

The rule of seniority, as might be expected in so homogeneous and equalitarian a society, plays an important part in all Tale social relations. When a group of boys are out herding cattle the oldest among them are in charge. The women of a household defer to the most senior by generation, age, or marital status among them. In all collective activities of men the places of honour are taken by the most senior men, the *kpɛm*. Seniority commands deference at all times.

---

[1] Cf. my paper 'The Significance of Descent in Tale Social Structure', *cit. supra*; also Forde, op. cit. and his previous papers cited there; and a brilliant discussion of this point in E. E. Evans-Pritchard's *The Nuer*, ch. 3.

[2] I owe this valuable concept to R. G. Collingwood's *Autobiography*.

PLATE XI

(a) The grave of Tɛndaan Gɛnɔt and the space believed to have been occupied by his homestead and Mosuor's, now the sacred dancing ground, Giŋgaaŋ Puhug, at Tongo. Note that it is not cultivated.

(b) A miniature homestead symbolizing the ancestral home of a maximal lineage or clan. Note the lineage bɔyar against the outside wall.

PLATE XII

(a) The head of a medial lineage, Siiyɛŋ biis of Tongo, about to sacrifice to the lineage *bɔyar* on formally taking over the headship of the lineage. The *bɔyar* is in front of him in the broken pottery vessel.

(b) A sacrifice to the *dugni* (maximal lineage) *bɔyar* of one of the component maximal lineages of Zubiuŋ. Only elders of the lineage are present.

THE LINEAGE IN THE LOCAL COMMUNITY

Seniority (*kpɛmɔt*) is defined by four criteria, singly or in combination according to the situation and the group involved. These are age, generation, social maturity, and status. A youth of 18 is always a 'child (*bii*)'; a man of 40 calls himself a 'child' if his father is still alive, but will be counted among the *kpɛm* if he is head of a nuclear lineage. A chief is always a *kpeem* irrespective of his age or generation.

Succession to lineage headship depends on one very important rule.[1] Within the range of recognized generation differences—that is, at the widest the medial lineage—succession goes by generation, not by age. The son begotten by an old man towards the end of his life takes precedence over his much older grandson. Beyond that range succession goes by age. This is summed up in the maxim 'Generation differences do not cross the *dug* (*dɔyam pu yakɔt dug la*)'. This rule is a source of frequent discord.

No doubt because of their equalitarian social system and their segmentary social structure, Tallensi attach exceptional prestige value to the attainment of lineage headship, especially in the higher orders of lineage segmentation. Rival claims to headships of greater than medial lineages are based on varying interpretations of the rule of seniority. Thus Yinyɛla of Tɔŋ-Puhug (see pp. 195–6) claimed seniority by generation over all the other elders of Lɛbhtiis yir and demanded redress for having been cheated, as he said, of succession to the headship of Puhug thirty-five years or so before. The other elders declared that Puhug had 'spread' genealogically (*ɛŋ yalɔŋa*) so much since the time of Yinyɛla's grandfather that succession by seniority of generation no longer held outside the inner lineage.

In every maximal lineage (or among Mosuor biis, sub-clan) there is a hierarchy of lineage heads corresponding to the hierarchy of segments and the hierarchy of *bɔyar* shrines. Obviously a particular lineage head may be head of several segments of different orders. Thus Deemzeet (see p. 194) is head of his nuclear lineage, his medial lineage, and of the whole section of Puhug. At the apex stands the head of the maximal lineage or sub-clan whose status practically always carries with it politico-ritual office. This has an important bearing on the working of the lineage system. Every head of a less than maximal lineage stands for his segment, sometimes in opposition to other segments of the lineage. The head of the maximal lineage is raised above the sectional interests of the segments by his politico-ritual office. He is bound by that office to think of himself as representing the whole maximal lineage and its common interests, irrespective of the segment to which he happens to belong. This is symbolized by his having custody of the focal ancestor shrine of the maximal lineage and is sanctioned by the investment of his position with special ritual status. Though only *primus inter pares*, like all lineage heads, he has the added moral and ritual authority of his office, due to his being identified with the founding ancestors.[2]

[1] This rule and its far-reaching implications are fully discussed in the next volume of this study.

[2] This has often misled Administrative officers faced with rival claimants to jurisdiction in certain areas. When a chief or tɛndaana says of another 'I gave

226 THE LINEAGE IN THE LOCAL COMMUNITY

Tallensi say that lineage headship is conferred by inheritance of, or succession to (the same term, *vaa*, vb. is used for both), firstly, the custody of the founding ancestor's shrine (*bɔɣar*), and secondly the patrimonial property (*faar*), in particular the home farm (*saman*) of the lineage. Within the nuclear lineage, or at most the inner lineage, both conditions apply; beyond that limit lineage headship does not confer title to land, except in a few special cases; it is determined solely by succession to the custody of the *bɔɣar*. The rules of inheritance and succession are backed by the most powerful sanctions of the ancestor cult and supported by the whole fabric of the social system. Within the medial lineage inheritance disputes occur so rarely as to be negligible. This is a reflection of the strong solidarity of this unit, and of the recognition of classificatory fatherhood within it. Beyond that range succession disputes are settled either by the arbitration of the maximal lineage head or by an appeal to the ancestors through divination or an oracle test.

The range of application of the two conditions of *kpɛmɔt* define the gradation of powers and functions discharged by lineage heads. Within the nuclear (or at most inner) lineage the head has paternal authority[1] associated with his control of the farm-land and of the labour of his dependants. He has corresponding jural and ritual responsibilities for the junior members of the lineage. Formally, his is the decisive voice in all matters in which the lineage emerges as a corporate unit—for example, in the disposal of the daughters in marriage and in the payment of bride-price for sons' wives. Beyond the nuclear lineage the lineage head's powers and authority are purely moral and ritual. He cannot, for instance, command the services of any member of the lineage (outside his nuclear lineage) as of right, nor is he responsible for any of them in such matters as bride-price payments. And the degree to which he commands the loyalty of his lineage co-members depends considerably on his personality. They will always support him unhesitatingly where the common interests of the lineage are concerned, but they might not, in private matters, treat him with the confidence due to his status if he lacks tact or tries to be dictatorial. A lineage head represents the lineage. He is the pivot of its corporate unity. Everything he does as lineage head is for and on behalf of the lineage. Hence he never takes action in corporate affairs without consulting and obtaining the consent of the heads of all the component segments of the lineage. In fact a lineage head very rarely takes action in corporate matters without the presence of all the senior male members of the lineage. Thus it is common for the initiative and drive in corporate activities to come from younger men of intelligence and forceful personality, though they are carried out by, or in the name of, the lineage head. This is especially the case when, as often happens, lineage heads are old and infirm. Tinta'alɔm's senility did not diminish the respect and affection in which he was held by all the people

him land to dwell on and therefore I am his superior' he must not be taken literally. He is referring to a tradition of settlement going back to the founding ancestors of their lineages.

[1] We analyse the function of classificatory fatherhood and of paternal authority in the lineage more fully in the second volume of this study.

THE LINEAGE IN THE LOCAL COMMUNITY 227

of Tɔŋ-Kuorəg. The practical duties of his office were carried out by his sons and other elders of the section. The decrepitude of age does not make a chief or tɛndaana any the less a chief or tɛndaana. The activities of the office are simply taken over by his sons.

Tallensi never undertake anything of importance,—for instance, a marriage transaction or the building of a new shrine or making a new bush farm—without the knowledge of the other members of the medial lineage and without consulting or at least informing the head of their section or maximal lineage. The home of the lineage head is the centre of the social life of the lineage members and their families. There is a constant coming and going of members of the lineage at the lineage head's homestead. There they often congregate in the dry season to gossip or discuss their affairs under his shade tree. Visiting kinsmen and affines of lineage members from other clans usually call to greet him there. This applies especially to the medial lineage but also to maximal lineages and sections in a slightly lesser degree. The lineage head himself, if he is able-bodied, often goes to see other members of the lineage. The bonds of solidarity, mutual interest, and knowledge of one another's affairs are thus constantly being knit together within the lineage.

Though a lineage head has no judicial authority, he is often asked to arbitrate in disputes or conflicts between segments of the lineage. What he generally tries to do is to bring about a compromise and reconciliation, for he has no powers of enforcing his decision. When he is successful in adjusting differences, it is on account of his prestige and because he has the public opinion of the lineage on his side. No lineage head would attempt to adjust a dispute in the lineage without the advice and backing of the other elders of the lineage.

The sanction of a lineage head's position is the ancestor cult. Even a chief has, in the native social order, no judicial or economic sanctions to support his authority. A tɛndaana has, in addition, the sanction of the Earth. The role of the lineage head in corporate affairs, his duties, responsibilities, and privileges all arise from the fact that he has custody of the lineage bɔyar. The strength of this sanction depends not only on the natives' belief in the mystical powers of the ancestors but also on the crucial function of the ancestor cult as the ideology around which lineage relations are organized. The cult of the lineage ancestors is the supreme centripetal force in lineage relations. Many men live far away from their lineage homes. They maintain their lineage bonds on account of their dependence on the ancestor cult. Individuals may transgress the norms of lineage unity and amity with apparent impunity. Their death, when it comes, is conceptualized as a punishment from the ancestors and this serves to reaffirm the norms of lineage solidarity.

Because of this, sacrifices to the lineage bɔyar form the key mechanism for maintaining lineage cohesion and affirming the status of the lineage head. The first of these sacrifices made by a new lineage head (in a lineage of a high order) when he formally takes over the custody of the bɔyar is of outstanding significance. Not less than three or four and sometimes ten to fifteen years elapse between successive ceremonies of this sort. They are occasions of special solemnity marking the re-establishment of

228 THE LINEAGE IN THE LOCAL COMMUNITY

the proper structural form of the lineage around a new lineage head after its temporary disturbance by the death of his predecessor. Not only do all the adult members of the lineage attend, each bearing a fowl to be sacrificed on behalf of himself and his segment, but representatives of other branches of the clan and very many extra-clan kin, descendants of daughters of the lineage, also attend. The pattern of the rites is the same as that of any sacrifice to the *bɔyar*, but all who participate feel them to be a specially binding sacrament. An atmosphere of great goodwill and fellowship prevails, particularly during the festive episodes of sharing out the meat and the beer.

In addition, the funeral of a lineage head is an event that mobilizes the entire lineage structure and demonstrates the power of the religious sanctions as the bulwark of his position. Special rites are performed, in many clans, to detach his social personality from the lineage shrines. And it is often in the divination sessions at the funerals of lineage heads that suppressed intra-lineage conflicts are brought into the open. The religious sanctions against intra-lineage conflict are thus set in motion and reconciliations brought about.

A mere catalogue of the chief privileges and responsibilities of the head of lineage of a high order is sufficient to indicate his social role as chief representative of the lineage in relation to other lineages and to the ancestors. No ceremonial or jural transaction in which the lineage is concerned as a whole can take place without the presence of the lineage head or his deputy. When the carcass of an animal slaughtered for ritual or ceremonial purposes is divided up, the best part of the portion allotted to a particular lineage is reserved for the *kpeem*. When a member of the lineage kills an animal in the hunt, one hind leg and sometimes the skin are the perquisites of the lineage head (of the medial or maximal lineage), and the skull and horns are deposited with him. In these and similar situations the *kpeem's* privileges are regarded as a means of apprising the ancestors of the event and winning their blessings. The meat he gets, for instance, is 'set out for the ancestor spirits (*zien kpiim*)' before it is consumed.

Certain sacrifices to the lineage ancestors are obligatory on every man of advanced years. They are both a sign of gratitude to the ancestors and a symbol of the common interest of the whole lineage in the giver's welfare and possessions. Thus a man must sacrifice one of the cows he receives for his eldest daughter's bride-price to the lineage *bɔyar* of his medial lineage; and the lineage head receives a hind leg and the skin as well as other parts of the animal. Similarly if a man wishes to set up a new ancestor shrine he must first inform his lineage ancestors by means of a sacrifice to the *bɔyar*. Hence Tallensi say that one of the advantages of being the head of a medial or maximal lineage is that there is always meat in the house. But this privilege, they add, is a compensation for the responsibilities of lineage headship. Not the least of these is the *kpeem's* duty to make frequent sacrifices to the ancestors in order to preserve their goodwill towards the lineage.

All interlineage jural and ritual transactions take place formally through the lineage heads. Thus if a man seduces the wife of a member

THE LINEAGE IN THE LOCAL COMMUNITY 229

of another medial or maximal lineage of his own or a closely allied clan, hostility between the two units is aroused and their normal relations are thrown out of gear. But usually steps are very quickly taken to set matters right. Either the head of the wronged lineage sends to protest to the head of the seducer's lineage, and the latter, backed by the lineage elders, makes the seducer confess and agree to apologize, or else the culprit himself, aware that public opinion would reprove his action, begs the head of his nuclear lineage to get the head of their medial or maximal lineage to intercede on his behalf with the head of the wronged lineage. It is at the homestead of the latter that the rites of reconciliation are performed by representatives of the two lineages. This is typical of inter-lineage jural relations.

A woman who commits adultery exposes her husband and children to mystical dangers. Among Namoos she is haled to the homestead of the head of her husband's medial lineage and subjected to the ordeal of entering the gateway (*zanɔr*). If she confesses she may enter safely. If not, the lineage ancestors will cause her to get ill if she enters the gateway. This is a very powerful sanction of marital fidelity among women and is one reason why adultery is not very common. Tallensi sum up the role of the lineage head in the sentence, 'All our (lineage) affairs are conducted at the gateway of our lineage head's homestead (i.e. the lineage *zanɔr*—cf. p. 208) (*Ti yɛla kama maana ti kpeem yir zanɔne*)'.

In the old days the men of a medial lineage all assembled at the *kpeem's* homestead before going out to fight. There they all took part in sacrifices to the ancestors and 'ate (*di*)' protective medicine to fortify themselves against the enemy's arrows. Nowadays they do the same before setting out on a communal hunting expedition, for there are many dangers to be faced—accidental arrow wounds, fire, and wild beasts. This is the service for which the *kpeem* is rewarded when he is given a hind leg of every animal slain by the sons of the lineage.

The *kpeem's* functions are most conspicuous in relation to the wives and children of the lineage, for they stand for the greatest common interest of the lineages. It is the reproductive powers of the wives and the existence of children that secure the perpetuation of the lineage and the immortality of the ancestors. The handling of a woman who commits adultery illustrates this. Similarly the lineage elders must be informed of, and the lineage head give his formal consent to, the re-marriage of a widow of any member of the lineage. A widow is in theory entitled to reject a husband chosen for her by her late husband's nuclear lineage and to choose any member of his clan of the right generation. If she does this she must get the consent of the head of his medial lineage and this is binding on the whole medial lineage. Her late husband's nuclear lineage cannot then object to her marrying out of that lineage.

The head of a medial or maximal lineage comes into the formalities of marriage for every member, man or woman, of the lineage, in his capacity as its chief representative in interlineage jural relations. The right to dispose of a girl in marriage is vested in her guardian the head of her nucleur lineage. It is he who receives and owns the bride-

230   THE LINEAGE IN THE LOCAL COMMUNITY

price;[1] and conversely, it is he who is directly responsible for the payment of bride-price for the wives of members of the nuclear lineage, and for any other outlay entailed by the marriage formalities. But for all these transactions the formal consent (which is in fact never withheld) of the medial lineage head is required. This has the force of a blessing. When the bridegroom's people send the placation gifts (*lu sɛndaan*) by which the marriage is regularized, the messenger goes first to the head of the girl's medial or maximal lineage, and gives him a live cock, the most important item among the placation gifts.[2] By accepting the live cock the lineage head signifies the acquiescence of the whole lineage in the marriage and the blessing of the ancestors thereon. Whether or not bride-price is paid, the girl is thereafter the jurally recognized wife of the bridegroom. As a rule it is perfectly safe for the lineage head to accept the cock, as placation gifts are only sent when the head of the girl's nuclear lineage consents. But cases do occur in which they are sent without the knowledge of the latter as a dodge by which to compel him to acquiesce in the marriage. Then if the head of the medial lineage accepts the live cock, the head of the girl's nuclear lineage must perforce acquiesce. This makes the marriage binding but does not secure it against dissolution through action taken by the head of the girl's nuclear lineage.

In the same way, when a woman's father's people come to demand the payment of bride-price from her husband's nuclear lineage, they go first to the head of the husband's medial lineage. He conducts the messengers to the head of the husband's nuclear lineage and formally presides over the negotiations.

Marriage transactions illustrate a very important principle of Tale jural relations. They are always relations between lineage units. Even when they appear to involve only particular individuals the lineage framework is implicit in the transaction. But this does not mean that all Tale jural relations are based on the concept of collective responsibility. On the contrary, jural responsibility is precisely fixed on particular individuals or exactly defined corporate units. This is graphically summed up in many Tale maxims. Thus they say 'A pipe sounds best in its owner's mouth (*Yiig m-mah ka daana nuoni*)'—that is, an action should be answered for by the person directly responsible for it. What we find, rather, is that all jural relations involve a configuration of rights on one side and a configuration of responsibilities on the other, both corresponding to the range of lineage segments involved. And no jural transaction is complete until the whole configuration of rights and responsibilities, on both sides, is brought into action. Though marriage formalities involve primarily the nuclear lineage and medial lineage, they presuppose the entire framework of maximal lineage and clan relations; and this is the case with most other jural relations among the Tallensi.

[1] Subject to limitations that will be detailed in our next volume.

[2] In many clans there is an arrangement between pairs of medial or maximal lineages that have some special tie of kinship by which the *sɛndaan* cock for a girl of one lineage is delivered to the *kpeem* of the other lineage and vice versa. E.g. this arrangement obtains between Lɛbhtiis yidɛm and Kabuu yidɛm at Tɔŋ-Puhug and is a sign of their close kinship as lineages sprung from one original progenitrix (see p. 212).

CHAPTER XIII

THE FORM OF TALE SOCIETY

The Socio-geographic Region

OUR survey of the macroscopic structure of Tale society has led us from the consideration of the natives' habits of grouping themselves by name, through an analysis of Tale clanship, to the ritual institutions that form the crowning mechanism of co-ordination in the system, and finally to the internal structure of the settlement and the lineage. An ethnographer accustomed to think of a native society as a unit of social organization marked off by precise territorial, political, or cultural boundaries might protest against our frequent references to 'Tale society'. But this habit of thought, appropriate enough in dealing with island communities, nomadic tribes, or territorially organized states, must be discarded if we wish to understand the structure of societies like that of the Tallensi. For the concept of a society as a closed unit, a sort of thing distinguishable from like things in the same way as one house is distinguishable from another or one animal from another, we must substitute the concept of society as a socio-geographic region, the social elements of which are more closely knit together among themselves than any of them are knit together with social elements of the same kind outside that region. We must substitute a relative and dynamic concept for an absolute and static one. If we look at the area of Voltaic culture as a whole, we can imagine innumerable currents of social life flowing through it in all directions. There are major currents and tributary currents. They intersect in all sorts of ways. But at particular places the forces of which the currents are an expression act in such a way as to draw together a large number, if not all, of the major currents. These regions of maximum confluence would correspond to what we have called a socio-geographic region, or a society. If we follow any single current from a region of maximum confluence it leads us right out of that region into another region. It is only if we look at the region from within that we see the coherence it has as a result of the confluence of many social currents.

But metaphors are proverbially treacherous and we must return to our proper subject-matter. The concept of society we have formulated enables us to see clearly the most characteristic feature of Tale society. It is a segmentary[1] system. At bottom this is a consequence of the fact that the Tallensi have not got a centralized, unified, political organization. This is clear if we compare the Tallensi with some other African peoples such as the Tswana of Bechuanaland Protectorate,[2] the Bemba of Northern

---

[1] Cf. Fortes, M., and Evans-Pritchard, E. E. (editors), *African Political Systems*, 1940, 'Introduction', and Evans-Pritchard, E. E., *The Nuer*, 1940.

[2] Cf. Schapera, I., *Handbook of Tswana Law and Custom*, 1938, and 'The Political Organization of the Ngwato', in *African Political Systems*, cited above.

232   THE FORM OF TALE SOCIETY

Rhodesia,[1] or the Ashanti of the Gold Coast.[2] These peoples have a pyramidal social structure corresponding to their pyramidal form of government. From the village to the tribal unit we find a hierarchy of territorial-political units, the greater made up of a collection of the lesser, and culminating in the whole tribal unit. This is associated with a corresponding hierarchy of political offices, from the village headman to the paramount chief at the apex. Among the Tallensi[3] there is no single person or body of persons vested with supreme executive and administrative authority over the whole of Taleland. Government is laterally distributed amongst all the corporate units that make up the society, instead of being vertically distributed as in pyramidal societies. All the corporate units are, broadly speaking, politically equal; all are segments of the same structural order.

This is one aspect of what is meant by describing Tale society as segmentary in form. But the concept has further implications. The corporate units that compose Tale society are not a casual agglomerate of discrete bodies, but are socially articulated and interconnected with one another; and they are thus interrelated in a segmentary series. This principle of association between defined social units runs right through the structure of Tale society. It means that small units of a particular form are, like cells, associated together into larger units of the same general form, and these again associated into still larger units of analogous or identical form, and so on up to the limits of the system. This rule holds whether the associations are temporary, for a particular end, or form permanent groupings. Furthermore, the principles according to which the associations occur are either uniform for a whole series of segments of increasing dimension or are so related to one another that principles operating on one level presuppose the principles operating on a lower level.

This is an architectural way of looking at the structure of Tale society. It is the line we have largely followed in the preceding chapters, where we have been concerned with the largest corporate units into which the Tallensi are organized. Our attention has been fixed mainly on the permanent edifice in which social relations and activities are congealed rather than on their emergence in process. We have been analysing the product of social segmentation rather than the process itself. To distinguish between product and process is, however, merely an analytic convenience in dealing with social facts. In reality what we denote as a product is a set of regularities and recurrences of process. A corporate unit is really the sum total of corporate relations and activities occurring amongst a defined group of individuals. We can think of a maximal lineage as an architectural segment of a composite clan in the same way as we can picture one storey of a modern building as a lateral segment of the whole. A maximal lineage, however, differs from a part of a building of brick and wood in that it is not always 'there', tactually and visibly.

[1] Cf. Richards, Audrey I., 'The Political System of the Bemba Tribe', in *African Political Systems*, and *Land, Labour and Diet in Northern Rhodesia*, 1939.

[2] Cf. Rattray, R. S., *Ashanti Law and Constitution*, 1929.

[3] A fuller analysis will be found in the 'Introduction' and in my article on 'The Political System of the Tallensi' in *African Political Systems*.

THE FORM OF TALE SOCIETY

It emerges when certain social processes and activities are in play; it is potential when they are not in play. Difficult as it is to convey this to a reader, it is something which the observer is constantly aware of. A maximal lineage emerges only in relation to other maximal lineages, and a clan in relation to other clans. When we speak of lineages being segmentarily related to one another and to the composite clan embracing them, we mean that their relations are mutual, symmetrical, and summative. A is related to B in the same way as B is related to A and the sum of their interrelations gives us a set of relations of the same kind but of higher order.

Putting it thus abstractly, however, leaves out a point of the utmost importance. The relations between individuals and between groups in which corporate units like the maximal lineage emerge are social relations. They are subject to jural, moral, and ritual norms; they are the means of achieving human purposes, of getting a livelihood, of marrying and procreating, of expressing emotional attitudes, organizing the intercourse of people, and so forth. A maximal lineage emerges in terms of jurally, morally, and ritually defined ties and cleavages that exist between it and other specified maximal lineages. A segmentary relationship between lineages or any other social units implies the existence of specific ties and cleavages which have the effect of making each unit a determining factor in the emergence of the other units. This is the basis of the concept of a field of social relations which we have used to describe the way in which lineages are differentiated from and articulated with one another.

The concept of a field of social relations has enabled us to see how clanship acts as a factor of social integration. Through the overlapping of the fields of clanship of adjacent maximal lineages chains of clanship ties interlinking a whole group of lineages are established. Thus each lineage can be regarded as the centre of a series of zones of clanship of increasing amplitude and diminishing integration. The clan is the central region of such a system, a wider community like that of the Hill Talis constitutes the next region, and beyond that lie still wider regions of diminishing importance for the members of the lineage that is taken as the starting-point.

We have seen that there are three major sub-regions within the sociogeographic region we have called Taleland, within each of which there is a greater degree of interarticulation of lineages and clans, and therefore closer integration, than there is between them. But the three sub-regions overlap with each other and with adjacent non-Tale regions. They have a particularly important connecting system in the chain of sub-clans of Mosuor biis.

This system of regions or communities constituted primarily by the operation of the ties and cleavages of clanship is the foundation of a scheme of ritual values and relationships which serves to reinforce the clanship organization by means of mystical sanctions and by co-ordinating the interrelations of lineages and clans at a higher level. Among the Tallensi the web of clanship and the web of ritual relationships take the place, as mechanisms of social integration, of a constituted governmental

234   THE FORM OF TALE SOCIETY

framework in politically centralized societies. Tale political relations are dominated by the facts of genealogical connexion on the one hand, and by the bonds of ritual interdependence on the other.

Looking only at the macroscopic structure of Tale society, therefore, we realize that it is a very complicated mosaic in which every tie between corporate units is counterbalanced by cleavages between them, all loyalties between corporate units are kept within bounds by loyalties towards other units, and all common interests are set off by divergent interests. The Tallensi provide an interesting example of a society in which there is a very strong tendency towards a general equilibrium in the collective life. What we have called Tale society is a social region demarcated by the range of the dynamic equilibrium that prevails within it. Non-Tale means simply outside this equilibrium; or rather, to be precise, it means on and beyond the circumference of this equilibrium. This is the essential difference between societies like the Tallensi and those that derive their unity from defined territorial boundaries and subjection to a common, all-powerful government. That does not mean that a segmentary social structure and a pyramidal social structure are necessarily mutually exclusive. It is quite possible for the subdivisions of a centralized state to have a segmentary social organization.

Re-examination of the Major Cleavage: Warfare

Through this mosaic, however, runs a major cleavage of great significance, as we have learnt. It is most conspicuous in the Tongo area. For this there may be historical reasons, but we have no means of discovering them. What is beyond question is that this fact is a fundamental feature of the existing structure of the society. Tongo is the most important centre of Namoo settlement; the Tong Hills area is the pivot of the ritual cults and values which play so dominant a part in Tale political relations. In consequence, the cleavage upon which the whole politico-ritual system hinges is most conspicuous there.

When Tallensi discuss the cleavage between Namoos and non-Namoos, they often hark back to the wars of former days. There are still old men living who took part in the last of those wars, and many middle-aged men and women tell tales of the fighting they saw as children or heard of from their parents; these wars are also a common theme of funeral dirges.

But the Tallensi are not one of those warlike African peoples who have a hypnotic effect even on anthropologists. Like most peasants who wring a bare subsistence from the soil, they have much too prosaic an attachment to their homes, their families, and their farms, and much too lively an appreciation of the perils of commonplace living to overrate the warrior. Not that Tallensi are lacking in physical courage or combativeness. They are quick to resent a trespass on their rights and readily snatch up a weapon or missile if they are provoked. In the old days a fearless and successful fighter (*zai*, pl. *za'ab*) was admired. The deeds of some of these great fighters of old are still recounted with pride. To kill an enemy in war was something to boast of. It was a mark of manliness as well as an important service to the clan. But there was a dark side

THE FORM OF TALE SOCIETY

to it; and nowadays the natives lay more stress on this than on the ancient glory of success in war. There was the mystical danger of reprisals from the spirit of one's victim (*gil*) following one all one's life. There was the hate created in the dead man's kin, agnates and extra-clan kin, including probably some of one's own clansmen or clansmen's wives. At best they might try to injure one by means of bad medicine; at worst it meant that one could never take part in a sacrifice or meal in which they shared. If one did, their hidden hatred had a mystical power to kill one. Nor did a man who had excelled in war derive any social, economic, or political advantage from it. It did not add to his wealth or give him more influence in the councils of the community. Soon even the fame of his prowess became dim, for it is bad form to talk publicly, during his lifetime, about the deeds of a man who has slain an enemy. It 'whitens (*pɛlɔg*)' him—that is, exposes him to the wrath of his victim's spirit which resents public comment on his defeat. A great fighter is praised in dirges and speeches after his death. But in the past, as now, it was the good farmer and not the bold fighter who was held up as the ideal of a worthwhile life.

Tallensi speak of fighting with weapons, for whatever reason, as one of the necessary evils of the old days. They look back without regrets on the passing of warfare. They regard the shedding of human blood, even in self-defence or in justifiable anger, as sinful. To kill a man in war was not homicide; one did not have to make heavy expiatory sacrifices to the Earth for it, yet one could never get rid of the blood taint (*ziem*). In 1936 two of the oldest men I knew died. There was much whispered talk about them. People pointed out that they had died in utter penury, lacking even a sheep for their grave-clout. Yet at different times in their long lives they had owned many cattle and had had several wives. Worse still, they had died leaving only one or two young children, the survivors of large families. Their lives had been tragically futile, by Tale standards. And why? Because they had both been redoubtable fighters in their young days; they had killed men in war; and this was the nemesis. All the animals they had sacrificed in expiation had been in vain, in the long run.

The most heinous sin of all was to instigate (*sa*) a war. It did not matter if the man had justice on his side. In the long run he paid for his sin with sickness and death, and the tale of misfortune might follow his descendants in the male line for generations. When Siiyɛlib died, the diviner consulted to find out the cause of his death revealed an unexampled story of misfortune going back twenty-five years. One after another, Siiyɛlib's wives and children had died; rinderpest had wiped out his cattle; and at last he himself had died without a son to mourn him and in extreme poverty. All this went back to his part in the Tong Hills Expedition of 1910–11, of which, the natives believe, he had been one of the prime instigators.

Before the arrival of the British the Tallensi, in common with their neighbours, had no judicial system. This was in keeping with their lack of a centralized form of government. As far as there was a 'rule of law'— that is, general observance of rights and obligations in property relations, in person-to-person relations, in intra- and inter-group relations subject

236 THE FORM OF TALE SOCIETY

to enforcement by explicit or implicit sanctions—it prevailed only within the clan or a cluster of closely interrelated clans, or between individual kinsfolk of different clans. Even so, every line of social cleavage was a source of weakness to the sanctions of right. It needed very little temptation or provocation for men of different clans or maximal lineages, however close the links between their respective groups, to lay violent hands on one another's property, person, or dependants. There was a general atmosphere of non-cognizance of rights *as such*. Times of crisis, such as famine, brought about a relapse into lawlessness.

In consequence the ultimate sanction of jural rights outside the clan was self-help. If a man could not recover a wife who had been abducted or a bride-price debt owing to him through the intermediation of the elders of his clan and those of the abductor's or debtor's clan, he had the right to use self-help and make a raid on the cattle of the offender's clan. This was legitimate and reprisals were not allowed. If the offender were to attempt any, his clansmen would not support him. But these raids might result in an armed clash with the cattle herds. Men might be killed; and then war flared up.

But raiding (*ŋɔk*), as a measure of self-help, in itself was not an act of war. It led to war if men were killed, but not if there were no bloodshed. Sometimes, even if a raid ended in an affray and men were killed, a reconciliation was made before an interclan fight could develop. The Tallensi distinguished precisely between raiding, as a method of self-help which they considered a legitimate jural device for redressing a wrong, and warfare. The custom of raiding reinforced warfare because it provided occasions for armed clashes and because of the habit of mind that lay behind it. Though this habit ran counter to the moral repugnance of the Tallensi to shedding human blood, it tolerated the use of violence as the proper ultimate means of asserting one's rights. This attitude still survives, to some extent. Men still carry their weapons when they go on a journey. Disputes over wives or unpaid debts sometimes bring the parties to the brink of a sanguinary fight. One reason why these fights are suppressed by the natives themselves before they become serious is the fear of the white man with his armed police in the background. Another and more powerful reason is the system of chiefs' tribunals and District Commissioners' courts imposed by the British. This judicial system has become an established part of native life. It has provided an effectively sanctioned alternative to self-help and made the latter obsolete (cf. p. 13). But in the past the attitude of mind we have described led the natives to think of warfare in its corporate aspect as a mechanism for redressing wrongs that could not otherwise be put right. Considering their lack of a single, all-embracing government and their segmentary social structure, it was inevitable that conflicts should often arise that could only be settled by fighting.[1]

---

[1] In this connexion it is worth noting that the Tallensi have only one term, *zabɔr*, for every kind of fighting, from a quarrel between co-wives to a war. But, in addition, war was distinguished by referring to it euphemistically as 'arrows' (*peema*). Thus a war is identified as 'the arrows of so-and-so', after its chief instigator.

THE FORM OF TALE SOCIETY

Forty years ago, when no man ventured outside the bounds of his own settlement without weapons, when it was a common thing for a little group of armed men to raid the cattle of another clan in settlement of a debt, when a passing member of a different clan could be set upon and robbed, if he was unprotected, a trivial argument might lead to blows in the twinkling of an eye. Thus many fights occurred between clans and lineages. But general wars, involving all the Tallensi, were less frequent. Only three seem to have taken place in the last three or four generations.

These general wars always took place between Tale clans or between some Tale clans and neighbouring non-Tale clans. The Tallensi never united for defence or offence against other 'tribes'. Wars began between adjacent clans which were not united by direct or indirect ties of clanship, and then spread by mobilizing the opposing forces along the lines of structural interconnexions which we have described. This was a basic feature of warfare. Tongo could not fight Gorogo directly, for to get at the men of Gorogo the Tongo warriors would have to cross the hostile territory of Gbeog and Wakii. Tɛnzugu could only fight Tongo if Wakii and Soog gave their men passage and took their side. A general war therefore inevitably followed the line of major cleavage between the Namoos and non-Namoos. An example will show how this occurred.

Some fifty years ago a quarrel between a Yaɣazuor man and a Kpatia man led to a general war. It began in the way many of those wars did, with an argument about a wife. There was dancing at Yaɣazuor one night and a Kpatia man who was present was accused of trying to abduct the wife of a Yaɣazuor man. Next day one of the annual communal game drives took place. A bush turkey was brought down and both a Yaɣazuor man and a Kpatia man claimed it. Such disputes were and still are common at these big game drives, when it is often difficult to determine whose club or arrow inflicted the death blow on an animal. In the circumstances, with the competitive spirit at its highest pitch, with men standing beside their clansmen with weapons in hand, with the excitement of the chase as a stimulus, words soon led to blows. Besides, the squabble of the previous evening over the woman was still rankling. So fighting broke out between the men of Yaɣazuor and the men of Kpatia.

Next morning the alarum was raised at both settlements. Ba'ari at once came out to help its *sunzɔp* the Yaɣazuor men. Namɔɣalug and Sie rallied to the side of their fellow Namoos at Kpatia. Yamɔlɔg followed suit. Tongo, to assist Sie and Yamɔlɔg, attacked Ba'ari. Gbeog then attacked Tongo to help Ba'ari; Wakii and Soog, followed shortly by Tɛnzugu, came out to support their kin, the Gbeog people; Zoo immediately set out against the Hill Talis in support of Tongo, and Zubiuŋ, hitherto neutral, followed suit. Then Gorogo came to the help of Gbeog; and Sii and Yinduuri, mindful of their ties with Tongo through the chiefship of Sii, attacked Gorogo from the rear. All this happened in two or three days. Then the Gbizug and Wakii tɛndaanas, armed with their ritual peacemaking powers, intervened and compelled the combatants to lay down arms. Tongo and Wakii made peace and the news was broadcast from clan to clan. Once two important representative clans made peace thus, all the others had to stop fighting. The ties of clanship

238 THE FORM OF TALE SOCIETY

which brought a particular unit into the fight compelled it also to retire when its allied clan made peace.

The fighting lasted only a few days, but many men were killed, the old men say, and much grain and live-stock destroyed. The Namoos suffered badly. So the following year, at the usual time for fighting, just before the commencement of the sowing season, while the granaries were still full, the then Chief of Tongo 'set up arrows (*sa peema*)'[1] again to revenge their defeat. Thus the 'debt was cancelled (*samər lɛrigya*)'.

In these wars the major cleavage of Tale society came into operation in its most acute form, and they give us a particularly clear insight into its meaning. The major cleavage between Namoos and non-Namoos is not an insuperable barrier like that which separates castes or races in some societies. It should rather be regarded as the coping-stone of the whole complex system of differentiation and integration of corporate units in Tale society by means of the structural ties and cleavages inherent in it.

Wars, among the Tallensi, were not acts of political policy, as we understand it. They were not fought for the sake of acquiring territory, of extending the authority of one group over another, of taking captives, or of pillage. Indeed pillage to enrich oneself was strictly tabooed. Tale wars were not even calculated acts of aggression. They usually arose out of impulsive acts of retaliation by individuals or small groups of clan brothers for attacks, as often as not unpremeditated, on their kin, their property, or their self-regard. If the parties involved in the quarrel belonged to clans on opposite sides of the major cleavage, the whole system of clanship and ritual ties might be swung into activity and the result would be a general war. It could not be otherwise, given the native system of genealogical relationships and the sentiments connected therewith.

The structure of Tale society as a dynamically integrated social region is incompatible with warfare directed towards political or economic domination. One consequence of their segmentary social structure was that they had no regular military organization. In war all the able-bodied men turned out carrying their bows and quivers of poisoned arrows, their adzes, and other weapons, and hung around with medicines, exactly as they do to-day to go hunting. All the fighting men of a clan, the men of each major segment forming a separate contingent, went out in a mob to meet the enemy at the outskirts of the settlement. Their women folk, many of whom were daughters of the enemy clans, carried water to them, dragged away casualties, and urged on the fighters with their shrill, trilling *kpɛləmət* cries. The fighting consisted of uncoordinated sorties and skirmishes by individuals or small parties, without fixed leadership and with no other purpose than to rout the enemy and thus reassert the flouted rights or restore the injured pride of the victors. Their principal weapon, a bow strung with a slither of bamboo firing an unfeathered poisoned arrow, made it necessary for a man to get within about 50 yards

---

[1] A clan-head could initiate a just war of revenge, with the consent of all the clan elders, and after consulting a diviner, in theory without incurring mystical blood-guilt. And yet, in after years, misfortunes falling on his descendants might be ascribed to this act.

THE FORM OF TALE SOCIETY

of an enemy in order to hit him. Fighting went on all day in spasms. At nightfall the men retired to their settlements to feast, dance, sing boastful songs, lament the dead, and rest. This was kept up for two or three days at most and then peace was made.[1]

Tale warfare inevitably took this form, since no single segment of the society and neither of the two major groups of clans had political power superior to any other segment or the other group. There is no institutional framework that could be extended so as to make any one segment paramount over the others as a result of a successful war. Every segment holds its allotted place in the whole system in virtue of complementary politico-ritual ties with the other segments, in particular with segments that would be opposed to it in war. They have common values and are subject to common ritual sanctions. Besides, their marriage rules and kinship system spread a wide network of affinal and cognatic relations between clans and lineages. Every Taləŋ has cognatic or affinal kin in every clan within a radius of four or five miles of his own. Though corporate loyalties to his lineage and clan override his private loyalties to his kinsfolk of other clans, whenever the corporate interests of his unit are at stake, they do not extinguish them. Hence a man had to be very careful, in a fight, to avoid killing or injuring any of his own kinsmen who might be on the other side. Hence, also, the prohibition of pillage for one's own advantage. If the enemy was routed, the victors might descend on their settlement, set fire to the homesteads, burn the stored grain, slaughter and eat the live-stock; they could not carry off any of the enemy's possessions. A Namoo clan might fight a Talis clan; but it would be a grave sin against kinship morality for an individual Namoo to plunder or to take captive individual Talis, since they would most likely be the cognates or affines of members of his own clan and therefore indirectly of himself. The idea of killing the women folk or children of the enemy clan—who might easily be one's clan sisters or nephews—would have seemed monstrous.

Last, but not least, Tale economic organization is incompatible with warfare for material gain. There was and is no such thing as a tribe-wide or clan economy. Occupational differentiation, other than the division of labour between the sexes and in accordance with age, has barely emerged. Local trade is becoming increasingly important, but there was in the past no commerce other than barter and occasional petty trade. The Tallensi were and are still sedentary cultivators, using a primitive

---

[1] Tallensi often say that many men were killed and wounded in these fights. As they never counted their casualties it is impossible to get accurate figures from them. But taking account of the weapons used, the manner of fighting, and the duration of the fights, it is difficult to believe that casualties were in fact very heavy. As far as I can estimate, no more than three to four thousand men, fighting in scattered contingents of about 20 to 50 men, would be engaged in a general war. A settlement like Tongo, the largest in Taleland, would turn out between 200 and 300 fighting men at the outside. Putting together all that I was told, I would say that three or four men killed and a dozen wounded would have been regarded as a very heavy casualty list for Tongo in a day's fighting. It must be remembered, though, that the mortality from wounds was probably high, as the main non-magical treatment used was to suck the poison and pus out of the wound.

240   THE FORM OF TALE SOCIETY

and stationary form of hoe culture in which the volume of output is a direct product of human skill and muscle. The family group which produces the food, shelter, raiment, utensils, and weapons needed for its own subsistence can work only a limited amount of land. Wage labour is only sporadically employed for very short periods and to a negligible extent; twenty or thirty years ago it was almost non-existent. For technical and climatic reasons it is generally impossible for a subsistence unit to produce a regular surplus over current needs. And any surplus produced during any year is used up in meeting social or ritual obligations, in renewing the household's productive and living equipment, or in purchasing small numbers of live-stock destined to be used up, sooner or later, for obtaining wives or discharging social and ritual obligations.

The most valuable durable economic resource of the Tallensi is land; but as no rent, tax, or tribute is paid for the use of land, it would not profit a man to buy land he and his family could not work even in those parts where the sale of land is not a sacrilege. Nor would it be to the advantage of the head of a maximal lineage or clan to have authority over the land of another clan. He received no tax or tribute from his own clansmen, and the idea of exacting any such payments from others would never have occurred to him. In any case he had no means of enforcing such demands.

The scale of differences in wealth is narrow and was narrower in the past when there was no possibility of obtaining money by labour abroad or local trade. The stage has not yet been reached where a family group which has more resources than its neighbours thereby endows its members with permanent economic advantages or acquires, for any of them, special political or social powers and privileges.[1] The economic organization of the Tallensi was entirely, and to a great extent still is, a non-competitive, little differentiated, self-sufficient, stationary, subsistence economy. It acts as a stabilizing factor in the social system. It does not give rise, as yet, to social ties and cleavages cutting across those established by genealogical, local, and ritual principles. Economic incentives and interests did not influence the relations of clans with one another in the past, and did not therefore influence the course or aims of warfare.

That Tale warfare was a function of the segmentary structure of the society and not of political or economic ambitions is even clearer from the records of small-scale fights. It happened, quite often, that clans which were allies in general wars by reason of clanship or other structural ties fought among themselves. Like general wars, these local, interclan fights were kindled by such things as the abduction of a wife, quarrels over bride-price payments, the slaying of a man in a dispute between members of different clans or in a cattle raid, or simply by young men flaunting the corporate unity and independence of their clan in the face of another clan. Once started they followed the usual course of all social activities by setting the lineage system in motion and involving the patri-

---

[1] Except for a handful of chiefs and the Gɔlibdaana mentioned later; but even in their case the absence of facilities for investing wealth in land or other durable (capital) goods means that their wealth is rapidly dissipated by sons and grandsons.

PLATE XIII

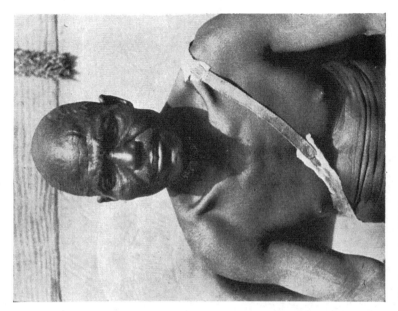

(a) Yikpemdaana of Tongo, the *kpeem* of Tɔŋ-Kuorɔg.

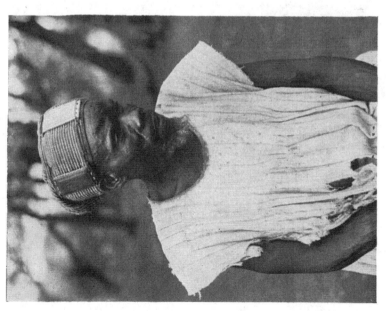

(b) Lɔyani, a highly respected junior elder of Zubiuŋ.

PLATE XIV

(a) *Sunzɔp m-maan yɛla.* A Gbizug elder performs a ritual service for Zubiuŋ-Yakɔra by sewing the sheepskin loin cover for the dead at a funeral.

(b) Elders representing all the component maximal lineages of Ba'ari assemble for the burial rites of the Ba'at-Sakpar tɛndaana at his homestead.

THE FORM OF TALE SOCIETY 241

lineal kin of both parties. One of the best-remembered fights of this kind broke out between Gorogo and Wakii in the very year that the British appeared on the scene of Tale life. It occurred in circumstances that made it a mystical calamity which these two clans are still expiating.

On the day that marks the climax of the *Gɔlib* Festival, all the Talis and thousands of non-Talis from the rest of the country congregate on the summit of the Tong Hills for a great ritual dance. It is in the main a dance of the men of the Hill Talis clans. They come up and dance in clan contingents, wearing festive garb and carrying their weapons. The tumult is indescribable. The throngs of spectators, men, women, and children, milling backwards and forwards, the rhythmic thud of stamping feet, the harsh lilt of the choruses pulsating against the babel of the crowd, the shimmer of sweating bodies and gaudy attire, the ritual officers in their finest skins and black caps, the swift, snake-like convolutions of the dancers, all this makes a scene of thrilling excitement. The taut bodies and tense expression of the dancers show that they are keyed up to the highest pitch of enthusiasm; and as they dance in separate clan contingents, an intense feeling of clan unity and pride is created in each group.

Each clan contingent accompanies its dancing with choruses for which new verses on topical themes are made every year. And the point of most of these songs is the superiority of that particular clan to all other people. There is a strong feeling of rivalry between the various clan contingents, which grows keener and keener as the day advances. The old men say that careful watch must always be kept lest any of the young men start fighting. For though there is a ritual truce on all forms of strife throughout Taleland during *Gɔlib*, passions are easily inflamed during the dances.

These were the circumstances in which the fight between Gorogo and Wakii took place. The two contingents were dancing near each other. The Gorogo men sang, defiantly, '(We are like) the adder, woo! If others wish to, let them tread on its tail and see'. The Wakii contingent flung back '(We are) a beehive, woo! If others wish to, let them touch us and see'. The dancing became more furious and the two groups drew nearer and nearer each other. And then, suddenly, they clashed. In the mêlée several men were killed and many wounded before the tɛndaanas and men of other clans could separate them.

Bloodshed during *Gɔlib* is a dreadful sacrilege; bloodshed on Tɛnzugu on the day of the most important ceremonies and during the dancing is a religious enormity that cannot be compared to anything else in the Tale calendar of sins. The people of Gorogo and Wakii atoned for their sacrilege by the sacrifice of many cattle and sheep to the Earth, but they have not yet freed themselves of its consequences. The Earth still exacts the toll of death after death from the sons and grandsons of the original sinners. No reprisals were taken by either clan and their relations with each other were not affected by this fight.

Such fights could not develop into general wars because they took place between clans that are closely linked together by ties of clanship or ritual collaboration, or are connected through an intercalary unit that

R

242 THE FORM OF TALE SOCIETY

acts as peacemaker. But in principle they go back to the same facts as general wars, the structural differentiation of maximal lineages and clans.

We can see that Tale wars were in fact a kind of intestine feud within a single homogeneous social region, rather than wars in our sense. We have refrained from calling them feuds because they were usually short and sharp and never led to a long series of mutual reprisals. If one war was followed a year later by a war of revenge, as in the instance given in this chapter, that was the end of it. One might even describe them as a kind of civil war, since they sprang from the cleavages inherent in the social structure, particularly the cleavage between Namoos and non-Namoos. They served to keep these cleavages alive, to defend the corporate unity of the maximal lineage and clan and the corporate rights associated with it, against other like units. They were, at bottom, a mechanism for resolving tensions within the society[1] and not an instrument of political action against outsiders. The ever-present possibility of war was a potent factor in maintaining the segmentary structure of the society. It achieved this by enhancing to the utmost both aspects of the social differentiation of maximal lineages and clans—the demarcation of unit from unit by genealogical and local criteria, and the corporate solidarity of each unit in its own right. However much the Tallensi deplored bloodshed among them, as in civilized nations, in warfare all personal interests were subordinated to the common interest of the clan or maximal lineage, whether its cause was just or not. All normal activities were suspended and every man, woman, and adolescent child took some part in the fighting or in caring for the wants of the fighters. Clan patriotism reached a pitch of fervour which no other occasion could evoke. It was felt as passionately by the women and girls carrying water to the fighters and dragging the wounded away, and by the old men at home who tended the wounded and went around from shrine to shrine making sacrifices to the ancestors, as by the fighting men. Something of this spirit comes out to-day in the inaugural ceremonies of an important elder's funeral, when the whole clan turns out for a pageant mimicking the activities of war.

Yet there was never any danger of wars or smaller fights breaking the society up into a number of anarchic fragments. They were inhibited from doing so by the countervailing influence of the strong social ties between traditionally hostile groups. Indeed their very occurrence stimulated the reassertion of the overriding common interests of the society and the reaffirmation of the bonds of unity between the factions. In a war between Namoos and non-Namoos peace had to be made quickly and the *status quo ante* restored because the two groups are so closely interconnected by ties of marriage and kinship that the majority of members of one group have bonds of duty, affection, and mutual interest with members of the other; because they are such close neighbours; above all, because they are bound together by ties of politico-

[1] These tensions persist, though they are kept well in check by fear of the British Administration. The new judicial system provides a safety valve to some extent; but they break through, chiefly in the form of political intrigue, as we shall see in the next section.

ritual collaboration in a series of complementary relations the proper maintenance of which they believe to be indispensable for their common welfare. This is the basis of the ritual sanctions against instigating war and shedding blood and of the moral repugnance associated with them. A war temporarily upset the equilibrium of Tale society; it could not destroy it.

The social system of the Tallensi, in its widest extent, is held together by its religious superstructure. Its unity is none the less real because it appears only on the highest plane of common religious values known to the natives. As we have noted, the complementary politico-ritual offices of the chiefship, which is typically a Namoo office, and the tendaanaship, typically an office found amongst non-Namoos, constitute the focus of the institutions that maintain this unity; and the annual cycle of the Great Festivals are at once the chief sanction and the supreme expression of it. The coming of the white man has made very little difference to the way these institutions operate in relation to the fundamental structure of Tale society. They continue to be the crowning mechanism of equilibrium in Tale society, because its segmentary social structure has kept its traditional form and vitality. It is possible, though not demonstrable, that only a strong and universally accepted religious sanction could hold such a society together. In practice the equilibrium is achieved by the distribution of mutually complementary offices among the segments of the society, all of which are essential for the performance of definite ritual duties.

It is a significant index of the type of social system presented by the Tallensi that the widest range of social solidarity found among them is evoked by their Great Festivals. Great stress is laid on the ritually sanctioned truce to all fighting or discord between clans or maximal lineages during the Festivals. That is why marriages are forbidden during the Gɔlib Festival. The Festival Cycle begins with the Harvest Festivals. These are celebrated by single clans or groups of linked maximal lineages independently of one another and serve to enhance the sense of clan and lineage solidarity. The climax is the Gɔlib Festival, immediately before the rains. This gives ritual sanction and dramatic expression to the idea of the close-knit interdependence of all the Tallensi with one another. Its reiterated themes are the common interests of all the Tallensi—food, peace, and fecundity—which must be achieved if they are to survive, and the supreme common values—the cult of the ancestors and of the Earth—by which the whole of Tale social life is steered. The lesson of Gɔlib, to the Tallensi, is that men cannot realize their greatest common interests or pursue their greatest common purposes in mutual enmity. Gɔlib is the most powerful counterweight to war and to the tendency of each clan and maximal lineage to set its own corporate interests above the common interest of the whole society. It is noteworthy that the Great Festivals do not presuppose the suspension of the primary loyalties of the segments that make up Tale society. They represent a synthesis, for the time being, of these primary loyalties—a synthesis that is possible only by giving full scope to the feeling of clan and maximal lineage unity and singularity in each group. Gɔlib emphasizes the mutual dependence of Namoos and Talis, but it does this by simultaneously enhancing the

244 THE FORM OF TALE SOCIETY

feeling of politico-ritual difference between them. It is the same within each cluster. The elders inaugurate the Festival season with many sacrifices asking the ancestors and the Earth to prevent fighting from breaking out between the young men, in spite of the truce, and they always depute a number of reliable young men to keep a good look-out during the dances lest unruly spirits stir up trouble. Thus the greater solidarity is built up on the lesser solidarities; and this principle applies throughout the social system.

The rhythm of Tale social life is contained within an annual cycle. It swings between two poles. For most of the year the sectional interests of lineage and clan dominate the pattern of collective life. But for one month the greater solidarity of the whole society prevails.

In relation to the mechanisms of unity and equilibrium Tale warfare appears as a negative sanction that reinforces their effects. It was the obverse of these mechanisms, the polar opposite of the idea of unity, arising out of the very same balance of social forces that makes that unity possible. Both in time and at a given time the equilibrium of Tale political life swung (and still swings) between two poles: on the one hand, the extraordinarily consistent and precise differentiation of social segments; on the other, the strong sense of unity created by the religious bonds of the society.

War or, more often, the threat of war was the most drastic means of bringing to a head and working off the frictions that inevitably arose from the action of the principle of social differentiation of corporate units; its effect, however, was to bring the opposite principle into action, and thus it served to strengthen the forces of social cohesion in the society at large.

Equilibrium and Solidarity within the Clan and Lineage

The pattern of solidarity we have been discussing applies at all levels of Tale social structure. Tensions similar to those we have discerned in the corporate relations between clans underlie corporate relations within clans and maximal lineages. Centrifugal tendencies and centripetal tendencies pull against one another. Conflicts within corporate units tend to follow the lines of lineage and local segmentation. They take the form of opposition between the solidarity of the segment and the wider solidarity of the lineage or clan. And the greater the relative autonomy of the segment, the deeper does the conflict tend to be. Hence conflicts in a composite clan tend to go deeper than conflicts in a genealogically unitary group such as a sub-clan of Mosuor biis. But, as in the social structure at large, the bonds of common interest, of mutual dependence in ritual and secular matters, and of local unity tend to prevail in the long run. However deep a breach may be, the dissidents never repudiate membership of the larger unit, for this would be tantamount to repudiating the ancestors. The ancestor cult is the supreme sanction of lineage and clan solidarity. Thus, at the best, conflicts are resolved by the eventual restoration of the *status quo ante*. At the worst, a new balance is struck between the centrifugal tendencies of lineage segmentation and the centripetal emphasis of the lineage structure as a whole backed by the ancestor cult. It is in this way that the structure of a lineage or clan is

THE FORM OF TALE SOCIETY

adapted by stages to changes in its internal composition due to the passage of time or the cumulative effects of social and economic pressure, without bursting its form.

Solidarity within the clan or the lineage is governed by the field principle. It is a function of the situation; and it is a function, also, of the segmentary relationship of each unit involved to other like units, to more inclusive units, and to the whole social structure. The complex of thought, feeling, action, and expression we designate as the sentiment of solidarity is evoked in different degrees in accordance with the sector of the social structure engaged. It reflects the range of common interests evoked in the situation and the strength of the common values.

Within the clan, or any segment of it, the sentiment of solidarity is a constant motive of conduct and a regular criterion by which the individual evaluates the behaviour of others. We have seen how it grows out of the lifelong association of lineage kin in daily life. Hence a Taləŋ identifies himself by reference to his clan settlement and the segment of his clan to which he belongs. He speaks of his clansmen as 'our folk (*ti yidɛm*)' and of their wives and children as 'our wives (*ti pɔyaba*)' and 'our children (*ti biis*)'. In the old days of warfare, as in market brawls or hunting expeditions to-day, a Taləŋ never stops to question the rights or wrongs of an argument in which a clansman of his is involved with a non-clansman, or a close agnate with a distant agnate. He immediately takes his clansman's or close agnate's part.

The unity of a clan or a lineage is not only a vital fact of experience for its members but the principal concept by which other corporate groups define it in jural, political, and ritual relations. Thus in the old days a creditor could raid the live-stock of any clansman of his debtor, but not those of a neighbour of his debtor who belonged to a different clan. In the latter case a reprisal raid was the penalty. In the former case the victim of the raid could demand restitution from his clansman, the original debtor; and I know of men who pawned a child or sold him into slavery in order to find the means of repaying a clansman who had been raided, rather than let the affair become a source of conflict in the clan. This is a good illustration, incidentally, of the statement previously made that collective responsibility is not a principle of Tale jural relations. It is not the clan but the debtor himself who is responsible for his debt. Self-help is a technique for putting pressure on a debtor through the mechanisms of clan and lineage cohesion.

The same principle appears in the abduction of wives of distant unrelated clans. Thus Pal of Zubiuŋ abducted the wife of a Yinduuri man. He claimed that this was merely 'cancelling a debt (*lɛrag samar*)'. Some years earlier a distant clansman of the Yinduuri man had abducted the wife of one of Pal's clansmen and this 'debt' had now been cancelled. The point is, not that all Yinduuri was held responsible for the original wrong, but that every wife is a gain to the clan as a whole and the loss of a wife is a loss to the clan as a whole. If a clan wishes to avoid reprisals such as those taken by Pal, men of the clan must not countenance the abduction of wives by any of their fellows. It is like the avenging of a clansman's death at the hands of men of another clan in the old days.

THE FORM OF TALE SOCIETY

Some sixty years ago a Tamboog man was killed by a group of Yamələg men with whom he quarrelled at a dance. Two or three years later a couple of Tamboog men met a Yamələg man alone in the bush and slew him in revenge. The Yamələg people understood that this was a case of 'wiping out a debt' and the matter was regarded as closed.

The principle of representative status enhances the sense of lineage or clan solidarity. We have seen how, in ceremonial situations, any member of a lineage or clan is regarded as representing the whole unit. I have often seen men refuse gifts of meat or food at ceremonies because these had no precedent and accepting them would be equivalent to committing their lineage or clan to reciprocate in the same way at some future time.

Co-operation in ceremonies, especially in funerals, brings to light the institutional machinery of lineage and clan solidarity. Its basis is the distribution of duties and privileges among the different segments of the lineage or clan concerned in the situation, in accordance with their segmentary relationship to the group principally affected. Thus in funerals, in accordance with the maxim 'Brother lineages take charge of one's affairs (*sunzɔp m-maan yɛla*)', members of a close brother lineage of the bereaved lineage supervise the ceremonies. In addition, all the segments of the maximal lineage or clan concerned send prescribed food contributions and receive prescribed shares of beer, meat, and food distributed during the ceremonies. Funerals are important because the death of a person may entail a rearrangement of social relations in a segment and this is a matter of common interest to the whole clan.

These obligatory reciprocal services and privileges constantly remind the individual of his dependence on his clansmen for the proper management of the critical events of his life. In consequence the obligation of reciprocity is strongly felt, in both secular and ritual matters, the strength of the feeling being relative to the lineage relationship of the parties. When a man invites a collective hoeing party (*pooh kpa'arəp*) it is always co-members of his medial lineage who turn up in largest force. Distant clansmen only come if they have ties of personal matrilateral kinship with him. And the motive usually given for responding to such an invitation is 'To-morrow I may need the help of a hoeing party'. Public opinion is critical of those who do not conform to the conventions of mutual assistance, and when they find themselves compelled to call for assistance in collective hoeing or housebuilding or some similar activity, they are left in the lurch.

Intra-clan disputes involving lineages of a higher order than the nuclear lineage very rarely arise over economic affairs—that is, in effect, over the ownership of land or live-stock. Disputes in higher order lineages arise over the inheritance of widows or marriage with a woman who was formerly the wife of a member of a different segment of the clan. Members of the deceased husband's medial lineage feel they have a prior claim to a widow's hand and sometimes object to her marrying a man of a different branch of the clan. And if a marriage is dissolved, no matter what the reason may be, it is regarded as a grave breach of clan solidarity for any other member of the husband's clan to take her to wife. It arouses suspicion of collusion between the woman and the second

THE FORM OF TALE SOCIETY 247

husband. In both types of case conflicts reflect the importance of wives as a common interest of the lineage and clan.

But the chief source of intra-clan discord is rival claims to priority in the exercise of rights of a politico-ritual nature, which are generally vested in lineages and are associated with the dominant values of the society. The conflict may be precipitated by a clash of personalities. But very often the underlying pressure comes from a change in the internal constitution of the lineage that has been taking place gradually with the passage of the generations and is not yet recognized. In the course of two or three generations an inner lineage may ramify so widely that its members claim the status of a medial lineage when it comes to succeeding to the headship of a more inclusive lineage, and this claim may be resisted by the other branches of the more inclusive lineage. It is such conflicts that eventually get resolved by the setting up of a new equilibrium in which the change is recognized by the redistribution of reciprocal rights and obligations. Intra-clan discord is often due to the universal human propensity to resist infringements of one's recognized social rights or one's self-regard; or to the complementary tendency for individuals to assert themselves by aggressive action. But it is probably more often a phase in the structural development of a lineage or clan, a symptom of a hitherto unrecognized internal change in its structure. This does not make the conflict less acute or disturbing while it lasts; but it does mean that there are always social forces at work that counteract the conflict even while it is going on and will prevent it from disrupting the corporate group entirely.

These processes are so characteristic of the social system of the Tallensi that they could be illustrated from the contemporary history of any clan or maximal lineage. Tallensi say that intra-clan conflicts have increased since the coming of the white man. They maintain that the suppression of warfare and of self-help, and the new freedom of movement, have greatly diminished lineage and clan solidarity. People no longer need the help of their kinsmen as much as they used to. But careful inquiry shows that intra-clan discord was as common forty or fifty years ago as to-day and sometimes more violent. Many of the most deep-seated and intractable antagonisms within and between lineages or clans to-day go back to conflicts that began fifty or sixty years ago.

A typical instance is the dispute between the Gbizug tɛndaana and the Gbeog tɛndaana which began with the immediate predecessors of the present tɛndaanas. The dispute concerns the degree of autonomy to which the Gbeog tɛndaana is entitled in his ritual jurisdiction over the tɛŋ of Gbeog (see p. 87). He claims full autonomy. The Gbizug tɛndaana as 'elder brother' (*bier*) in ritual status of the Gbeog tɛndaana, and head of the senior maximal lineage of the clan, citing ancient custom, claims to have an over-right over the Gbeog tɛndaana. He says that the Gbeog tɛndaana is simply his deputy and should therefore render to him the perquisites that a tɛndaana receives for the performance of such ritual services as marking out graves. The men of Gbizug are unreservedly on the side of their lineage head. The men of Gbeog are torn between their loyalty to their maximal lineage and the greater solidarity

248 THE FORM OF TALE SOCIETY

of the clan. They regularly attend sacrifices and ceremonies at Gbizug as their forefathers did, and continue to perform the duties and accept the privileges of close *sunzɔp* of Gbizug. But they are uneasy, the more so as the Gbizug tɛndaana never loses an opportunity of haranguing them, at ceremonies, about the disgraceful conduct of their tɛndaana. For a short while the inescapable demands of ritual collaboration brought the two tɛndaanas together again, when the Gbeog tɛndaana had to perform the principal rites at the installation of the new Gbizug tɛndaana. But soon afterwards their dispute revived again. It is, as elders of related clans declared, an insoluble dispute. Both tɛndaanas are right, they say. The Gbizug tɛndaana is going by 'what used to be (*dɛn daa a siem*)', the Gbeog tɛndaana by 'what is now (*dɛn a siem zinala*)'. It is a problem of adjusting the equilibrium of the clan to changes in the segmentary relationship of its component lineages. One day, it is said, there will be a Gbizug tɛndaana who will accept the present position. Then the two tɛndaanas will become reconciled and the quarrel will cease.

As this story shows, intra-clan conflicts dislocate the routine of co-operation and reciprocity and lead to anomalies in customary modes of conduct. Yinyɛla's refusal to co-operate in the affairs of Tɔŋ-Puhug led to many embarrassing situations; as when two men who were not members of Yinyɛla's segment came to assist his (classificatory) grandson with his house-building, in accordance with normal custom, and were publicly rebuked for this by the head of their family. Dislocation of the normal scheme of ritual and ceremonial co-operation in the ancestor cult and in public ceremonies such as funerals is particularly disturbing. It serves to focus attention on the interpretation of actions that damage lineage solidarity as offences against the ancestors. Public opinion, the point of view of the majority, which always favours the greater solidarity as the source of stability and normality in corporate relations, becomes critical. In due time one of the opponents of the dispute dies; and according to custom the mystical cause of his death is sought by divination. The technique and social setting of the divining session make it a reflection of public sentiment. The diviner brings the simmering conflict in the lineage into the open and relates the death to it. His verdict, coming ostensibly from the ancestors, concludes with commands from them to put the situation right by means of sacrifices and a ritual reconciliation. This is the commonest way in which the ancestor cult emerges as a sanction of reintegration in the lineage or clan. But it presupposes the existence of ritual ties and common ritual obligations among lineage and clan kin; and it comes as the culmination of a social reaction to the anomalies arising from intra-clan conflicts.

We have space only for one illustrative case history. Many years ago Gbalɔg of Tɔŋ-Puhug insulted the then Chief of Tongo. The chief pronounced a curse on him; and rather than apologize Gbalɔg went to settle in one of the peripheral settlements taking his younger sons with him. His oldest son, Naŋgbeog, dissociating himself from his father, stayed behind at Tongo. Years passed. There was a new Chief of Tongo. Yet Gbalɔg remained unrepentant. In 1937 he died, a very old man, boasting that after all he had got the better of the chiefs of Tongo. But the diviner revealed that the ancestors had caused him to die because of

THE FORM OF TALE SOCIETY

his quarrel with the chief of his clan. The diviner added that the ancestors demanded that Gbalɔg should be exhumed and re-buried at Tongo among his forefathers. This meant that Gbalɔg's sons should beg the Chief of Tongo's pardon and offer expiatory sacrifices to the clan ancestors. But Gbalɔg's second son, who had lived with him, scornfully refused to do this, and added the further sin of withholding from his older brother Naŋgbeog, the legitimate heir, the property their father had left. There was scathing criticism of his behaviour at Tongo but nothing could be done about it. There are no jural sanctions compelling a man to abide by custom in cases of this kind; and as the Tallensi often say, men do not fear to defy even the ancestor spirits, when their property or power is at stake.

But shortly afterwards the second son suddenly became ill and died. At once everybody drew the obvious moral: he had incurred the wrath of the ancestors for his double sin. And when the cause of his death was sought by divination public opinion was confirmed. Naŋgbeog, now the recognized heir, at once got some elders to plead with the chief on his behalf and the curse was withdrawn. Naŋgbeog gave a young bull and several small stock to be sacrificed to the clan ancestors in expiation of his father's sin. Since representatives of all branches of the clan have to be present at such sacrifices, this was equivalent to a ritual reconciliation. Naŋgbeog then exhumed and re-buried the bodies of his father and brother at Tongo. He brought home the live-stock and personal effects he had inherited from his father as well as the widows and children of whom he was now the proper guardian. Gbalɔg's defection was thus erased and his line wholly reunited to the parent stem.

Lineage solidarity, which in its widest extent passes over into clan solidarity, has great practical utility for the natives. But this is not the source of its strength and binding force. Their roots lie in the moral premisses of Tale society; the ideas of right and duty, in the idiom of Tale culture, are the formative elements in the sentiment and the display of lineage solidarity. The starting-point is the fundamental moral axiom of Tale social organization, the axiom that kinship is binding in its own right.[1] And the supreme sanction of lineage solidarity is, as we have seen, the ancestor cult, which is, for the natives, the objective, cultural embodiment of the social conscience.

This is evident not only from the preceding analysis but from a consideration of the rights and restrictions associated with lineage membership. There is the whole complex of rights, obligations, and prohibitions centred in the wives of the lineage members. Underlying it is the identification of lineage members with one another in virtue of their common agnatic descent. The right to inherit a clansman's wife is the correlative of the prohibition against adultery with a clansman's wife. Both rules spring from the notion of the social equivalence of siblings and from the common interest of the clan in the children of the clan. These are not matters of collective property rights but of moral norms. This is clear from the sanction against adultery with a clansman's wife, the belief that the adulterer is mystically dangerous to the injured husband if the latter gets ill.

[1] This subject is fully discussed in *The Web of Kinship among the Tallensi*.

250   THE FORM OF TALE SOCIETY

Similarly there is the prohibition against homicide within the clan. It is a moral prohibition, a taboo (*kihɔr*), the overt sanction being that the slayer's segment and the victim's segment cannot again sacrifice together. This is shown equally by the fact that vengeance is prohibited, in accordance with the maxim 'It is (as if) a cow had trampled its calf to death (*naah n-nɔ bu bii ku*)', and will be prevented by the elders if necessary by forcibly restraining the victim's segment brothers. Hence comes the prohibition, also, against raiding (*ŋɔk*) within the clan or between linked clans.

To sum up, there is an undercurrent of tension in every clan and lineage arising directly out of its segmentary structure. From time to time this breaks out in conflict. But in the long run lineage solidarity prevails. The pattern is the same as in the total socio-geographic region of Tale society.

Modern Factors of Disequilibrium

A. British Rule

The suppression of warfare is a symptom of the changed political circumstances of the Tallensi. New forces are beginning to affect their social structure, creating new internal tensions that threaten the supremacy of the ancient sanctions of cohesion. Though the traditional politico-ritual institutions are still the most powerful determinants of corporate relations within and between clans and maximal lineages, the tendency of the new forces is to work against the traditional social equilibrium. As we have seen, the natives themselves stress this.

The most pervasive and most powerful of these new factors is British rule. Its greatest achievement has been the enforcement of peace and the substitution of an embryonic judicial organization for the arbitrament of the bow and arrow. Up till 1933, when the reorganization of the system of local government in the Northern Territories was inaugurated, the Administration aimed at creating a centralized, pyramidal organization of executive authority among the clan heads of the Tallensi, under the leadership of the Chief of Tongo. To further this aim the Administration gave its support to certain headmen and chiefs in their dealings with their own clans and with one another. These men were vested with powers which they had never previously held and which had no relation to the native social structure. Coercion and extortion were practised, under cover of meeting the requirements of the white man. Where these requirements were concerned, the system worked, though far from satisfactorily. But constant friction between the chiefs and headmen constituting this artificial hierarchy was inevitable owing to the contradiction between it and the segmentary pattern of the native social structure. For, as we have seen, the native social structure, like the traditional economy and the age-old ritual ideas and values of the people, has preserved its vitality in relation to the social interests and ends which it has always served and still subserves.

Whenever these interests and ends are paramount, as at the times of the Great Festivals, the factional rivalries stirred up by the new dis-

THE FORM OF TALE SOCIETY

pensation sink into the background, the sanctions inherent in the native social structure prevail, and the traditional ties of politico-ritual collaboration come into force. But when the new interests brought into being by the influence of the British Administration come to the fore, the traditional social ties and the sanctions associated with them no longer prevail. For among the Tallensi, as among ourselves, such ties and sanctions do not function at all times and in all circumstances. They work in the context of the scheme of social relationships of which they form a part and not in other contexts. These new interests mobilize the existing corporate units of Tale society. Thus they tend to deepen some of the cleavages that exist, and to weaken the countervailing ties, between lineages and clans. It is noteworthy that rivalry for the rewards of political power under the British Administration is most acute between clans that have close ties in the native social system. As was the case with war in former days, clans and maximal lineages that are widely separated from one another, either locally or in terms of their fields of social relations, cannot come into conflict or competition with one another. Thus political rivalry between the Chief of Tongo and his 'younger brother' the Chief of Yamɔlɔg is severe and has led to estrangement between these two branches of Mosuor biis. But there is no political rivalry between the Chief of Tongo and the Chief of Datɔk. Competition for politico-ritual office within clans is fiercer than it was in the past and less scrupulous, though it still follows the lines of cleavage in the lineage structure.

At the same time some chiefs have used their new powers to weld their clans into closer unity on the political plane than existed in the old days. This has happened at Tongo and at Sie. But it has not been to the benefit of the social balance in the greater society. By strengthening the autocratic ambitions of these chiefs, the closer unity of their clans has tended to aggravate the antagonisms between clans.

B. *Pecuniary Competition among the Hill Talis*

A new factor of disequilibrium that has had a very disturbing influence among the Hill Talis is pecuniary competition which has become associated with certain traditional institutions. Many families nowadays obtain driblets of money through members of the family working abroad, or by petty trade. But the pecuniary competition we are referring to concerns money on a scale unprecedented in Tale history; and its disruptive influence is due to its association with a traffic in ritual benefits comparable to that of the notorious Southern Nigerian oracles.

The centre of this traffic is the Tong Hills, and its disruptive influence has been greatest among the Hill Talis, where it has brought violent competition into the sphere of the common ritual interests and values which form the bulwark of their cohesion. The integration of the Hill Talis in the native social structure depends, as we have seen, on a meticulous balance of local, clanship, and ritual ties and cleavages focused in the politico-ritual offices vested in the heads of maximal lineages. So nicely calculated is the distribution of these politico-ritual functions amongst the various maximal lineages that none can claim

THE FORM OF TALE SOCIETY

precedence over the others. All are equally essential for the maintenance of the social equilibrium and competition between them is absolutely excluded. Now the possibility has arisen of acquiring unlimited wealth through these same offices, by a miracle, almost, and from external sources. They have become commercially valuable. And the Tallensi, perhaps because of their great poverty of material goods, their general equality of wealth, and their undifferentiated productive system, are extremely acquisitive. Some of them have shown a natural cupidity for riches and power, and a skill in the pursuit of these gratifications, for which their native way of life formerly gave little scope.

In our references to the cult of the External Bɔyar we discussed chiefly the significance of the Bɔyar for the interrelations of the Hill Talis clans among themselves. But, as we have mentioned, the cult also has an important role in the external relations of these clans. Each Bɔyar has a well-defined sphere of influence in one or other of the tribes adjacent to the Tallensi, or within easy access of the Tong Hills, the Mamprusi, the Bulisi, the Woolisi, the Gɔrisi, and even some of the Mossi sub-tribes. Thus a number of villages in the south-west of Mampurugu are in the sphere of interest of Bona'ab, the Bɔyar of which Kpata'ardɛm are the senior custodians, whereas many villages in the south-east of Mampurugu come into the sphere of influence of the Degal Bɔyar. The villages are further divided up so that each of the maximal lineages belonging to a Bɔyar congregation has several villages, or sections of several villages, as its particular clients. This aspect of the cult is by no means a mere side-line. It is an intrinsic and obviously old-established feature of it. The best proof of this is the fact that Hill Talis clans which claim to be of immigrant origin usually cite those parts of the adjacent non-Tale areas where they have client villages as their probable homes of origin. Similarly the ritual officials of these villages whom we mention below often explain their association with the External Bɔyar cult of the Talis by a myth of descent from an immigrant from the Tong Hills.

From these client villages, as we have already learnt, pilgrims come to the Bɔyar regularly, particularly in the dry season. They come individually to supplicate for health, prosperity, and especially for the boon of children. As children born in answer, ostensibly, to such requests are the spiritual wards of the Bɔyar, many pilgrims come as 'children of the Bɔyar' to offer thanksgiving gifts and sacrifices, or atonement sacrifices for a misdeed. But more important are the pilgrims who come annually as official representatives of their villages. They are usually the tɛndaanas of the villages, and they come to beg for the blessings of the Bɔyar on the village, for its health, and for a successful farming year; or if there has been sickness, or a failure of crops or any other misfortune in the past year, to bring atoning sacrifices to the Bɔyar. The ritual offices these men hold in their own villages are under the aegis of the Bɔyar; and through them the Bɔyar exercises considerable influence in the affairs of a client village. For to these outsiders the Bɔyar is an oracle as well as a shrine, manifesting itself through the medium of a mysterious subterranean voice, whose advice, admonitions, and demands are interpreted by its custodians.

THE FORM OF TALE SOCIETY

This aspect of the *Bɔyar* cult had great economic and social importance, in the past, for the Hill Talis. The pilgrims bring gifts of salt, cloth, hoes and so forth, nominally for the *Bɔyar*, that is, the Primordial Ancestor, who is believed to manifest himself in the oracular voice. Actually these gifts are secretly shared among the heads of the maximal lineages which own the particular *Bɔyar*. Nowadays these gifts are of small, though by no means negligible, worth, for all these commodities can be bought in any market, far more cheaply than in the past. But in the past they represented a valuable source of supply of scarce and highly prized goods.

Again, the visits of the pilgrims are annually reciprocated by a visit to the client village of representatives of the Talis lineage which is its sponsor with the *Bɔyar* to which it owes ritual allegiance. These ritual visits are made in order to consecrate local shrines representing the *Bɔyar*, to release pilgrims and children born to them from special taboos, and to perform the ritual shaving of the children by which they are formally placed under the spiritual guardianship of the *Bɔyar*. But these services are paid for in cowries and other gifts, and portions of the animals sacrificed are taken home and added to the meat supply of the sponsors. Young men go along on these ritual tours carrying fowls for sale in the client villages, and sometimes buy grain or yams in return.

The pilgrim traffic was, therefore, in former times an economic asset of the first importance as the Hill Talis and their neighbours themselves point out. It gave them also a wider range of social and cultural relationships than their own restricted community. People travelling to and from the Tong Hills on ritual errands carried the sacred emblems of the *Bɔyar* cult and were safe from molestation.

Some twenty years ago the pilgrim traffic took a new turn. Tallensi were coming into contact with Ashanti and the coast, and thus news of the Tong Hills 'fetishes' reached those areas. Men from the Hills, with a mixture of inborn business acumen and sincere faith in the magical powers of their oracle cult, advertised the cult quietly. A trickle of pilgrims from these wealthy and comparatively sophisticated areas began to flow northwards. And the trickle soon became a broad stream. Rich and poor, farmers, traders, chiefs, commoners, literate and illiterate, pagans and Christians joined the stream. To-day this traffic is a major industry of the Tong Hills.

These pilgrims[1] from the south come with extraordinarily varied wishes to lay before the *Bɔyar*. They beg for children, for health, for wealth, for power, for the success of farming and business enterprises, for victory in litigation, for help in a career or in the prosecution of political aims. Most important of all, Ashanti and Colony medicine men come to purchase the privilege of ritual clientship of the *Bɔyar*. They receive the right to

---

[1] I am indebted to Dr. M. J. Field, formerly Government Anthropologist, Gold Coast, for some information on the Colony end of this traffic. See also her *Religion and Medicine of the Ga People* for references to 'Nana Tongo' and her paper 'Some New Shrines of the Gold Coast and their Significance', *Africa*, xiii. 2, 1940. Rattray, op. cit., vol. ii, pp. 361 ff., gives a vivid description of the ceremony at the Tɔŋna'ab *Bɔyar* when hundreds of southern pilgrims come to present their pleas and register their vows.

254   THE FORM OF TALE SOCIETY

set up a shrine affiliated to Tɔŋna'ab at their own homes, and these shrines are used by them (*vide* Field, op. cit.) in their own ritual practice to cure witchcraft and dissipate other forms of magical misfortune or misdeeds.

This traffic is extremely profitable to the Hill Talis concerned in it. The pilgrims bring gifts in money and kind beside which the traditional gifts of Mamprusi or Bulisi client villages pale into insignificance. Those who have received benefits bring gifts. The medicine men who own affiliated shrines pay heavily for the privilege and bring periodical gifts in gratitude for benefits received. These vary from a pound or two to £10, £20, and in at least one case, for the authenticity of which I have good evidence, £100. In addition the pilgrims pay generously for their board and lodging and for animals which they offer in sacrifice at the *Bɔyar*.

From the beginning this traffic was monopolized by one maximal lineage of Tɛnzugu, Gɔlibdaan yidɛm of Bunkiuk. The head of this lineage, the Gɔlibdaana, a shrewd and resolute man of unbounded ambition, was, until the recent political reorganization of the country, recognized by Government as the headman of the Hill clans. He used his political authority to keep the pilgrim traffic with the south in his own hands, allowing only a minor share of the profits to go to his fellow ritual functionaries of the *Bɔyar* (Wannii) to which his lineage belongs. With the aid of the young men of his lineage and young men of other Tɛnzugu clans attracted to him by the lure of gain he has built up a complex organization for keeping contact with Ashanti and Colony pilgrims and clients and for stimulating the flow of pilgrims. By Tale standards he is a Croesus, but it would be hopeless for an outsider to attempt to estimate his wealth. It is enough to see his huge and well-kept homestead, his eighty wives, the sumptuous clothes he affects, the extravagance of his gifts to friends and adherents, to realize that he must derive an income of several hundred pounds a year entirely from this pilgrim traffic.

Though he is himself the principal beneficiary of this monopoly, all the members of his maximal lineage, except one segment, co-operate in running it and benefit from it. His closest partners are some of his own half-brothers and cousins, and their share of the profits is enough to make them considerably more wealthy than the average native. Two or three henchmen belonging to other Tɛnzugu clans and the other ritual functionaries of the *Bɔyar* whose presence is essential for the performance of the rites of accepting the pilgrims get about the same 'rake-off' as his near agnates. On a rough estimate I should say that the Gɔlibdaana keeps about half the profits and divides the other half among the other men interested in the business. This enables these others—his close agnates, his henchmen, and the other ritual functionaries of the *Bɔyar*— to have from five to nine wives each, where the ordinary native of similar age and status would have at most two or three wives; and the number of wives a man has is a good indication of his income in terms of food-supply and cash. The economic system of the Tallensi provides no outlets for this wealth in new economic enterprise. What cannot be invested in wives, live-stock, and clothes, or consumed in the form of

THE FORM OF TALE SOCIETY

food, beer, tobacco, kola nuts, and household and farming equipment, must be hoarded. One result has been that the Gɔlibdaana's ambitions have been enormously inflated. He has been striving to turn his wealth into prestige. He would fain be a great chief, and has for years been scheming and intriguing to this end. As is common in African societies to which European contact has opened up new economic opportunities that are wholly or partially divorced from their own social structure and economic system, the Gɔlibdaana's response to the opportunity offered by the pilgrim traffic has been a mixture of cupidity, calculation, and unbridled self-interest.

The point of interest here is the effect of the Gɔlibdaana's monopoly on the interrelations of the Hill Talis clans. All the other clans of the Hills view it with open envy, in particular Kpata'ar, the clan immediately contiguous with the Gɔlibdaana's clan, Bunkiuk. The people of Kpata'ar claim political superiority to Bunkiuk, on the strength of their being (as they assert) *primus inter pares* in the scheme of ritual collaboration among the Hill clans. They therefore demand the lion's share of the pilgrim traffic with the south, though they are now wholly excluded from it. The other clans of the Hills excluded from this traffic make similar but smaller demands. It is, in effect, a demand for a distribution of the profits of this new economic application of the *Bɔyar* cult on the same lines as the distribution of the traditional client villages. In the traditional arrangement the economic exploitation of the cult follows the accepted principles of equality and equilibrium in the social system. Each of the dozen or so *Bɔya* of the Hill Talis had its group of client communities exclusively reserved for it and there were no great variations between the profits of one *Bɔyar* and another.

An immediate result has been that the Gɔlibdaana no longer exercises undisputed headmanship, as the executive agent of the Administration, over all the Tɛnzugu clans. In 1933 he was in control of all the Tɛnzugu clans in all matters falling under the jurisdiction of the Administration. He called out the young men for road building or rest-house repairs; exacted a tribute from all independent householders living on top of the Hills or entitled to live there; and judged all cases brought against Tɛnzugu people or sent on cases from Tɛnzugu to other headmen or chiefs. Since 1936 the Kpata'ar faction has refused to submit to his control in these matters. Meanwhile the Administration has ruled that neither the Gɔlibdaana nor the Kpata'arna'ab shall be recognized as headman of the Tɛnzugu clans until the people have settled among themselves which of them is rightfully entitled to the post. So there are now two headmen.

To-day a silent feud, taking the form of intrigue and conspiracies to undermine one another's reputation with the Administration, rages among the Hill Talis. On one side stands the Gɔlibdaana and his faction, the nucleus of which is the majority of his own maximal lineage; on the other the factions hostile to him, chief of which is the maximal lineage of the Kpata'arna'ab. The struggle has become so acute, on several occasions, that bloodshed was only prevented by the fear of stern intervention by the District Commissioner.

The feud follows the lines of cleavage between clans and maximal

256 THE FORM OF TALE SOCIETY

lineages inherent in the native social structure. The majority of the Gɔlibdaana's own maximal lineage share in the profits of his monopoly and are solidly behind him; the maximal lineages of the leaders of the opposition are solidly against him; but many of the maximal lineages that have clanship or ritual links with both sides are split. Many of the young men of these lineages side with the Gɔlibdaana—enticed, their elders say bitterly, by his lavish gifts. The older men are uneasily neutral or tacitly opposed to the Gɔlibdaana because he has brought dissension to the Hills and has flouted some of the ancient ritual customs. Both parties try to manœuvre the opposition into a position which will set the Administration in motion against them; the leaders of both parties say that the white man's authority is the only force that will help them to victory. And they feel particularly bitter because the vigilance of Administrative officers has frustrated all their efforts to exploit this potent sanction.

At the same time they try to use the sanctions of their own social structure to gain their aims. For outside the struggle for control of the pilgrim traffic, the ties of clanship, kinship, and ritual collaboration remain valid as before. During the Great Festivals the feud sinks into temporary abeyance. The Gɔlibdaana and the Kpata'arna'ab speak with hatred of each other when it is a question of political power or the pilgrim traffic; they continue to perform those rites of the Great Festivals and of the Earth cult in which they are ritually obliged to collaborate, with apparent cordiality. This is a 'separate thing' they declare. It would be an appalling sin bringing catastrophe on the whole country, they say, if they threw over these bonds.

But the new alinements in the pecuniary struggle and the traditional social structure cannot be kept apart in watertight compartments. The Kpata'arna'ab and the Gɔlibdaana try to coerce each other through their mutual ritual obligations. They try to put pressure on each other through maximal lineages that are intercalary between their lineages; and to win over the other maximal lineages with which they have clanship or ritual ties.

Experienced elders maintain, with the sceptical candour that is one of the few charms Tallensi have for an ethnographer, that this can never decide the issue. Putting it at its highest, the bonds of clanship, kinship, and ritual collaboration are a double-edged weapon. If Kpata'ar tries to coerce Samiit to side with it by refusing to collaborate with Samiit in the rites of their common External Bɔyar, the ancestors might well blame Kpata'ar and punish them. Tallensi are not—so the old men say—restrained from doing something to their personal advantage by the fear of mystical penalties. 'Who fears death before death comes upon you?' It is only after a death occurs that the survivors see in it signs and omens referring to their social relations with one another.

Whenever a death occurs in any of the Hill clans, especially if it is the death of an important person, the chronic discord between them is openly recollected. It is both a symptom of the general feeling of uneasiness and a move in the game of attempted mutual coercion by mystical sanctions. A funeral almost inevitably causes this feeling to be ventilated. For people of all the Tɛnzugu and many other clans are present, as kinsfolk, affines,

PLATE XV

(*a*) A mimic war parade at Ba'ari to inaugurate an elder's funeral.

(*b*) The widest politico-ritual community includes all the Tallensi. Part of the vast gathering of people from all over Taleland who come to take part in or watch the concluding ceremonies and dances of the Gɔlib Festival. Note the dust cloud raised by the dancers.

THE FORM OF TALE SOCIETY

neighbours, and friends of the deceased. They feel the contradiction between their mutual bonds of amity with one another as kin or friends and their latent hostility, in other situations, as members of opposed corporate units. Thus it often happens that when a diviner is publicly consulted about the mystical cause of the death, he attributes it to the anger of the ancestors or the Earth over the disharmony on the hills. Even if this is not the diviner's verdict, the faction opposing that to which the dead man belonged will interpret his death in this sense. Thus when the Sakpee tɛndaana died, the men of Kpata'ar, including some of his own matrilateral kinsmen, were secretly almost jubilant. They were convinced that this death was a punishment, and a warning from the ancestors, for his defection from the Kpata'ar party to the Gɔlibdaana's side; for the Sakpee tɛndaana is one of the ritual officers of the External Bɔyar of which Kpata'ardɛm are the senior custodians, as we have previously seen.

Up to now these mystical warnings have not been heeded. They have, at most, reinforced the tendency for the heads of maximal lineages to aline themselves on the same side as the maximal lineages with which they have ties of clanship and of ritual collaboration. For obviously these ties have greatest efficacy for the individuals who hold the offices through which they are normally expressed. The rank-and-file members of the lineages concerned often persist in the path of greatest self-interest. Nor have these warnings helped to mitigate the struggle between the Gɔlibdaana's maximal lineage and the other lineages which take the lead in opposing him. To-day, as in the days of warfare, a man can keep up cordial personal relations with a kinsman in the opposite camp. He will not, because of his personal kinship ties with the enemy, contract out of his own lineage in issues affecting its corporate unity—least of all when the motive of profit is added to the bonds of lineage solidarity.

The disturbing effects of the Gɔlibdaana's pecuniary enterprise have not been limited to Tɛnzugu. He has come into conflict with Yinduuri by claiming jurisdiction over a section of Zandoya that has always been regarded as coming within the field of social and politico-ritual relations of Yinduuri (see p. 163). He is not on speaking terms with the Bɔyaraana of Sii, who claims to be the senior ritual functionary of the Wannii Bɔyar as well as the senior chief of all the Talis, and therefore demands control of the pilgrim traffic with the south. He has gravely offended the Chief of Tongo, his own brother-in-law, by wrongfully assuming the insignia and aping the etiquette of a superior chief, and by bribing the Paramount Chief of the Mamprusi to invest him with the rank of a chief of high status. But for the intervention of the Administration this particular quarrel would already have led to serious disturbances, for the people of Tongo are extremely jealous of the rank and status of their chiefship and unanimously resent the Gɔlibdaana's presumption. It is notable that they do not in the least envy the Gɔlibdaana his pecuniary monopoly. Frankly despising the fertility and oracle aspects of the Bɔyar cult as a piece of fraudulent magic, they look on the money gained through the pilgrim traffic as tainted. In this matter Namoos and Talis have not got a sphere of common interests within which they might be rivals. The interests of Tongo and Bunkiuk intersect only in relation to the

S

258 THE FORM OF TALE SOCIETY

Chiefship of Tongo, to which the Golibdaana's office has a politico-ritual relationship.

The point that must be stressed, however, is that the Golibdaana's monopoly has not yet thrown the existing scheme of structural alinements into complete disorder. It is a factor of disequilibrium and may, in the course of a few more years, make serious rents in the complex fabric of the social and politico-ritual relationships of the Hill Talis. Up to the present the native social structure, and in particular the web of ritual collaboration, has resisted the corruption and kept in check, to a very considerable extent, the dissensions due to this new force. This might well go on as long as the Administration keeps the ring impartially, and as long as the Golibdaana and his maximal lineage accept the politico-ritual values on which the integration of the Hill Talis rests, and abide by the principal jural and moral norms of the society. So far the struggle has not given rise to new corporate associations running counter to those of the existing social structure. In fact, it has on the whole been canalized along the lines of cleavage laid down in that structure. It has deepened some of the existing cleavages and sharpened some of the inherent tensions of the system; but it has also accentuated some of the ties and enhanced the dominant values of the system. Thus the only section of Kpata'ar that has vacillated, at times, in its loyalty is Nak-y-eet yidɛm, the assimilated lineage. They have been influenced by their lineage differentiation from Kpata'ar proper, their consequent subsidiary interest in the politico-ritual status of the head of Kpata'ar proper, their clanship ties with the Sakpee section that has gone over to the Golibdaana, and the greed of their lineage head. But their intercalary structural position between the two factions is shown in their divided counsels. Some of the older men are whole-heartedly for Kpata'ar, one or two adhere publicly to the Golibdaana, several try to keep on good terms with both parties. When they have to take a stand as a corporate unit, their bias is towards the Kpata'arna'ab in ritual and intra-clan affairs, and towards the Golibdaana in matters of law and government coming within his purview as a headman under the Administration. On the other hand, the ancient ties between Kpata'ar and Gundaat have been greatly strengthened, the bond of goodwill between Kpata'ar and Tongo, based on their politico-ritual interdependence, given a new meaning, and moves to defend the traditional social order stimulated.

POSTSCRIPT

THIS book has dealt with the constitution and interrelations of the corporate groupings found in Tale society. But this is only one major aspect of Tale social structure. There is another major aspect of no less importance, the system of interpersonal social bonds that constitutes the Kinship System in the strict sense. The lineage and clan organization forms the permanent framework of social relations in Taleland. But it is based on certain fundamental categories of thought and axioms of conduct that derive from a different cross-section of Tale social life, the domestic organization. The well-worn simile of the warp and the woof is apposite here. We can think of the lineage and clan organization as the warp of the social fabric of the Tallensi. Interwoven with it, sustaining it, and in turn shaped and regulated by it, is the intricate web of interpersonal relations we have described as the Kinship System in the strict sense. Kinship ties grow directly out of the biological, psychological, and social relations of men, women, and children in the domestic nucleus of Tale social life, the agnatic joint family. Unlike lineage ties, they involve the equal and parallel recognition of descent through both parents; and because of this bilateral criterion of social identification in kinship relations, they cut across the lineage structure.[1]

This second major aspect of Tale social structure, the Kinship System, is the subject of our next volume, *The Web of Kinship Among the Tallensi*. Our aim will be not a detailed analysis of all Tale interpersonal relationships through all the levels of social behaviour, but an investigation of their place in the social structure in relation to the lineage and clan organization.

[1] Cf. my previously cited paper on 'The Significance of Descent in Tale Social Structure'.

INDEX

Abduction of wife, 42, 90, 245.

Adultery, ordeal, 229.

Agnatic, ancestor, 31, 35; descent, 45 *see* Patriliny; notion of unilineal — descent, 47.

Agriculture, Tale —, 9.

Alinement, funeral ceremonies as criteria of social —, 121.

Amity, 105; common sacrifice as pledge of mutual —, 98.

Ancestor, psychological value of — cult, 9; agnatic —, 31 *see* Agnatic; in lineage structure, 31; cult as calculus of lineage system, 33, 130; sacrifices to founding —, 43, 98, significance of, 52 see also *bɔyar*; Mosuor as common —, 22, 43; graves and shrines as focus of sub-clan's unity, 55; anonymity of — in totemic myths, 68, 128 ff.; blasphemy against, 130; —s as sanction of lineage unity, 135, 144, 215, 244, 248; symbolism of immortality of —s, 143; attributes of —s and their symbolism, 145; —s symbolized by animals, 145; —s in relation to farm-land, 178; founding —'s homestead as sacred spot, 208, 218; sites of —s' graves, 209; obligatory sacrifices to lineage —s, 228.

Animals, division of — at funeral ceremonies, 44; transformation of, 68; most commonly tabooed, 140, not of one class, 141; symbolism, 142, 145.

Autochthonous communities in Voltaic region, 6, 7.

Avoidances, *see* Taboo, Totemic.

Ba'ari, relation to Zubiuŋ, 82; clanship ties of, 87, 118; internal constitution, of, 88; joking partnership, 91; ritual collaboration, 101, 120.

Ba'at Da'a, 101, 116; see *tɔŋgban*.

bayɘr (pl. *baya*) = shrine of ancestor or other spirit, 52, 142.

Beer, division of — at funeral ceremonies, 44.

Bégué, L., 1 (note).

biis (sing. *bii*) = children, 33 *see* Lineage.

Binger, Capitaine, 16 (note).

Biuk, 39, 42; links with Gɔrisi, 60.

Biuŋ, 28; Chief of —, 73, 162; *see also* Zoo; size and layout of —, 74.

Bona'ab *see* External *Bɔyar*.

Boundaries, absence of — between tribes, 16; Tongo has no fixed territorial —, 160; social — of a settlement, 161 ff., 169; social — of Tongo, 161, 170; social — of Tɛndaana's *tɛŋ*, not defined, 185, 186, shaped by social relationship, 187.

Boundary, disputes, 163, cases of, 164.

Bɔyar, External (pl. *Bɔya*) = common shrine of all ancestors of constituent maximal lineages of a clan, 100; of the Talis, 57, 220; Duunk-palɘg as ritual focus of clan, 79; complementary to Earth shrine, 80 ff., 100; symbolizes lineage continuity, 81; as apex of ancestor cult, 100, 137; as unifying force in social structure, 101, 110; initiation cult, 104; organization of cult of, 104; as polar principle to Earth cult, 104 ff., 108, 182; names of, 106; Bona'ab, 106, 109–12, 130, 252; parochial and universal aspect of —, 106; as organizing principle of social structure, 108; totemic avoidances connected with —, 130, 137, 138; ritual and moral sanctions in — cult, 131; pilgrim traffic to —, 131, 252; in relation to patriliny, 131; spiritual wards of, 132; client clans outside Taleland, 132, 252; oath by —, 138; destroys perjurer, 138.

bɔyar (pl. *bɔya*) = shrine of founding ancestor, 42, 52 (note 2); of clans and lineages, 43, 213; — of Sie-datɔk, 47; chief of Tongo owns Mosuor's —, 52, 54; succession disputes, 70; significance of — in clanship, 98.

dugni bɔyar, = lineage shrine, 81; relation to External *Bɔyar*, 81; definition of, 100; description of, 101; inheritance of, 150, role of women in, 149, 150; of fathers' and mothers' lineage, 197, 200.

Bɔyaraam, *see* Festival, Harvest.

Bride-price, responsibility for, 230.

British, influence of — rule, 10; — rule as factor of disequilibrium, 250.

Brotherhood, see *sunzɔt*.

Brothers (*sunzɔp*), see *sunzɔp*; residential relations of —, 207.

Brothers (*soog*), *see* Uterine; residential relations of —, 207.

Bunkiuk, clanship ties of, 89, 254.

262 INDEX

Cardinall, A. W., 2 (note); 6 (note 2).
Cemeteries, 184; of Hill Talis, 220.
Chain, principle of clan linkage, 40, 75, 90.
Chief, Paramount — of Mampurugu, 6, 29; authority of —s, 13, 250; of Tongo: owns Mosuor's bɔyar, 54, relations to Gbizug tɛndaana, 95, ritual power over rain, 95, highest in Taleland, 182, 189; political relation between —s, 73; political jealousies between —s, 94, 251; ritual definition of social personality of —, 144; boundary disputes between —s and headmen, 163; politico-ritual functions of —s, 182 ff.; —s predominantly Namoos, 184; meaning of, 184.
Chiefship, of Tongo, 43; of sub-clan, 43; in Sie district, 119.
Children, importance attached to, 68.
Cicatrization, facial —, 16.
Clan, see also Sub-clan; dispersed —, 42, 62; organization, 45; unity: factors of, 48, basis of, 81; internal differentiation of, 49; equilibrium of, 49, internal, 216, 244; not a closed genealogical unit, 49; — segmentation, 49; definition of —, 61, 85; as local unit, 62, 85; clanship ties between —s, 87; moral coercion between —s, 95; significance of —s, 98; —s as largest corporate units in political matters, 103; membership based on lineage membership, 137 see Lineage; ritual focus of —, 218, 220; solidarity, 244, 249, sanction of —, 244; reprisals between —s, 245; reciprocity of rights and duties in —, 246; disputes within —, 246, dislocating effect of —, 248, how set right, 248; homicide within — prohibited, 250; composite —: definition of, 62, 74, status of component lineages of, 82, social boundary of, 169.
Clanship, see also Exogamy, Levirate, Lineage, War, Wives; chains of — ties, 40, 75, 90; war in relation to —, 42, 62; patriliny as basis of, 45; norms of, 47; reciprocity in, 48; rights and duties at funeral ceremonies, 56, 58, 83; field of — defined, 61, 63, 87; exogamy as mark of —, 62, 84; maximal lineage as centre of field of —, 62, 89; defined, 63, 90 ff.; in relation to spatial and genealogical distance, 63; rules of raiding in relation to —, 73; field of — among Namoos, 76; consanguinity in relation to —, 79;

extra-clan ties of —, 82; field of — of Zubiuŋ lineages, 82; gradation of — ties, 83, 90; adaptation of — ties to changing conditions, 85; pattern of — among Talis, 85; mesh of — among Talis, 87; cult of Earth shrine in relation to —, 87; linking Tallensi and Gɔrisi, 88; quasi —, 91, 133; rationalization of —: by fictions of kinship, 46, 96, 97, ties by a token of ritual ties, 97; as bridge between levels of social structure, 103; ties correlated with spatial and ritual ties, 109; totemic avoidances not precisely correlated with — ties, 124, 127; as factor of social integration, 233.
Clanswomen (pɔyayabɔlis), see also Women; definition and status of, 147 ff.; privileges of, 148; rights of, 148; funeral of, 148; concealed rivalry between — and male agnates, 149; recognition of —'s status, 149; in relation to lineage bɔyar, 149; co-operation amongst—, 151; duties of — at funerals, 151, 152; contrasted with wives at funeral, 151; as intermediary between paternal and husband's clans, 152; build up network of kinship ties, 153.
Cleavage, symbols of social —s, 26 ff.; signs of — between Namoos and non-Namoos, 28, 78, 238 ff.; major — between Namoos and Talis, 103.
Climate of Northern Territories, 1.
Collaboration, see Ritual.
Collective, concept of — responsibility, 230, 245.
Colour, skin — of Tallensi, 7.
Communications in Northern Territories, 4.
Community, basis of interconnexion with locality, 171; tɛŋ as —, 180, 181; integration of —, 181; prosperity of — depends on chiefs and tɛndaanas, 183; see Chief, Tɛndaana.
Composite clan, see Clan.
Consanguinity (dɔyam), defined, 61, in relation to clanship, 79; see also Kinship.
Contiguity, influence of local —, 76.
Contraposition, technique of, 17, 27, 36; definition of, 18.
Corporate, representation of — units, 99; types of — activities within lineages, 217.
Cowrie shells, three — as ritual decoration, 66; oath by —, 66, 125.
Crops, in Northern Territories, 3; social significance of plentiful —, 173.

INDEX

263

Cult, of the Earth, 7 *see* Earth; ancestor —, 9 *see* Ancestor.
Culture, influence of — contact on Tallensi, 10, 11.
'Custodian of the Earth', *see* Tɛndaana.
Custom, variation in — as factor of social integration, 21, 25; similarity and divergence of —, 21; sanctions of —, 25.

Da'a, rite, 21, 124 *see* Festival, Harvest.
daboog = original home-site, 42, 208; *see* Ancestor.
Dagbane, Mole — speaking groups, 6, 14.
Dagomba, tribe, 2, 6.
Datɔk, size and layout of —, 74; structure of —, 221.
Death as corporate concern, 218.
Dee = war march at funeral ceremonies, q.v.
Deemzeet, 209.
Dekpieŋ, segment of Tongo, 213.
Delafosse, M., 4, 107.
Demographic factors, in structure of settlement, 155 ff.; in relation to clan structure, 217.
Dim Delobsom, A. A., 6 (note 2).
Diseases, endemic, 3, 8.
Disequilibrium, British rule as factor of —, 250; pecuniary competition as factor of —, 251; *see* Equilibrium.
Divination, technique of, 130.
dɔyam = consanguinity, *see* Kinship; definition of, 61, 116, 117; in relation to clanship, 79.
dug = 'room', 33, 100, 202; *see* Lineage; definition of, 203 ff.
Duunkpalɔg, *see* External *Bɔyar*.
Duusi, clan structure of, 119.

Earth *(tɛŋ)*, Custodian of the —, 7, 20, 80 *see* Tɛndaana; ancestors sprang from the —, 22; symbolizes common values, 81; universal mystical power of —, 175, 181; native attitude to —, 176; homicide as sin against —, 177, 188; other sins against —, 188; sacrifices of expiation to —, 177; as sanction of social solidarity, 177; indivisible powers of —, 185; cult of the —, 80, 101, External *Bɔyar* as polar principle to —, 104 ff., 108, 182, localized at sacred spots, 104 see *tɔŋgban*, parochial and universal aspect of, 106, as organizing principle of social structure, 108; taboos of the —, 142, 188, symbolism of, 143, observances of, 175, on bloodshed, 176.

Earth shrine = *tɔŋgban*, of Zubiuŋ as focus of clan unity, 80; complementary to External *Bɔyar*, 80 ff., 100; cult of — in relation to clanship, 87; significance of —s in social structure, 107; supreme — at Gbizug, 108.
Ecological adjustment between clans, 168.
Economic system as stabilizing factor, 240.
Efficiency, conditions of productive —, 173.
Equilibrium, of lineages, 31, 32, 244; tendency to — in Tale society, 47, 234, 243; internal — of clan, 49, 216; social — among Talis, 180; structural — and land tenure, 180.
Evans-Pritchard, E. E., 14 (note 1), 231 (note 1).
Exogamy, 47; rule of, 41; as mark of clanship, 62; in relation to clanship, 84.
External *Bɔyar*, see *Bɔyar*.

Family, as growing-point of lineage, 32; joint — defined, 195, 198; expanded — as basis of lineage segment, 204.
Farming, as basis of Tale livelihood, 172; unit, 177.
Farm-land, kinds of —, 172; in relation to ancestors, 178; owned by lineage, 178, 180; sales of —, 178, 189, tabooed in some areas, 189; pledging of —, 179; borrowing of —, 179; redeemable —, 180.
Festival:
Great —, —s as criterion of classification, 19; traditional reference to ancestors during —s, 25; cycle, 28, 53, 103; meaning and function of — cycle in social structure, 105, 113, 243; role of Doo in —s, 112; as index of widest community, 243; fighting tabooed during —s, 243.
Harvest —, *Bɔyaraam*, 19, 21, 104, 106, 124, initiation cult, 104; *Tɛŋɔn-lɛbɔgɔt*, 21; *Da'a*, 21, 124.
Sowing — (*Gɔlib*), 19; centred on Earth cult, 105; bloodshed during — tabooed, 241; as counterweight to war, 243.
Field, Dr. M. J., 253 (note).
Field, of clanship, 47, 61, 63, 76, 82, 87 *see* Clanship; of social relations, 103, 137, defined, 233, principle of — governs lineage solidarity, 245.
First-born child, avoidances of —

264 INDEX

among Namoos, 66; fowl taboo of, 69, 132.

Firth, R., xii.

Folk-lore of Tallensi, 141.

Food, division of — at funeral ceremonies, 44.

Forde, Daryll, 199 (note 1).

Fowl, see Taboo.

Funeral ceremonies, see also Rites; among Talis, 20; among Namoos, 20, 66; war march (dee) at, 27; significance of, 31; rights and duties of clans at, 44, 83, 84; division of meat, beer, and food at, 44, 72; at Sie, 46; clanship in, 56, 58, 122; as criteria of social alinement, 121; as sacred duty, 122; as quasi totemic avoidances, 122, 136 see Totemic; symbolic value of, 123; significance of local variations in, 123, 124; structural correlations of, 124; for woman, 148.

Gambaga scarp, 3.

Gbaləg, case history of, 248.

Gbambee, outpost of Tongo and Zoo, 162.

Gban, clanship ties of, 56, 57; as composite clan, 61, 62.

Gbeog, relation to Zubiuŋ, 82, 87; tɛndaana, 247.

Gbizug, clanship rights and duties of, 57; myth of origin of — tɛndaana, 58 see also Tɛndaana; relation to Zubiuŋ, 82; clanship ties of, 87; politico-ritual relationship with Tongo, 95; ritual bonds of, 101 ff.; supreme Earth shrine at —, 108; as peacemaker, 121; politico-ritual status of, 162; tɛndaana dispute with Gbeog tɛndaana, 247.

Genealogies, as mnemonics of lineage system, 31; no historical validity of, 36; function and significance of, 65.

Genealogical: distance, 37, 63; — differentiation, 124; — relationships, 134 see Kinship; — knowledge of Tallensi, 216.

Generation, recognition of — differences, 204.

Gɛnət, primordial Gbizug Tɛndaana, 22, 110, 218.

Goatskin, loin cover for the dead, 66, 122 see Namoos.

Gorogo, connexion with Tongo, 57; fight between — and Wakii, 240.

Gɔlib, see Festival.

Gɔlibdaana, disrupture influence of, 113, 163 ff., 254; monopolizes pilgrim traffic from south, 254; political feud with Kpata'ar, 25, 255.

Graves, ancestral —, 55; sociological significance of, 220.

Gundaat, clanship ties of, 89, 110.

Guŋ, section of Tongo, 213.

Harvest, see Festival.

Headmen, 192; authority of, 13; boundary disputes between chiefs and —, 163.

Heaven and Earth are one, 22.

Hill Talis, see Talis.

History, absence of — among Tallensi, 24, 26.

Homicide, as sin against the Earth, 177; between clans, 177; within the clan, 177, prohibited, 250.

Immigrant, communities in Voltaic region, 6; Hill Talis as —s, 23.

Initiation, External Bɔyar and — cult, 104.

Joking as compensation for structural tensions, 94 ff.

Joking partnership, definition of, 91; among Talis, 91; conventional modes of expression of, 91; compared with brother-in-lawship, 92; structural significance of, 92; Namoo equivalent of, 93; connexion with clanship, 96.

Judicial, present day — system, 236.

Jural, relations of lineage, 229, 230; relations not judicial, 235; status of sanctions of — rights, 236.

Jurisdiction, ritual — over land of tɛndaana, 164.

Kaləŋkaa yidɛm, accessory lineage of Sie, 46.

Kinship (dɔyam) = consanguineous — in clan, 45, 52, 61, 117.

Kinship (mabiirət = — in the wide sense), 61, 117; web of, 19; and warfare, 42; fictions in ritual collaboration, 102; as model of all social ties, 114; fictions in social structure, 116; quasi —, 133; relations as dominant ideology of social relations, 134; terms, 192, 193.

Kparəg, annual hunt in — bush, 73.

Kpata'ar, political feud with Gɔlibdaana, 25, 255; clanship ties of, 89, 109; senior custodians of Ḍoo, 111 see Ḍoo; loyalty to —, 112.

Kuŋkɔŋto'o yidɛm, attached lineage of Tongo, 57.

Kuŋkye, ancestor of Sie, 39, 45 ff.

Kuorəg, section of Tongo, 213.

INDEX

265

Labour migration, 10, 156.

Labouret, H., 6 (note 2), 107 (note), 141 (note 1).

Land, *see also* Farm-land; forms of ownership of —, 177, 178; religious sanctions of — ownership, 178; prosperity of —, 183.

Land tenure, 177; determined by social organization, 180, 181; security of —, 180.

Languages, Sudanic —, 6.

Legends, counterfeit history, 26.

Levirate, 41, 47, 83.

Lɛbhtiis yidɛm, custodians of shrines of Tongo ancestors, 54; segment of Tongo, 195 ff.

Ligər yidɛm, assimilated lineage, 57; ties with Tongo, 57; myth of origin of, 58.

Lineage, *see also* Clanship; paradigm of — system, 26, 30 ff.; definition of — as patrilineal descent group, 30; solidarity, 31, 204, 244, 249, sanctions of, 244; equilibrium of, 31, 32, 244; as temporal system, 32; fission in, 33; nomenclature of —s, 33, 195; — segmentation, 33, 193, rules of, 201, grades of, 205; — *sunzɔp*, 37, 201; corporate interests and activities of, 37, 217, 226, 227 ff.; of slave descent, 49; as fundamental social unit, 62; definition of field of clanship of a —, 63; significance of — structure, 98, 224; membership as determinant of social relations, 135; totemic and funeral taboos as symbolic expressions of — membership, 135, 136, 139; norms absolutely binding, 135; membership as determinant of individual conduct, 136; membership as basis for individual's field of social relations, 137; membership in relation to External *Bɔyar* cult, 139; localization, 143, 207 ff., 209; ties determine structure of settlement, 166 *see* Settlement; land rights of, 178; principle in structure of settlement analysed, 191; span of, 30, 194; internal organization of, 192 ff., order of, 194; differentiation of —s, 195; — *bɔyar*, 197, 209 see *bɔyar*; residential relations correlated with — ties, 197, 207 ff.; influence of family pattern in, 198; patri- and matri-segments of, 198; founding ancestor of, 201; representative, 201; progenitrix, 201; medial and inner —s, 202,

229, defined, 205; zones of — relations, 203; reaction to incest and adultery within —, 204; patrimonial land in relation to, 205; segments are *soog* segments, 212; time factor in — structure, 224; initiative in, 226; obligatory sacrifices to — ancestors, 228; jural relations of, 229, 230; nuclear —, 229; adaptation of — structure, 244; changes in — structure, 247.

Accessory lineages, definition of, 40; at Sie, 46, 49; disabilities of, 51; status of, 55; with intercalary relations, 59.

Assimilated lineage, definition of, 40; status and traditions of, 51, 52, 53, 57; origin of, 51; Nɔŋsuur yidɛm as —, 44, 53.

Attached lineages, definition of, 40, 50; status and traditions of, 51, 52, 57, 87; origin of, 51; disabilities of, 52.

Authentic lineages, definition of, 40, 51.

Intercalary lineage, status of —s at Tongo, 57, 59; —s at Sie, 58; Nɔŋsuur yidɛm as, 78.

Maximal lineage, definition of, 30; *sunzɔp* of —s, 32; as exogamous unit, 33; as core of every clan, 62; as smallest corporate units in political action, 103.

Minimal lineages, definition of, 30; as source of primary segmentation, 32; effective — defined, 192, 198.

Lineage Head, 208; among Talis has fixed homestead, 220; definition of, 224; rules of succession, 225; succession ceremony, 227; status of, 225, 228; hierarchy of —s, 225; moral and ritual authority of, 225, 226; and lineage property, 226; office determined by custody of lineage *bɔyar* (q.v.), 226; responsibilities of —, 178, 226, 228, sanctions of, 179; as centre of social life, 227; no judicial authority, 227; religious sanctions supporting —, 227; privileges of, 228; funeral of, 228.

Lineage Home, 208, 215, 220.

Local, variations in Sudanese Zone, 3; ties as function of clanship, 59; clan as — unit, 62, 85; influence of — contiguity, 76; relationships parallel with clanship ties, 89; settlement as —ly fixed community, 157, 158.

Locality, as basis of interconnexion

266 INDEX

with community, 171; in relation to kinship, 221; *see* Lineage.

Loin cover, ritual value of sheepskin — for Talis, 122; ritual value of goatskin — for Namoos, 66, 122; oath by, 125.

Lynn, C. W., 1 (note), 7 (note).

mabii (pl. *mabiis*) = mother's child, definition of, 116 ff.; see *mabiirǝt*.

mabiirǝt = 'kinship in the wide sense', definition of, 61, 117; *see* Kinship.

Malinowski, B., xii.

Mamprusi, 2, 6, 14; myth of origin, 39; status of — at Tongo, 45.

Mampuru, 6, 39.

Mampurugu, Paramount Chief of —, 6, 22, 29, 39.

Marriage, importance of — among Tallensi, 68; regulations define zones of lineage relations, 204; formalities, 229.

Matrilateral, kin, 52; totemic avoidances as personal taboos of — kin, 132 ff.; descent in lineage structure, 200, 202; antithesis between — and patrilateral ties, 201.

Meek, C. K., 107 (note).

Migration, in Voltaic region, 7; labour — in Northern Territories, 10, 156; to peripheral settlements, 163, 221.

Mole, — Dagbane speaking groups, 6, 14.

Money, value of, 10.

Monteil, Charles, 107 (note), 140 (note).

Moral, coercion between clans, 95, 96.

Mortuary, *see* Funeral ceremonies.

Mossi, 4, 6.

Mosuor, founder of Tongo, 22, 39; custody of —'s grave, 42; as common ancestor, 43; thanksgiving sacrifice to, 53; —'s grave described, 219.

Mosuor biis, dispersion of, 39, 42, 62; chain of four sub-clans of, 40, 43; constitution of, 43, 60, 191; as maximal lineage, 43; rights and duties of — at funeral ceremonies, 44; as open system, 55; numerical preponderance of, 64; as backbone of Tale political organization, 65.

Mythology of totemic avoidances, 128 ff.

Myths of origin, of Namoos, 22, 39; of primordial tɛndaanas, 22, 58; function of, 23, 24, 26 ff.; counterfeit history, 26; and new social tensions, 27; of totemic avoidances, 67, 128 ff.; of Zoo, 72.

naditib, — clans in Sie district, 119.

Namoos, taboos distinguishing Talis and —, 20; myth of origin, 22, 39; signs of cleavage between — and non-—, 28, 78, 238 ff.; funeral rites and totemic observances of, 46, 66; distribution of —, 66; common Mampuru origin for, 66; avoidances of first-born among —, 66, 69; distinctive taboos of —, 66, 68; totemic oaths of —, 66, 69; fowl taboo among —, 69, 125; clans, 71 ff.; in Sie district, 75; meaning of, 76; field of clanship among —, 76; ties with Talis, 76; ritual relations in — clans, 98; cult of founding ancestor among —, 100; major cleavage between Talis and —, 103, 242.

Natural history, knowledge of — among Tallensi, 159.

Nomenclature, of social identification, 17, 21; of lineages, 33.

Northern Territories, of the Gold Coast, 1; communications in —, 4; political reorganization of, 13.

Nɔŋsuur yidɛm, assimilated lineage of Tongo, 44, 53, 99, 213; relationship to Zubiuŋ, 59; as intercalary lineage, 78.

Daaŋ yidɛm, accessory lineage of Sie, 46.

Ŋkoog, avoidances of people of —, 66; ties with Tongo, 74; ritual collaboration at —, 99.

Doo, supreme Earth shrine of Tɛnzugu, 111; Kpata'ar as senior custodians of —, 111; role in Great Festivals, 112.

Oaths, totemic — of Namoos, 66, 69, 125, of Talis, 125; by External Bɔyar, 138; see also Bɔyar, Funeral ceremonies, Totemic avoidances.

Oribi, loin cover of — skin for the dead, 122.

Origin, myths of — of clans, 21 ff.; *see* Myths.

Ownership, concept of — analysed, 171; of land, 171, 177 ff.

Parent, funeral ceremonies as sacred duty of son to —, 122.

Paternity, illegitimate, significance of, 51, 52.

Patrilateral, antithesis between — and matrilateral ties, 201.

Patriliny, 200; as basis of clanship, 45; symbolic value of totemic taboos in relation to —, 69, 130, 133; External Bɔyar cult in relation to —, 131; significance of patrilineal de-

INDEX

scent for individual, 134, 202; as basis of social order, 139; *see also* Agnatic.

Peace, Gbizug as — maker, 121.

Place-names, 157; derivation of, 167.

Political, organization of Voltaic tribes, 6, 13; reorganization of Northern Territories, 13; Tale — organization, 14; structure of widest politico-ritual community among Tallensi, 107; spatial relations and politico-ritual relations, 107; politico-ritual relations, 108.

Population, density of — in Zuarungu district, 2 ff.; distribution of — in Northern Territories, 3, 154; of Taleland, 4, 19; density of — and its influence on settlement structure, 155; increase of — of Taleland, 156.

pɔyayabɔlis (sing. *pɔyayabɔlɔg*), *see* Clanswomen.

Progeny, importance of — among Tallensi, 68.

Psychology, Tale —, 142.

Public, calamities, 174, and Earth, 175.

Puhug, section of Tongo, 203, 212, 218.

Raiding (*ŋɔk*), as method of self-help, 72; rules of — in relation to clanship, 73, 90, 245; as sanction of rights, 236.

Rationalization, of clanship by fictions of kinship, 96, 97; of clanship ties by token of ritual ties, 97.

Rattray, R. S., 6, 141 (notes), 232 (note 2).

Reciprocity in clanship, 48.

Refugee, disabilities of, 52.

Region, three major —s in Taleland, 29 *see* Taleland.

Religious values as reflex of social structure, 134, 243; *see also* Ritual.

Representation, principle of unit —, 44, 246.

Reprisals between clans, 245.

Richards, Audrey I., 232 (note 1).

Rites, *ŋma ma'ala*, 123; *kpe kpiintaŋ*, 124; *Da'a*, 124.

Ritual, as mechanism of social organization, 103; Talis clan field of — relations, 103; installation of — functionary, 104; ties between Talis clans, 108; deviations from common — explained, 122; prohibitions and — injunctions, 122; function of — observances in social structure, 133 *see* Totemic avoidances; jurisdiction over land of tendaana, 164; focus of clan, 218, 220; as mechanism of social inte-

gration, 233; limitations of — sanctions, 256.

Ritual collaboration, correlation of — with clanship, 98, 99; among Talis, 100 ff., significance of, 114; as expression of corporate identity of lineage and clan, 101 ff.; kinship fictions in —, 102; underlying principles of —, 102; among Hill Talis, 103; as articulating mechanism among Talis, 113.

Sacred, spots, 104, 208; groves, 80, 220 *see* Earth shrine; funeral ceremonies as — duty, 122

Sacrifice, on graves of ancestors, 19; enemies must not — together, 98; common — as pledge of mutual amity, 98; as corporate activity, 218; obligatory —s to lineage ancestors, 228.

Samiit, 97, 110.

Sanction, —s of custom, 25; Earth as — of social solidarity, 177; religious —s of land ownership, 178; ancestors as — of lineage unity, 135, 244; limitations of ritual —s, 256; *see also* Land tenure.

Saɣabazaa, Tongo elder, 44, 53.

Sawalɔg, 24.

Section (*yizug*), definition of, 166; —s of Tongo described, 167, 203; structure analysed, 211.

Security, social, 175; of land tenure, 180.

Segmentary, Tale society as — system, 231; system defined, 232.

Segmentation, in Voltaic society, 16, 17; order of lineage —, 31 ff., 33, 193, rules of —, 201; clan —, 49; process of — in relation to land tenure, 180; principle of —, 198.

Seligman, G. S., xii.

Seniority, rule of —, 224.

Settlement, peripheral —s, 28; social structure of —, 154; two types of —s, 154; geographical and demographic factors in structure of —, 155 ff.; described, 155; topography of, 156; as locally fixed community, 157, 165; economic influences in structure of —, 158; boundaries of Tongo, 159; migration to peripheral —s, 163; definition of, 164; lineage ties determine structure of —, 166; internal structure of peripheral —s, 166, 221; continuity and stability of —, 191; lineage principle in structure of — analysed, 191; *see also* Community.

Seug, section of Tongo, 213.

268 INDEX

Sheepskin, loin cover for the dead, 122 see Talis.

Shrine, ancestral —, 55; see *bayər*, *Bɔyar, bɔyar.*

Sie (clan), 24, 42; Kuŋkye, ancestor of —, 39, 45; internal differentiation of —, 45, 48; major segments of —, 45; accessory lineages at —, 46, 49; intercalary lineages at —, 58; branch of Mosuor biis, 60.

Sie (district), funeral ceremonies and totemic observances in —, 46; Namoo clans in —, 75; structural ties in —, 118; structure of clans in —, 119; congeners of Talis in —, 119.

Sie-datɔk, section of Sie, 46; ties of clanship of, 48, 56.

Sister (*tau*), 40, 148.

Sister's son (*ahaŋ*, pl. *ahɔs*) = sororal nephew, 40, 47; status of lineages derived from, 59; as founding ancestor, 82.

Sister's son, of divorced sister = (*tau bii*), 40; descent from —, 47.

Slave, lineages of — descent, 40, 49; disabilities of, 52.

Social, symbols of — cleavages, 26 ff.; lineage as fundamental — unit, 62; meaning of — philosophy of Tallensi, 116; ritual symbolism of — personality, 145; boundaries of settlement correlated with structural ties and cleavages, 161 ff.; significance of plenty of crops, 173.

Social structure, adjustment in —, 53; External *Bɔyar* and Earth cult as organizing principles of —, 108; External *Bɔyar* as unifying force in —, 110; kinship fictions in —, 116; functions of ritual observances in —, 133; religious values as reflex of —, 134; of settlement, 154; tenacity of, 258.

Society, see Tallensi.

Socio-geographic, 14, 29; Tale society as — region, 231.

Solidarity, within clan and lineage, 31, 244, 249; machinery of clan —, 246; ancestor cult as sanction of —, 246, 248; lineage — fundamentally a moral fact, 249.

Son, funeral ceremonies as sacred duty of — to parent, 122.

Soog, clan structure, 89; clanship ties of, 89, 109.

soog (uterine kin), 200, 207, 212.

Span of a lineage, 30, 194, 202.

Spatial, see Local; distribution of Tale settlements, 18, significance of, 167; relations parallel structural rela-

tions, 48, 83, 89; distance of clanship, 63; influence of — proximity, 76; relations and politico-ritual relations, 107.

Spirit-guardian (*sɛyar*), 131.

String, in mortuary rites, 122.

Structural, field of — relations, tendency to equilibrium, 47; correlations of funeral ceremonies, 124.

Sub-clan, chain of —s of Mosuor biis, 40, 43; chiefship of —, 43; rights and duties at funeral ceremonies, 44; ancestral graves and shrines as focus of —'s unity, 55; defined, 61 ff.

Succession, rights of, 52.

sunzɔp (sing. *sunzɔ*) = brothers, 32, 43; see Clanship, Lineage; duties and privileges of lineage —, 37, 246; rights and duties of — at funeral ceremonies, 44; by courtesy, 72, 90, 92; rights of *fɔ*, 74; definition of, 116 ff.

sunzɔt = brotherhood, 32; definition of, 61; ties of, 84; see Lineage.

Symbolism, animal —, 142; of functional differentiation in the social system, 143.

Symbols, of social cleavages, 26 ff.; totemic taboos as — of moral value, 69, 142; definition of social —, 136.

Taboo, —s distinguishing Talis and Namoos, 20, 66; relaxation of, 25; fowl —, 67, 69 see Namoos; —s of first-born child, 66, 69, 132; analysis of concept of —, 122; animal and food —s in Voltaic culture, 142; animal —s in Tale religion, 142; —s of the Earth, 142, 188, symbolism of, 143, observances of, 175; —s on bloodshed, 176; see Totemic avoidances.

Tale, see Tallensi.

Taleland, population of, 4, 19, increase in, 156; typical of trans-Volta region, 13; as socio-geographic area, 14, 29, 231; sketch-map of, 15; three major regions in, 28, 233; differentiation into social regions, 29, see Region, Social.

Talis, 14 (note 2); definition of 'real —', 19, 21 see Tallensi, Clanship; taboos distinguishing — and Namoos, 20; — of the Plain, 21; Hill — as immigrants, 23; *Bɔyar* cult of the —, 57; totemic taboos of the —, 70; ties with Namoos, 78; joking relationship among —, 91;

INDEX 269

major cleavage between Namoos and —, 103; field of ritual relations of — clan, 103; social equilibrium among —, 113; congeners of — in Sie district, 119; unity of —, 121; as cohesive group, 121; Hill — return from exile, 181; cemeteries of Hill —, 220; conflicts and competition amongst Hill —, 251.

Tallensi (sing. Talɔŋa, adj. Tale), 1, 21; cultural affinities of, 4; physical characteristics of, 7; standards of living of, 8, 11 (note); main characteristics of — culture, 8 ff., 9, 130; influence of British rule and culture contact on —, 10, 13; resistance to British rule, 12; attitude towards white man, 12; meaning of, 14; orthography, 14 (note 2); political and social organization of, 14; distinctness of, 17; absence of history among —, 24; culture homogeneous, 67; importance of progeny and marriage among —, 67; clanship linking — and Gɔrisi, 88; meaning of social philosophy of, 116; folk-lore of, 141; dependence on face-to-face communications, 211; genealogical knowledge of, 216.

Tale society, highly homogeneous and integrated, 28, 143; as sociogeographic region, 231; as segmentary system, 231 ff.; equilibrium in, 234; major cleavage in, 27, 234, 238.

Talni dialect, 14.

tau = Sister, 40, 148.

Tauxier, L., 6 (note 2).

Tɛŋ (pl. *tɛs*) = Earth, 80; as social community, 164, 180; ritual significance of, 165, in relation to local distribution, 169; at its widest extent, 181; prosperity of —, 183; tɛndaana's —, 184, 187, boundaries not defined, 185 ff.; *see also* Earth.

Tɛndaana (Custodian of the Earth), 7, 20, 80; primordial —, myth of origin, 22, 58; represents lineage, 81; office of — in Sie district, 119; ritual jurisdiction over land of —, 164, 184 see also *Tɛŋ*; absence of precise boundaries between —s' lands, 164; politico-ritual functions of —s, 182 ff.; status of Gbizug —, 182; —s predominantly non-Namoos, 184; meaning of, 184; ritual services of —s, 188; status of —s, 189; dispute between Gbizug — and Gbeog —, 247.

Tɛndaanaship, 20; as ritual bond between clans, 102.

tɛndaanditib, — clans in Sie district, 119, 124.

Tɛŋən-lɛbəgət, see Festival, Harvest.

tɛŋənpiima, rules concerning —, 176.

Time factor in lineage structure, 224.

Tong Hills, 3, 17.

Tongo, chief of — owns Mosuor's *bɔyar*, 54; *see* Chief; forces of integration at —, 55; status of attached lineages at —, 57; neighbours of Zubiuŋ, 59; population and description of, 159 ff.; no fixed territorial boundaries, 160; social boundaries of, 161, 170; internal structure of, 167, 169, 215; analysis of lineage structure of, 191 ff.; sections of, 211; internal equilibrium of, 215; genealogical cleavages within, 216.

Tɔŋna'ab, External *Bɔyar*, 106.

Tortoise, as totemic animal, 20, 126.

Totemic, observances of Sie, 46; common — observances, 66; paramount moral values of — oaths of Namoos, 69; animals among Talis, 126; most commonly tabooed — animals, 140; significance of — animal symbolism, 145.

— avoidances, myth of origin of, 66, 67, 128 ff.; and funeral ceremonies, 122, 136 see also Funeral; and clanship ties, 124; not precisely correlated with clanship ties, 127; incidence of, 125; attitude of natives in, 125; oath by, 125 ff.; as reflex of social structure, 130; connected with External *Bɔyar* cult, 130, 137; as personal taboos of matrilateral kin, 132 ff.; deeper meaning of, 134; divergent — among Talis, 140; in Voltaic culture, 140.

— taboos, equivalence of Namoos and non-Namoos, 67; as symbols of moral values, 69, 70; of Talis, 70; as symbolic expressions of lineage membership, 135, 136; sanctions of, 138.

Totems, discriminative — of clans and lineages, 66; symbolic value of — in relation to patrilineal line, 69, 130, 135.

tɔŋgban (pl. *tɔŋgbana*) = Earth shrine, 80 *see also* Earth shrine; Ba'at Da'a, 101; sacred spots, 104, 220; meaning of, 106 (note).

Transformation, animal, 68.

Trees as ancestor shrines, 219.

270 INDEX

Unit, clan as local —, 62, 85; corporate —s, representation of, 99.

Uterine, (*soog* pl. *saarɔt*), kin, 23, 200.

Volta river system, 2.

Voltaic, tribes, 4; political organization of — peoples, 6; immigrant — communities, 6; autochthonous — communities, 6.

War, abduction of wife as cause of, 42; in relation to clanship, 42, 62; mutual assistance in — as criterion of structural relations, 121; ancient battle-ground, 160; preliminary ritual, 229; not admired, 234 ff.; killing in — sinful, 235; stimuli to —, 236; as mechanism for redressing wrongs, 236; stories of —, 237; as expression of major cleavage in Tale society, 238; nature of —, 238; described, 238; political significance of —, 239; kinship in relation to —, 239; economic aspect of —, 239; as function of segmentary system, 240; and interclan fights, 241; disintegrating effects of — limited, 242; as sanction of social cohesion, 244.

Westermann, D., 6.

Widows, rights of, 229; remarriage of, 246.

Wives, abduction of —, 42, 90, 245; ex-—, 42; mode of address for, 165; status of , 229.

Women, —'s clothes, 11 (note); avoid fowl, 125; role of — in lineage, 139; place of — in clan, 147 *see* Clanswomen; status of — in lineage, 150; descent through — in relation to patrilineal line, 150.

Yamɔlɔg, branch of Mosuor biis, 39, 42, 60.

Yidɛm = people of the house, 37, see *yir*, Lineage.

Yikpɛmdaan, Tongo elder, 209, 213.

Yinduuri, clanship ties of, 89.

Yinyɛla, 248.

Yir = house, 33, 202; *see* Lineage.

Yizug (pl. *yizugɔt*), *see* Section.

zanɔr (gateway), 208; lineage —, 208, 215.

Zoo, clan structure of, 71; ties with Tongo, 72; myth of origin of, 72.

Zoo-Yiraaŋ, clanship ties of, 82.

Zoonkpalɔg, lineage *bɔyar*, also External *Bɔyar*, 213.

Zuarungu, density of population in — district, 2; road system of, 4.

Zubiuŋ, neighbours of Tongo, 59; relationship to Nɔŋsuur yidɛm, 59; clan structure of, 78; situation and connexion with Tongo, 78; of diverse descent, 79; External *Bɔyar* of — as ritual focus of clan, 79; ritual differentiation and integration of, 80; clanship ties with Gbeog, Gbizug, and Ba'ari, 82; clan lineages of, 84; joking partnership, 91; ritual collaboration, 100, 122.